OSSAN IDOL! 06

MANGA ◆ ICHIKA KINO
ORIGINAL STORY ◆
MOCHIKO MOCHIDA
CHARACTER DESIGN ◆
MIZUKI SAKAKIBARA

STORY

MIROKU, A 270 LB UNEMPLOYED SHUT-IN WAS SPURRED ON BY THE POPULARITY OF HIS "LET'S TRY DANCING" VIDEO, JOINED A GYM, GOT IN SHAPE, AND TRANSFORMED INTO A MIDDLE-AGED HUNK IN NO TIME! ALONG WITH YOICHI AND SHIJU, HE CAUGHT THE EYE OF A FAMOUS PRODUCER, MR. LAVENDER, AND THE THREE MEN SUCCESSFULLY DEBUTED AS MIYOSHI! LATELY THEY'VE HAD MORE AND MORE GIGS WITH THE SUPER-POPULAR IDOL GROUP TENKA...

CHARACTERS

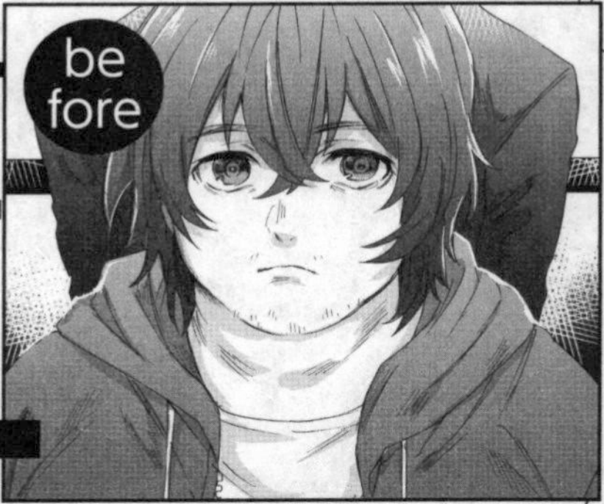
be
fore

MIROKU (36)

MIROKU OSAKI

UNEMPLOYED. SHUT-IN. VIRGIN INTERNET ADDICT. WEIGHS 270 LBS. GIVES OFF PHEROMONES UNCONSCIOUSLY

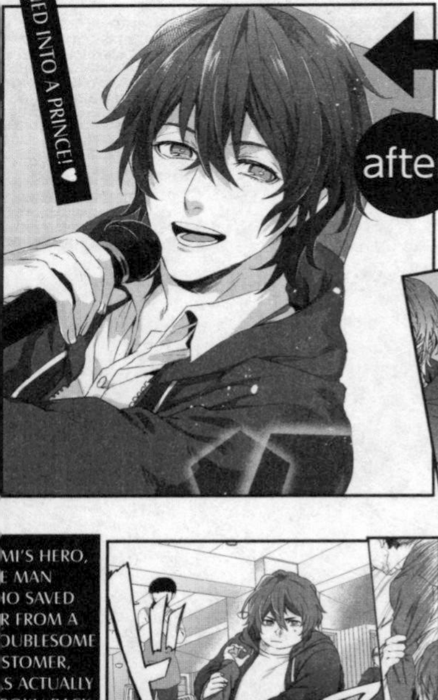
after
TURNED INTO A PRINCE!♥

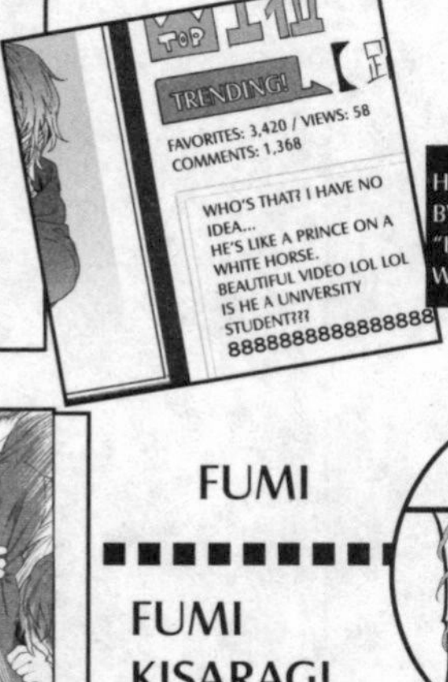
TOP
TRENDING!
FAVORITES: 3,420 / VIEWS: 58
COMMENTS: 1,368
WHO'S THAT? I HAVE NO IDEA...
HE'S LIKE A PRINCE ON A WHITE HORSE.
BEAUTIFUL VIDEO LOL LOL
IS HE A UNIVERSITY STUDENT???
8888888888888888

HE PRESSED "UPLOAD" BY MISTAKE AND HIS "LET'S DANCE" VIDEO WENT VIRAL!

FUMI

FUMI KISARAGI

YOICHI'S BUBBLY NIECE WHO WORKS AT HIS OFFICE. SHE ALWAYS PUTS HER ALL INTO HER WORK.

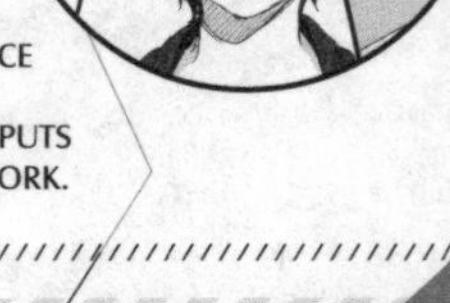

MI'S HERO, E MAN IO SAVED R FROM A OUBLESOME STOMER, S ACTUALLY ROKU BACK IEN HE WAS UBBY!

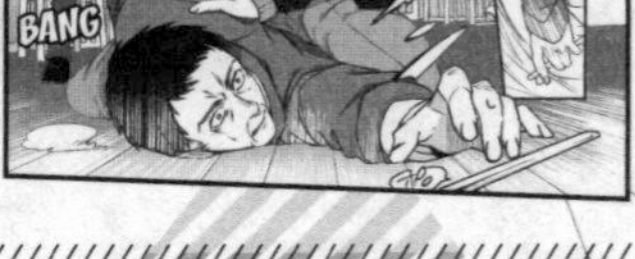
BANG

YOICHI (41)

YOICHI KISARAGI

HE WAS OVER 300 LBS, BUT NOW YOICHI IS THE CEO OF A SMALL ENTERTAINMENT COMPANY. HE AND MIROKU MET AT THE GYM. USED TO BE AN IDOL FOR THE SHINEEZ TALENT AGENCY.

SHIJU (40)

SHIJU ONOHARA

A FORMER DANCER AND HOST, NOW UNEMPLOYED AND LEADING A LIFE ON THE EDGE. HE WAS THE ONE WHO SUGGESTED THAT MIROKU TAKE PART IN THE DANCE COMPETITION, AND HE USED TO BELONG TO A LEGENDARY DANCE TEAM.

TENKA

SUPER POPULAR IDOLS IN THEIR TEENS THAT BELONG TO SHINEEZ, A MAJOR TALENT AGENCY.

KIRA

THE ULTIMATE PRINCE OF THE IDOL INDUSTRY. HE USED TO VIEW MIROKU AS AN ENEMY, BUT...?

ROU

HE LOOKS CUTE BUT IS SURPRISINGLY LEVELHEADED.

ZOU

DESPITE HIS COOL AND COLLECTED AURA, HE'S ACTUALLY AN IDIOT.

OSSAN IDOL!

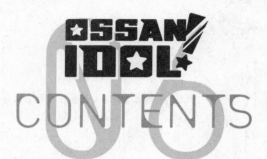

CONTENTS

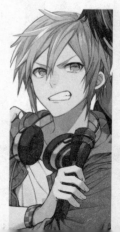

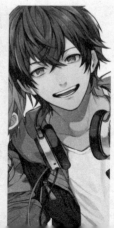

Chapter 31

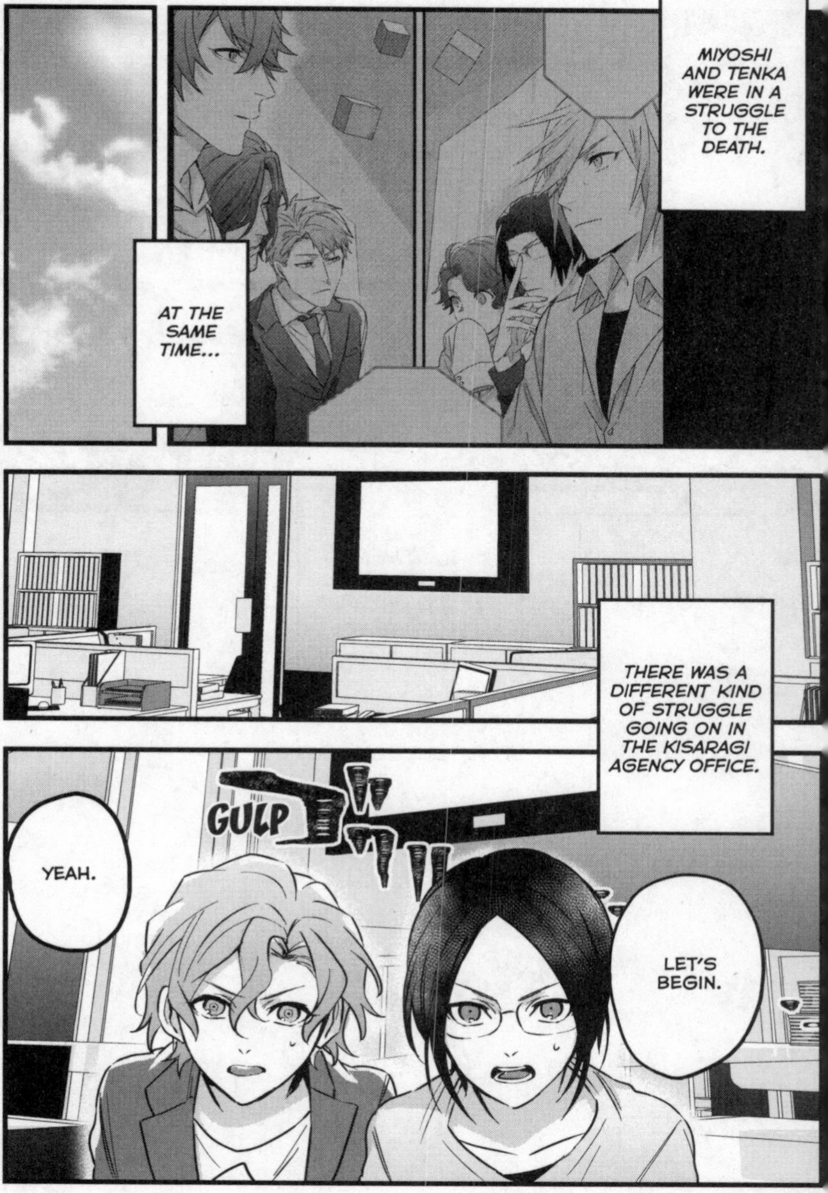
MIYOSHI AND TENKA WERE IN A STRUGGLE TO THE DEATH.
AT THE SAME TIME...
THERE WAS A DIFFERENT KIND OF STRUGGLE GOING ON IN THE KISARAGI AGENCY OFFICE.
LET'S BEGIN.
GULP
YEAH.

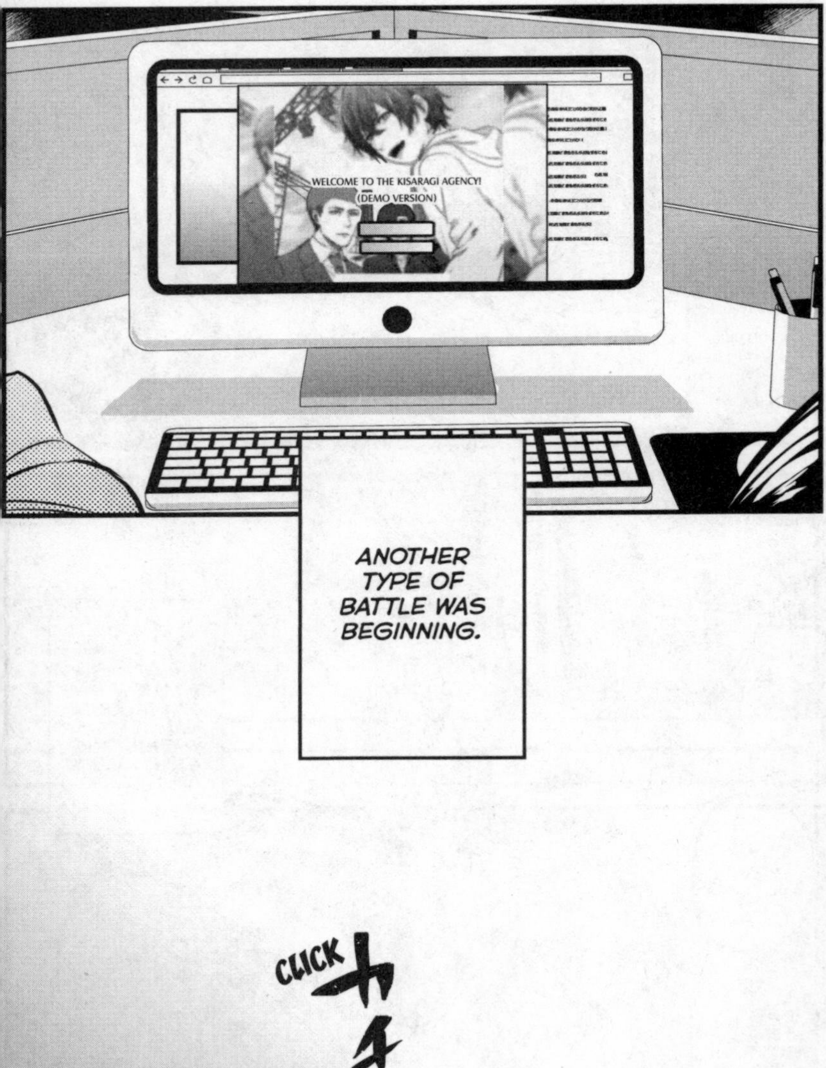
WELCOME TO THE KISARAGI AGENCY!
(DEMO VERSION)
ANOTHER TYPE OF BATTLE WAS BEGINNING.
CLICK

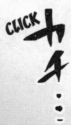

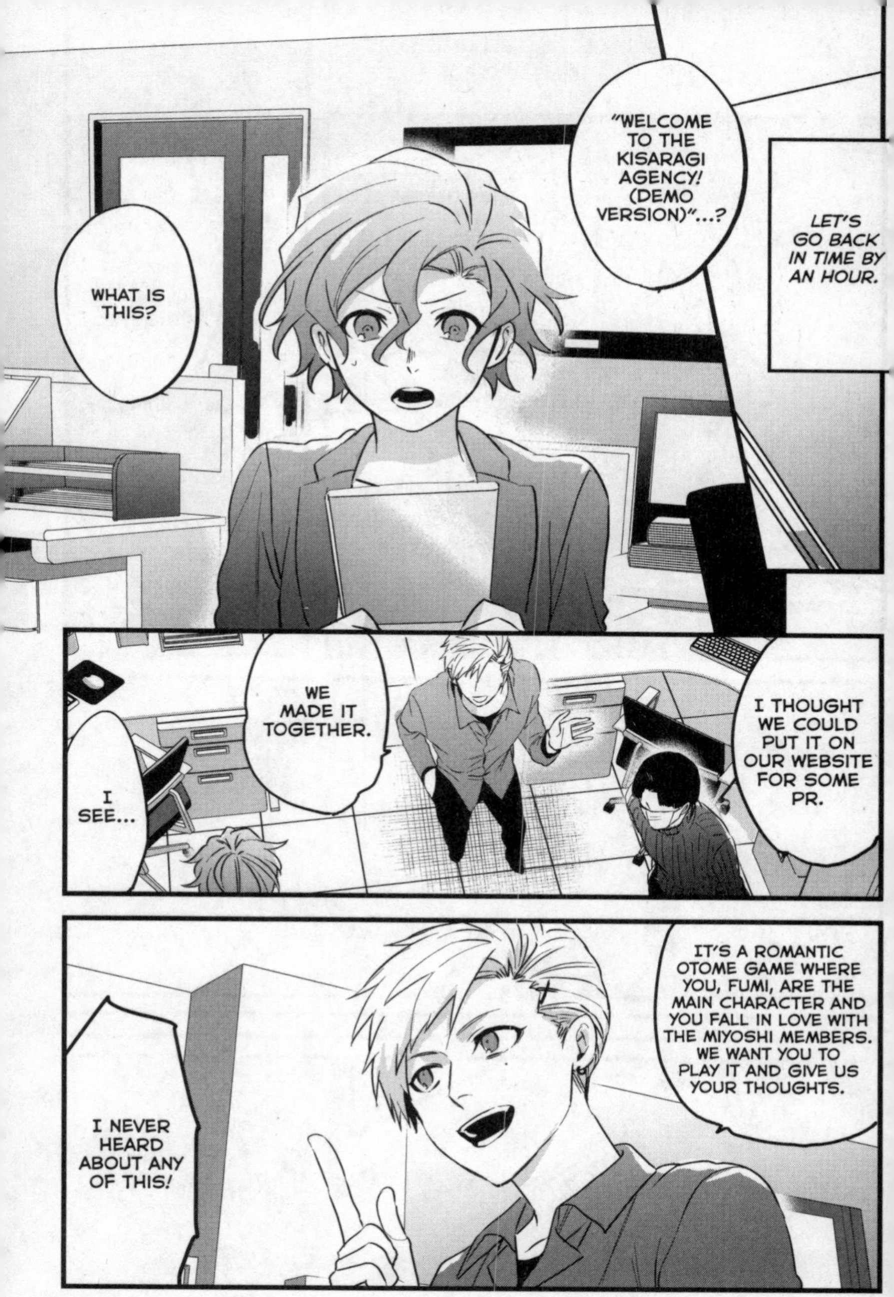
"WELCOME TO THE KISARAGI AGENCY! (DEMO VERSION)"...?
WHAT IS THIS?
LET'S GO BACK IN TIME BY AN HOUR.
I THOUGHT WE COULD PUT IT ON OUR WEBSITE FOR SOME PR.
WE MADE IT TOGETHER.
I SEE...
IT'S A ROMANTIC OTOME GAME WHERE YOU, FUMI, ARE THE MAIN CHARACTER AND YOU FALL IN LOVE WITH THE MIYOSHI MEMBERS. WE WANT YOU TO PLAY IT AND GIVE US YOUR THOUGHTS.
I NEVER HEARD ABOUT ANY OF THIS!

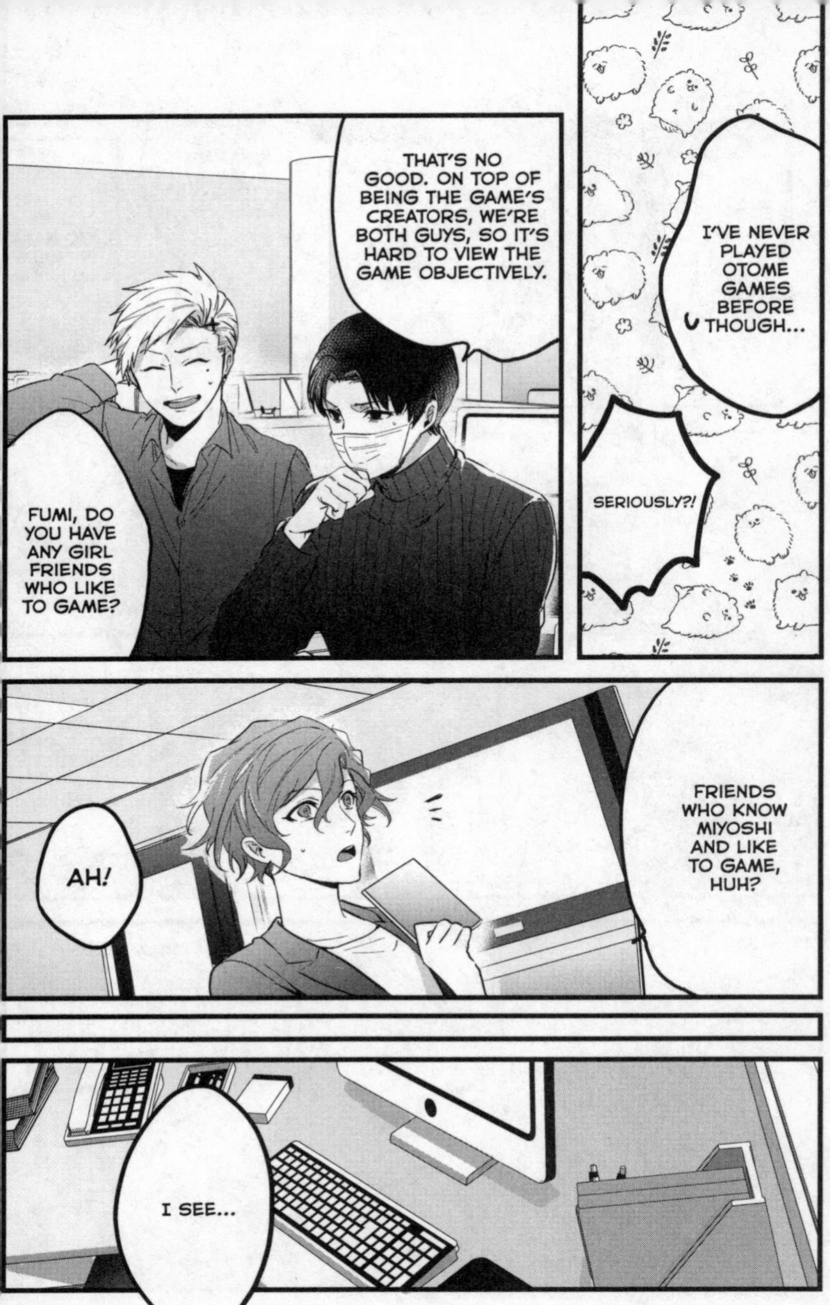
I'VE NEVER PLAYED OTOME GAMES BEFORE THOUGH...
SERIOUSLY?!
THAT'S NO GOOD. ON TOP OF BEING THE GAME'S CREATORS, WE'RE BOTH GUYS, SO IT'S HARD TO VIEW THE GAME OBJECTIVELY.
FUMI, DO YOU HAVE ANY GIRL FRIENDS WHO LIKE TO GAME?
FRIENDS WHO KNOW MIYOSHI AND LIKE TO GAME, HUH?
AH!
I SEE...

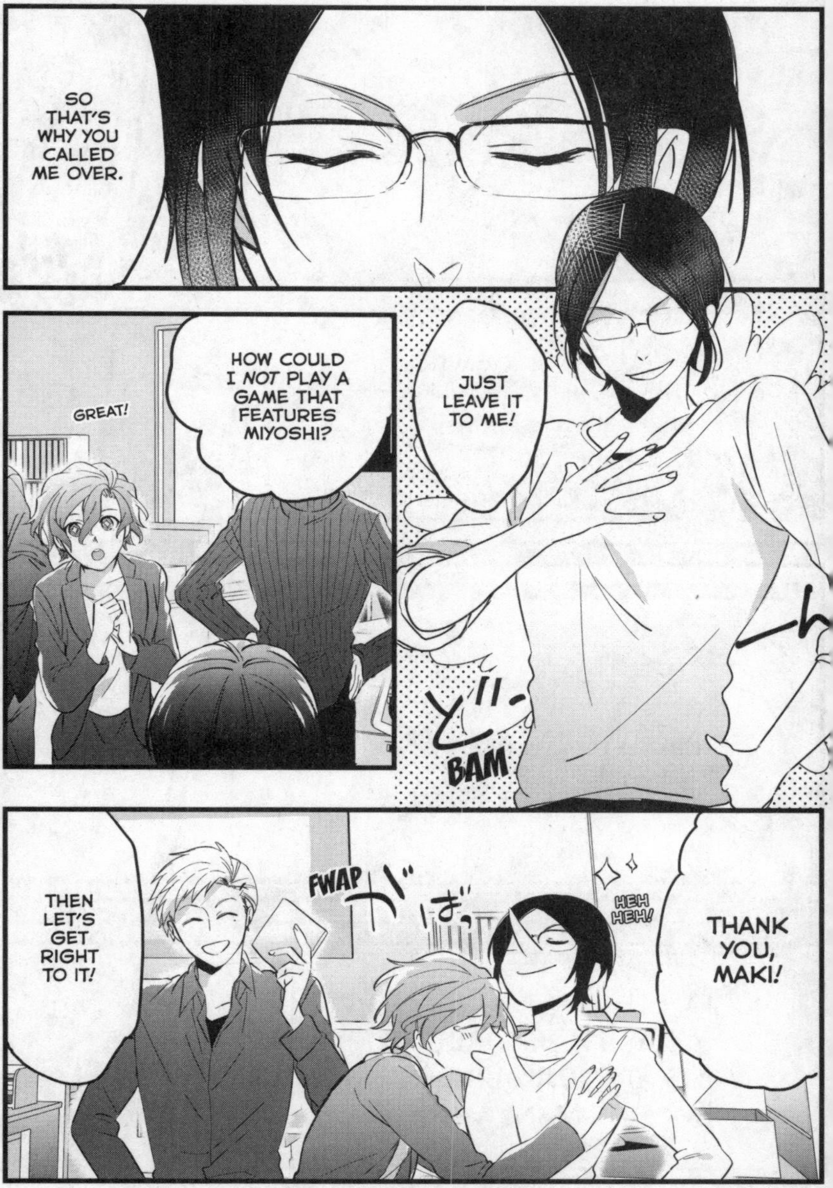
SO THAT'S WHY YOU CALLED ME OVER.
JUST LEAVE IT TO ME!
BAM
HOW COULD I *NOT* PLAY A GAME THAT FEATURES MIYOSHI?
GREAT!
THANK YOU, MAKI!
HEH HEH!
FWAP
THEN LET'S GET RIGHT TO IT!

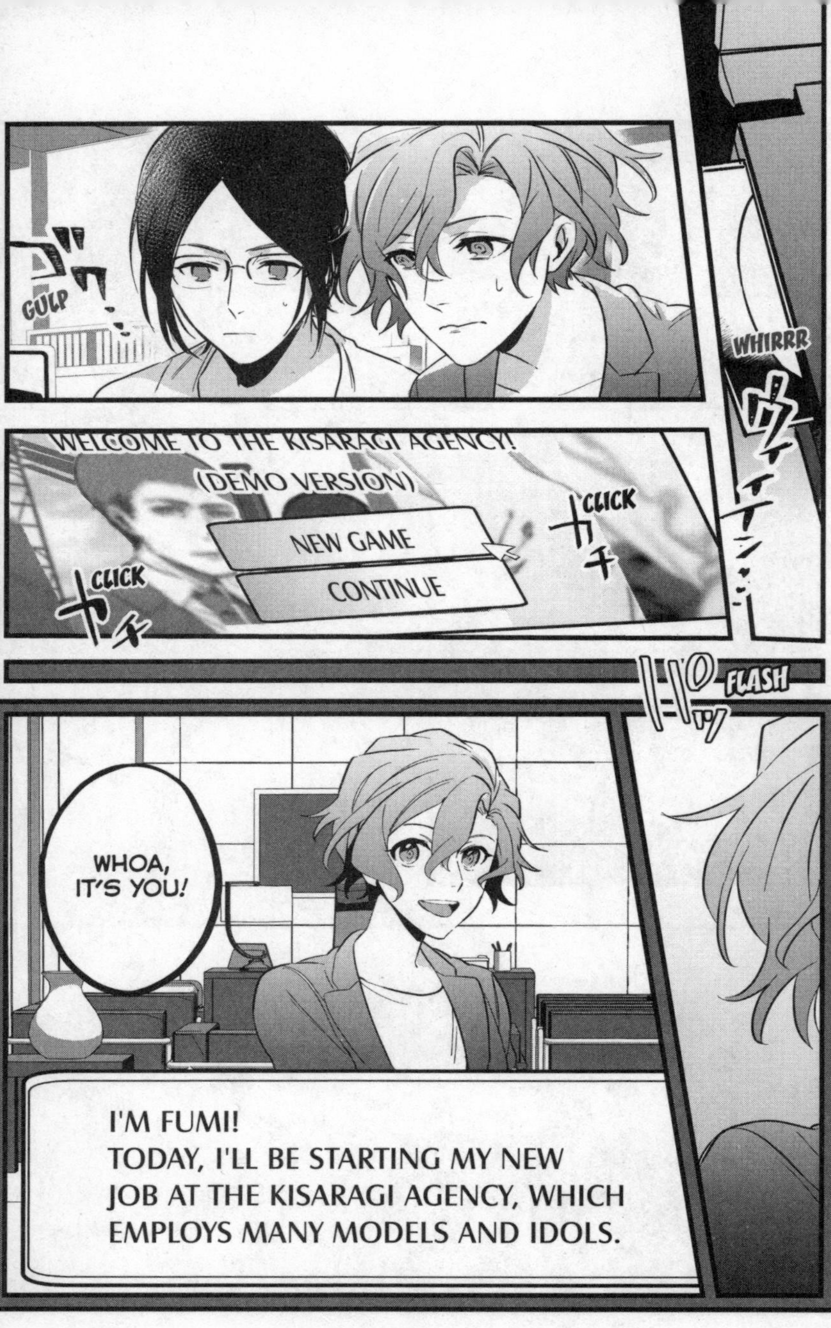
WHIRRR
GULP
WELCOME TO THE KISARAGI AGENCY!
(DEMO VERSION)
CLICK
NEW GAME
CONTINUE
CLICK
FLASH
WHOA, IT'S YOU!
I'M FUMI!
TODAY, I'LL BE STARTING MY NEW JOB AT THE KISARAGI AGENCY, WHICH EMPLOYS MANY MODELS AND IDOLS.

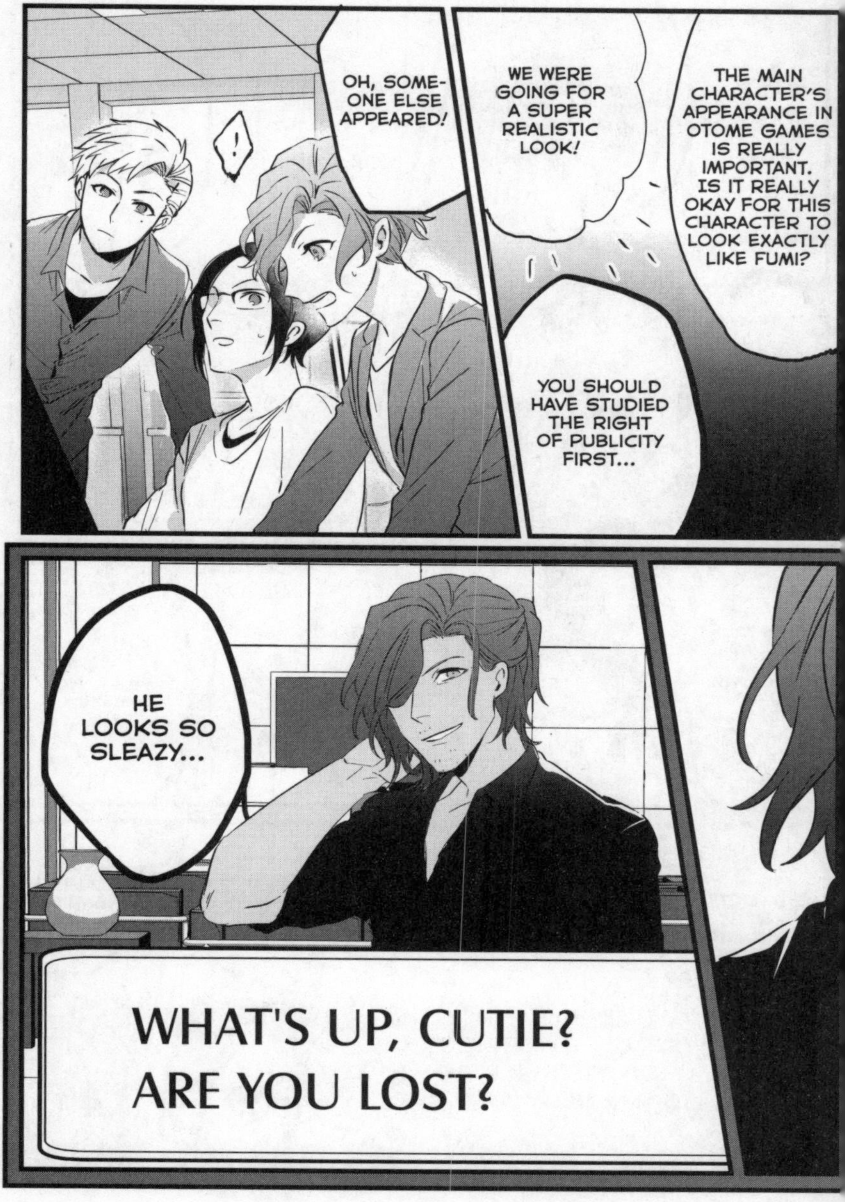
THE MAIN CHARACTER'S APPEARANCE IN OTOME GAMES IS REALLY IMPORTANT. IS IT REALLY OKAY FOR THIS CHARACTER TO LOOK EXACTLY LIKE FUMI?
WE WERE GOING FOR A SUPER REALISTIC LOOK!
YOU SHOULD HAVE STUDIED THE RIGHT OF PUBLICITY FIRST...
OH, SOME-ONE ELSE APPEARED!
!
HE LOOKS SO SLEAZY...
WHAT'S UP, CUTIE? ARE YOU LOST?

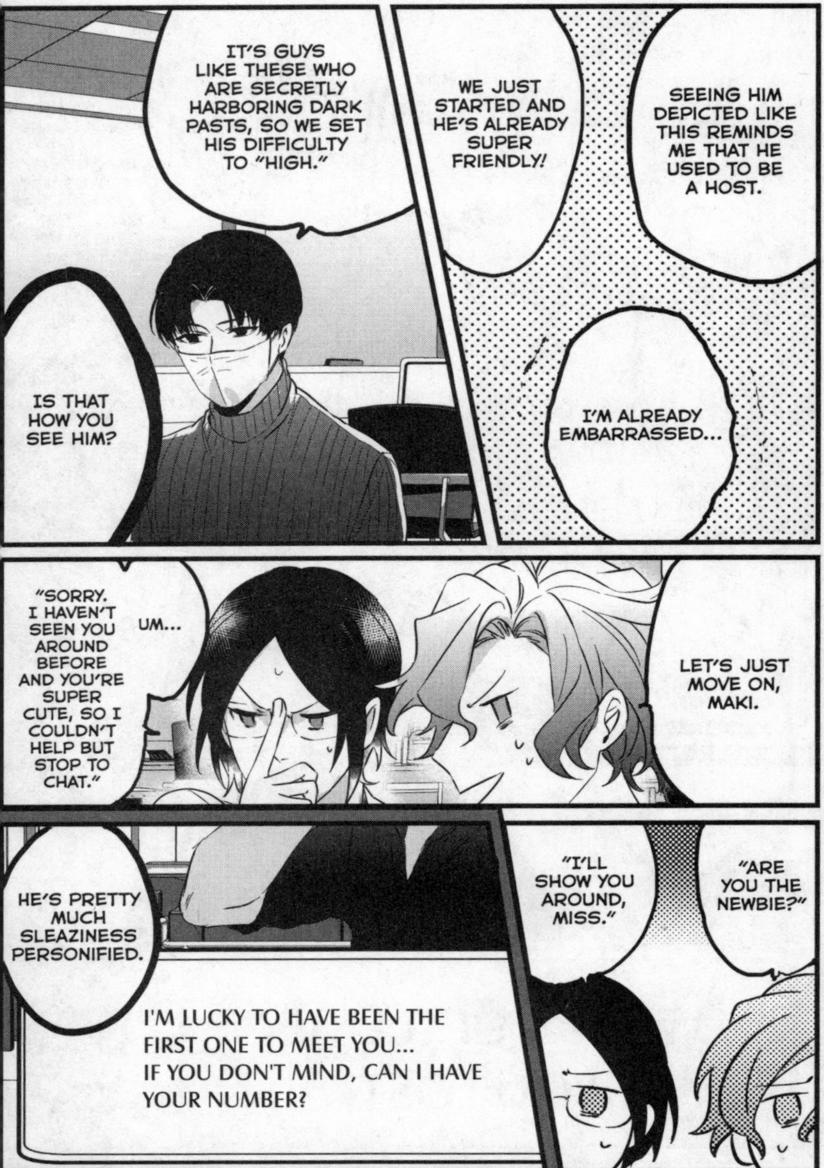
SEEING HIM DEPICTED LIKE THIS REMINDS ME THAT HE USED TO BE A HOST.
WE JUST STARTED AND HE'S ALREADY SUPER FRIENDLY!
I'M ALREADY EMBARRASSED...
IT'S GUYS LIKE THESE WHO ARE SECRETLY HARBORING DARK PASTS, SO WE SET HIS DIFFICULTY TO "HIGH."
IS THAT HOW YOU SEE HIM?
LET'S JUST MOVE ON, MAKI.
UM...
"SORRY. I HAVEN'T SEEN YOU AROUND BEFORE AND YOU'RE SUPER CUTE, SO I COULDN'T HELP BUT STOP TO CHAT."
"ARE YOU THE NEWBIE?"
"I'LL SHOW YOU AROUND, MISS."
HE'S PRETTY MUCH SLEAZINESS PERSONIFIED.
I'M LUCKY TO HAVE BEEN THE FIRST ONE TO MEET YOU... IF YOU DON'T MIND, CAN I HAVE YOUR NUMBER?

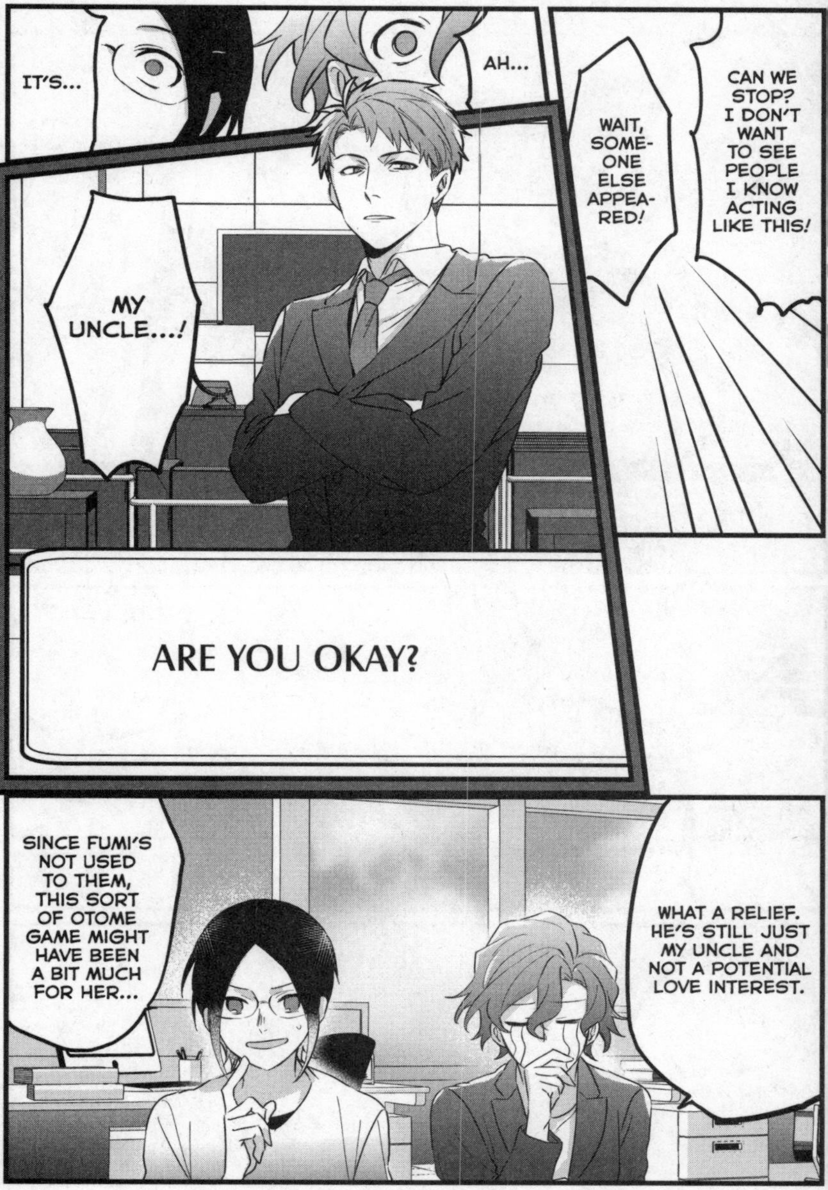
CAN WE STOP? I DON'T WANT TO SEE PEOPLE I KNOW ACTING LIKE THIS!
WAIT, SOMEONE ELSE APPEARED!
AH...
IT'S...
MY UNCLE...!
ARE YOU OKAY?
WHAT A RELIEF. HE'S STILL JUST MY UNCLE AND NOT A POTENTIAL LOVE INTEREST.
SINCE FUMI'S NOT USED TO THEM, THIS SORT OF OTOME GAME MIGHT HAVE BEEN A BIT MUCH FOR HER...

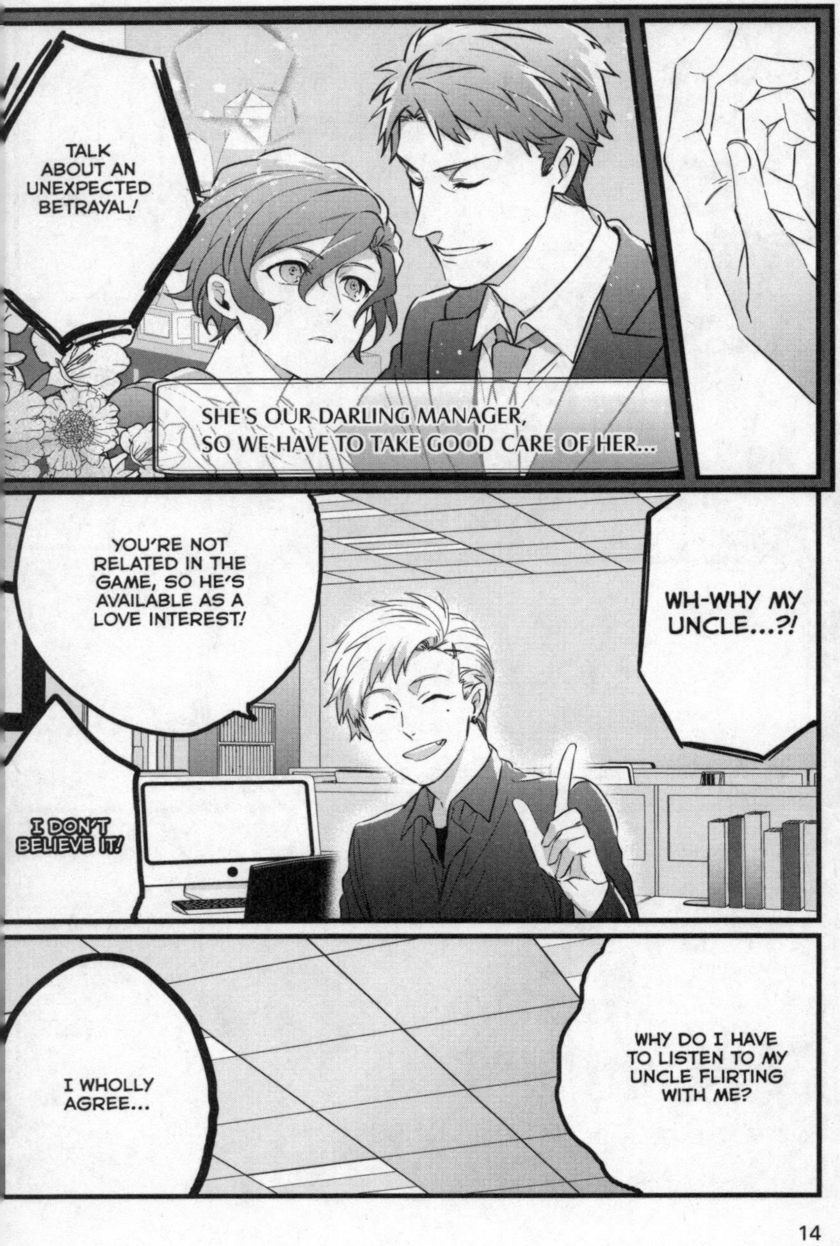
TALK ABOUT AN UNEXPECTED BETRAYAL!
SHE'S OUR DARLING MANAGER, SO WE HAVE TO TAKE GOOD CARE OF HER...
WH-WHY MY UNCLE...?!
YOU'RE NOT RELATED IN THE GAME, SO HE'S AVAILABLE AS A LOVE INTEREST!
I DON'T BELIEVE IT!
WHY DO I HAVE TO LISTEN TO MY UNCLE FLIRTING WITH ME?
I WHOLLY AGREE...

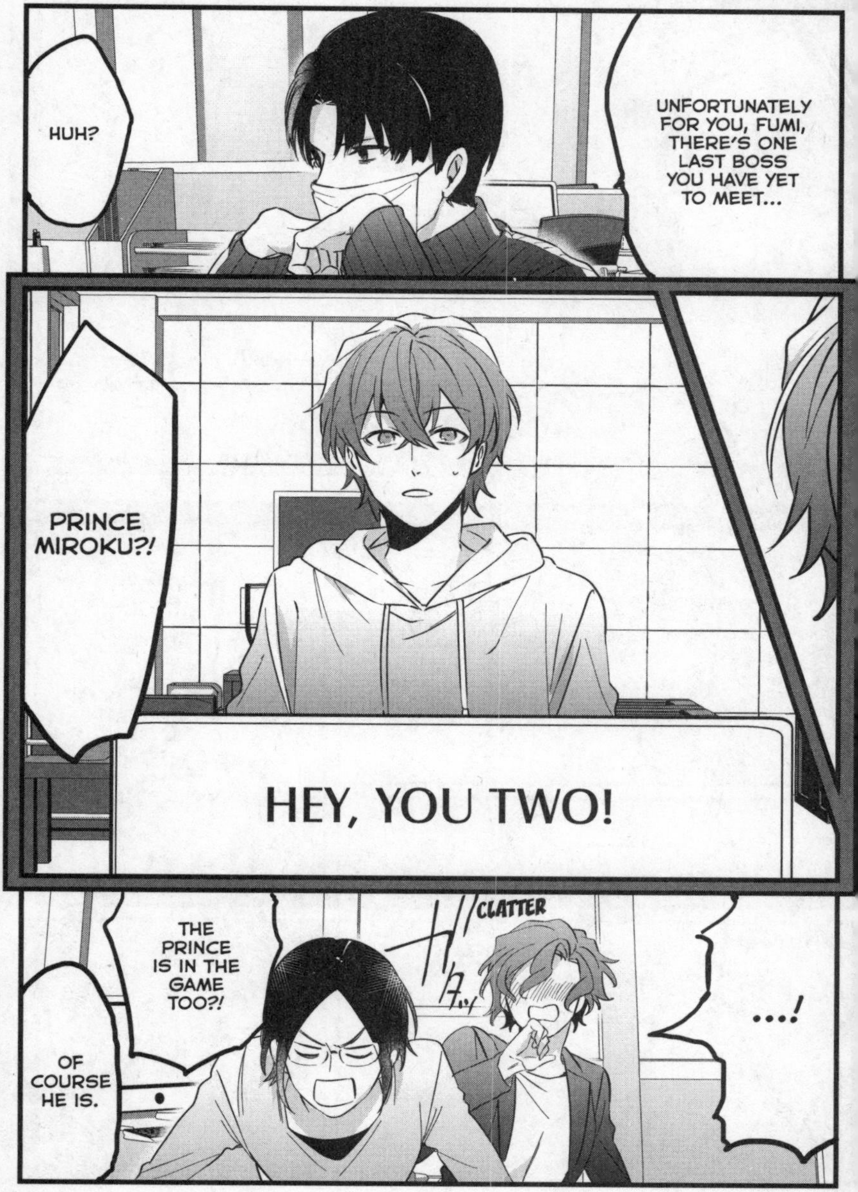
UNFORTUNATELY FOR YOU, FUMI, THERE'S ONE LAST BOSS YOU HAVE YET TO MEET...
HUH?
PRINCE MIROKU?!
HEY, YOU TWO!
...!
CLATTER
THE PRINCE IS IN THE GAME TOO?!
OF COURSE HE IS.

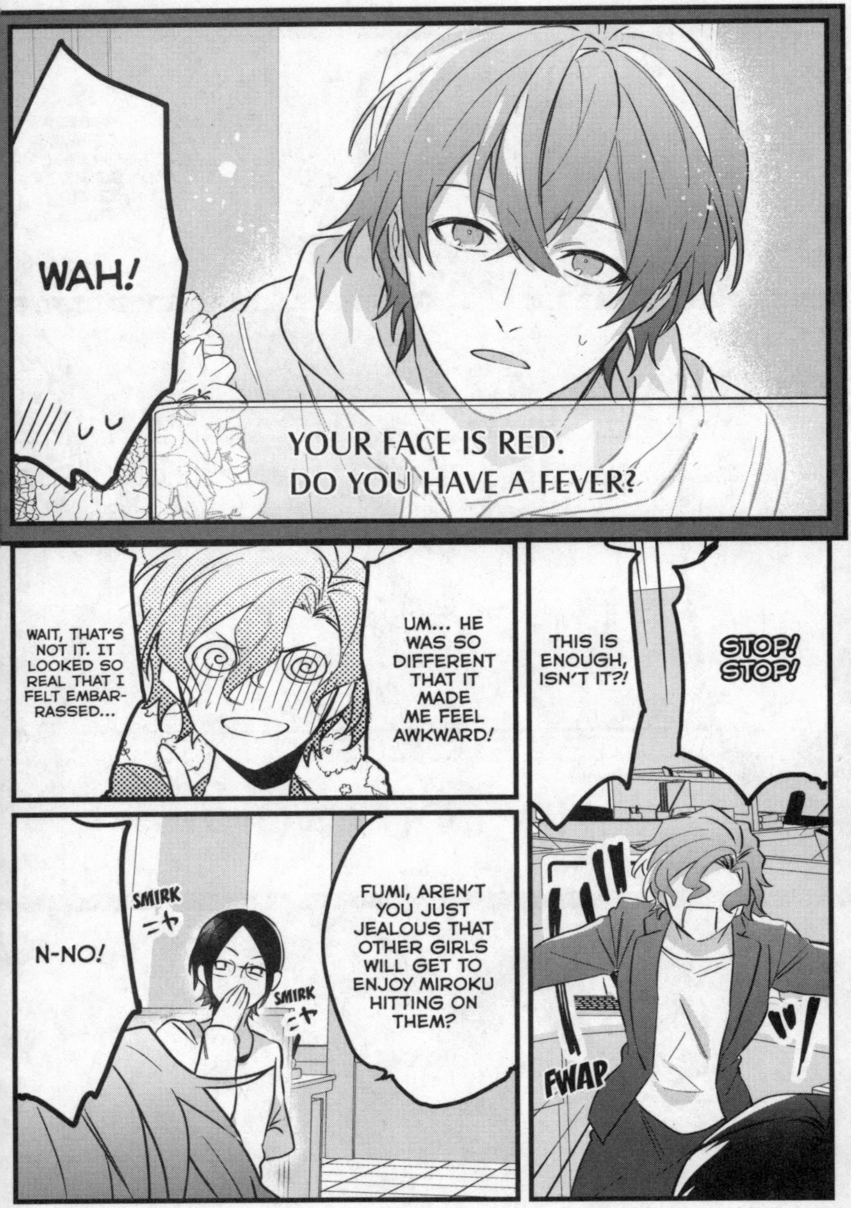
YOUR FACE IS RED.
DO YOU HAVE A FEVER?
WAH!
STOP! STOP!
THIS IS ENOUGH, ISN'T IT?!
FWAP
UM... HE WAS SO DIFFERENT THAT IT MADE ME FEEL AWKWARD!
WAIT, THAT'S NOT IT. IT LOOKED SO REAL THAT I FELT EMBARRASSED...
FUMI, AREN'T YOU JUST JEALOUS THAT OTHER GIRLS WILL GET TO ENJOY MIROKU HITTING ON THEM?
SMIRK
ニヤ
SMIRK
ニヤ
N-NO!

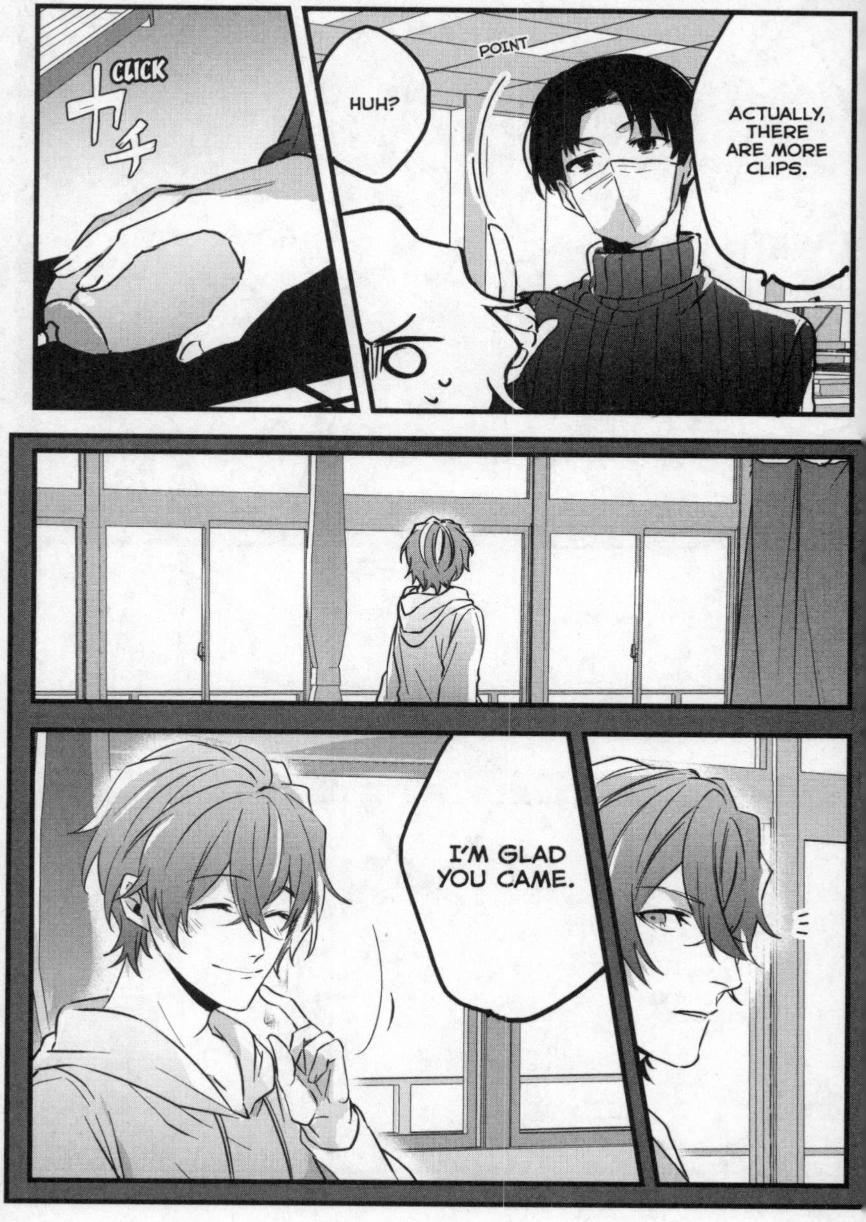
ACTUALLY, THERE ARE MORE CLIPS.
POINT
HUH?
CLICK
カチ
I'M GLAD YOU CAME.

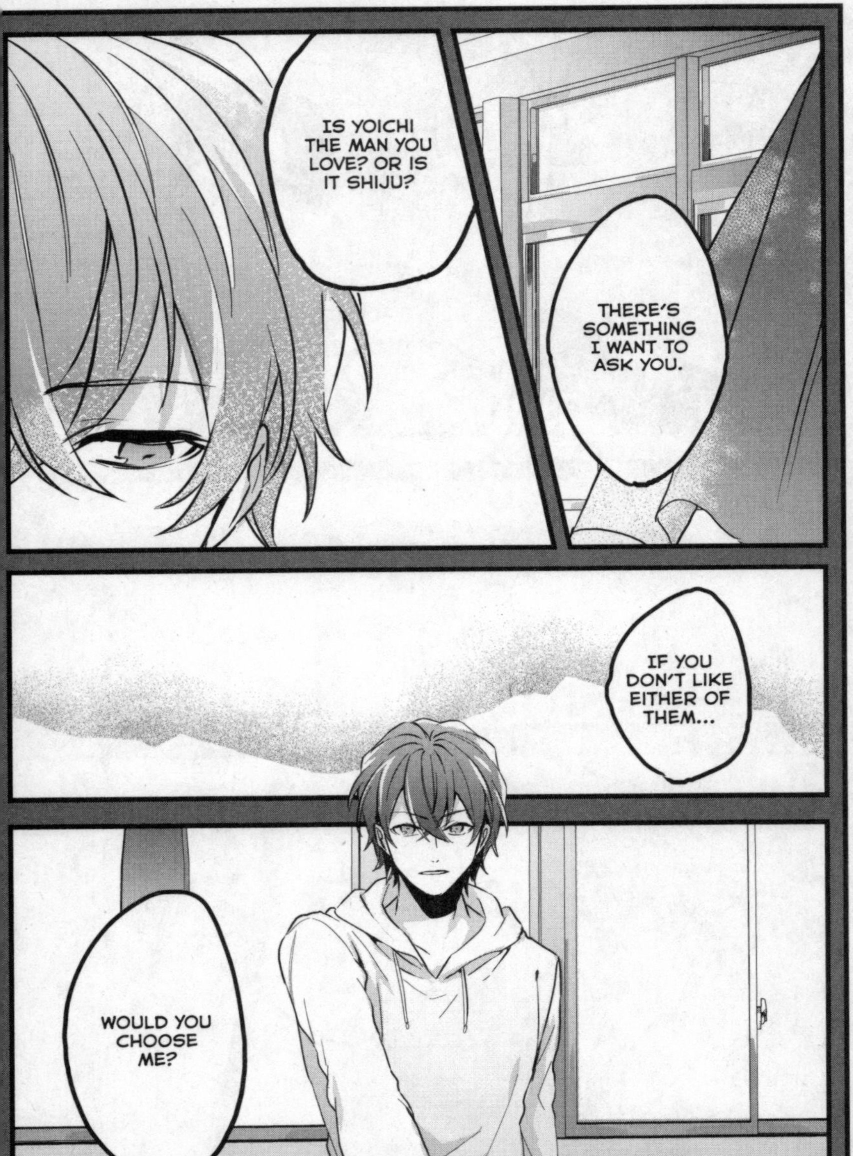
THERE'S SOMETHING I WANT TO ASK YOU.
IS YOICHI THE MAN YOU LOVE? OR IS IT SHIJU?
IF YOU DON'T LIKE EITHER OF THEM...
WOULD YOU CHOOSE ME?

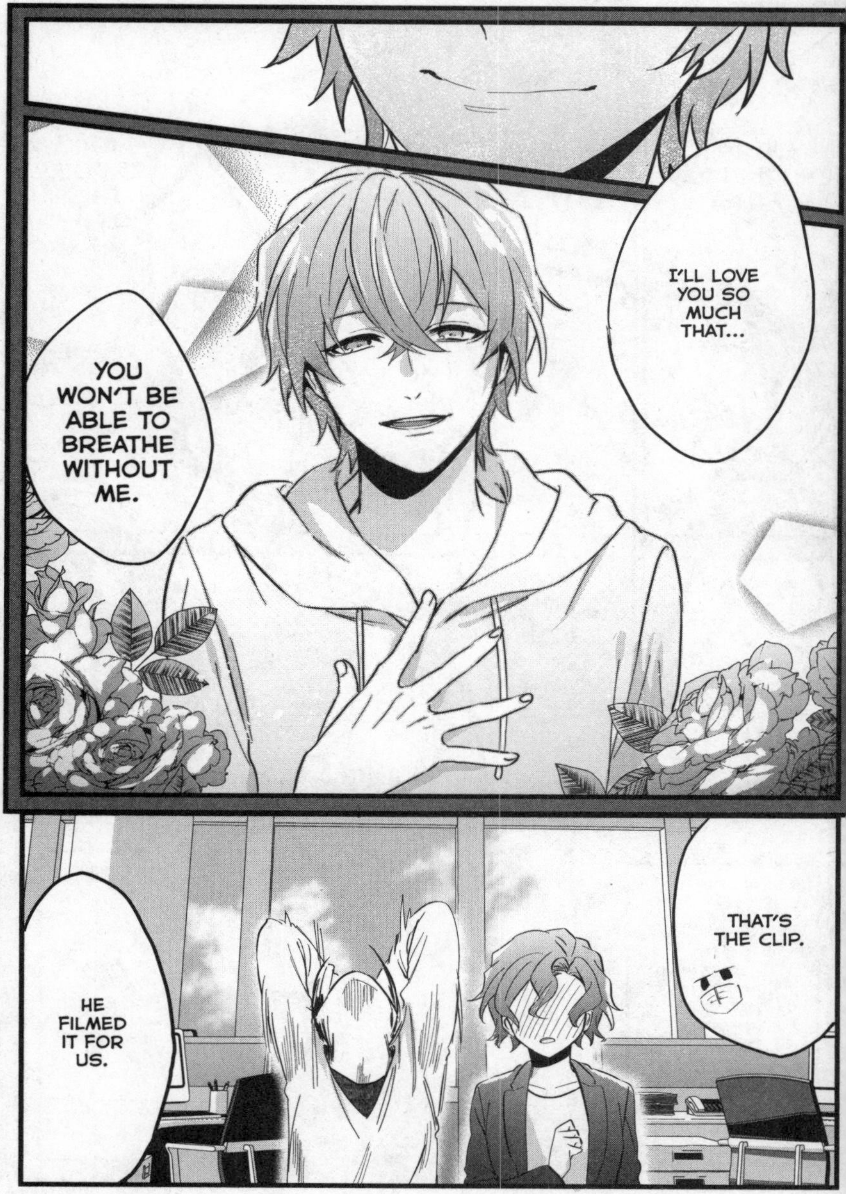
I'LL LOVE YOU SO MUCH THAT...
YOU WON'T BE ABLE TO BREATHE WITHOUT ME.
THAT'S THE CLIP.
HE FILMED IT FOR US.

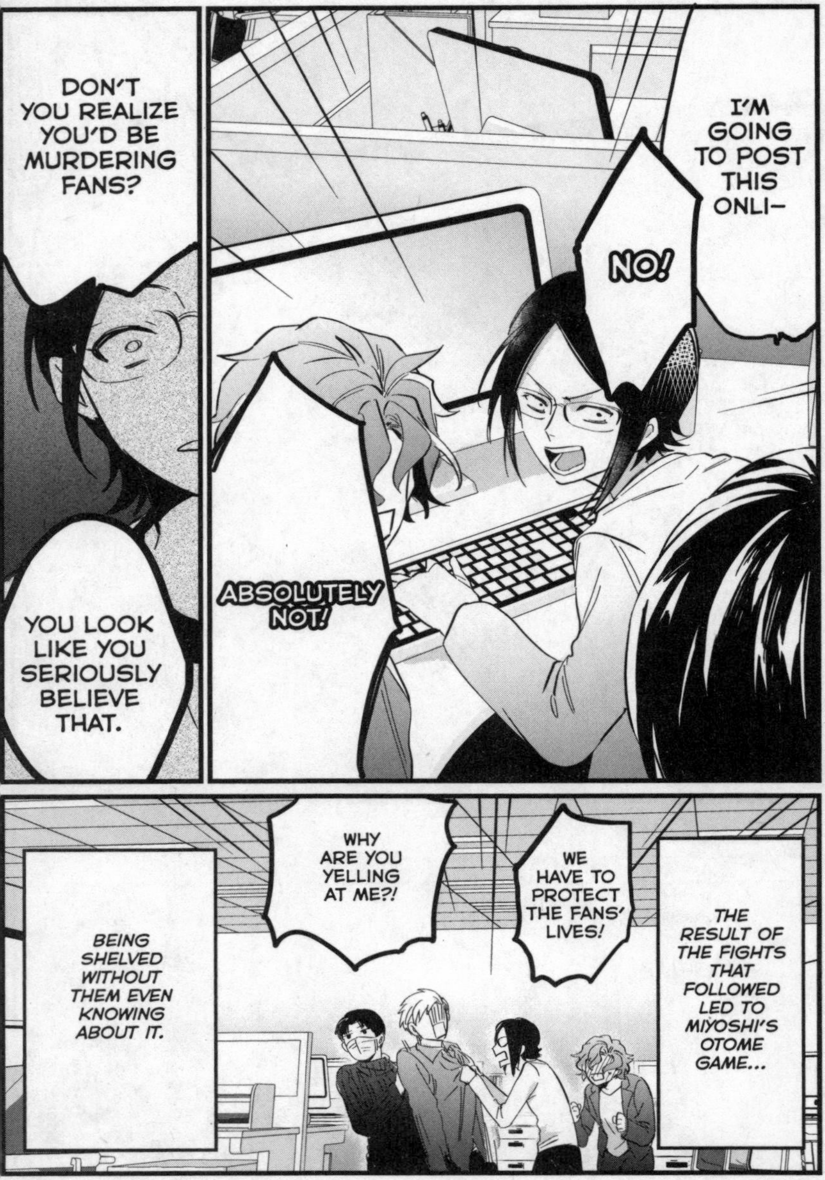
I'M GOING TO POST THIS ONLI—
NO!
ABSOLUTELY NOT!
DON'T YOU REALIZE YOU'D BE MURDERING FANS?
YOU LOOK LIKE YOU SERIOUSLY BELIEVE THAT.
THE RESULT OF THE FIGHTS THAT FOLLOWED LED TO MIYOSHI'S OTOME GAME...
WE HAVE TO PROTECT THE FANS' LIVES!
WHY ARE YOU YELLING AT ME?!
BEING SHELVED WITHOUT THEM EVEN KNOWING ABOUT IT.

Chapter 32

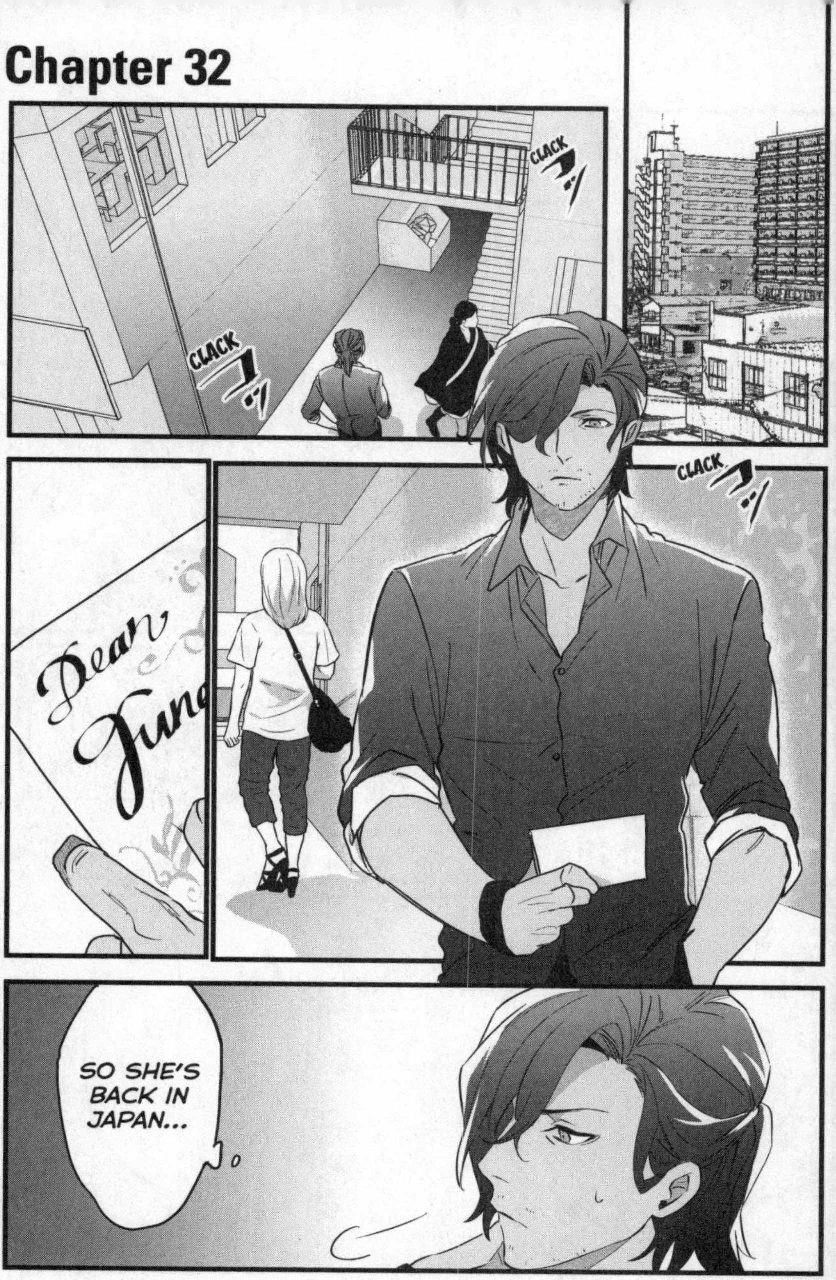
CLACK
CLACK
CLACK
Dear June
SO SHE'S BACK IN JAPAN...

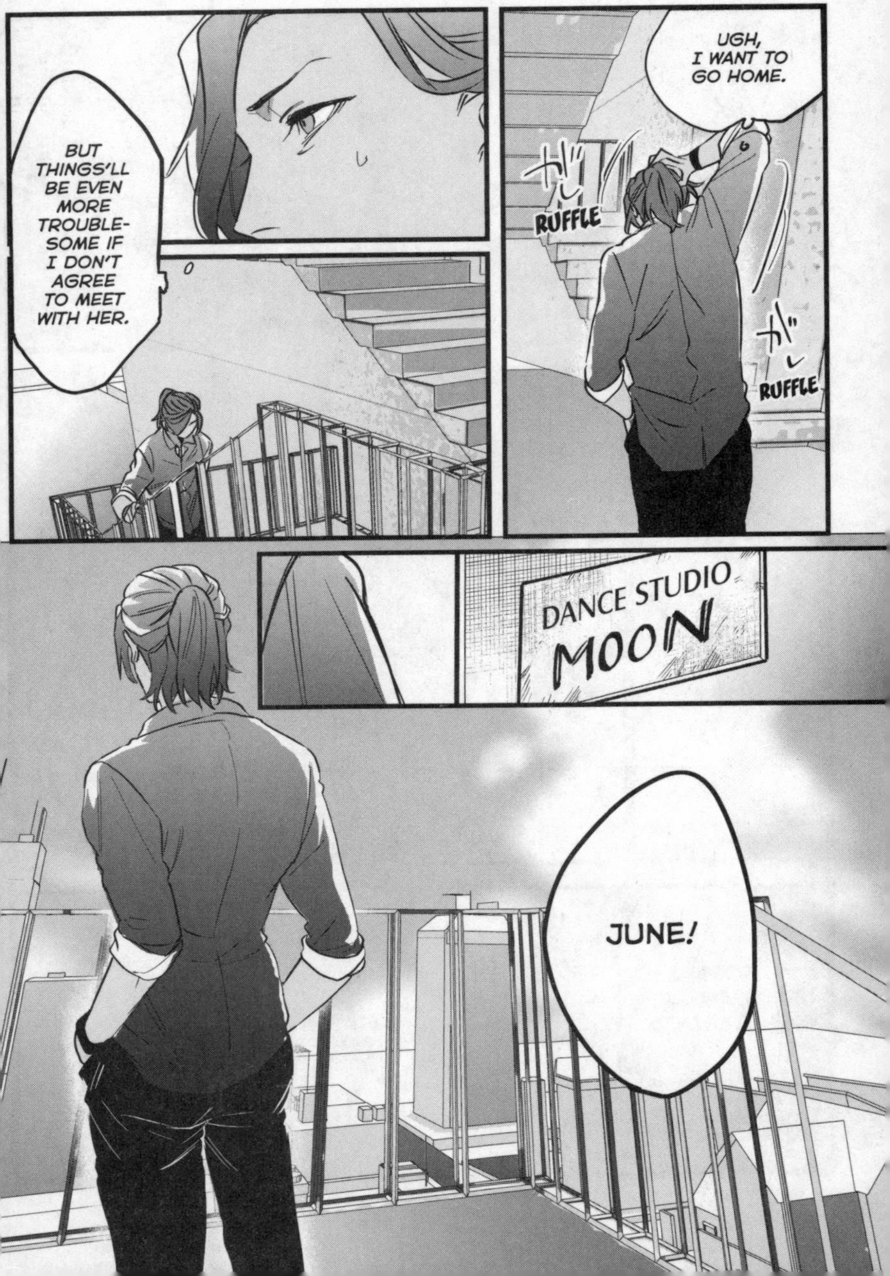
UGH, I WANT TO GO HOME.
RUFFLE
RUFFLE
BUT THINGS'LL BE EVEN MORE TROUBLE-SOME IF I DON'T AGREE TO MEET WITH HER.
DANCE STUDIO MOON
JUNE!

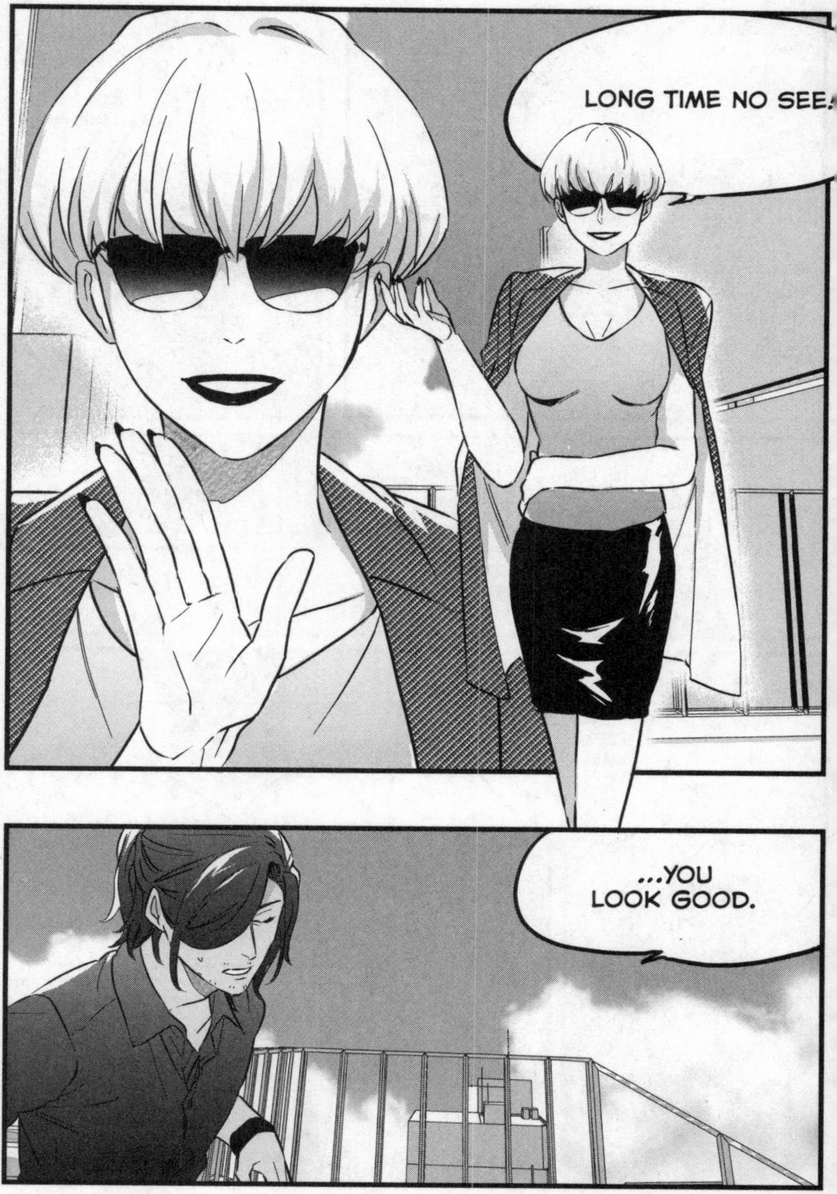
LONG TIME NO SEE!
...YOU LOOK GOOD.

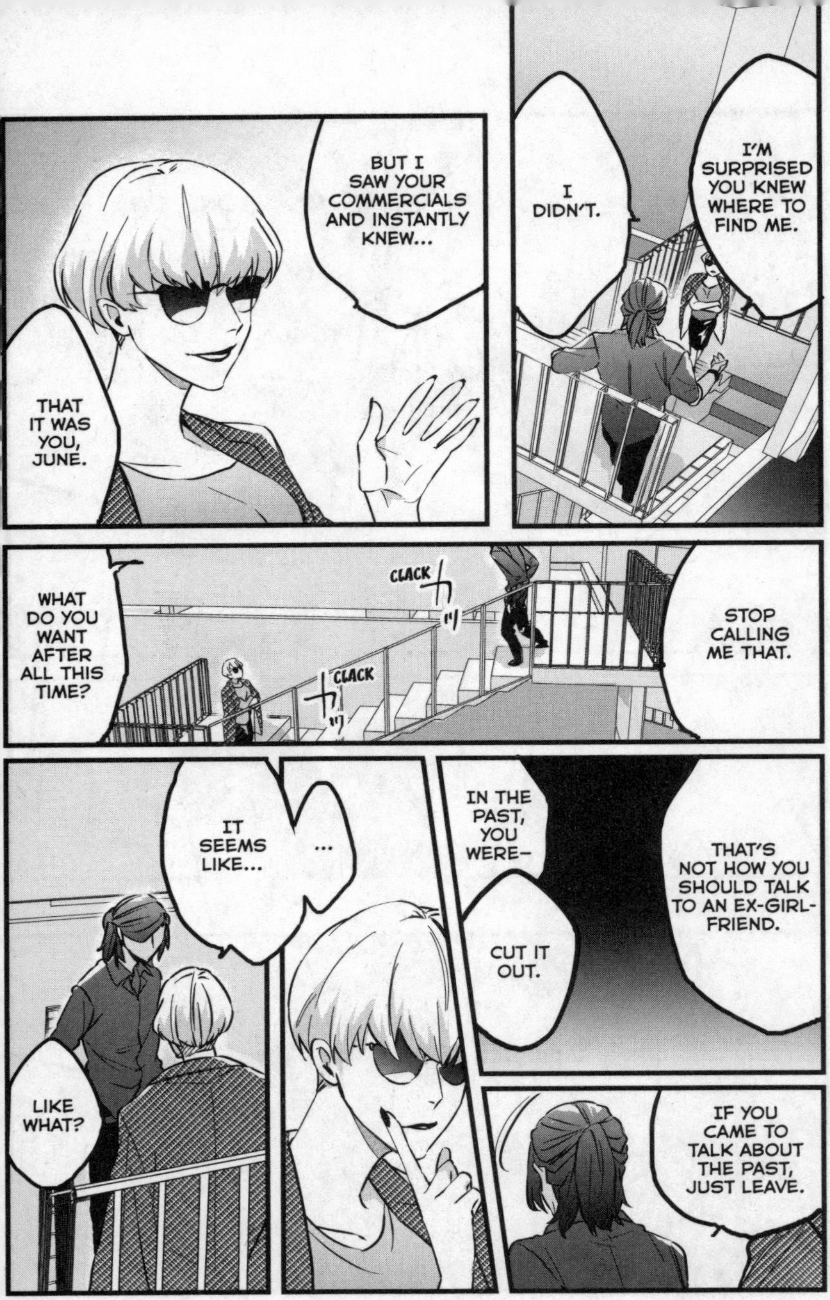
I'M SURPRISED YOU KNEW WHERE TO FIND ME.
I DIDN'T.
BUT I SAW YOUR COMMERCIALS AND INSTANTLY KNEW...
THAT IT WAS YOU, JUNE.
STOP CALLING ME THAT.
CLACK
CLACK
WHAT DO YOU WANT AFTER ALL THIS TIME?
THAT'S NOT HOW YOU SHOULD TALK TO AN EX-GIRL-FRIEND.
IN THE PAST, YOU WERE–
CUT IT OUT.
IF YOU CAME TO TALK ABOUT THE PAST, JUST LEAVE.
...
IT SEEMS LIKE...
LIKE WHAT?

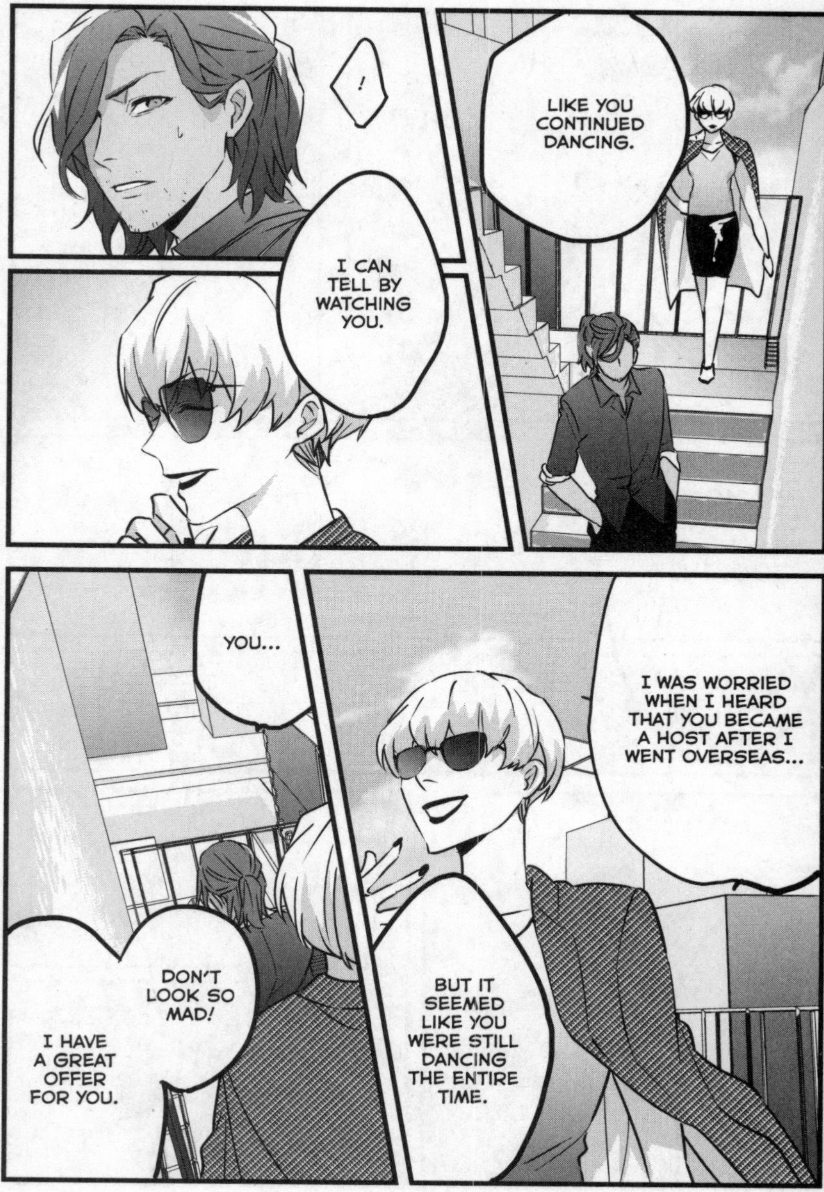
LIKE YOU CONTINUED DANCING.
!
I CAN TELL BY WATCHING YOU.
I WAS WORRIED WHEN I HEARD THAT YOU BECAME A HOST AFTER I WENT OVERSEAS...
BUT IT SEEMED LIKE YOU WERE STILL DANCING THE ENTIRE TIME.
YOU...
DON'T LOOK SO MAD!
I HAVE A GREAT OFFER FOR YOU.

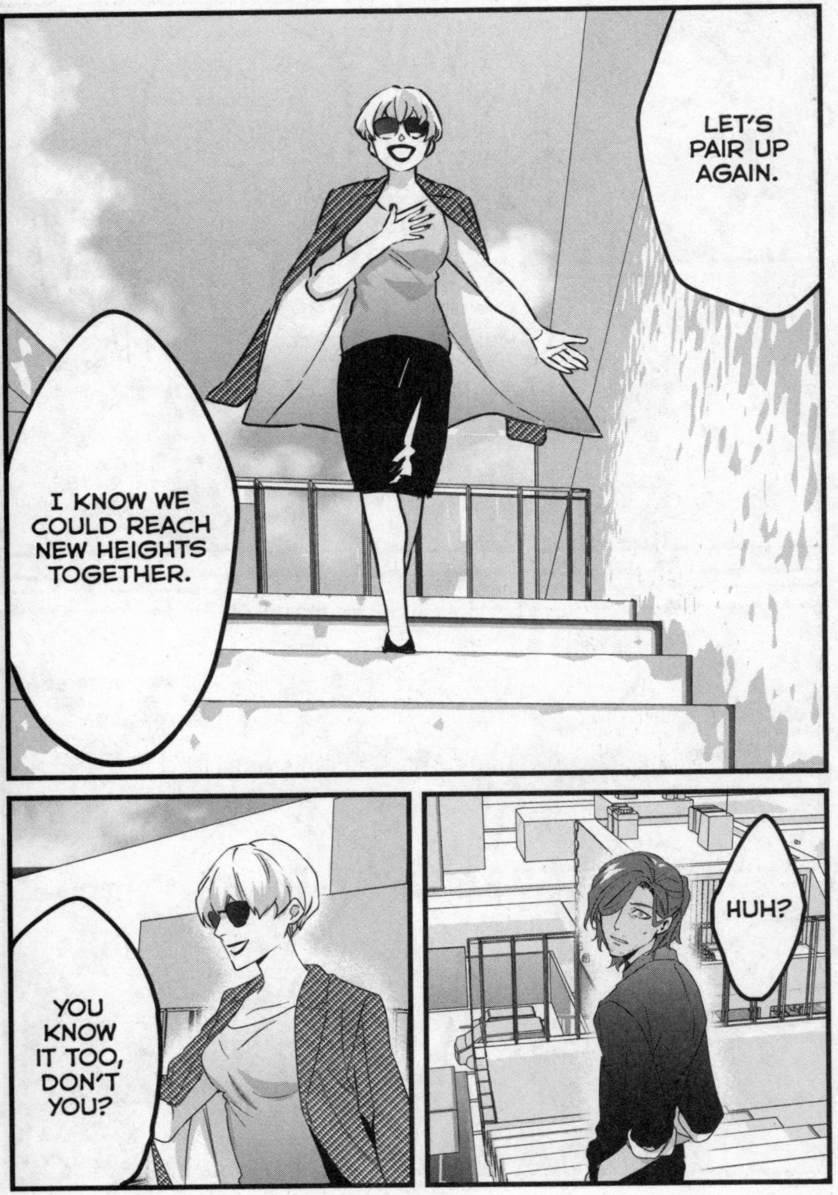
LET'S PAIR UP AGAIN.
I KNOW WE COULD REACH NEW HEIGHTS TOGETHER.
HUH?
YOU KNOW IT TOO, DON'T YOU?

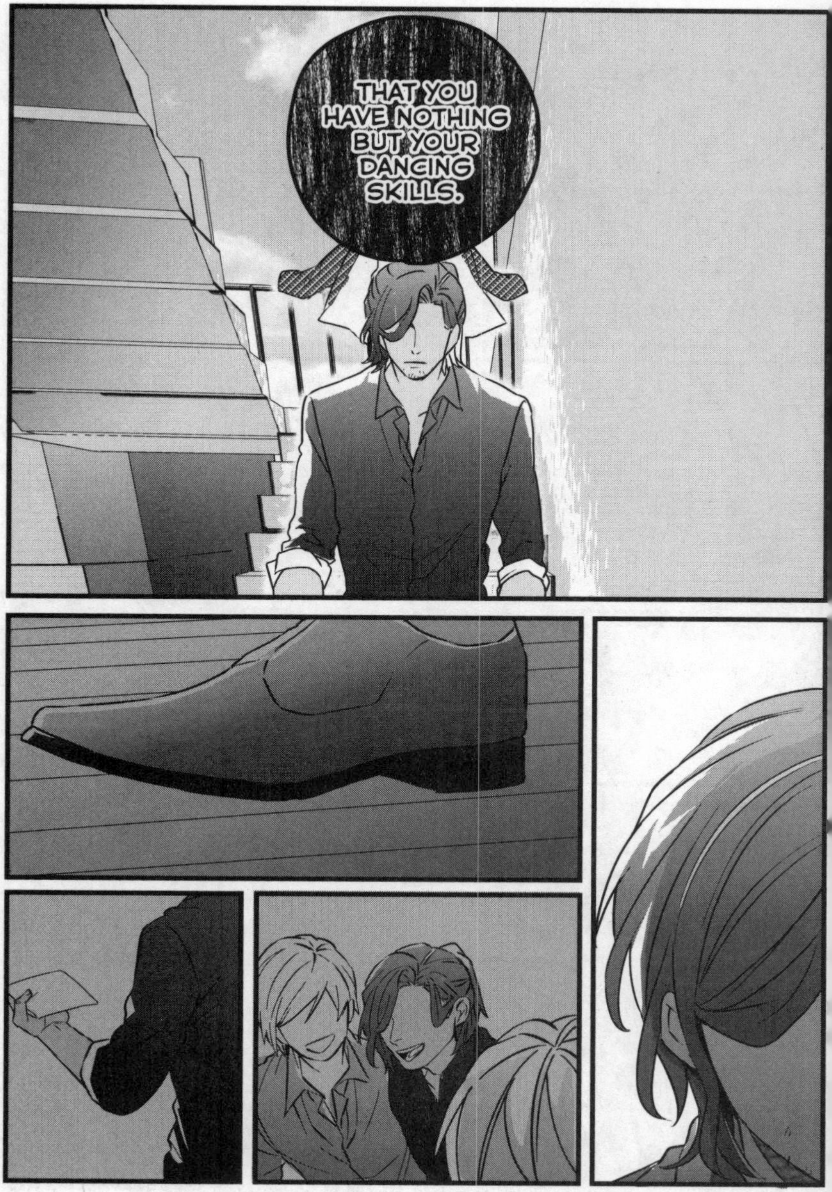
THAT YOU HAVE NOTHING BUT YOUR DANCING SKILLS.

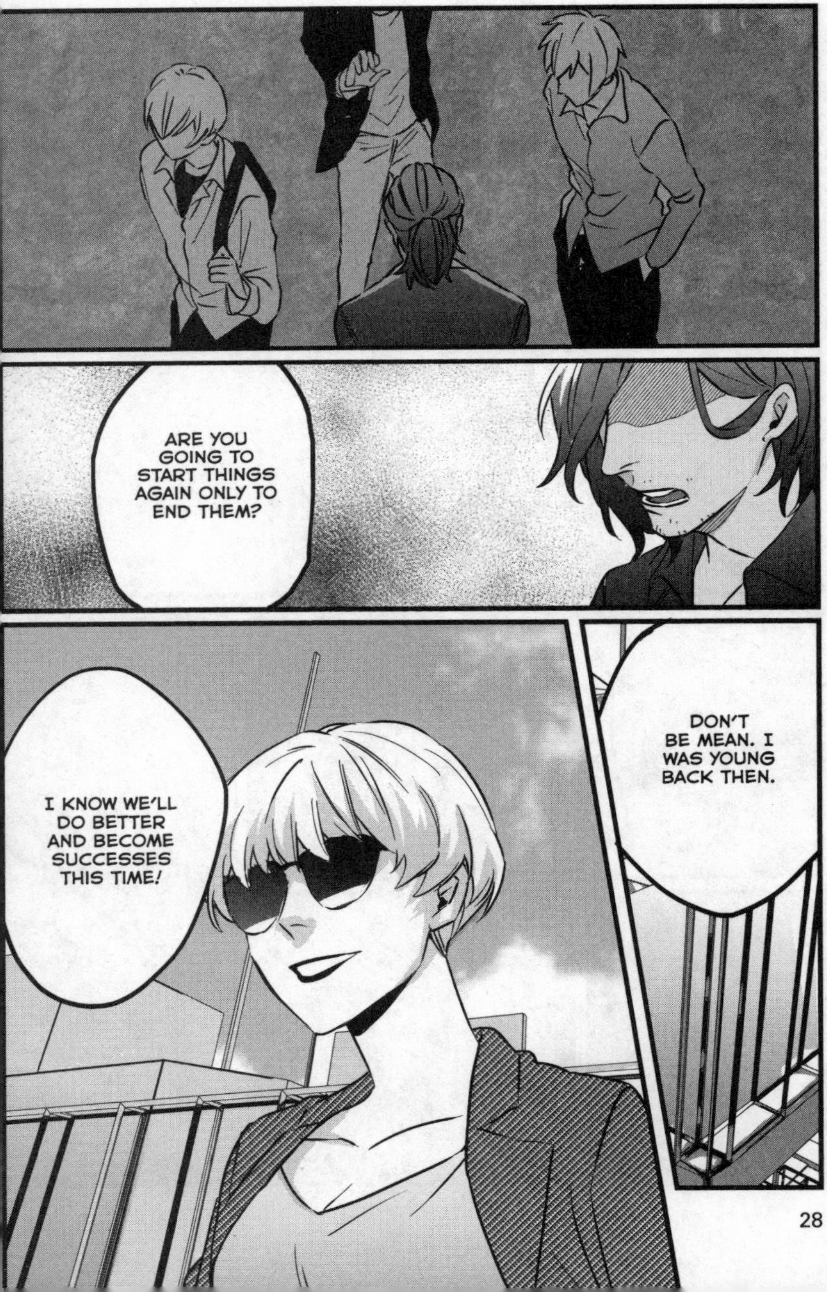
ARE YOU GOING TO START THINGS AGAIN ONLY TO END THEM?
DON'T BE MEAN. I WAS YOUNG BACK THEN.
I KNOW WE'LL DO BETTER AND BECOME SUCCESSES THIS TIME!

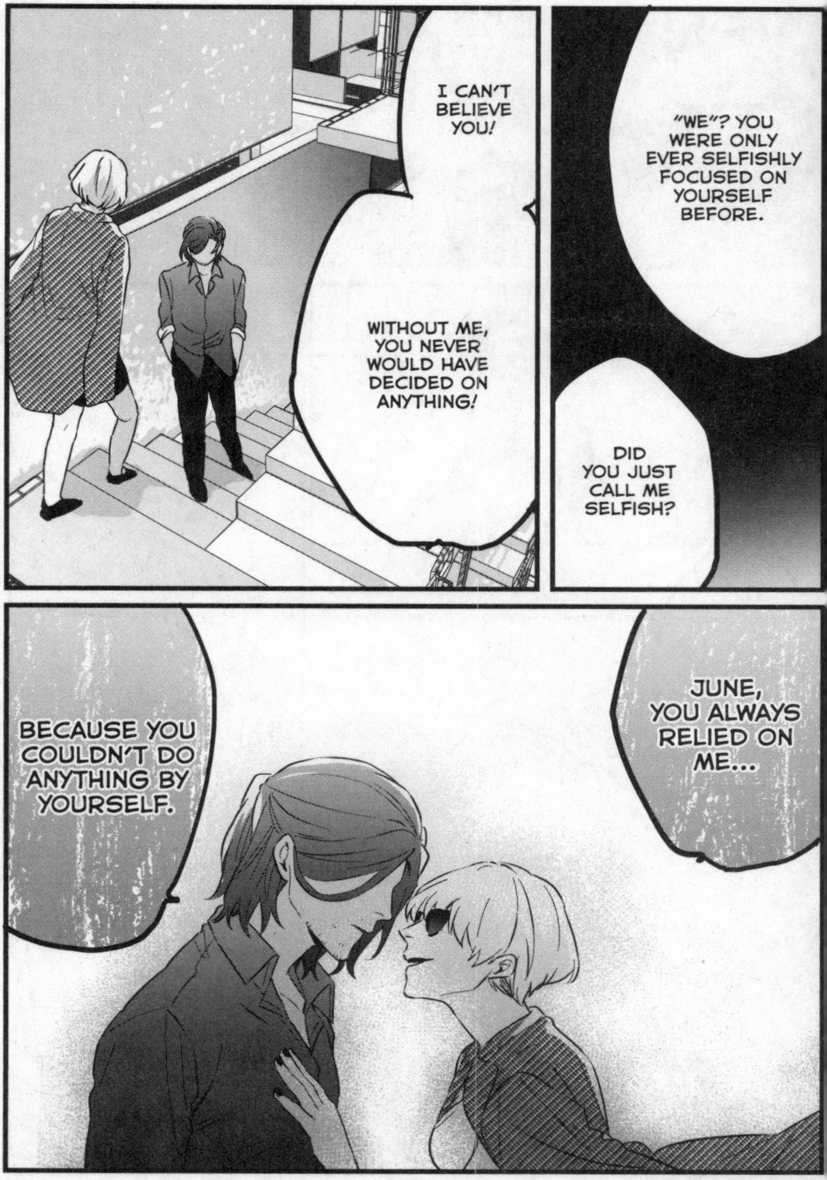
"WE"? YOU WERE ONLY EVER SELFISHLY FOCUSED ON YOURSELF BEFORE.
DID YOU JUST CALL ME SELFISH?
I CAN'T BELIEVE YOU!
WITHOUT ME, YOU NEVER WOULD HAVE DECIDED ON ANYTHING!
JUNE, YOU ALWAYS RELIED ON ME...
BECAUSE YOU COULDN'T DO ANYTHING BY YOURSELF.

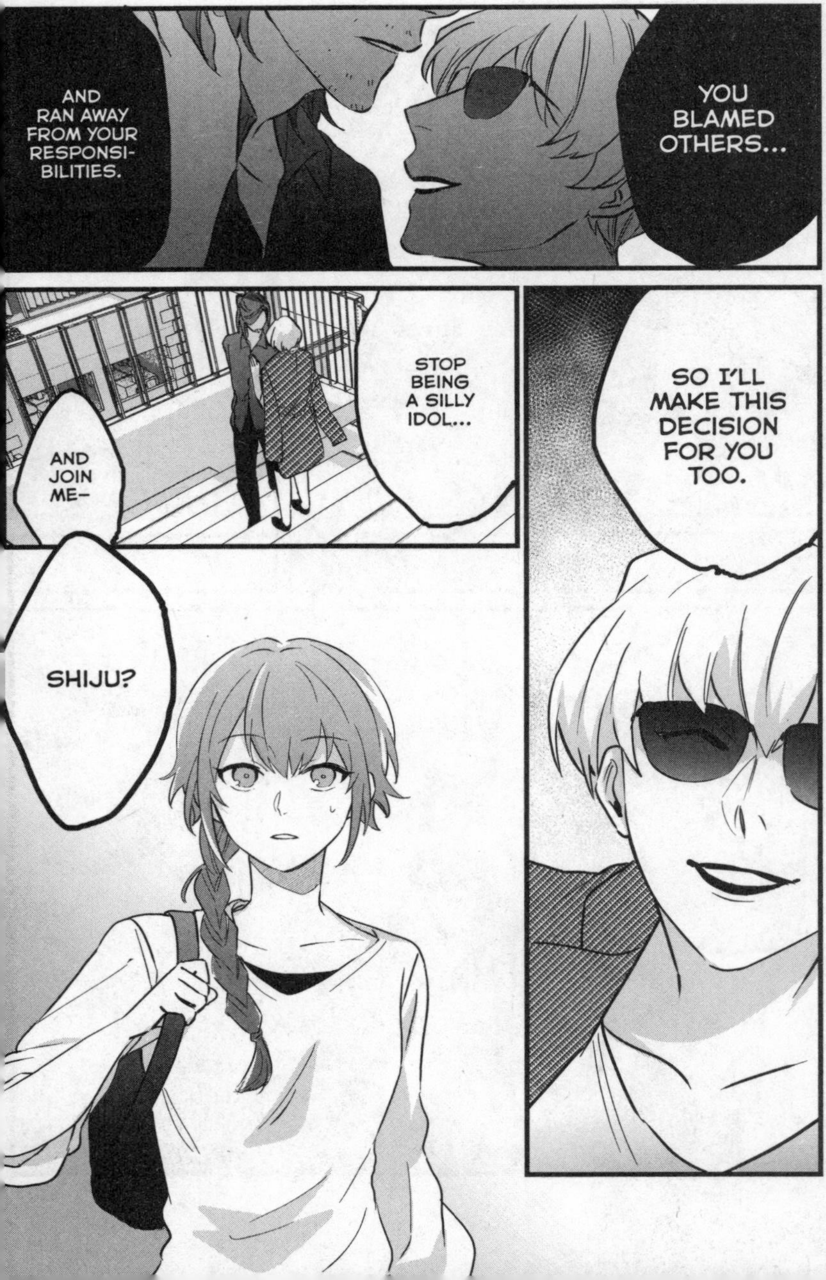
YOU BLAMED OTHERS...
AND RAN AWAY FROM YOUR RESPONSI-BILITIES.
SO I'LL MAKE THIS DECISION FOR YOU TOO.
STOP BEING A SILLY IDOL...
AND JOIN ME–
SHIJU?

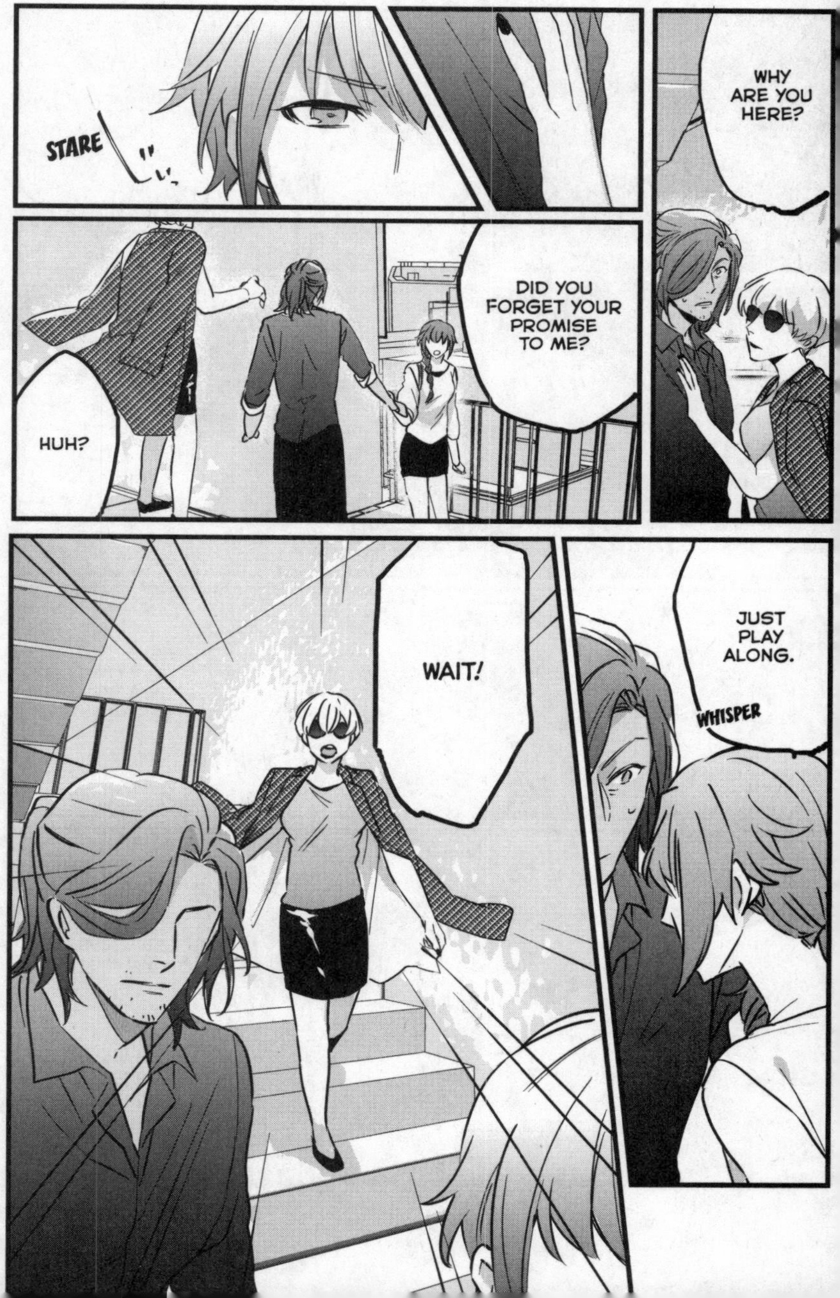
WHY ARE YOU HERE?
STARE
DID YOU FORGET YOUR PROMISE TO ME?
HUH?
JUST PLAY ALONG.
WHISPER
WAIT!

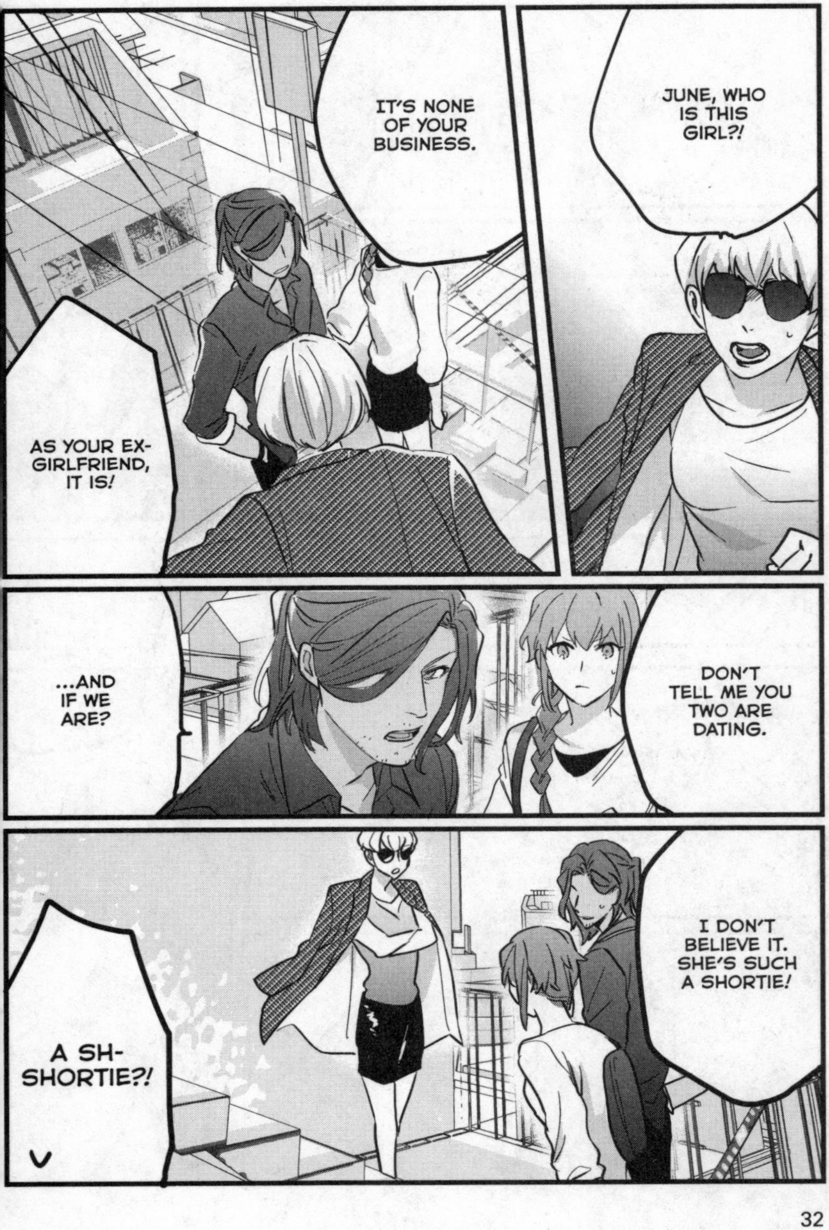
JUNE, WHO IS THIS GIRL?!
IT'S NONE OF YOUR BUSINESS.
AS YOUR EX-GIRLFRIEND, IT IS!
DON'T TELL ME YOU TWO ARE DATING.
...AND IF WE ARE?
I DON'T BELIEVE IT. SHE'S SUCH A SHORTIE!
A SH-SHORTIE?!

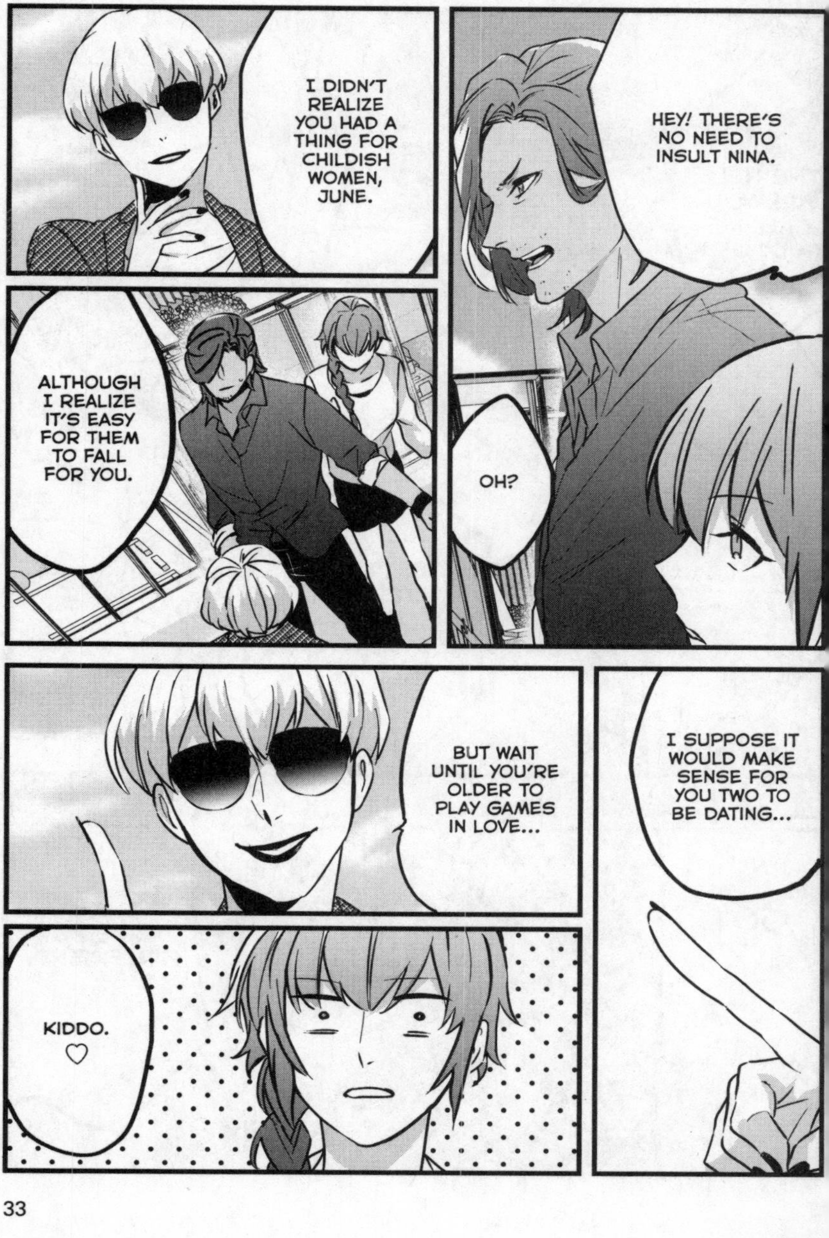
HEY! THERE'S NO NEED TO INSULT NINA.
OH?
I DIDN'T REALIZE YOU HAD A THING FOR CHILDISH WOMEN, JUNE.
ALTHOUGH I REALIZE IT'S EASY FOR THEM TO FALL FOR YOU.
I SUPPOSE IT WOULD MAKE SENSE FOR YOU TWO TO BE DATING...
BUT WAIT UNTIL YOU'RE OLDER TO PLAY GAMES IN LOVE...
KIDDO. ♡

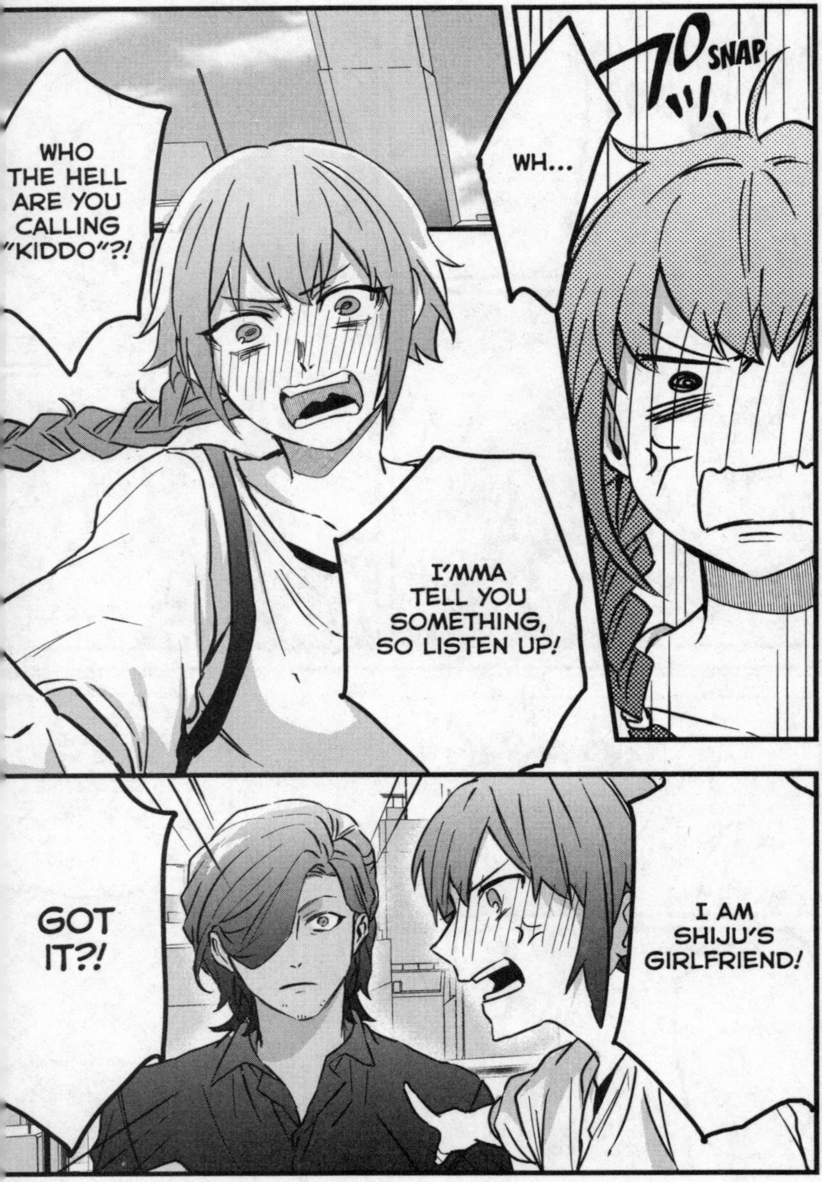
SNAP
WH...
WHO THE HELL ARE YOU CALLING "KIDDO"?!
I'MMA TELL YOU SOMETHING, SO LISTEN UP!
I AM SHIJU'S GIRLFRIEND!
GOT IT?!

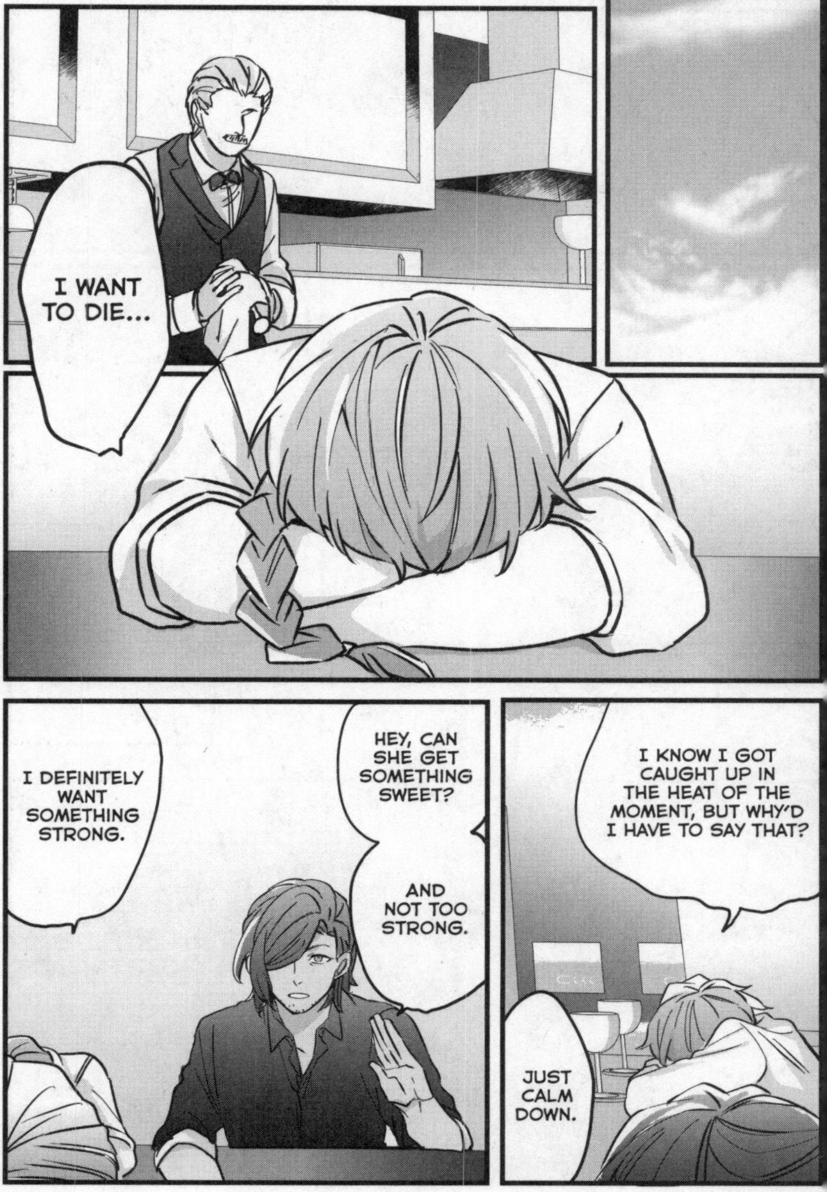
I WANT TO DIE...
I KNOW I GOT CAUGHT UP IN THE HEAT OF THE MOMENT, BUT WHY'D I HAVE TO SAY THAT?
JUST CALM DOWN.
HEY, CAN SHE GET SOMETHING SWEET?
AND NOT TOO STRONG.
I DEFINITELY WANT SOMETHING STRONG.

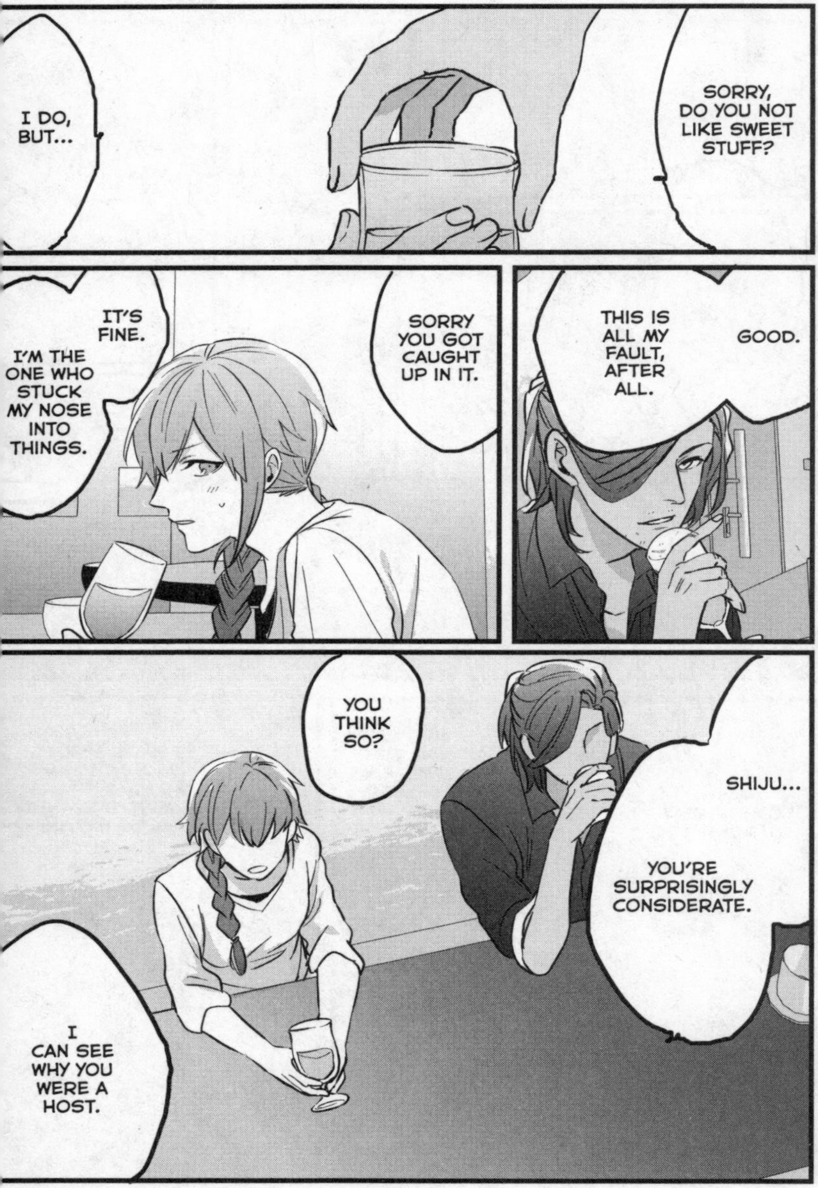
SORRY, DO YOU NOT LIKE SWEET STUFF?
I DO, BUT...
GOOD.
THIS IS ALL MY FAULT, AFTER ALL.
SORRY YOU GOT CAUGHT UP IN IT.
IT'S FINE.
I'M THE ONE WHO STUCK MY NOSE INTO THINGS.
SHIJU...
YOU'RE SURPRISINGLY CONSIDERATE.
YOU THINK SO?
I CAN SEE WHY YOU WERE A HOST.

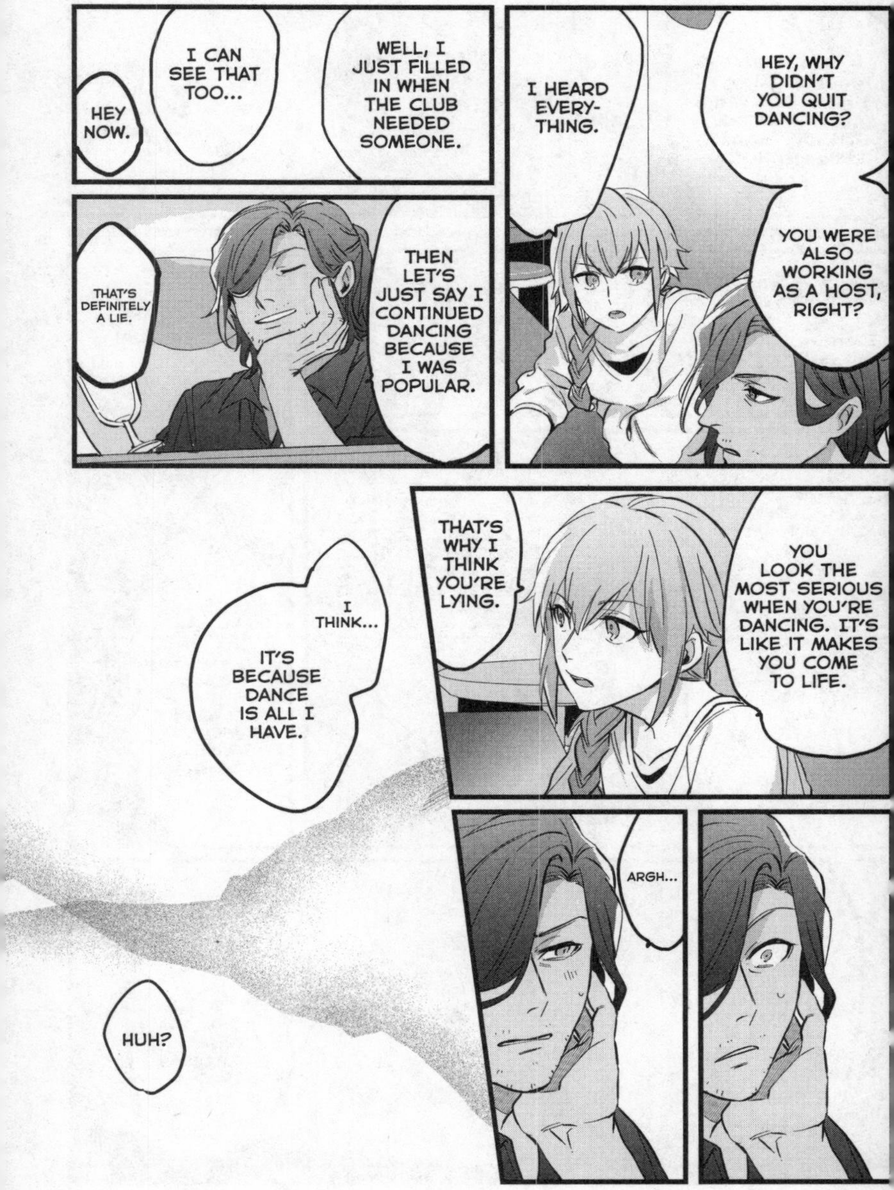
HEY, WHY DIDN'T YOU QUIT DANCING?
I HEARD EVERYTHING.
YOU WERE ALSO WORKING AS A HOST, RIGHT?
WELL, I JUST FILLED IN WHEN THE CLUB NEEDED SOMEONE.
I CAN SEE THAT TOO...
HEY NOW.
THEN LET'S JUST SAY I CONTINUED DANCING BECAUSE I WAS POPULAR.
THAT'S DEFINITELY A LIE.
YOU LOOK THE MOST SERIOUS WHEN YOU'RE DANCING. IT'S LIKE IT MAKES YOU COME TO LIFE.
THAT'S WHY I THINK YOU'RE LYING.
I THINK...
IT'S BECAUSE DANCE IS ALL I HAVE.
ARGH...
HUH?

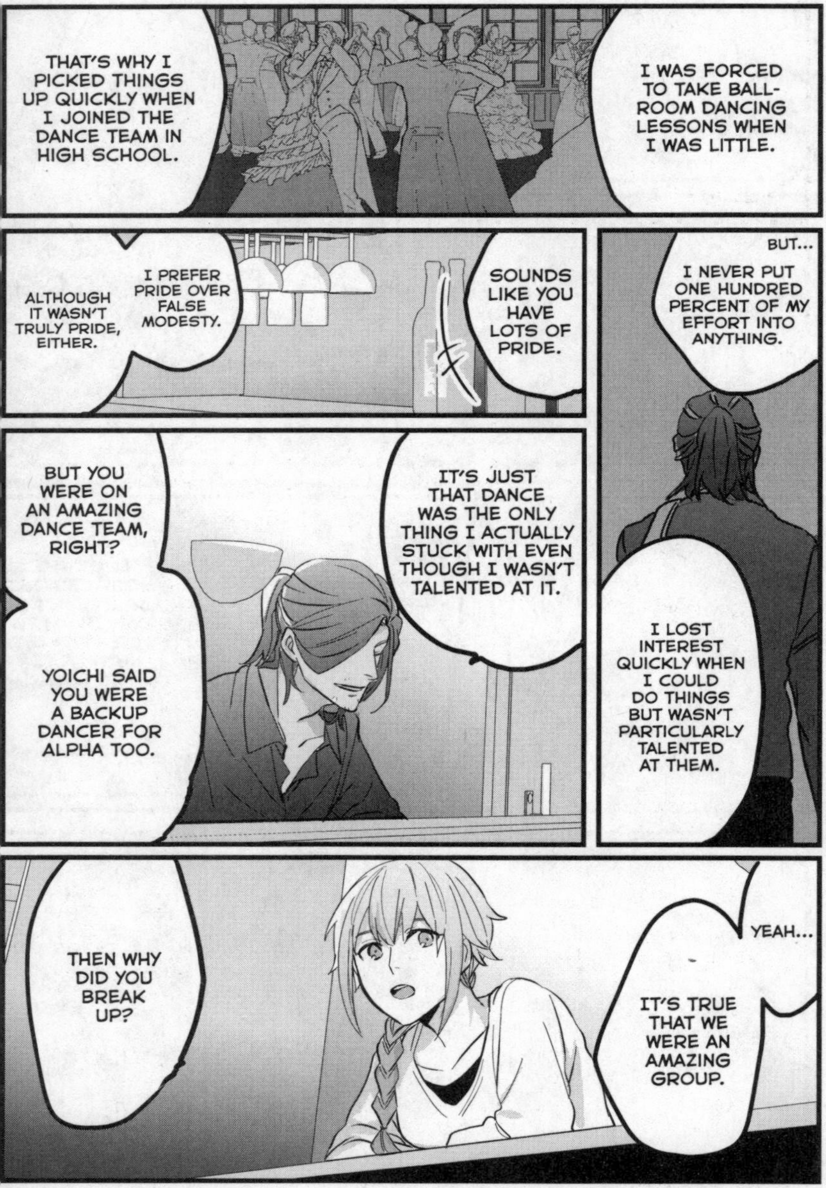
I WAS FORCED TO TAKE BALL-ROOM DANCING LESSONS WHEN I WAS LITTLE.
THAT'S WHY I PICKED THINGS UP QUICKLY WHEN I JOINED THE DANCE TEAM IN HIGH SCHOOL.
BUT...
I NEVER PUT ONE HUNDRED PERCENT OF MY EFFORT INTO ANYTHING.
I LOST INTEREST QUICKLY WHEN I COULD DO THINGS BUT WASN'T PARTICULARLY TALENTED AT THEM.
SOUNDS LIKE YOU HAVE LOTS OF PRIDE.
I PREFER PRIDE OVER FALSE MODESTY.
ALTHOUGH IT WASN'T TRULY PRIDE, EITHER.
IT'S JUST THAT DANCE WAS THE ONLY THING I ACTUALLY STUCK WITH EVEN THOUGH I WASN'T TALENTED AT IT.
BUT YOU WERE ON AN AMAZING DANCE TEAM, RIGHT?
YOICHI SAID YOU WERE A BACKUP DANCER FOR ALPHA TOO.
YEAH...
IT'S TRUE THAT WE WERE AN AMAZING GROUP.
THEN WHY DID YOU BREAK UP?

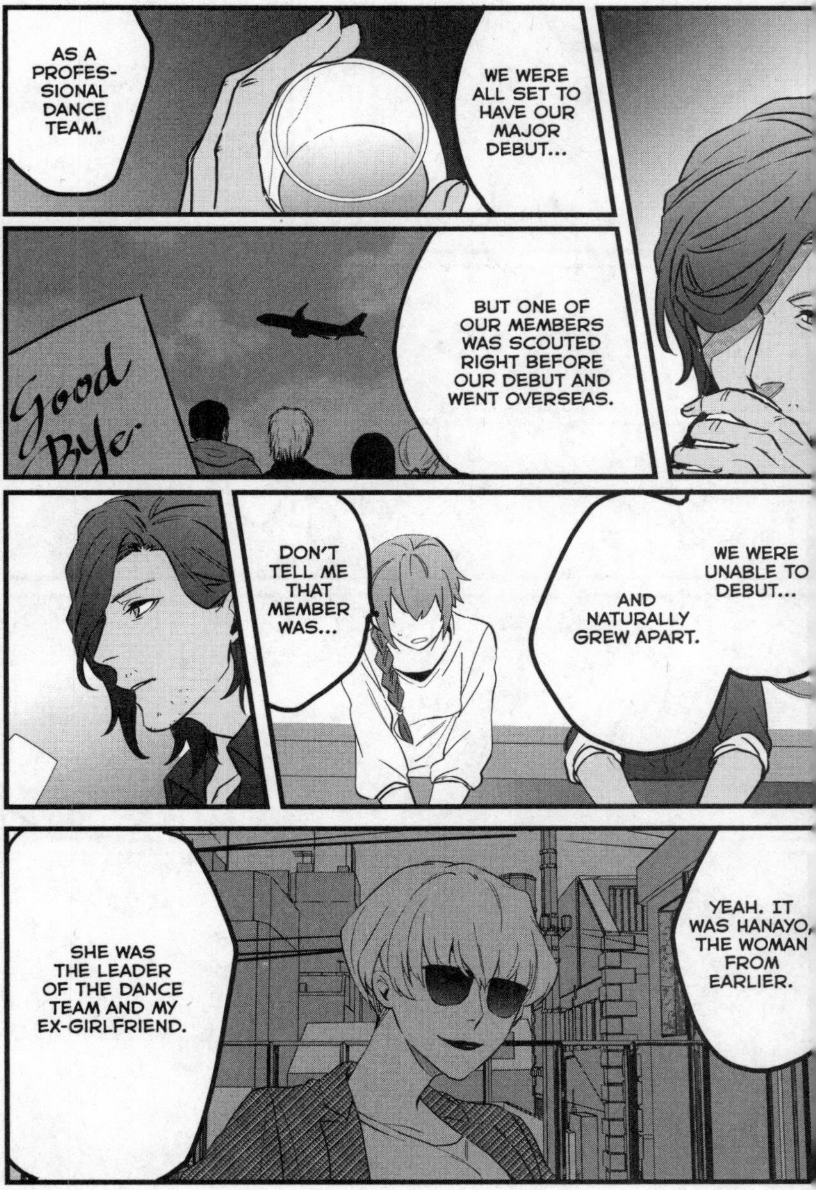
WE WERE ALL SET TO HAVE OUR MAJOR DEBUT...
AS A PROFESSIONAL DANCE TEAM.
BUT ONE OF OUR MEMBERS WAS SCOUTED RIGHT BEFORE OUR DEBUT AND WENT OVERSEAS.
Good Bye
WE WERE UNABLE TO DEBUT...
AND NATURALLY GREW APART.
DON'T TELL ME THAT MEMBER WAS...
YEAH. IT WAS HANAYO, THE WOMAN FROM EARLIER.
SHE WAS THE LEADER OF THE DANCE TEAM AND MY EX-GIRLFRIEND.

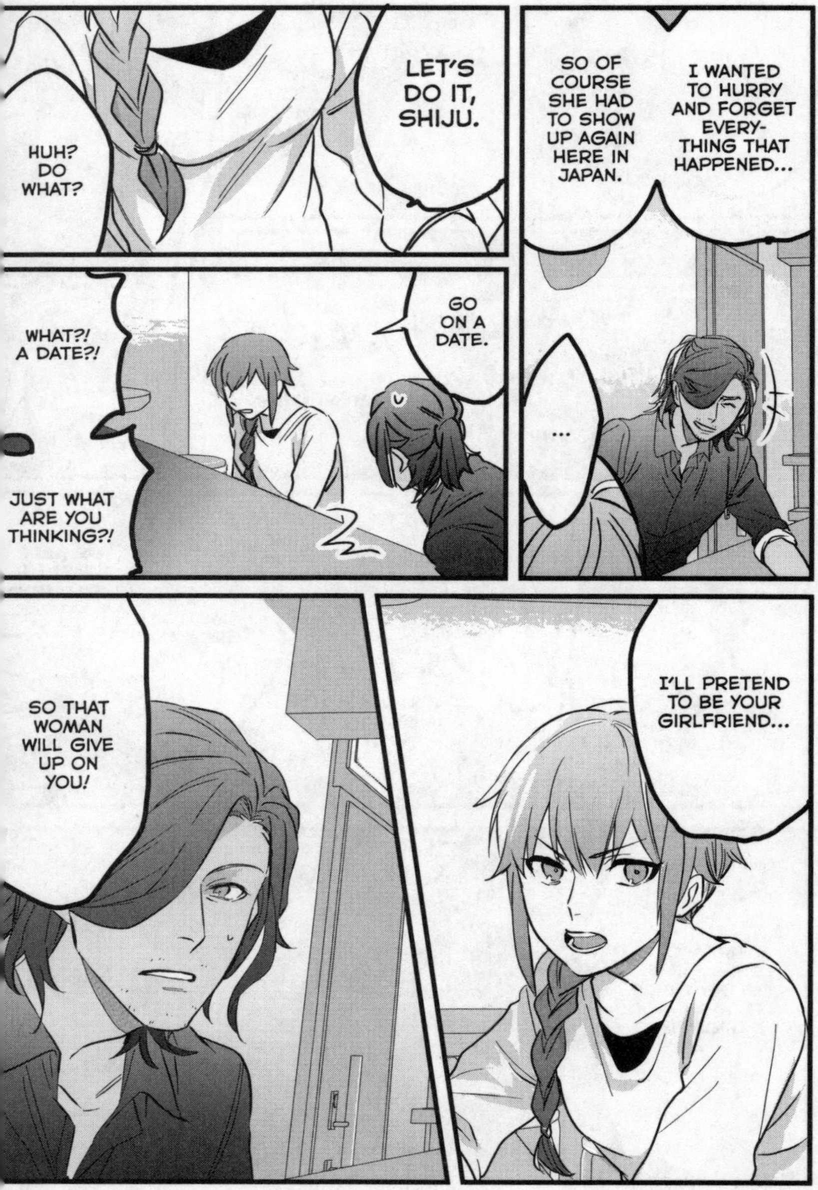
I WANTED TO HURRY AND FORGET EVERY-THING THAT HAPPENED...
SO OF COURSE SHE HAD TO SHOW UP AGAIN HERE IN JAPAN.
...
LET'S DO IT, SHIJU.
HUH? DO WHAT?
GO ON A DATE.
WHAT?! A DATE?!
JUST WHAT ARE YOU THINKING?!
I'LL PRETEND TO BE YOUR GIRLFRIEND...
SO THAT WOMAN WILL GIVE UP ON YOU!

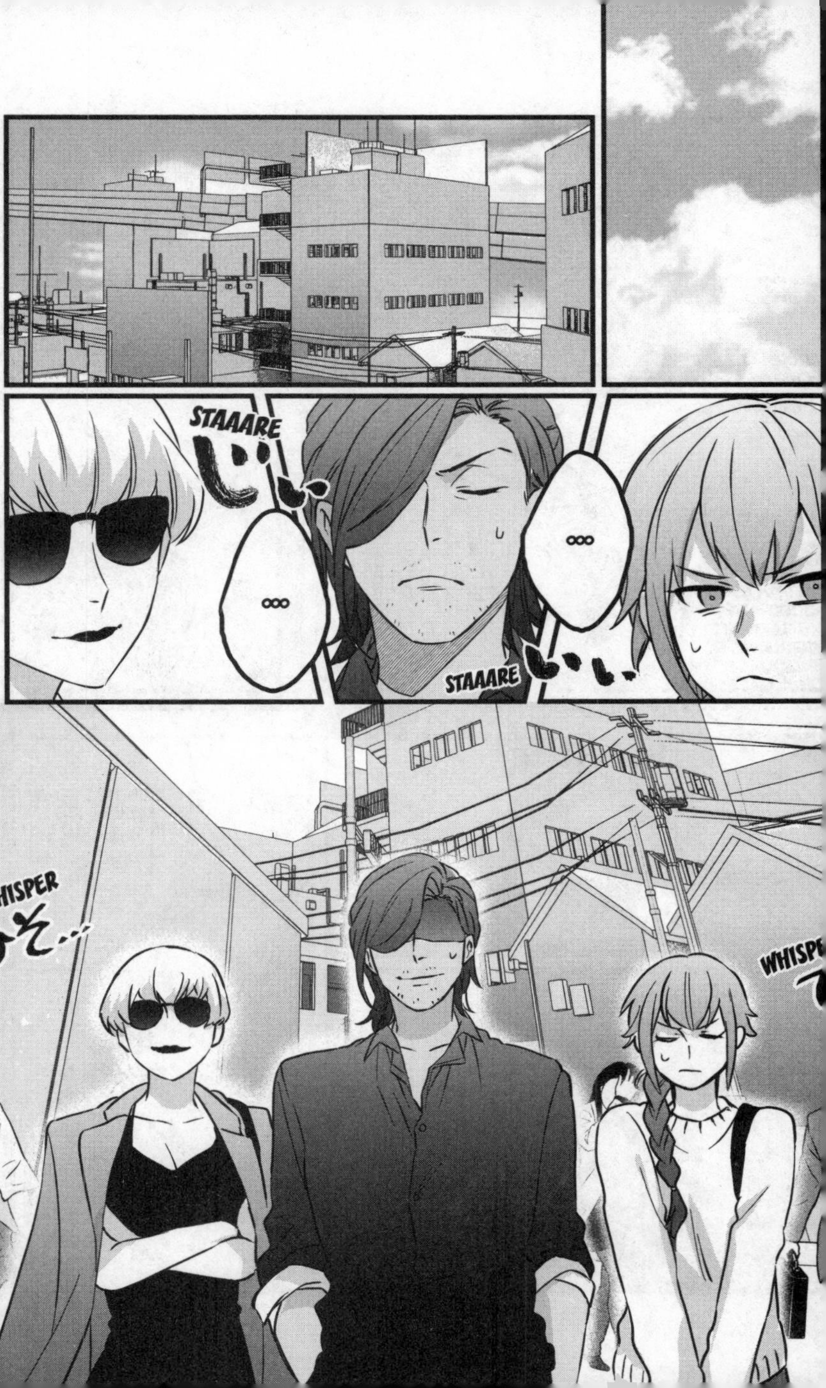
...
STAAARE
STAAARE
...
WHISPE
WHISPER
ひそ...

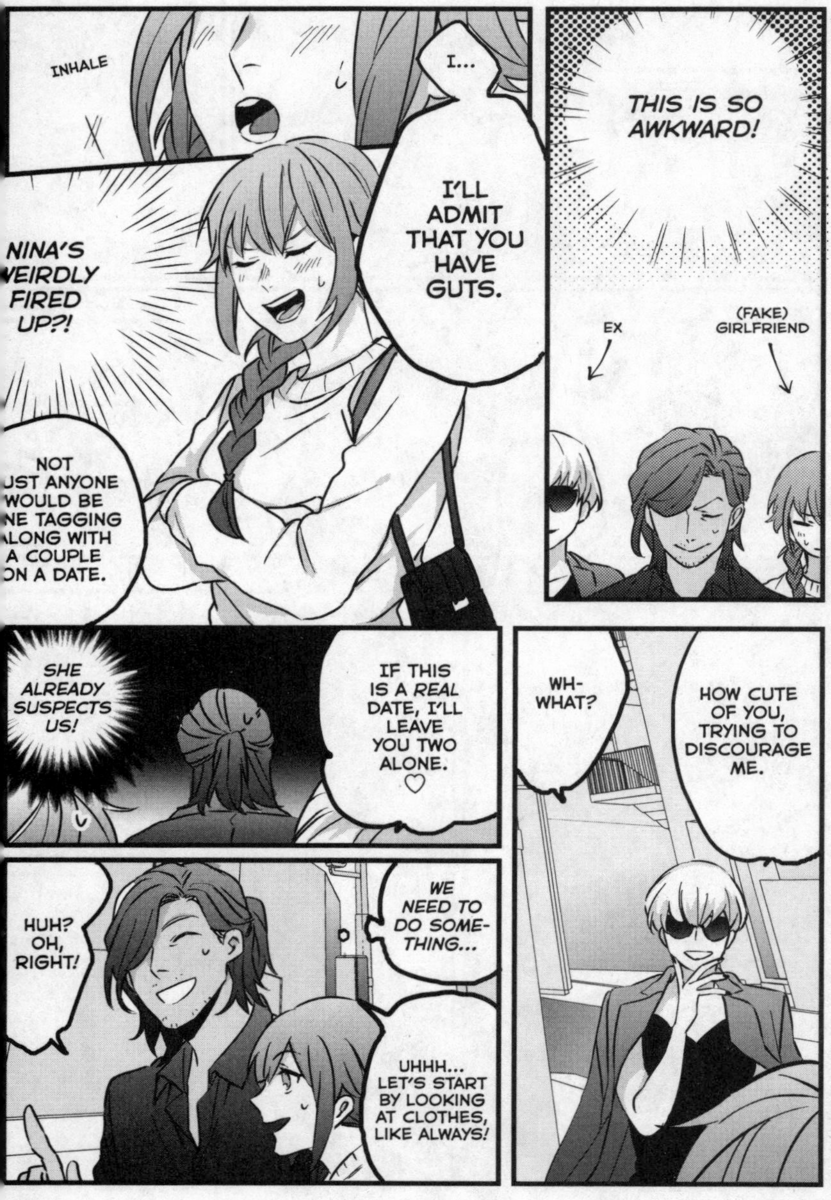
THIS IS SO AWKWARD!
EX
(FAKE) GIRLFRIEND
INHALE
I...
I'LL ADMIT THAT YOU HAVE GUTS.
NINA'S WEIRDLY FIRED UP?!
NOT JUST ANYONE WOULD BE THE TAGGING ALONG WITH A COUPLE ON A DATE.
WH- WHAT?
HOW CUTE OF YOU, TRYING TO DISCOURAGE ME.
IF THIS IS A *REAL* DATE, I'LL LEAVE YOU TWO ALONE. ♡
SHE ALREADY SUSPECTS US!
WE NEED TO DO SOME- THING...
HUH? OH, RIGHT!
UHHH... LET'S START BY LOOKING AT CLOTHES, LIKE ALWAYS!

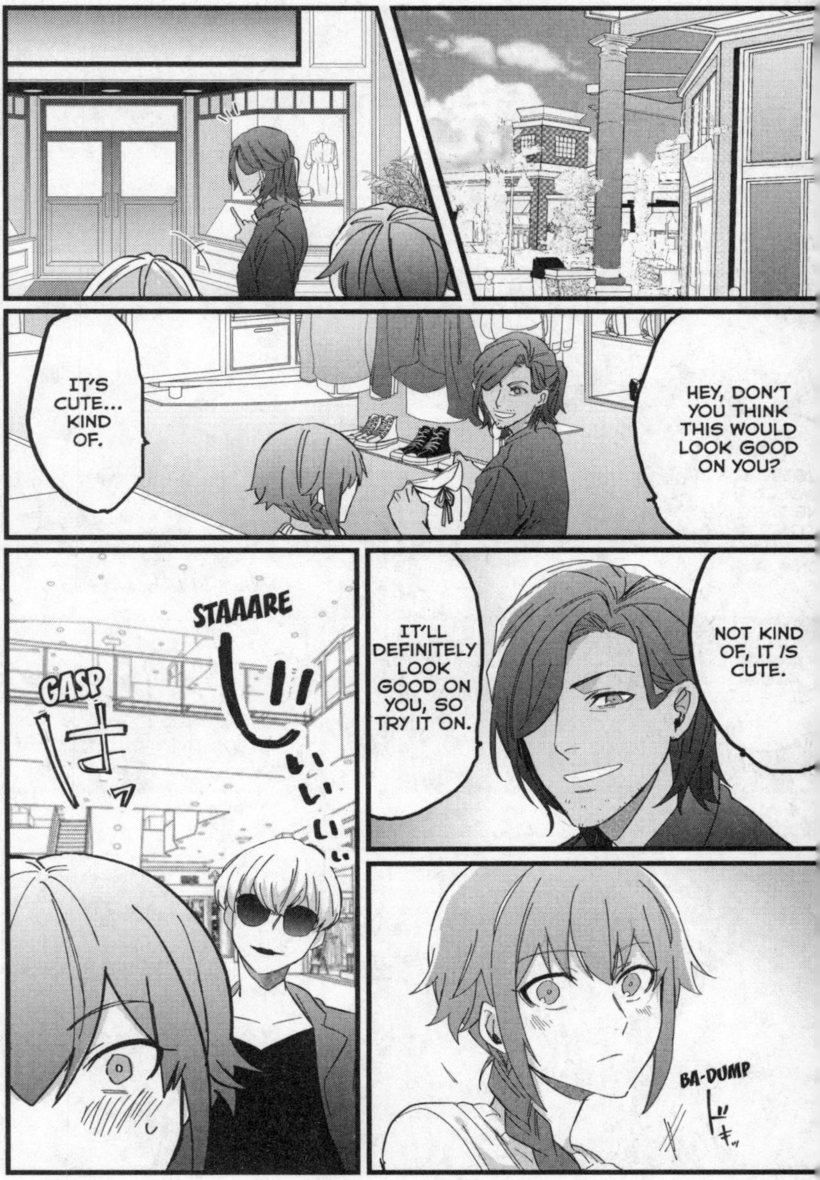
HEY, DON'T YOU THINK THIS WOULD LOOK GOOD ON YOU?
IT'S CUTE... KIND OF.
NOT KIND OF, IT *IS* CUTE.
IT'LL DEFINITELY LOOK GOOD ON YOU, SO TRY IT ON.
BA-DUMP
STAAARE
GASP

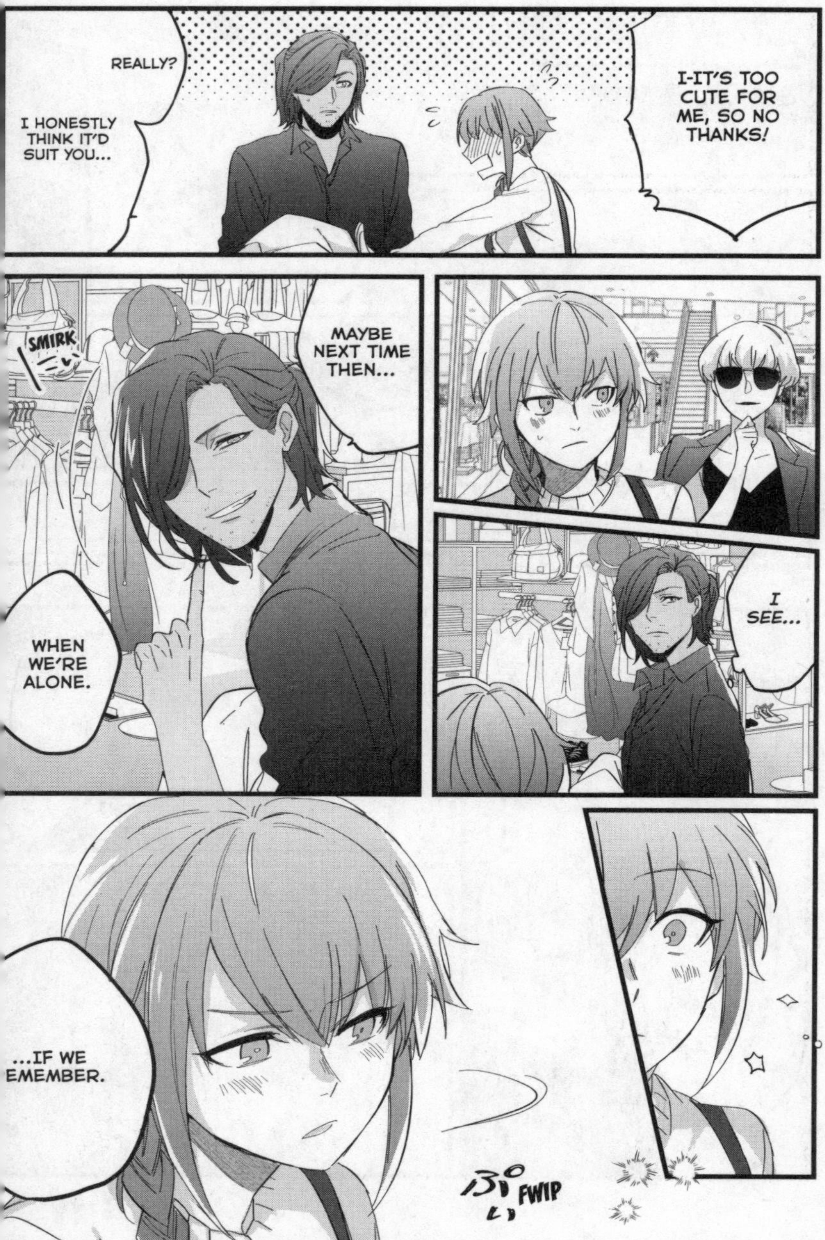
I-IT'S TOO CUTE FOR ME, SO NO THANKS!
REALLY?
I HONESTLY THINK IT'D SUIT YOU...
I SEE...
MAYBE NEXT TIME THEN...
SMIRK
WHEN WE'RE ALONE.
...IF WE EMEMBER.
FWIP

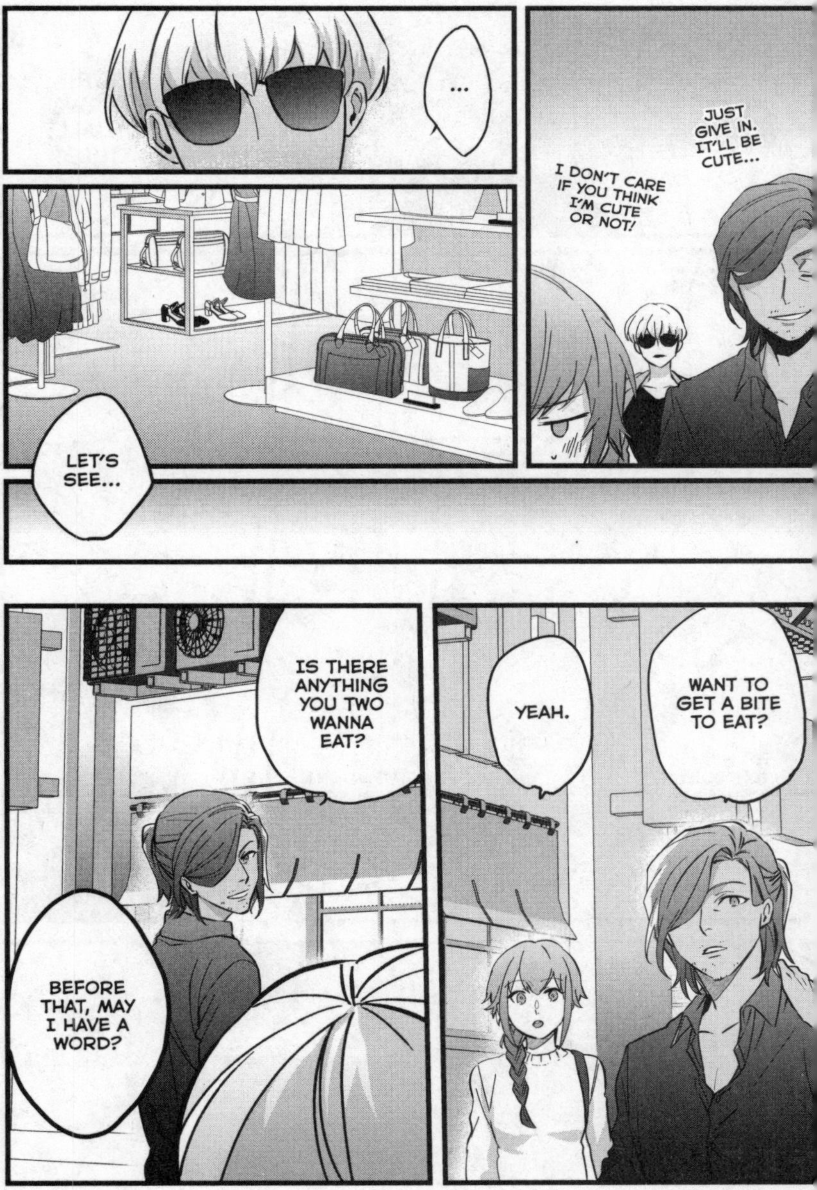
JUST GIVE IN. IT'LL BE CUTE...
I DON'T CARE IF YOU THINK I'M CUTE OR NOT!
...
LET'S SEE...
WANT TO GET A BITE TO EAT?
YEAH.
IS THERE ANYTHING YOU TWO WANNA EAT?
BEFORE THAT, MAY I HAVE A WORD?

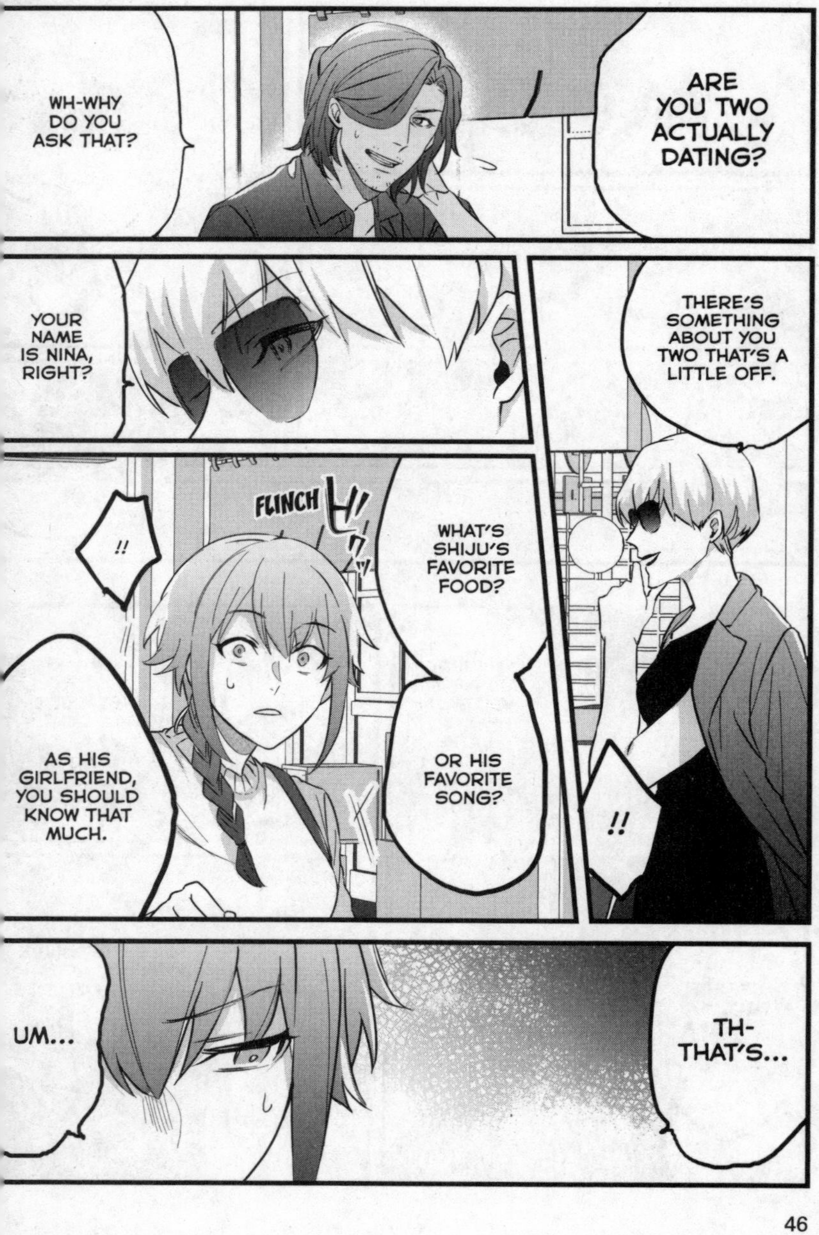
ARE YOU TWO ACTUALLY DATING?
WH-WHY DO YOU ASK THAT?
THERE'S SOMETHING ABOUT YOU TWO THAT'S A LITTLE OFF.
!!
YOUR NAME IS NINA, RIGHT?
WHAT'S SHIJU'S FAVORITE FOOD?
FLINCH
!!
OR HIS FAVORITE SONG?
AS HIS GIRLFRIEND, YOU SHOULD KNOW THAT MUCH.
TH- THAT'S...
UM...

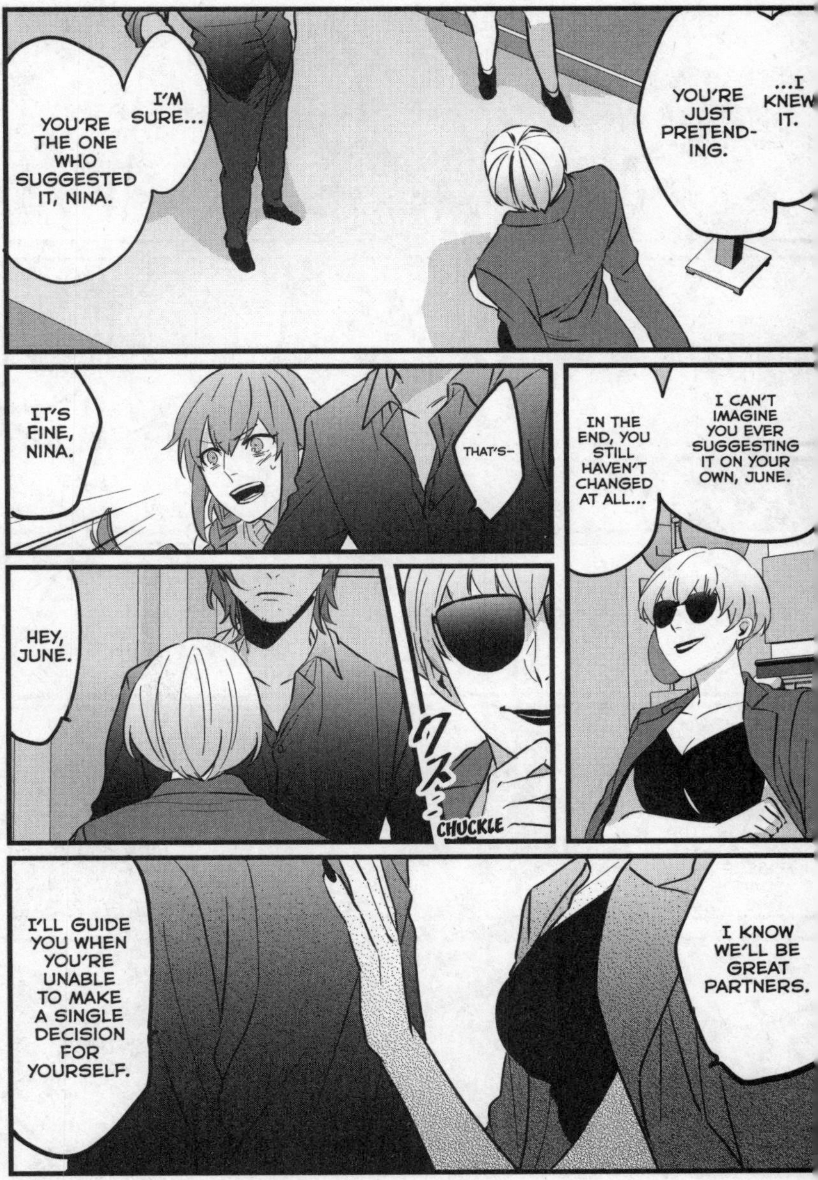
...I KNEW IT.
YOU'RE JUST PRETENDING.
I'M SURE...
YOU'RE THE ONE WHO SUGGESTED IT, NINA.
I CAN'T IMAGINE YOU EVER SUGGESTING IT ON YOUR OWN, JUNE.
IN THE END, YOU STILL HAVEN'T CHANGED AT ALL...
THAT'S—
IT'S FINE, NINA.
CHUCKLE
HEY, JUNE.
I KNOW WE'LL BE GREAT PARTNERS.
I'LL GUIDE YOU WHEN YOU'RE UNABLE TO MAKE A SINGLE DECISION FOR YOURSELF.

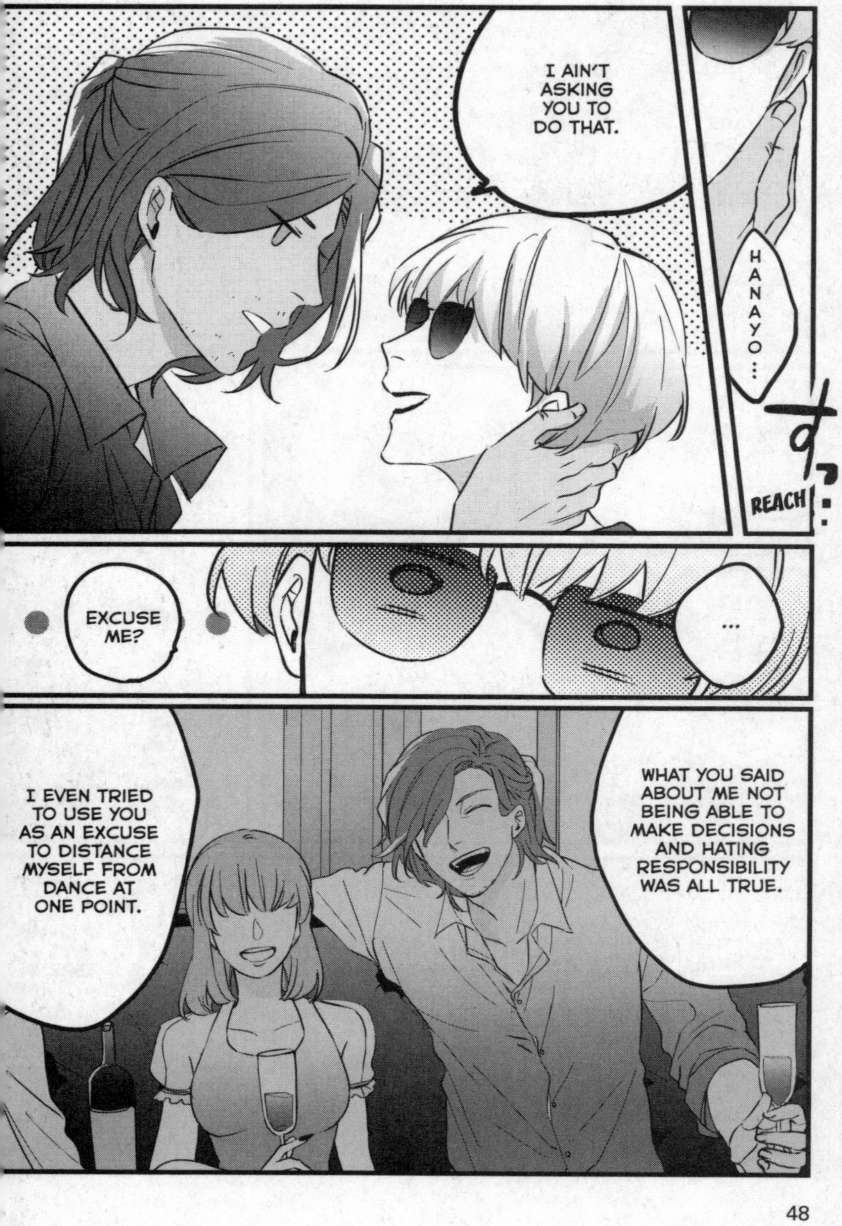
HANAYO...
す
REACH
I AIN'T ASKING YOU TO DO THAT.
...
EXCUSE ME?
WHAT YOU SAID ABOUT ME NOT BEING ABLE TO MAKE DECISIONS AND HATING RESPONSIBILITY WAS ALL TRUE.
I EVEN TRIED TO USE YOU AS AN EXCUSE TO DISTANCE MYSELF FROM DANCE AT ONE POINT.

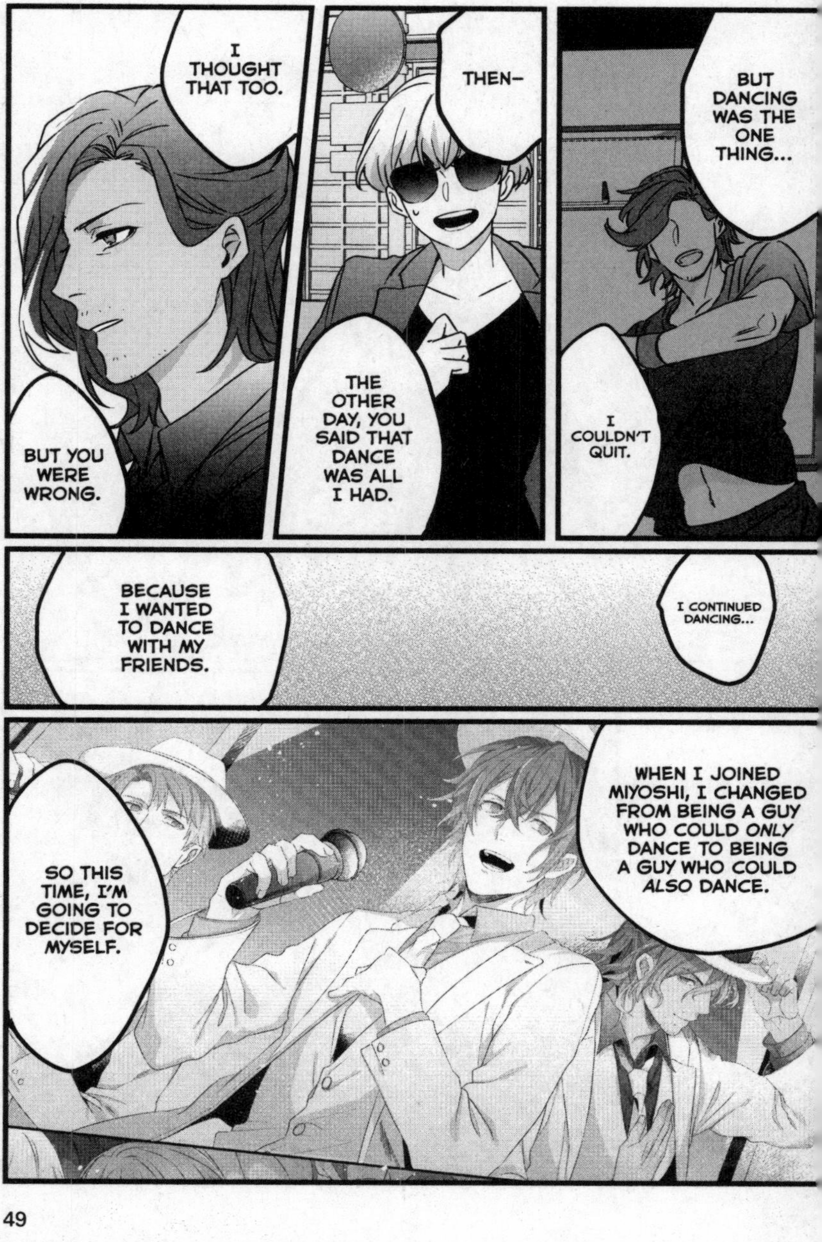
BUT DANCING WAS THE ONE THING...
I COULDN'T QUIT.
THEN—
THE OTHER DAY, YOU SAID THAT DANCE WAS ALL I HAD.
I THOUGHT THAT TOO.
BUT YOU WERE WRONG.
I CONTINUED DANCING...
BECAUSE I WANTED TO DANCE WITH MY FRIENDS.
WHEN I JOINED MIYOSHI, I CHANGED FROM BEING A GUY WHO COULD *ONLY* DANCE TO BEING A GUY WHO COULD *ALSO* DANCE.
SO THIS TIME, I'M GOING TO DECIDE FOR MYSELF.

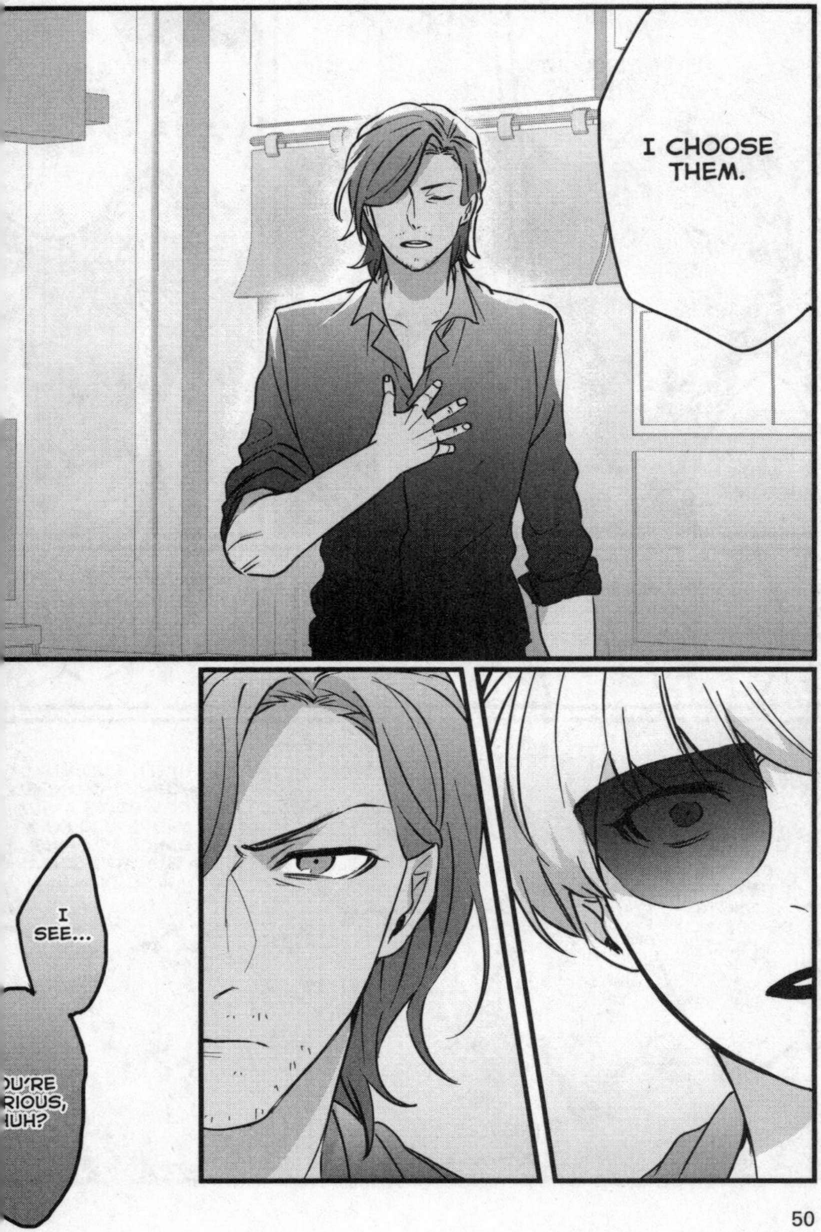
I CHOOSE THEM.
I SEE...
OU'RE RIOUS, HUH?

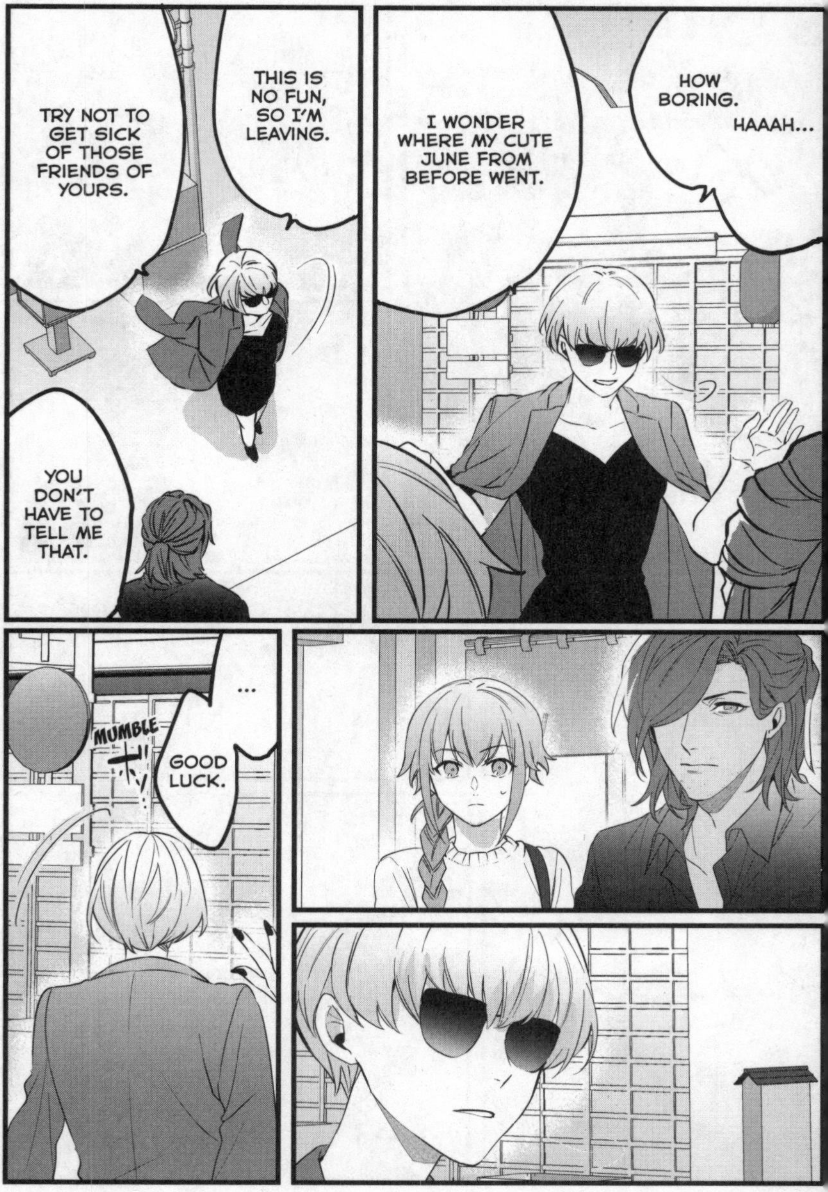
HOW BORING.
HAAAH...
I WONDER WHERE MY CUTE JUNE FROM BEFORE WENT.
THIS IS NO FUN, SO I'M LEAVING.
TRY NOT TO GET SICK OF THOSE FRIENDS OF YOURS.
YOU DON'T HAVE TO TELL ME THAT.
...
GOOD LUCK.
MUMBLE

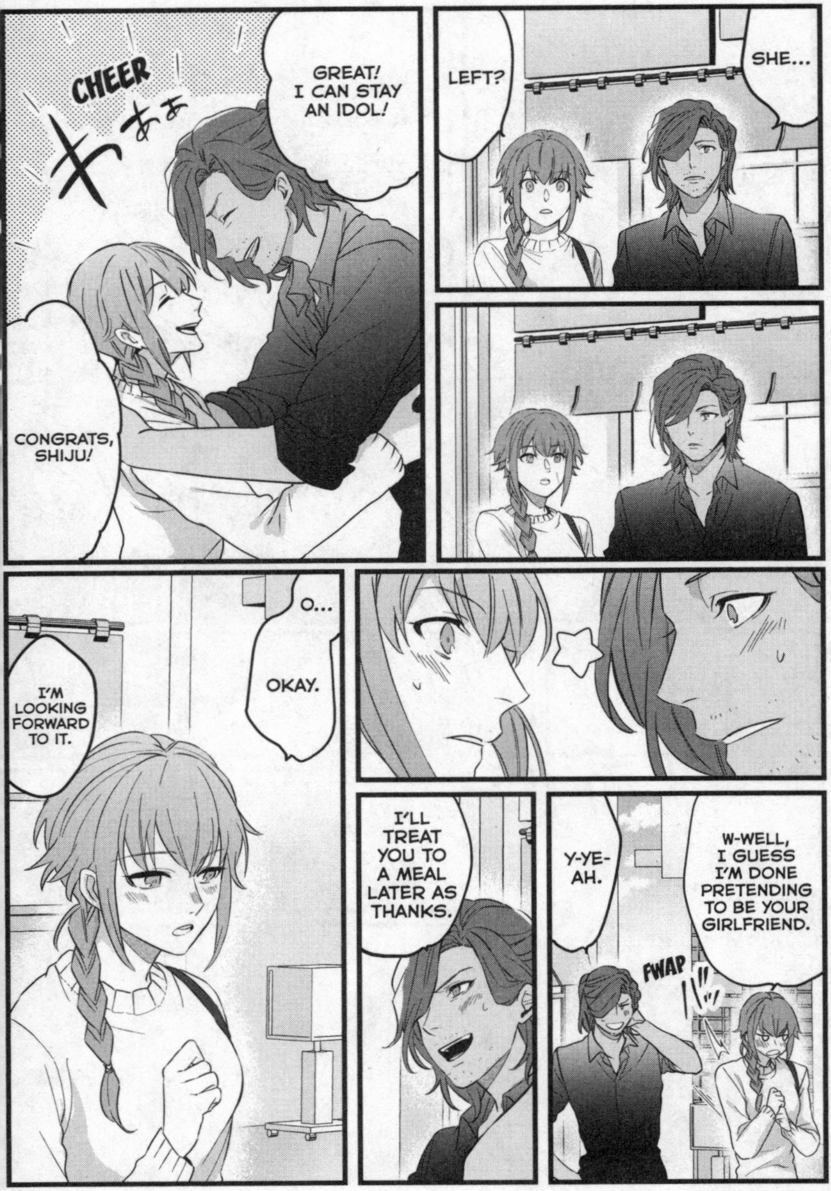
SHE...
LEFT?
GREAT! I CAN STAY AN IDOL!
CHEER
CONGRATS, SHIJU!
W-WELL, I GUESS I'M DONE PRETENDING TO BE YOUR GIRLFRIEND.
FWAP
Y-YE-AH.
I'LL TREAT YOU TO A MEAL LATER AS THANKS.
O...
OKAY.
I'M LOOKING FORWARD TO IT.

Chapter 33

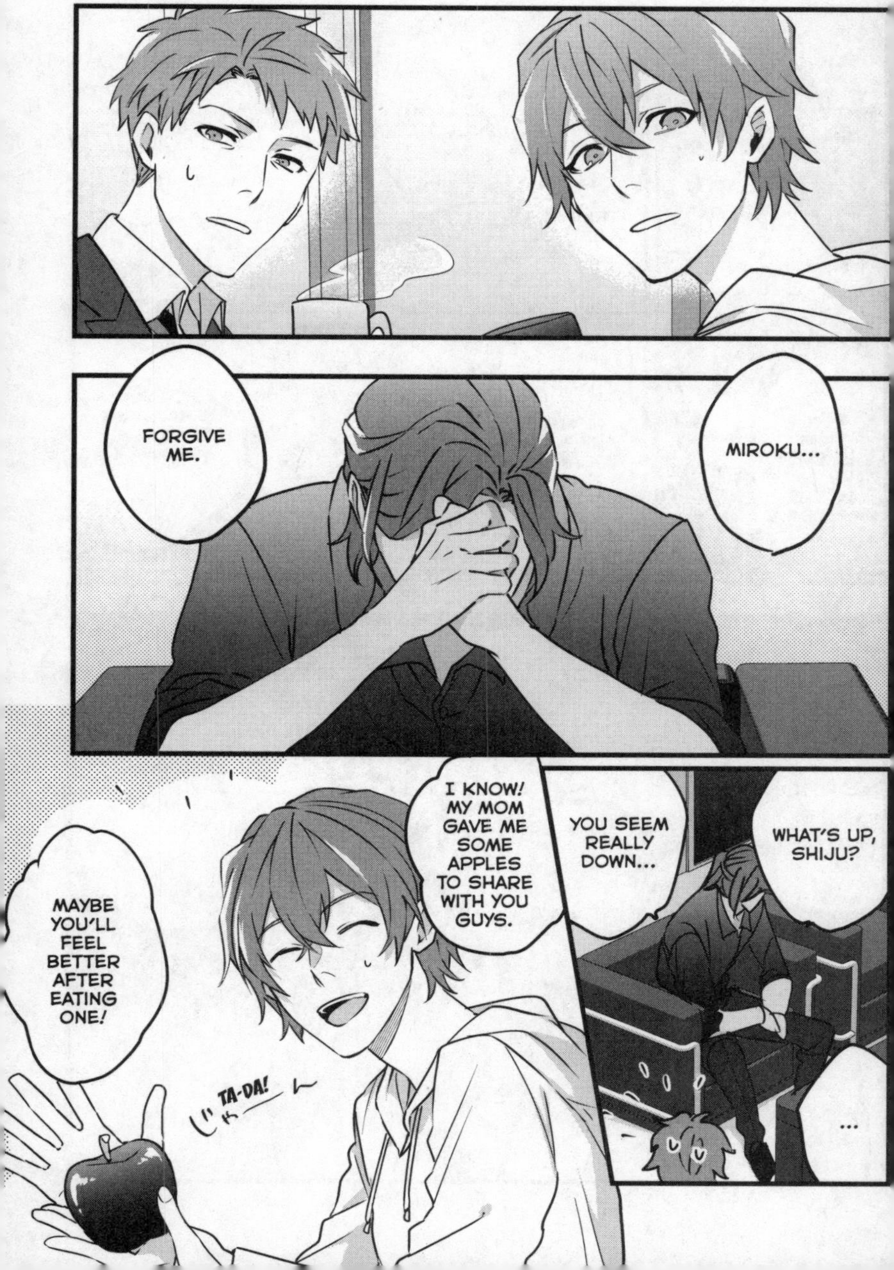
MIROKU...
FORGIVE ME.
WHAT'S UP, SHIJU?
YOU SEEM REALLY DOWN...
...
I KNOW! MY MOM GAVE ME SOME APPLES TO SHARE WITH YOU GUYS.
MAYBE YOU'LL FEEL BETTER AFTER EATING ONE!
TA-DA!
じゃーん

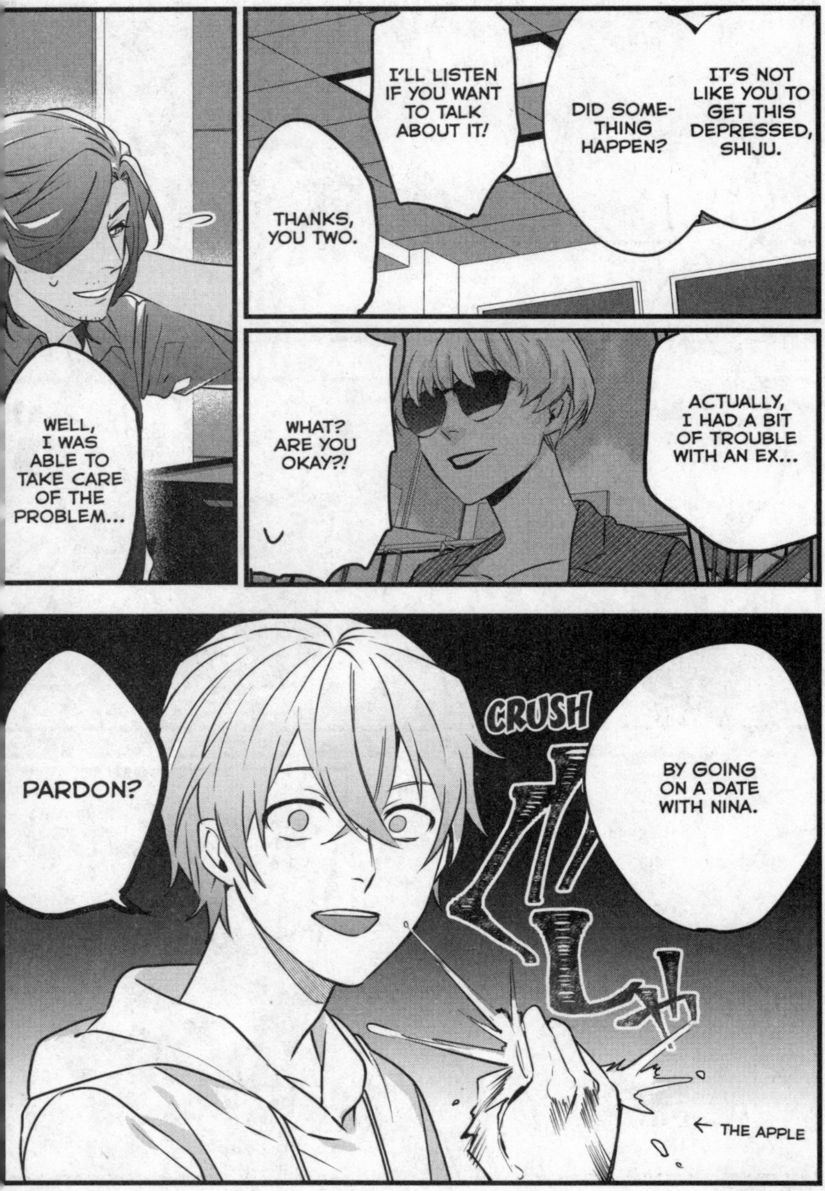

IT'S NOT LIKE YOU TO GET THIS DEPRESSED, SHIJU.
DID SOME-THING HAPPEN?
I'LL LISTEN IF YOU WANT TO TALK ABOUT IT!
THANKS, YOU TWO.
ACTUALLY, I HAD A BIT OF TROUBLE WITH AN EX...
WHAT? ARE YOU OKAY?!
WELL, I WAS ABLE TO TAKE CARE OF THE PROBLEM...
BY GOING ON A DATE WITH NINA.
CRUSH
PARDON?
← THE APPLE

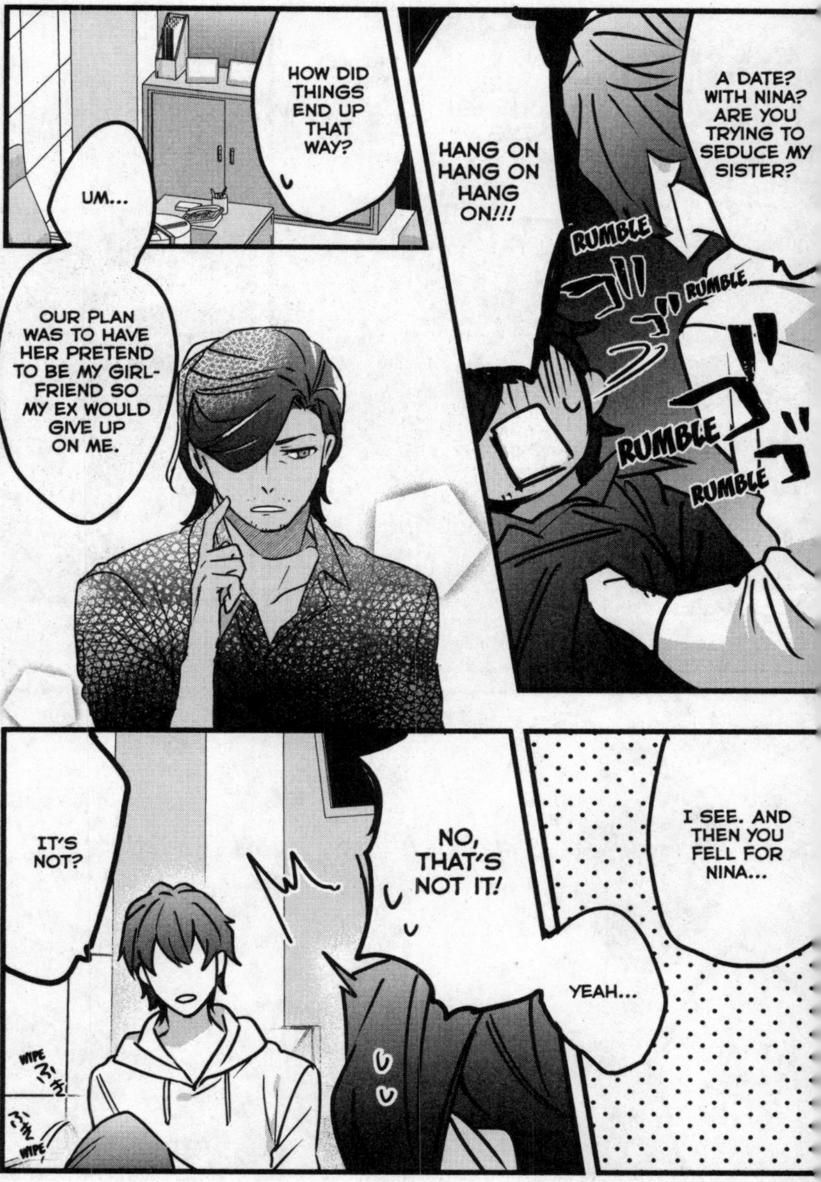

A DATE? WITH NINA? ARE YOU TRYING TO SEDUCE MY SISTER?
HANG ON HANG ON HANG ON!!!
RUMBLE
RUMBLE
RUMBLE
RUMBLE
HOW DID THINGS END UP THAT WAY?
UM...
OUR PLAN WAS TO HAVE HER PRETEND TO BE MY GIRL-FRIEND SO MY EX WOULD GIVE UP ON ME.
I SEE. AND THEN YOU FELL FOR NINA...
YEAH...
NO, THAT'S NOT IT!
IT'S NOT?
WIPE
WIPE

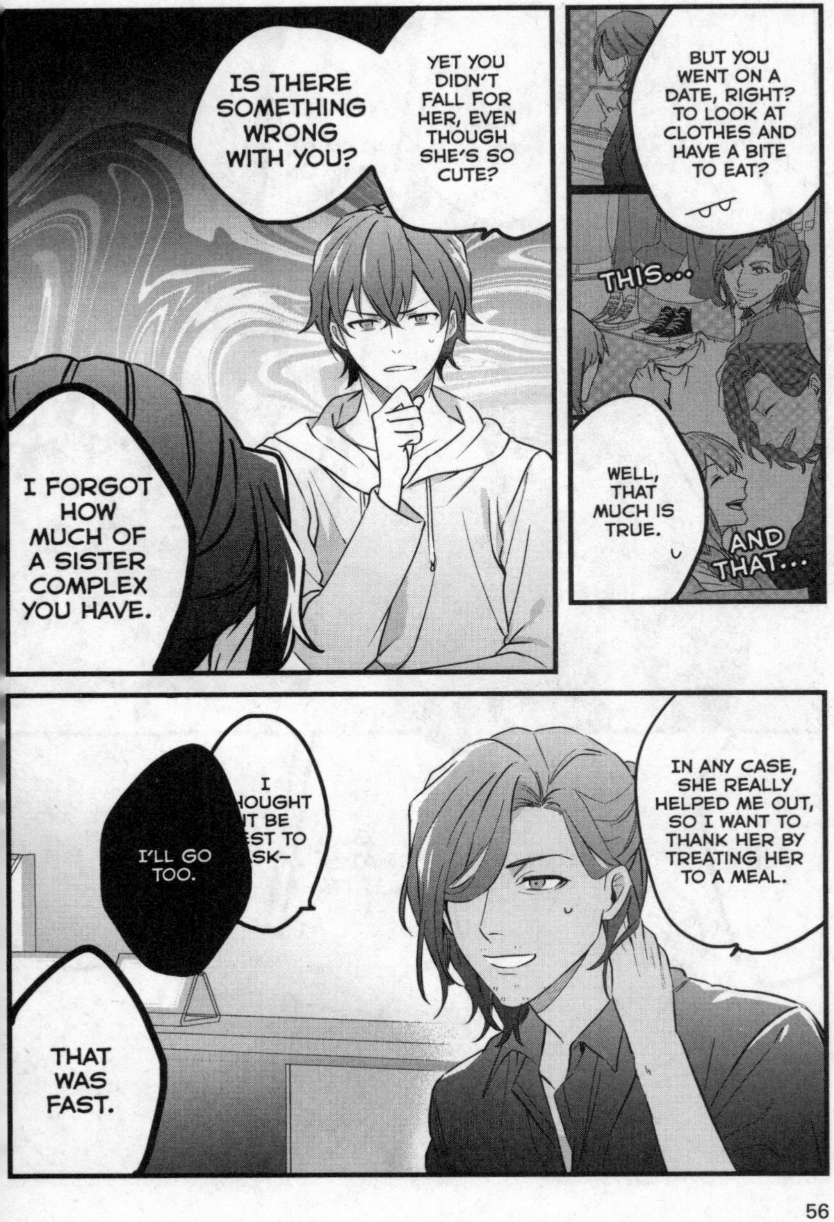
BUT YOU WENT ON A DATE, RIGHT? TO LOOK AT CLOTHES AND HAVE A BITE TO EAT?
THIS...
AND THAT...
WELL, THAT MUCH IS TRUE.
YET YOU DIDN'T FALL FOR HER, EVEN THOUGH SHE'S SO CUTE?
IS THERE SOMETHING WRONG WITH YOU?
I FORGOT HOW MUCH OF A SISTER COMPLEX YOU HAVE.
IN ANY CASE, SHE REALLY HELPED ME OUT, SO I WANT TO THANK HER BY TREATING HER TO A MEAL.
I'LL GO TOO.
THAT WAS FAST.

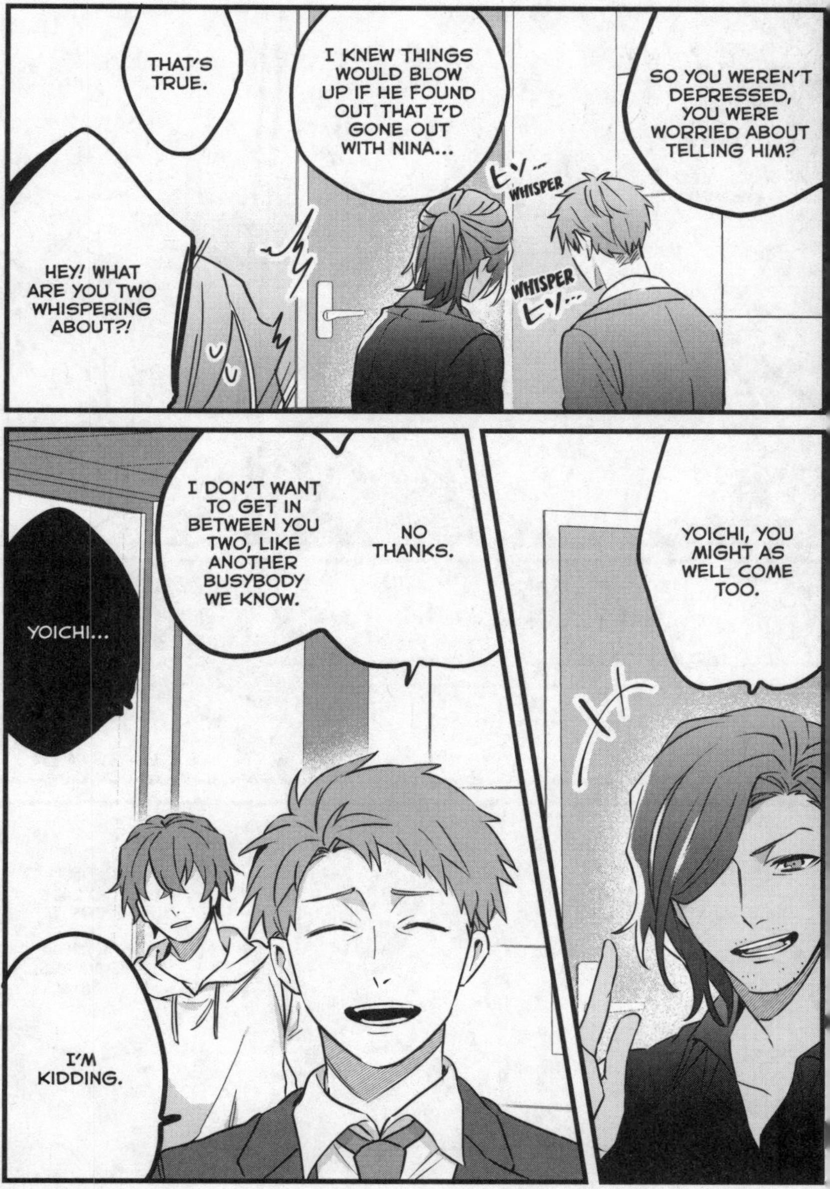
SO YOU WEREN'T DEPRESSED, YOU WERE WORRIED ABOUT TELLING HIM?
I KNEW THINGS WOULD BLOW UP IF HE FOUND OUT THAT I'D GONE OUT WITH NINA...
THAT'S TRUE.
ヒソ... WHISPER
WHISPER ヒソ...
HEY! WHAT ARE YOU TWO WHISPERING ABOUT?!
YOICHI, YOU MIGHT AS WELL COME TOO.
NO THANKS.
I DON'T WANT TO GET IN BETWEEN YOU TWO, LIKE ANOTHER BUSYBODY WE KNOW.
YOICHI...
I'M KIDDING.

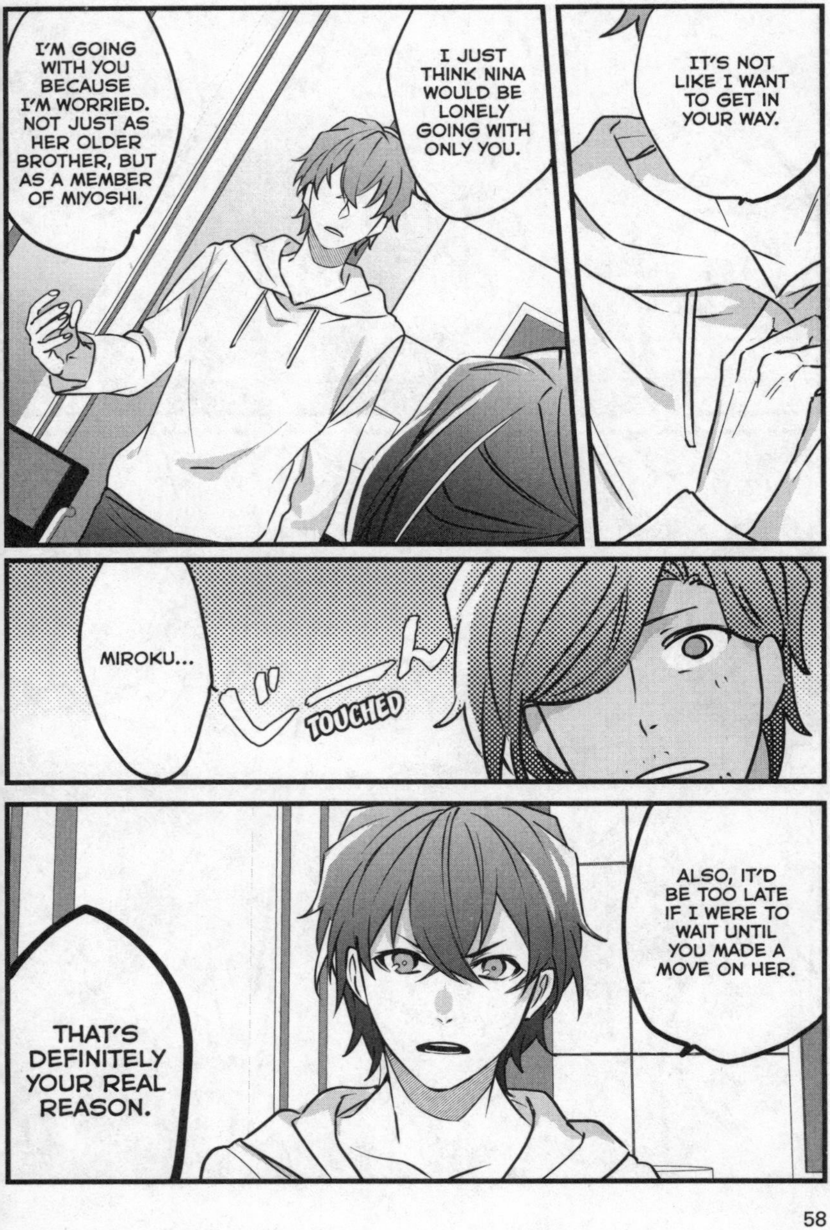
IT'S NOT LIKE I WANT TO GET IN YOUR WAY.
I JUST THINK NINA WOULD BE LONELY GOING WITH ONLY YOU.
I'M GOING WITH YOU BECAUSE I'M WORRIED. NOT JUST AS HER OLDER BROTHER, BUT AS A MEMBER OF MIYOSHI.
じーん
TOUCHED
MIROKU...
ALSO, IT'D BE TOO LATE IF I WERE TO WAIT UNTIL YOU MADE A MOVE ON HER.
THAT'S DEFINITELY YOUR REAL REASON.

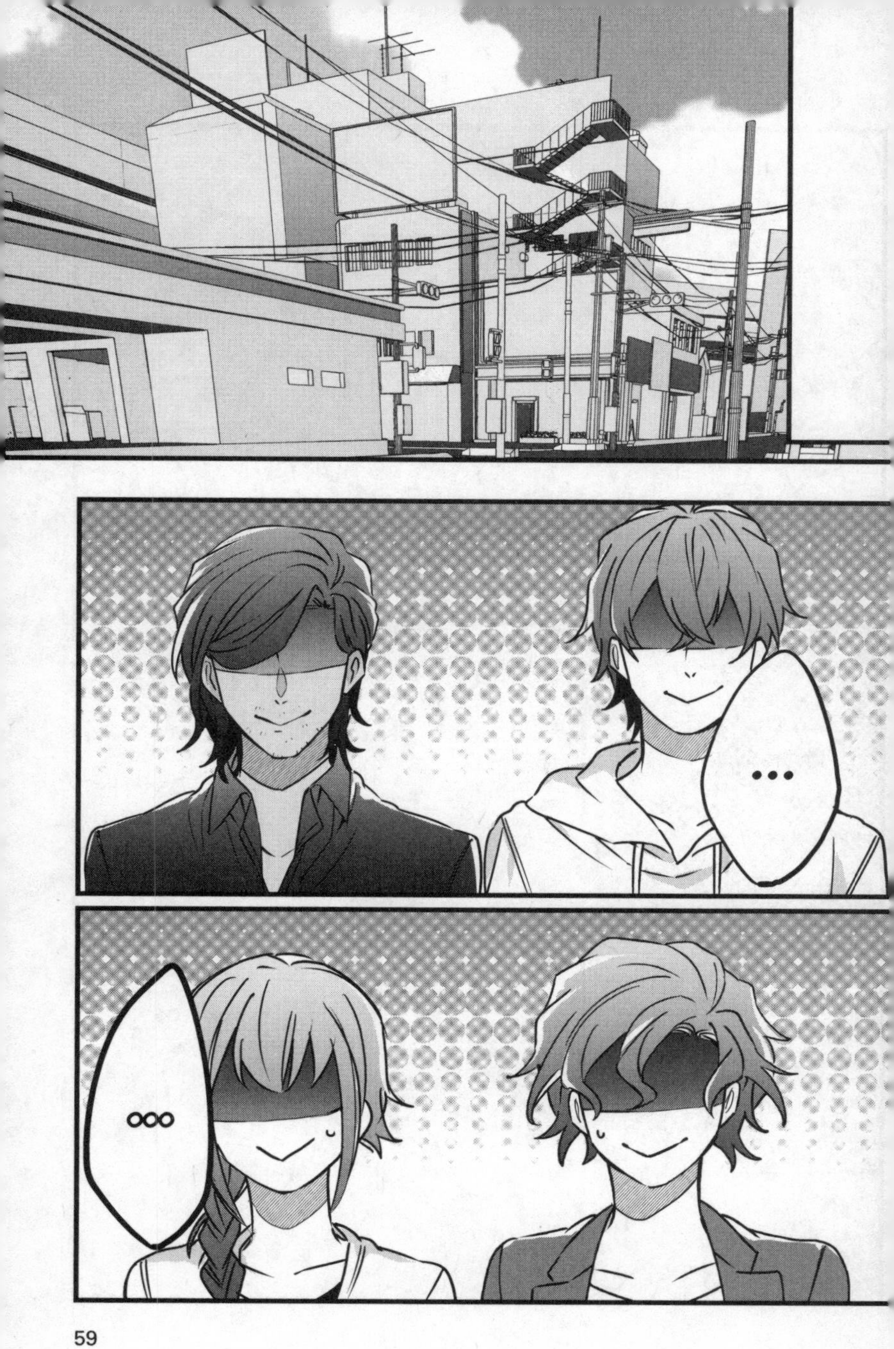
...
...

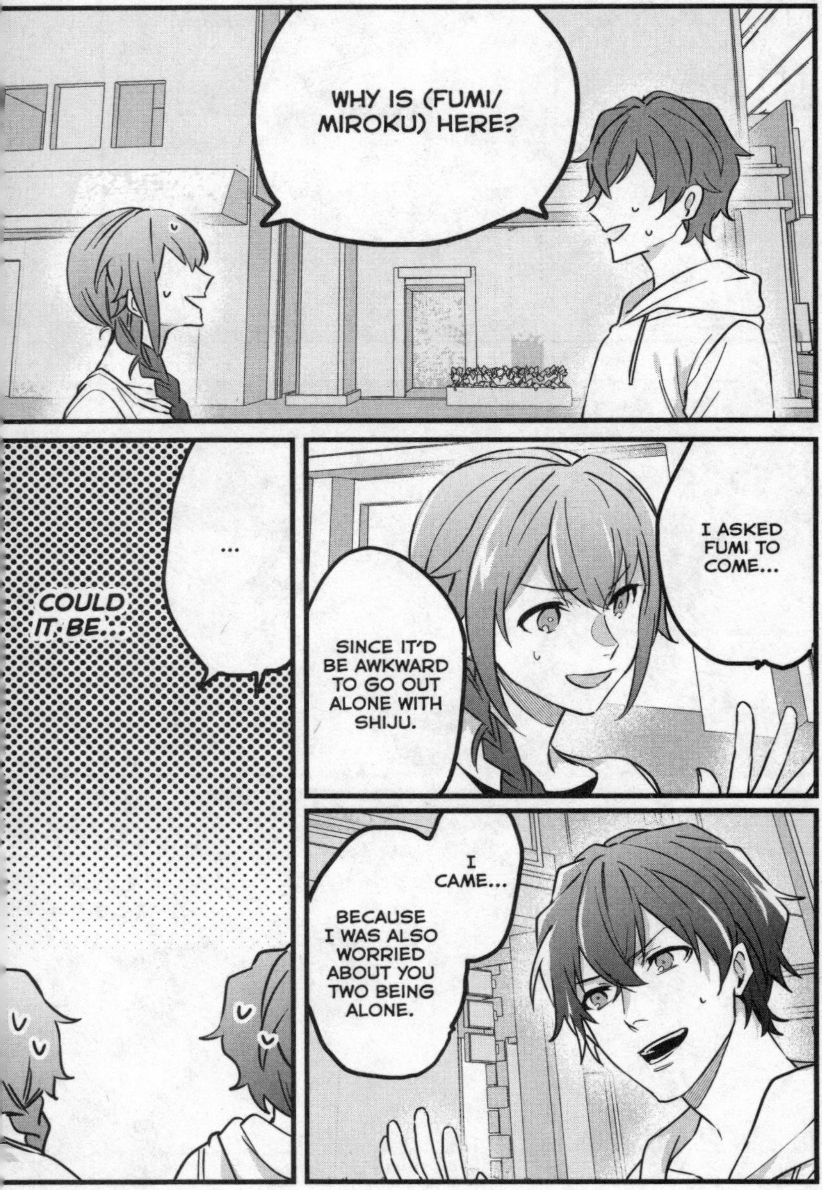
WHY IS (FUMI/ MIROKU) HERE?
I ASKED FUMI TO COME...
SINCE IT'D BE AWKWARD TO GO OUT ALONE WITH SHIJU.
I CAME...
BECAUSE I WAS ALSO WORRIED ABOUT YOU TWO BEING ALONE.
...
COULD IT BE...

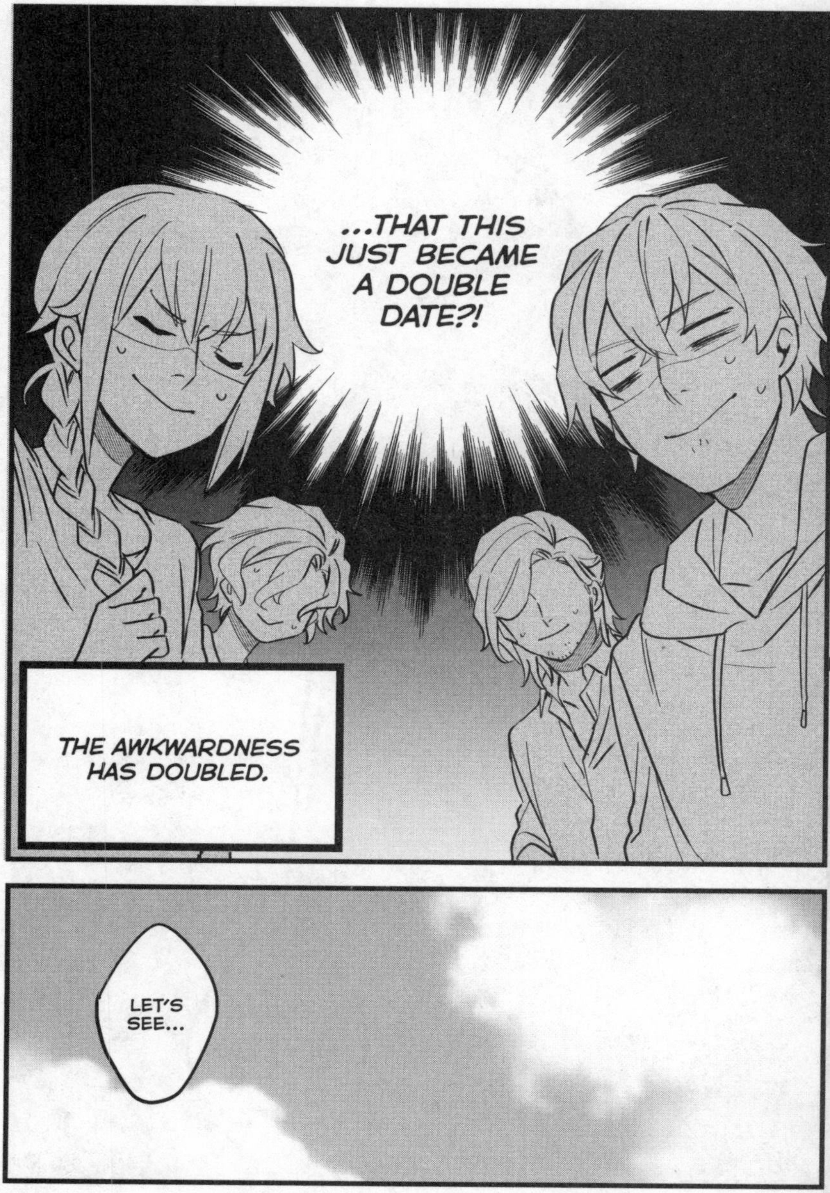
...THAT THIS JUST BECAME A DOUBLE DATE?!
THE AWKWARDNESS HAS DOUBLED.
LET'S SEE...

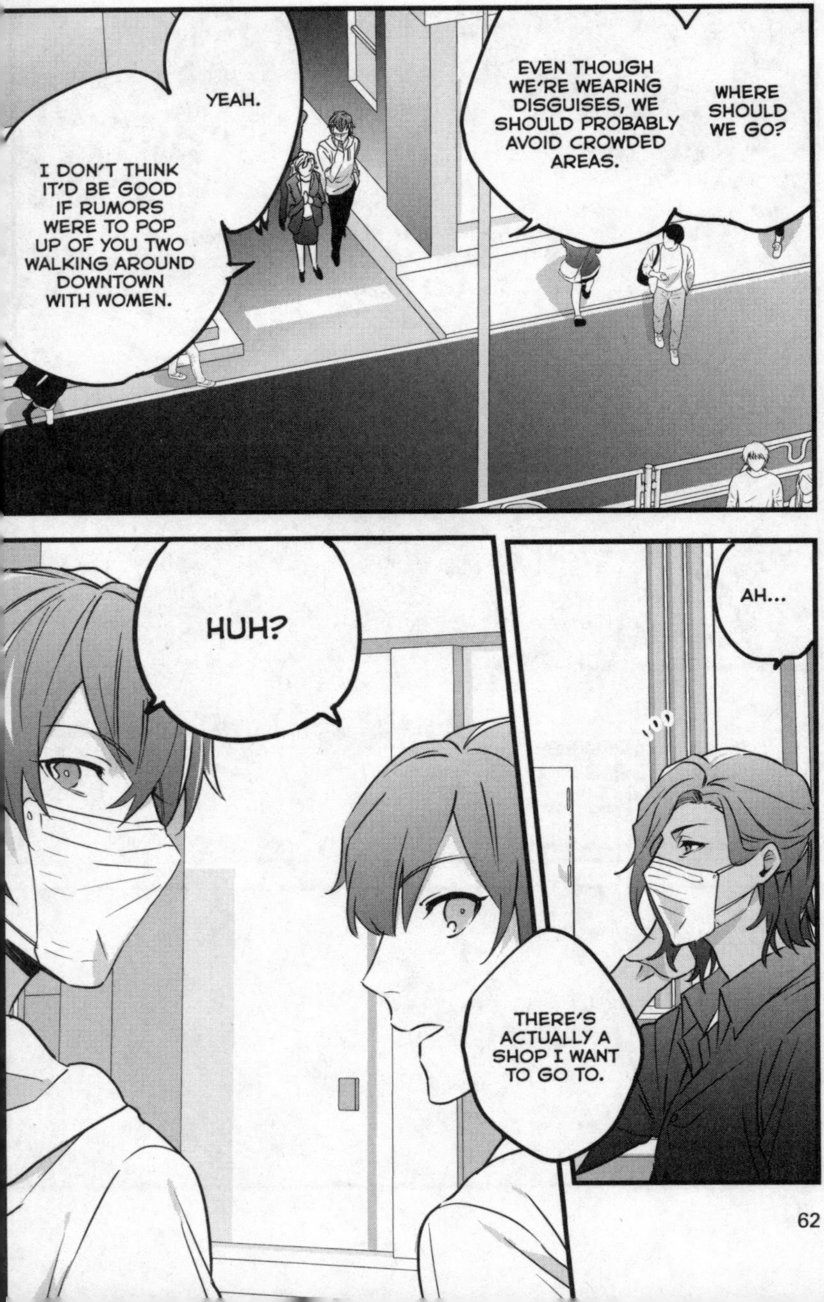
WHERE SHOULD WE GO?
EVEN THOUGH WE'RE WEARING DISGUISES, WE SHOULD PROBABLY AVOID CROWDED AREAS.
YEAH.
I DON'T THINK IT'D BE GOOD IF RUMORS WERE TO POP UP OF YOU TWO WALKING AROUND DOWNTOWN WITH WOMEN.
AH...
THERE'S ACTUALLY A SHOP I WANT TO GO TO.
HUH?

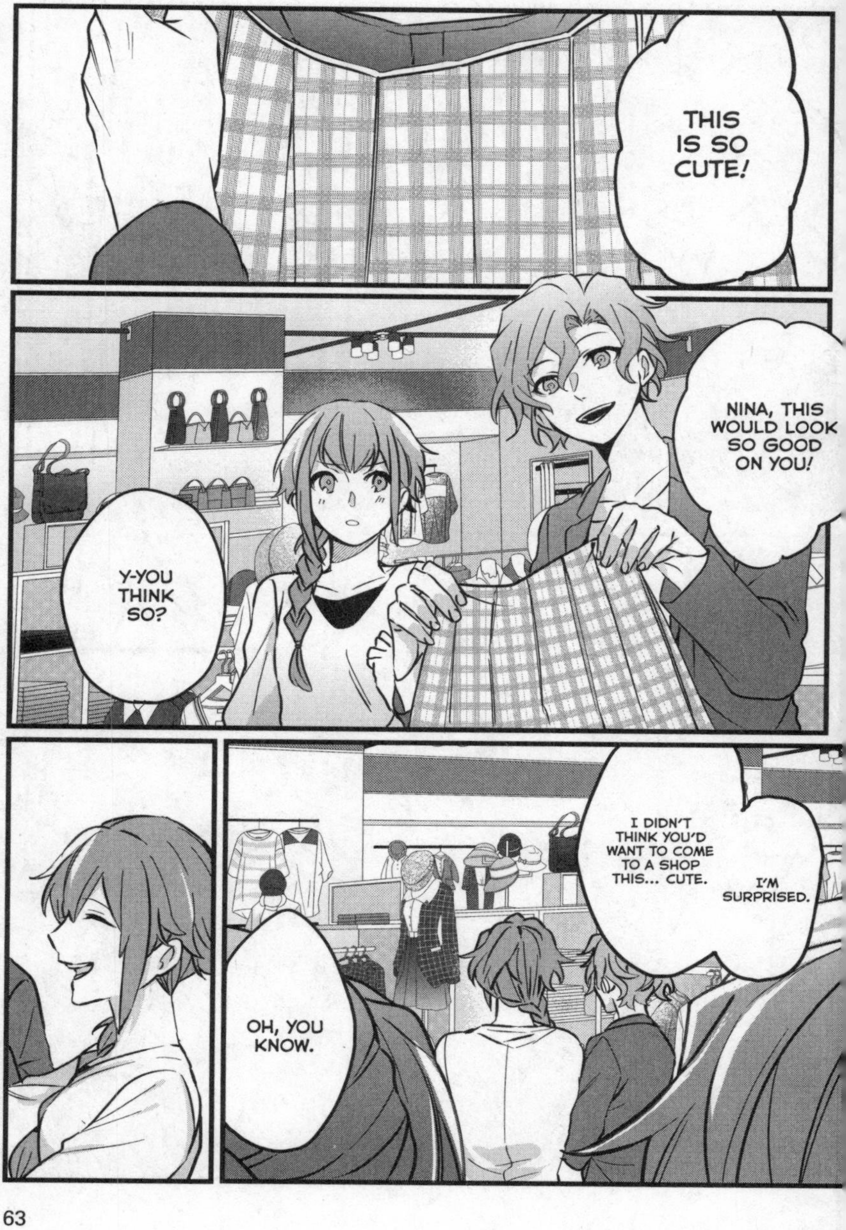
THIS IS SO CUTE!
NINA, THIS WOULD LOOK SO GOOD ON YOU!
Y-YOU THINK SO?
I'M SURPRISED.
I DIDN'T THINK YOU'D WANT TO COME TO A SHOP THIS... CUTE.
OH, YOU KNOW.

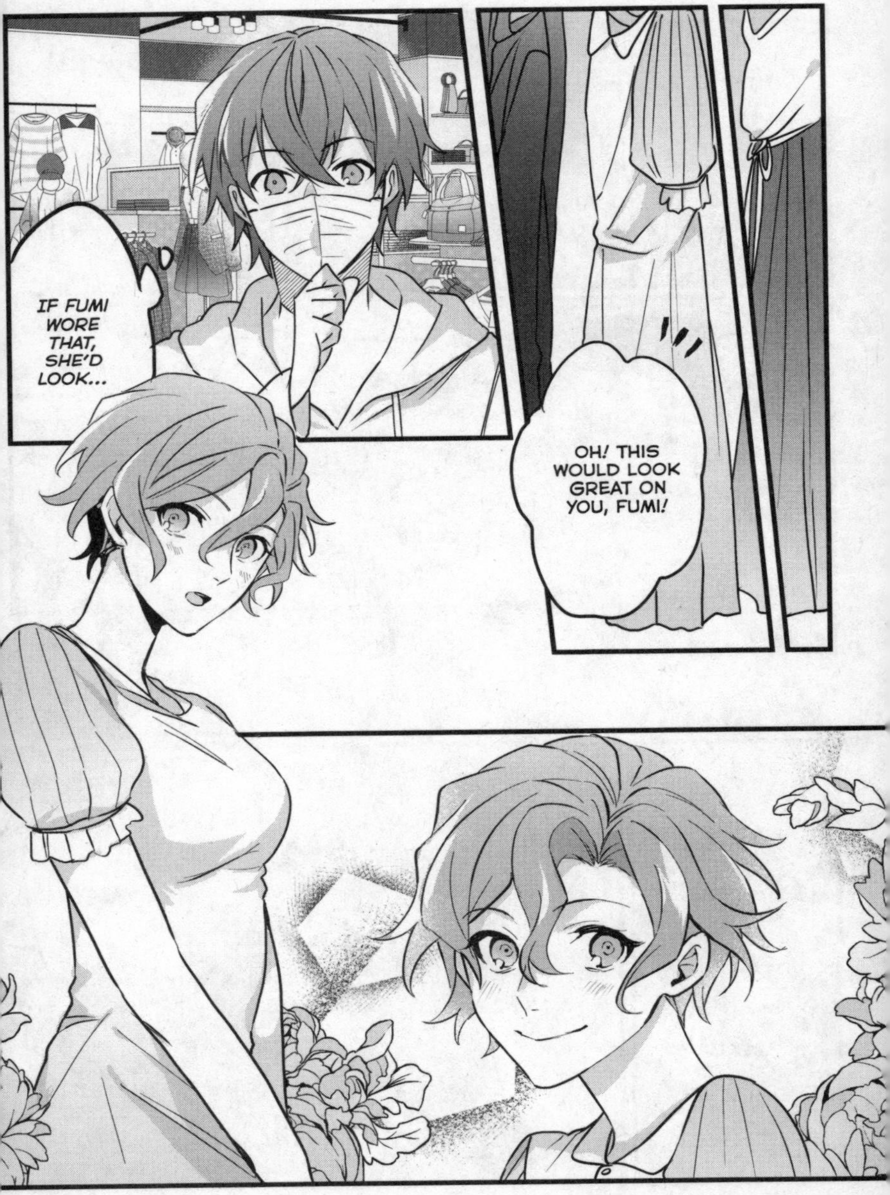
OH! THIS WOULD LOOK GREAT ON YOU, FUMI!
IF FUMI WORE THAT, SHE'D LOOK...

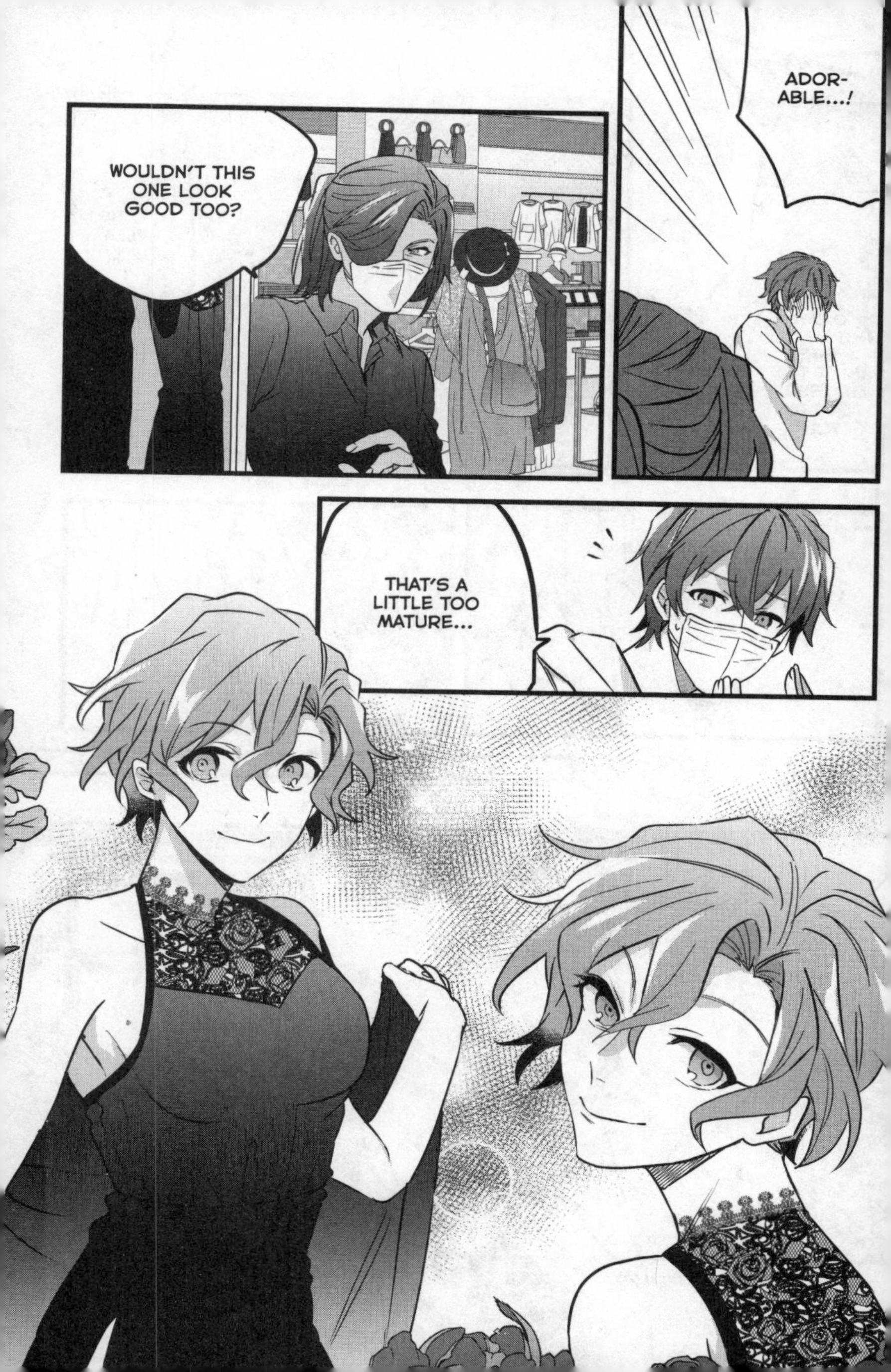
ADOR-ABLE...!
WOULDN'T THIS ONE LOOK GOOD TOO?
THAT'S A LITTLE TOO MATURE...

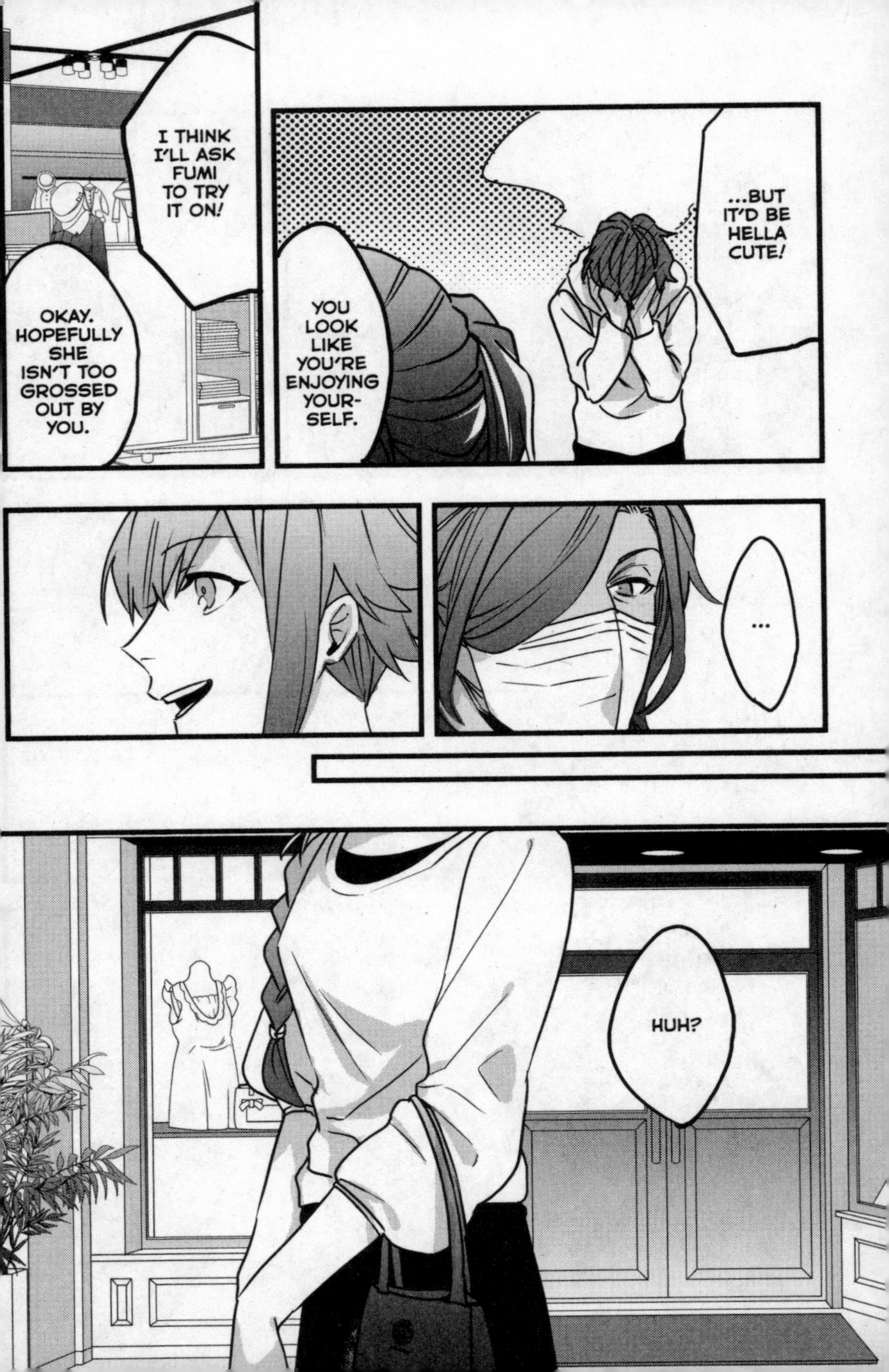
...BUT IT'D BE HELLA CUTE!
YOU LOOK LIKE YOU'RE ENJOYING YOUR-SELF.
I THINK I'LL ASK FUMI TO TRY IT ON!
OKAY. HOPEFULLY SHE ISN'T TOO GROSSED OUT BY YOU.
...
HUH?

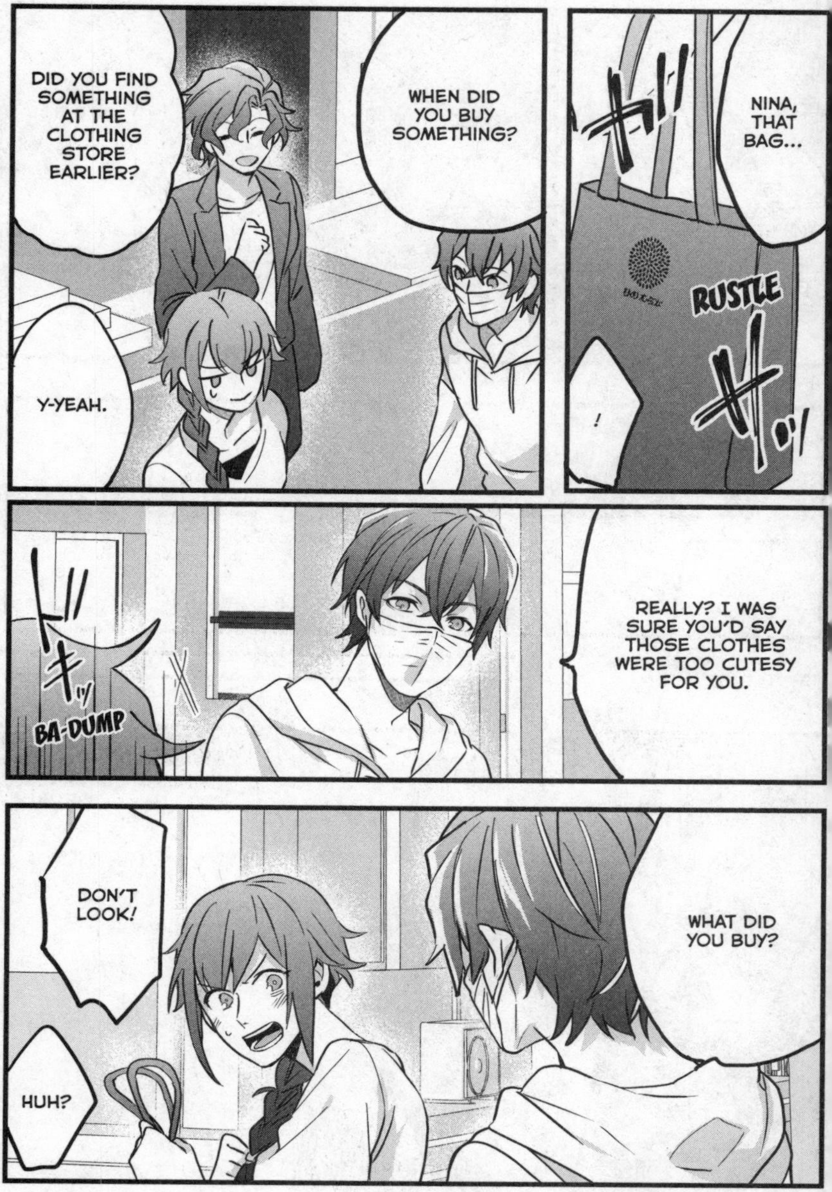
NINA, THAT BAG...
RUSTLE
!
WHEN DID YOU BUY SOMETHING?
DID YOU FIND SOMETHING AT THE CLOTHING STORE EARLIER?
Y-YEAH.
REALLY? I WAS SURE YOU'D SAY THOSE CLOTHES WERE TOO CUTESY FOR YOU.
BA-DUMP
WHAT DID YOU BUY?
DON'T LOOK!
HUH?

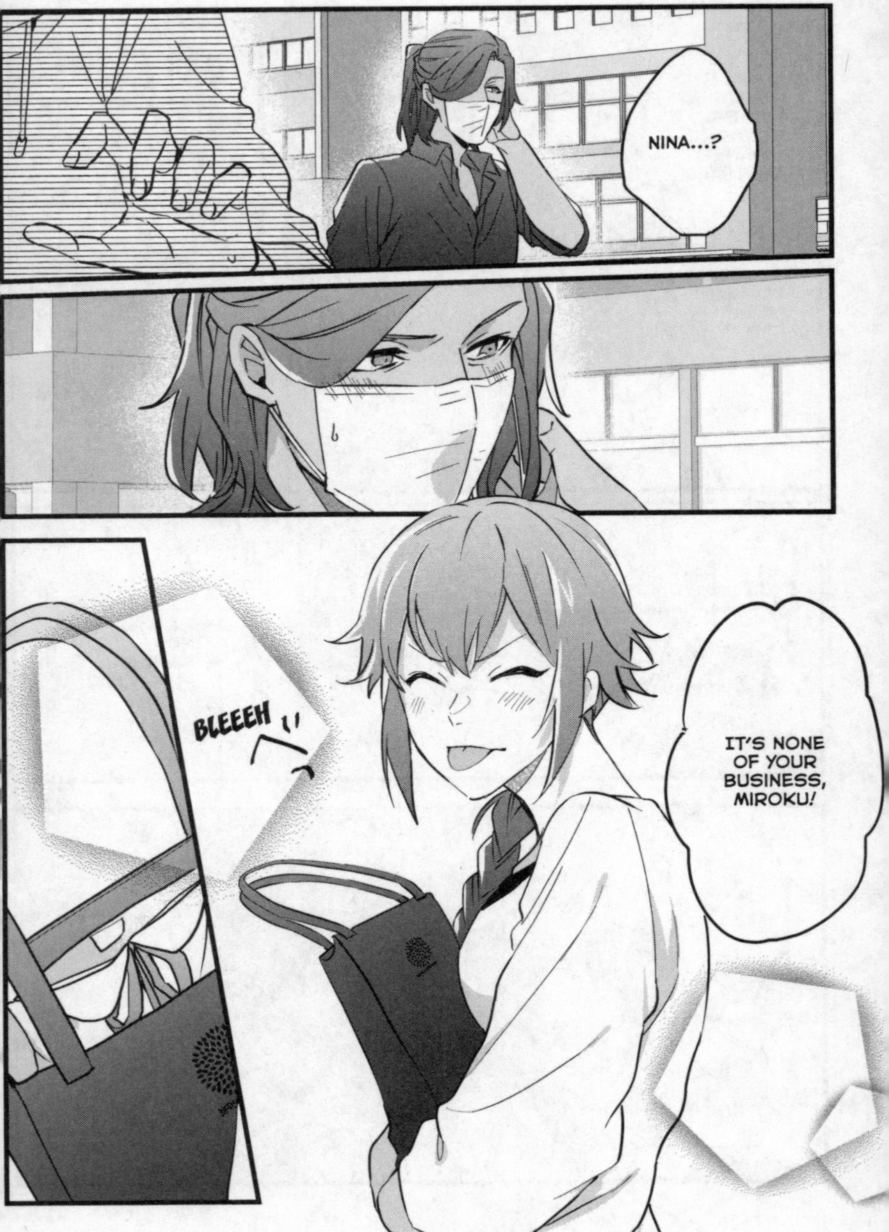
NINA...?
IT'S NONE OF YOUR BUSINESS, MIROKU!
BLEEEH

Chapter 34

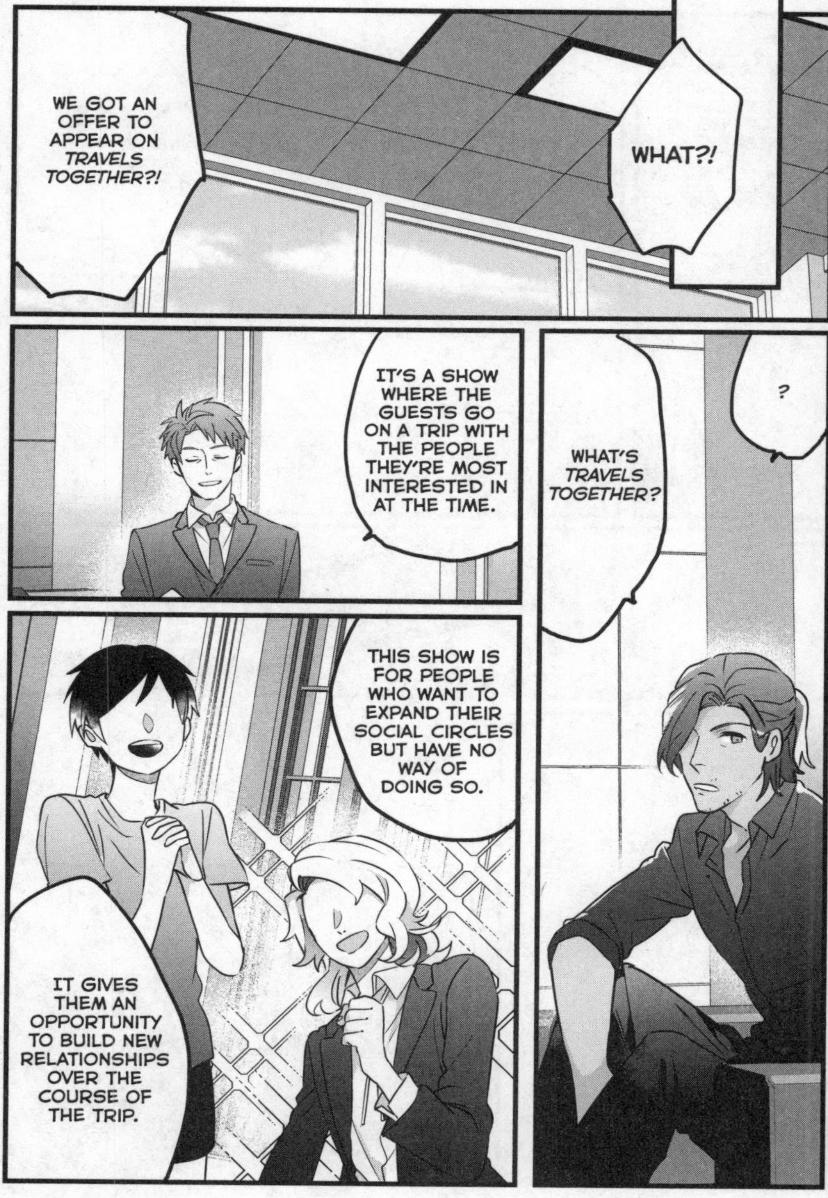
WHAT?!
WE GOT AN OFFER TO APPEAR ON *TRAVELS TOGETHER*?!
?
WHAT'S *TRAVELS TOGETHER*?
IT'S A SHOW WHERE THE GUESTS GO ON A TRIP WITH THE PEOPLE THEY'RE MOST INTERESTED IN AT THE TIME.
THIS SHOW IS FOR PEOPLE WHO WANT TO EXPAND THEIR SOCIAL CIRCLES BUT HAVE NO WAY OF DOING SO.
IT GIVES THEM AN OPPORTUNITY TO BUILD NEW RELATIONSHIPS OVER THE COURSE OF THE TRIP.

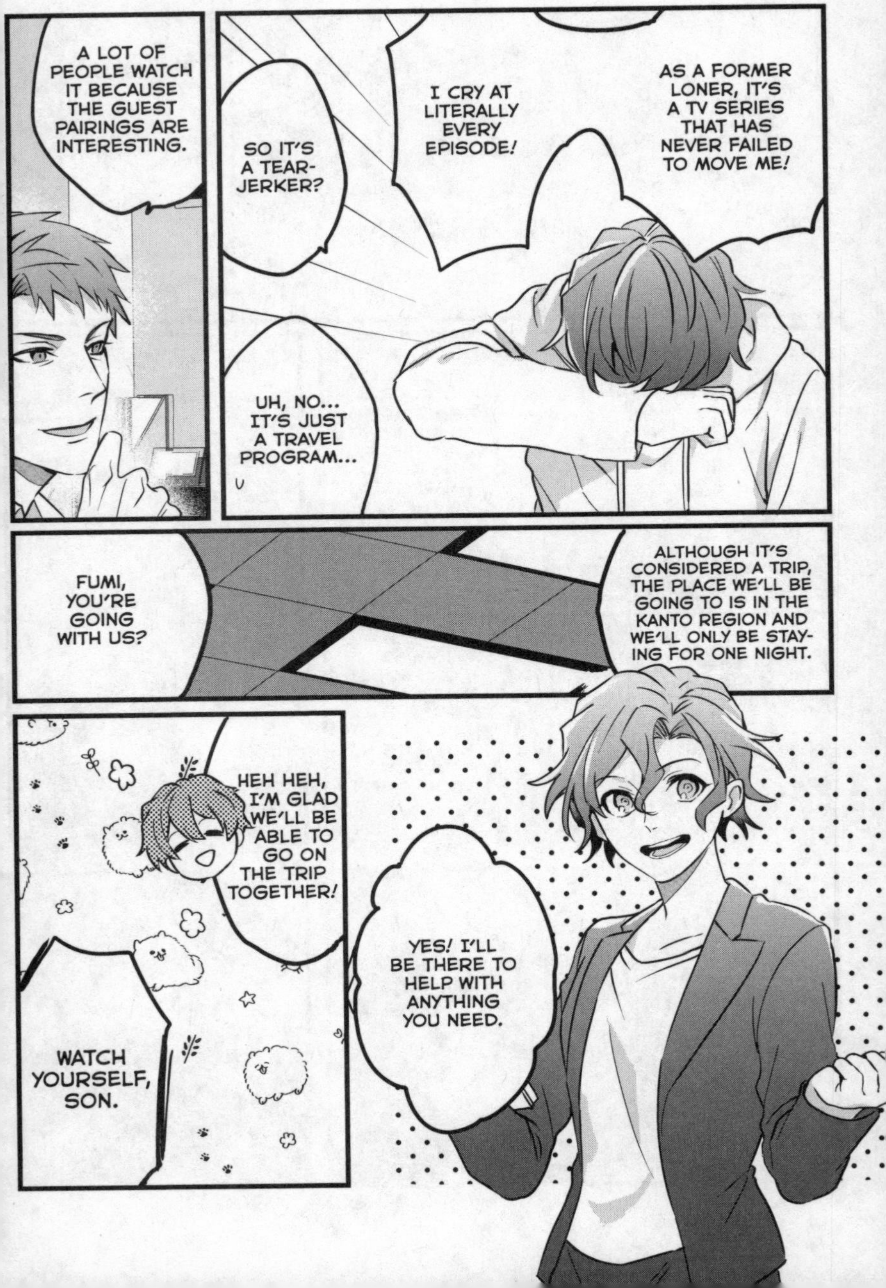
AS A FORMER LONER, IT'S A TV SERIES THAT HAS NEVER FAILED TO MOVE ME!
I CRY AT LITERALLY EVERY EPISODE!
SO IT'S A TEAR-JERKER?
UH, NO... IT'S JUST A TRAVEL PROGRAM...
A LOT OF PEOPLE WATCH IT BECAUSE THE GUEST PAIRINGS ARE INTERESTING.
ALTHOUGH IT'S CONSIDERED A TRIP, THE PLACE WE'LL BE GOING TO IS IN THE KANTO REGION AND WE'LL ONLY BE STAYING FOR ONE NIGHT.
FUMI, YOU'RE GOING WITH US?
YES! I'LL BE THERE TO HELP WITH ANYTHING YOU NEED.
HEH HEH, I'M GLAD WE'LL BE ABLE TO GO ON THE TRIP TOGETHER!
WATCH YOURSELF, SON.

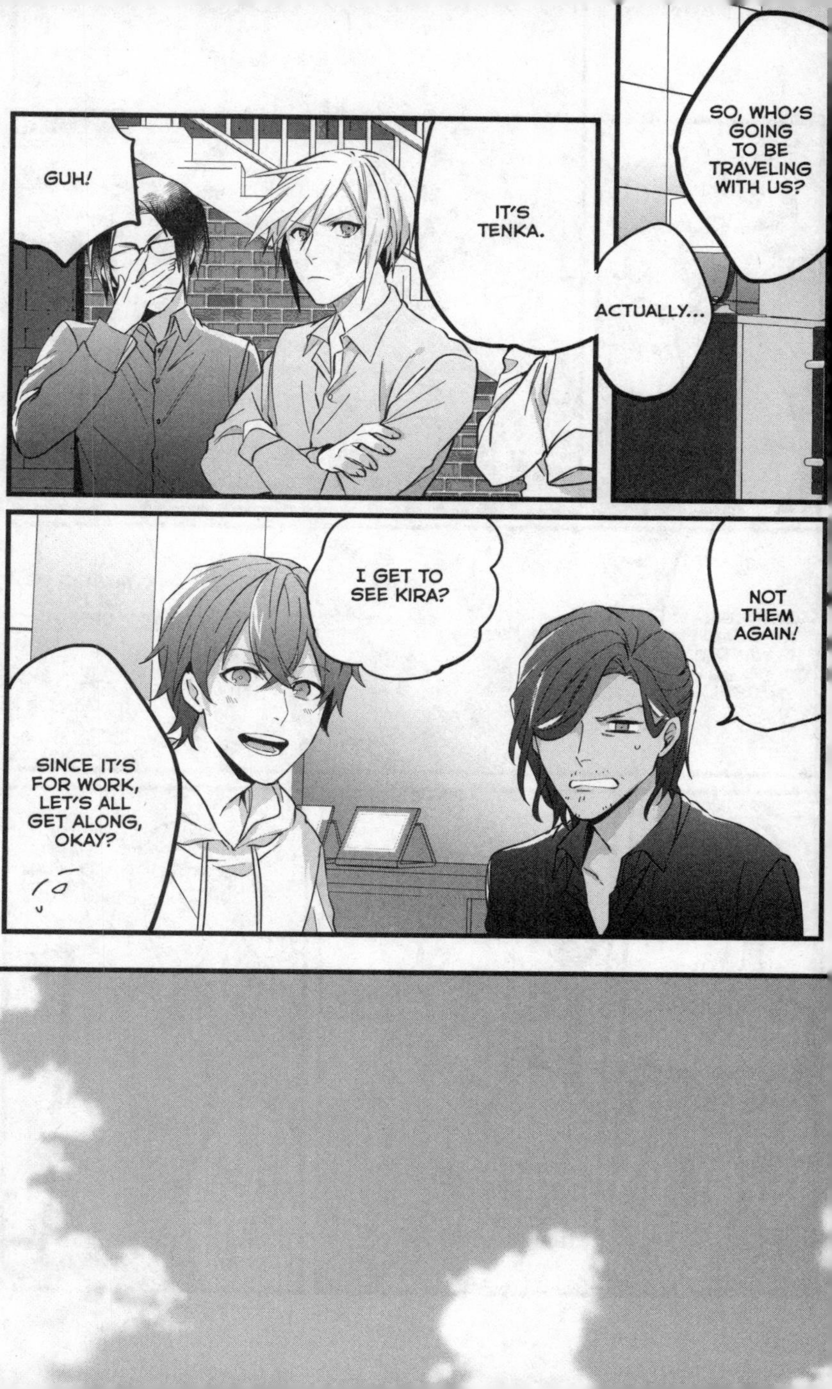
SO, WHO'S GOING TO BE TRAVELING WITH US?
ACTUALLY...
IT'S TENKA.
GUH!
NOT THEM AGAIN!
I GET TO SEE KIRA?
SINCE IT'S FOR WORK, LET'S ALL GET ALONG, OKAY?

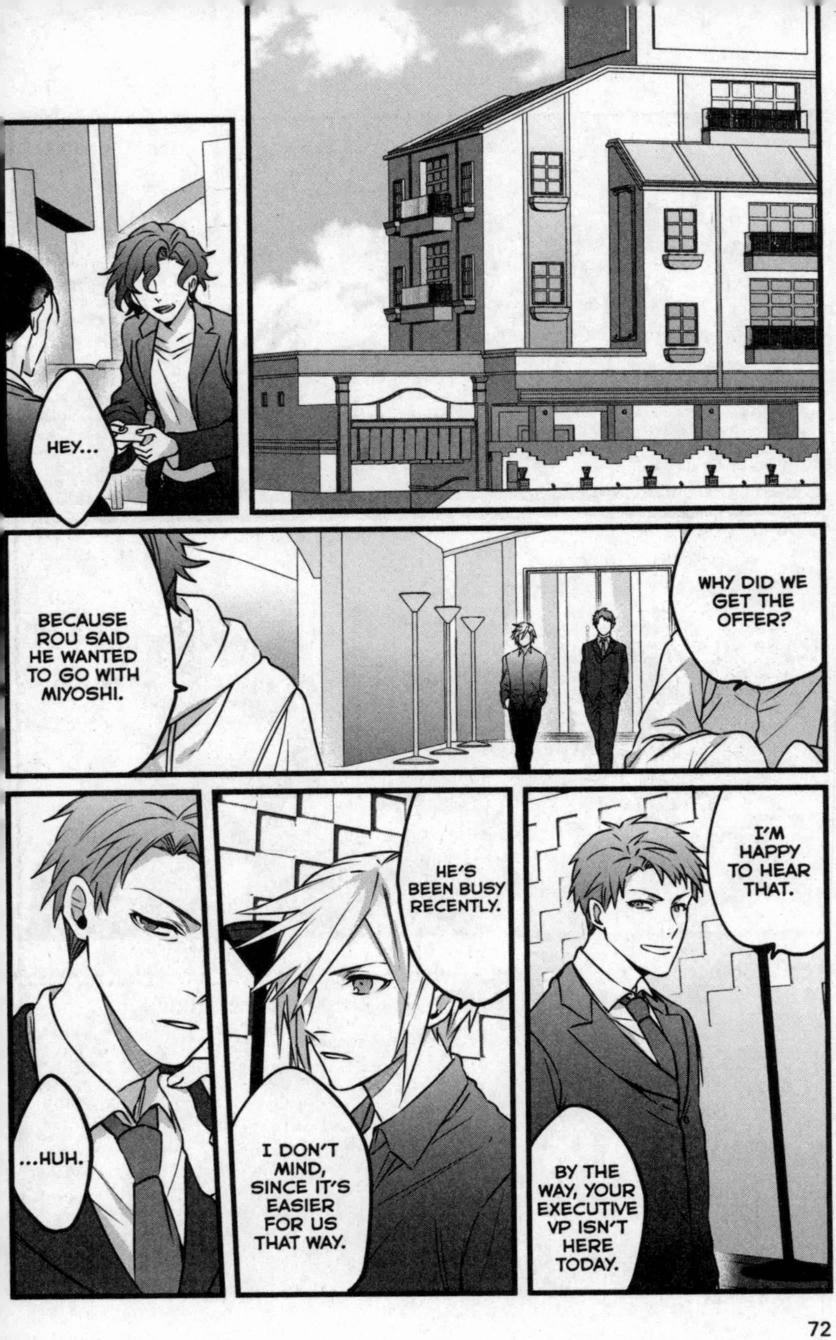
HEY...
WHY DID WE GET THE OFFER?
BECAUSE ROU SAID HE WANTED TO GO WITH MIYOSHI.
I'M HAPPY TO HEAR THAT.
BY THE WAY, YOUR EXECUTIVE VP ISN'T HERE TODAY.
HE'S BEEN BUSY RECENTLY.
I DON'T MIND, SINCE IT'S EASIER FOR US THAT WAY.
...HUH.

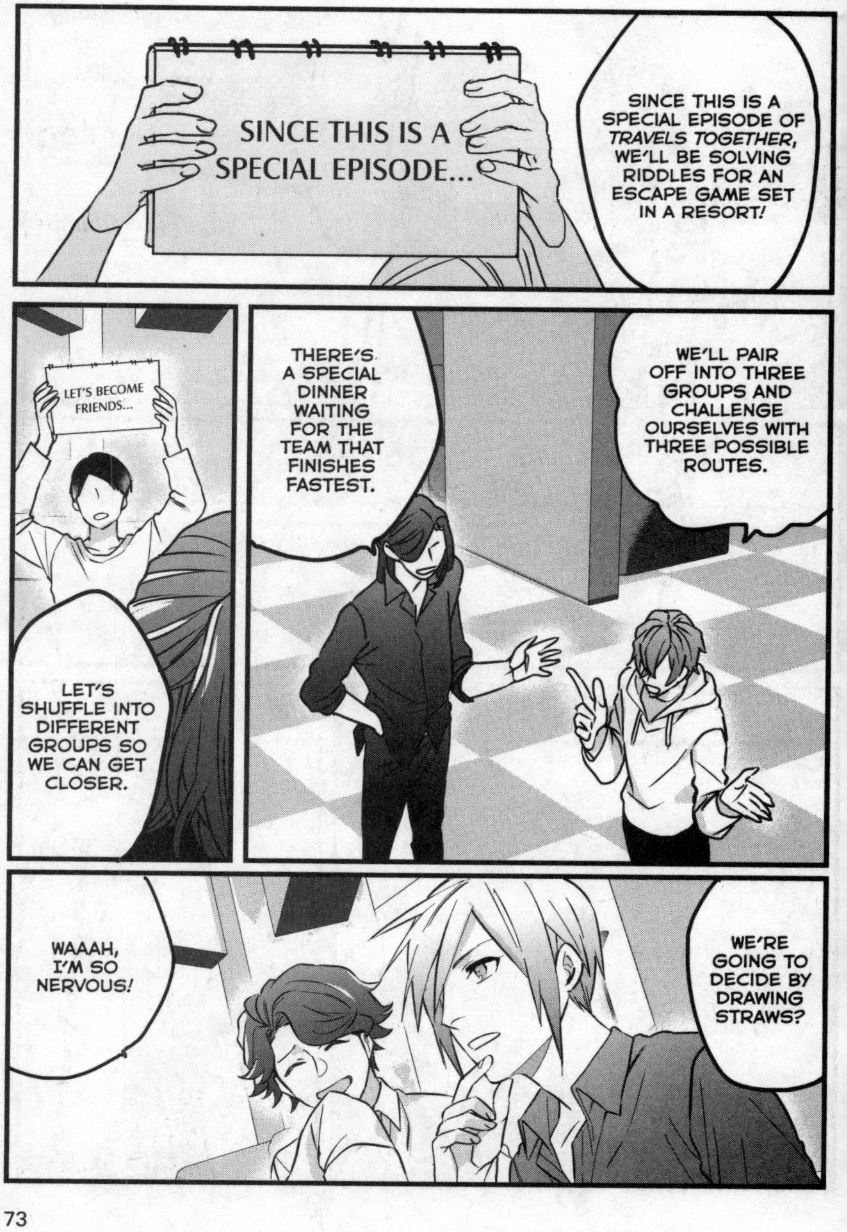
SINCE THIS IS A SPECIAL EPISODE OF *TRAVELS TOGETHER*, WE'LL BE SOLVING RIDDLES FOR AN ESCAPE GAME SET IN A RESORT!
SINCE THIS IS A SPECIAL EPISODE...
WE'LL PAIR OFF INTO THREE GROUPS AND CHALLENGE OURSELVES WITH THREE POSSIBLE ROUTES.
THERE'S A SPECIAL DINNER WAITING FOR THE TEAM THAT FINISHES FASTEST.
LET'S BECOME FRIENDS...
LET'S SHUFFLE INTO DIFFERENT GROUPS SO WE CAN GET CLOSER.
WE'RE GOING TO DECIDE BY DRAWING STRAWS?
WAAAH, I'M SO NERVOUS!

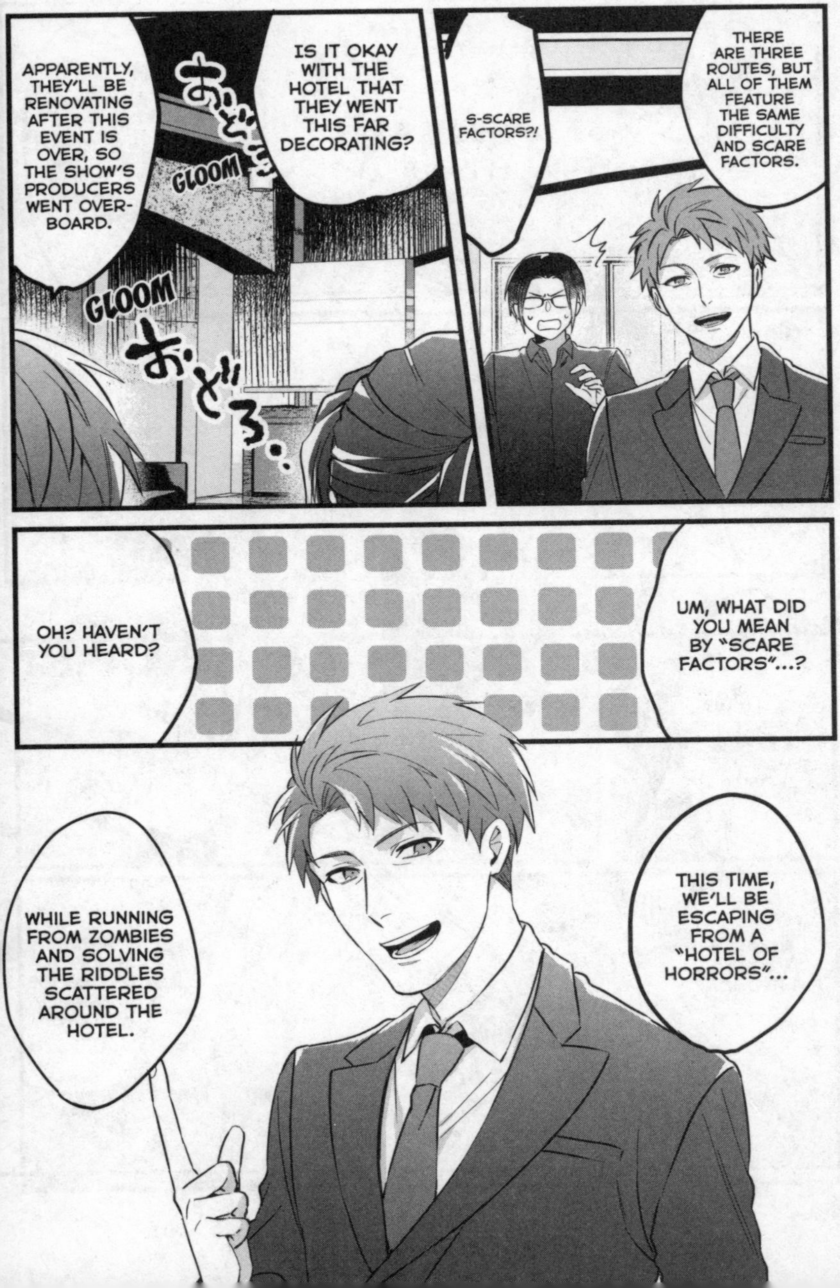
THERE ARE THREE ROUTES, BUT ALL OF THEM FEATURE THE SAME DIFFICULTY AND SCARE FACTORS.
S-SCARE FACTORS?!
IS IT OKAY WITH THE HOTEL THAT THEY WENT THIS FAR DECORATING?
APPARENTLY, THEY'LL BE RENOVATING AFTER THIS EVENT IS OVER, SO THE SHOW'S PRODUCERS WENT OVER-BOARD.
GLOOM
GLOOM
おどろ…
UM, WHAT DID YOU MEAN BY "SCARE FACTORS"...?
OH? HAVEN'T YOU HEARD?
THIS TIME, WE'LL BE ESCAPING FROM A "HOTEL OF HORRORS"...
WHILE RUNNING FROM ZOMBIES AND SOLVING THE RIDDLES SCATTERED AROUND THE HOTEL.

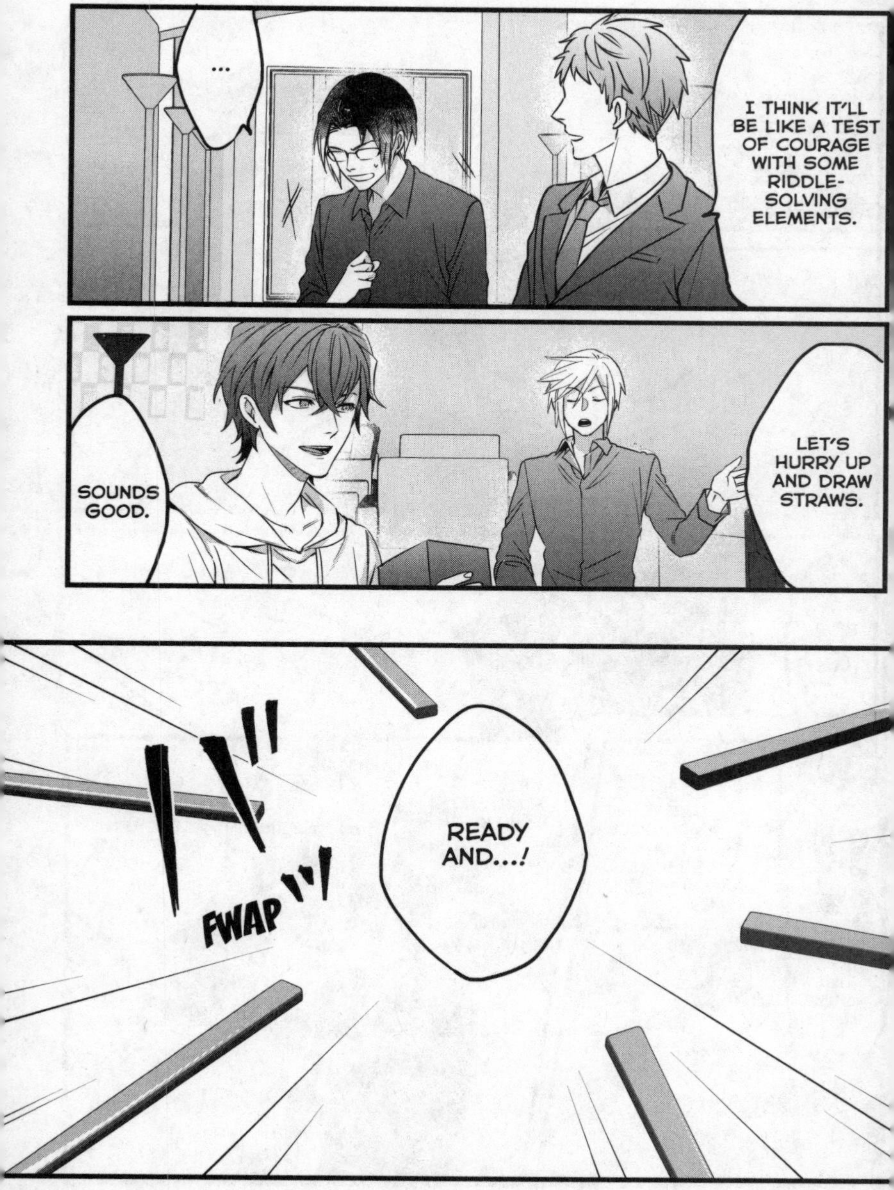
I THINK IT'LL BE LIKE A TEST OF COURAGE WITH SOME RIDDLE-SOLVING ELEMENTS.
...
LET'S HURRY UP AND DRAW STRAWS.
SOUNDS GOOD.
READY AND...!
FWAP

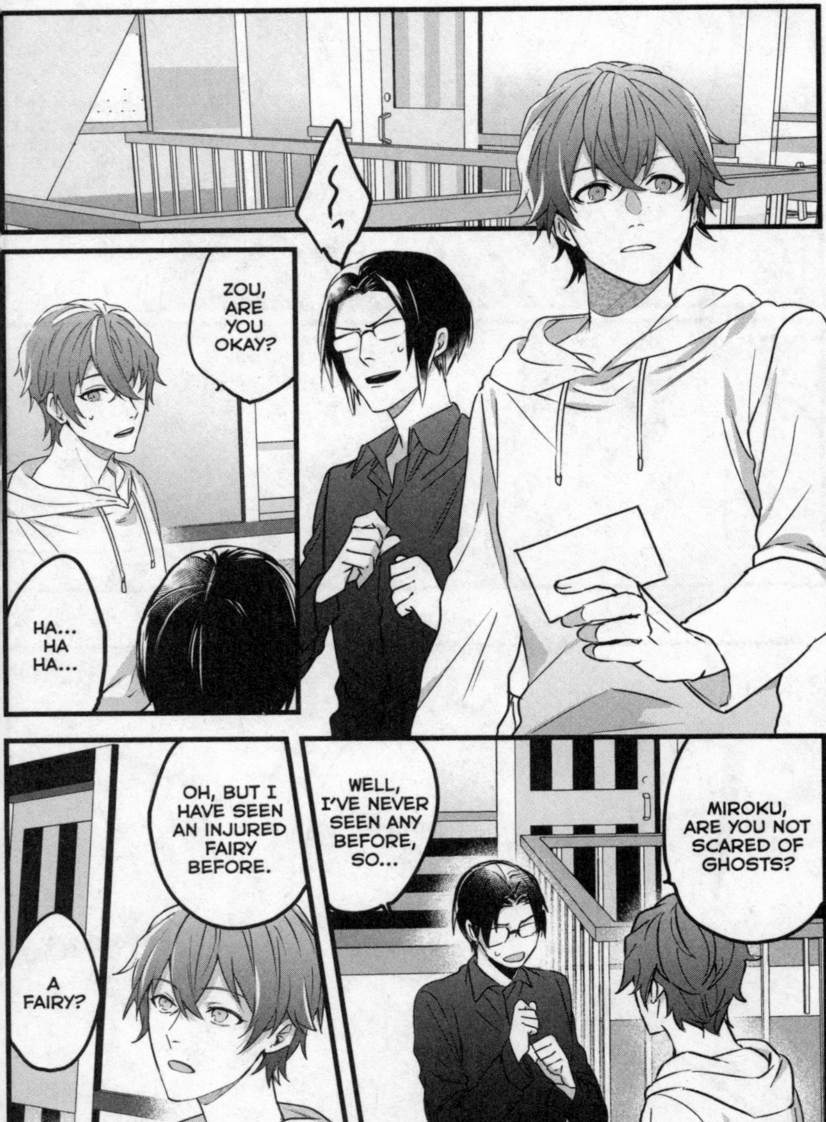
ZOU, ARE YOU OKAY?
HA... HA HA...
MIROKU, ARE YOU NOT SCARED OF GHOSTS?
WELL, I'VE NEVER SEEN ANY BEFORE, SO...
OH, BUT I HAVE SEEN AN INJURED FAIRY BEFORE.
A FAIRY?

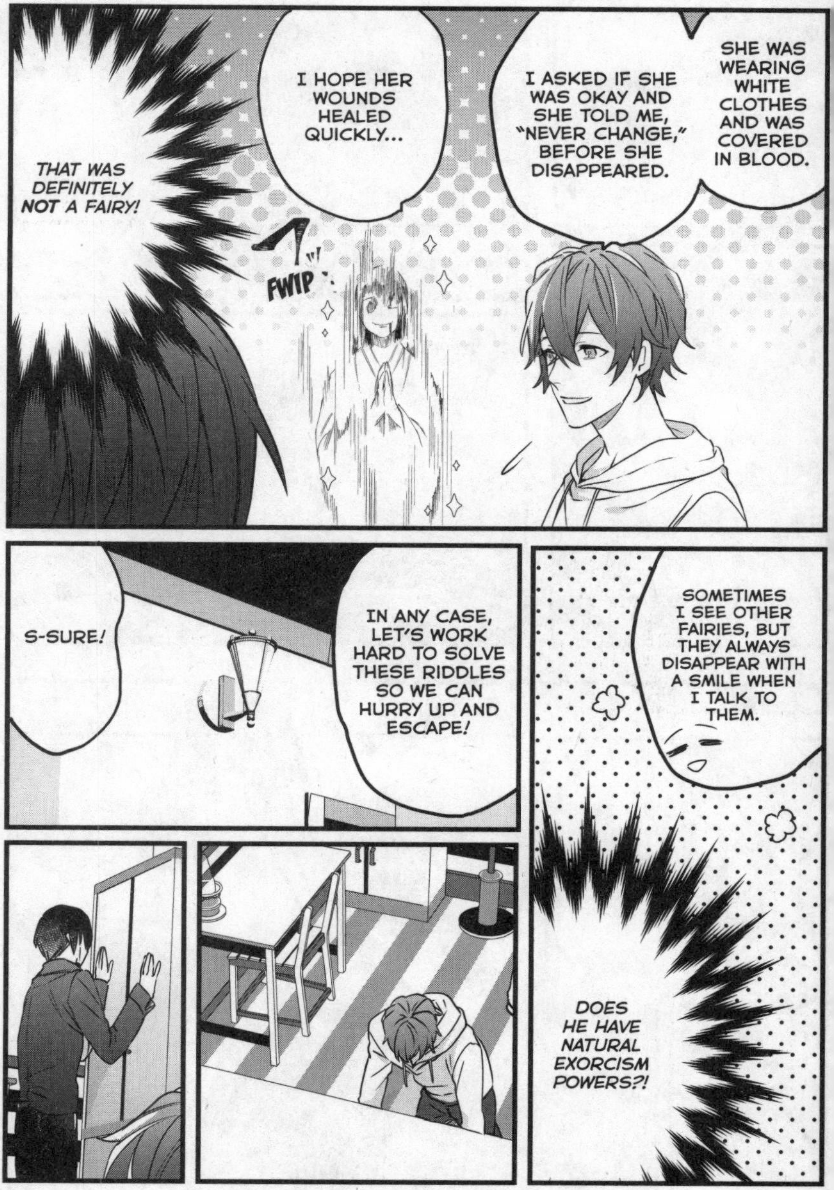
SHE WAS WEARING WHITE CLOTHES AND WAS COVERED IN BLOOD.
I ASKED IF SHE WAS OKAY AND SHE TOLD ME, "NEVER CHANGE," BEFORE SHE DISAPPEARED.
I HOPE HER WOUNDS HEALED QUICKLY...
FWIP
THAT WAS DEFINITELY NOT A FAIRY!
SOMETIMES I SEE OTHER FAIRIES, BUT THEY ALWAYS DISAPPEAR WITH A SMILE WHEN I TALK TO THEM.
DOES HE HAVE NATURAL EXORCISM POWERS?!
IN ANY CASE, LET'S WORK HARD TO SOLVE THESE RIDDLES SO WE CAN HURRY UP AND ESCAPE!
S-SURE!

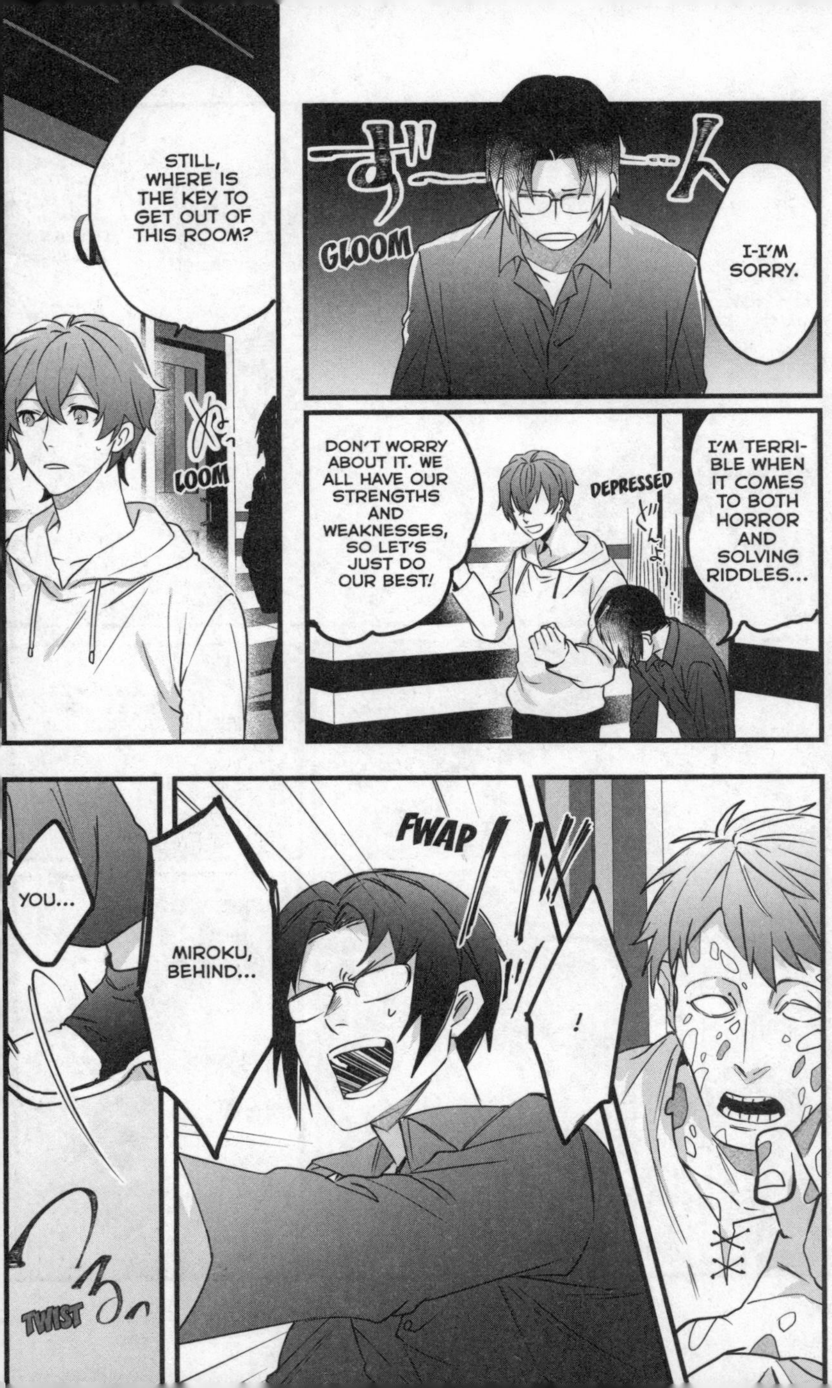
GLOOM
I-I'M SORRY.
I'M TERRIBLE WHEN IT COMES TO BOTH HORROR AND SOLVING RIDDLES...
DEPRESSED
DON'T WORRY ABOUT IT. WE ALL HAVE OUR STRENGTHS AND WEAKNESSES, SO LET'S JUST DO OUR BEST!
STILL, WHERE IS THE KEY TO GET OUT OF THIS ROOM?
LOOM
!
FWAP
MIROKU, BEHIND...
YOU...
TWIST

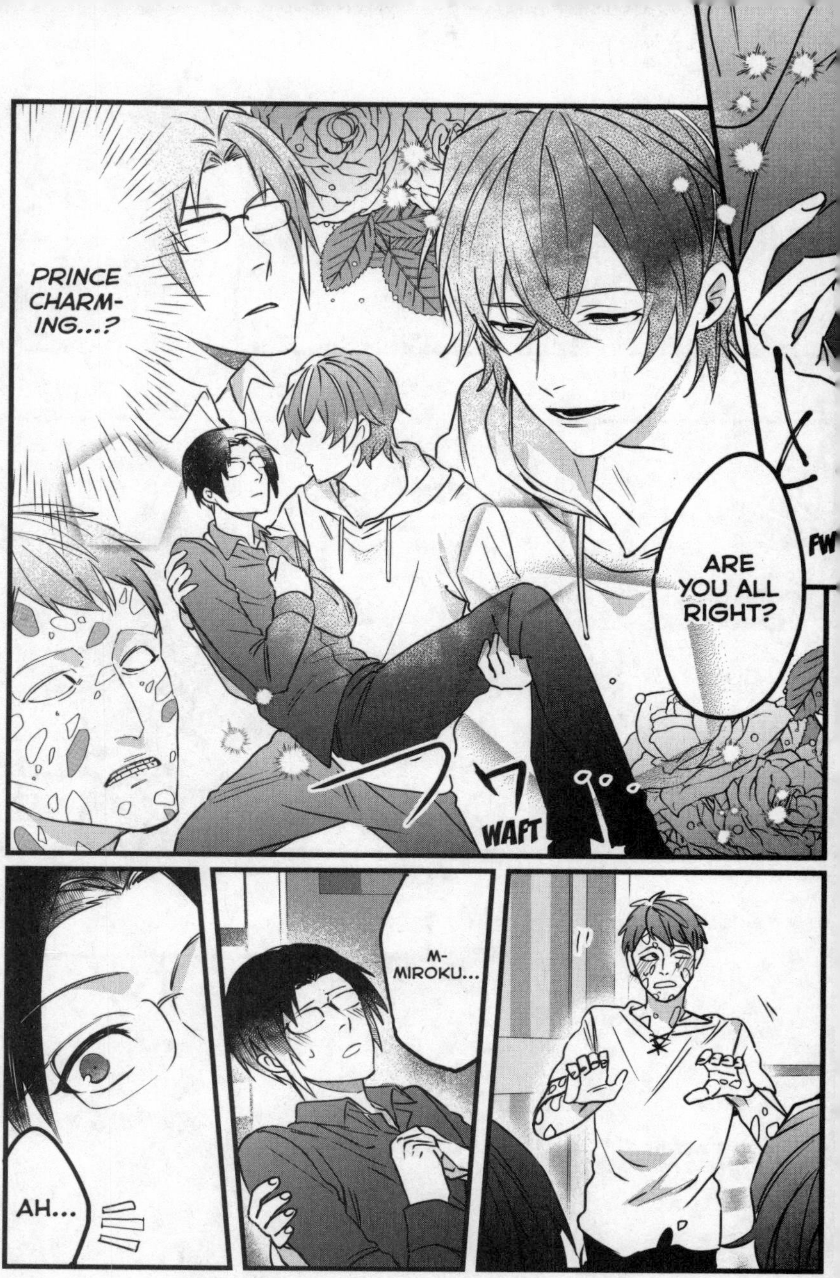
ARE YOU ALL RIGHT?
PRINCE CHARMING...?
WAFT
M-MIROKU...
AH...

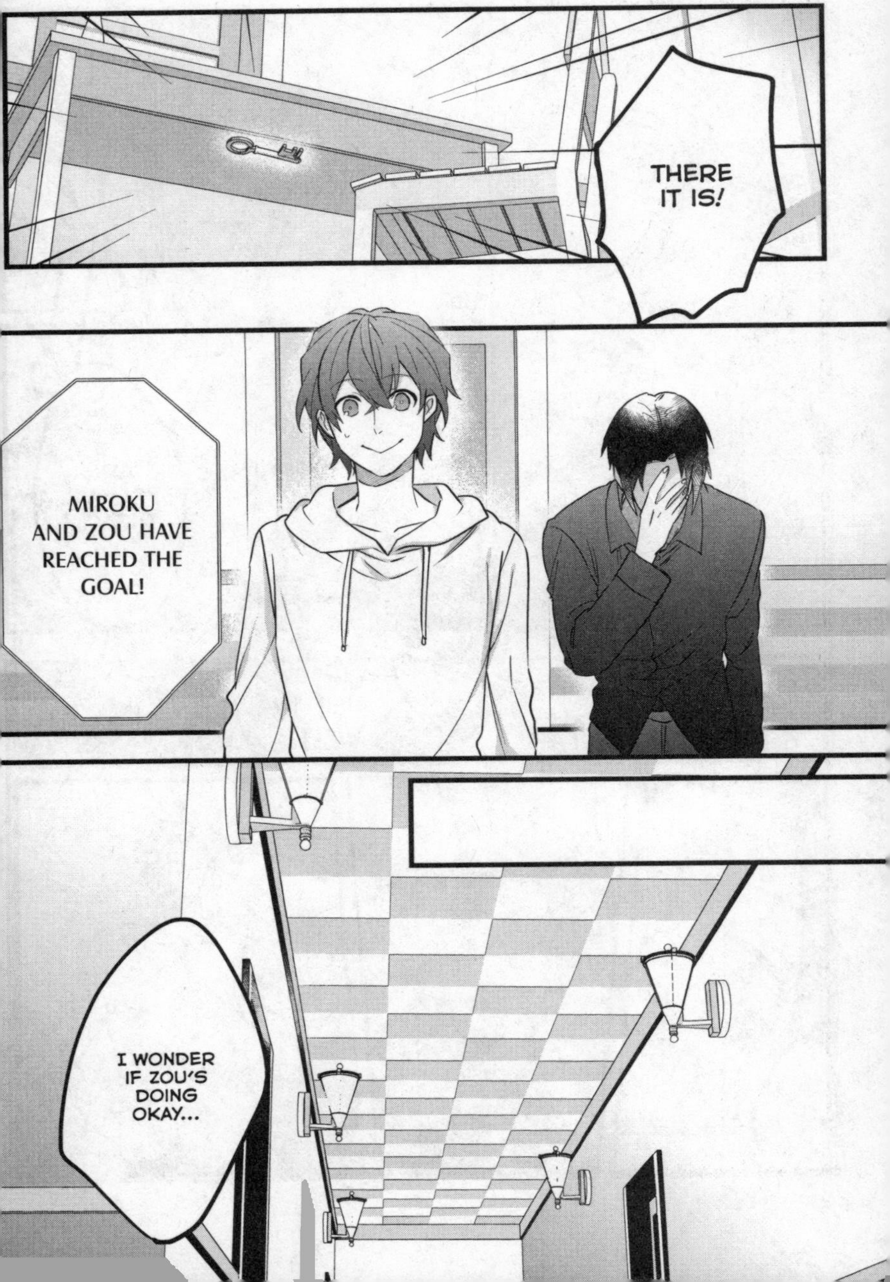
THERE IT IS!
MIROKU AND ZOU HAVE REACHED THE GOAL!
I WONDER IF ZOU'S DOING OKAY...

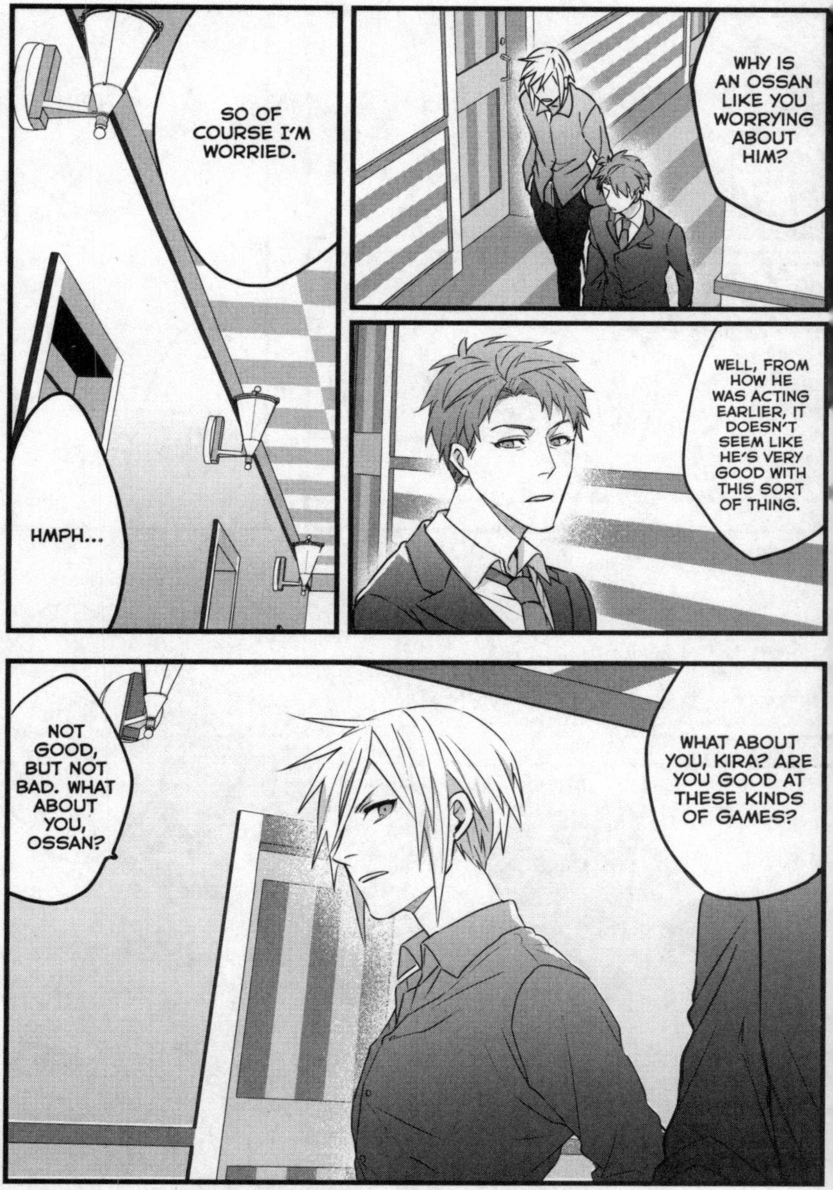
WHY IS AN OSSAN LIKE YOU WORRYING ABOUT HIM?
WELL, FROM HOW HE WAS ACTING EARLIER, IT DOESN'T SEEM LIKE HE'S VERY GOOD WITH THIS SORT OF THING.
SO OF COURSE I'M WORRIED.
HMPH...
WHAT ABOUT YOU, KIRA? ARE YOU GOOD AT THESE KINDS OF GAMES?
NOT GOOD, BUT NOT BAD. WHAT ABOUT YOU, OSSAN?

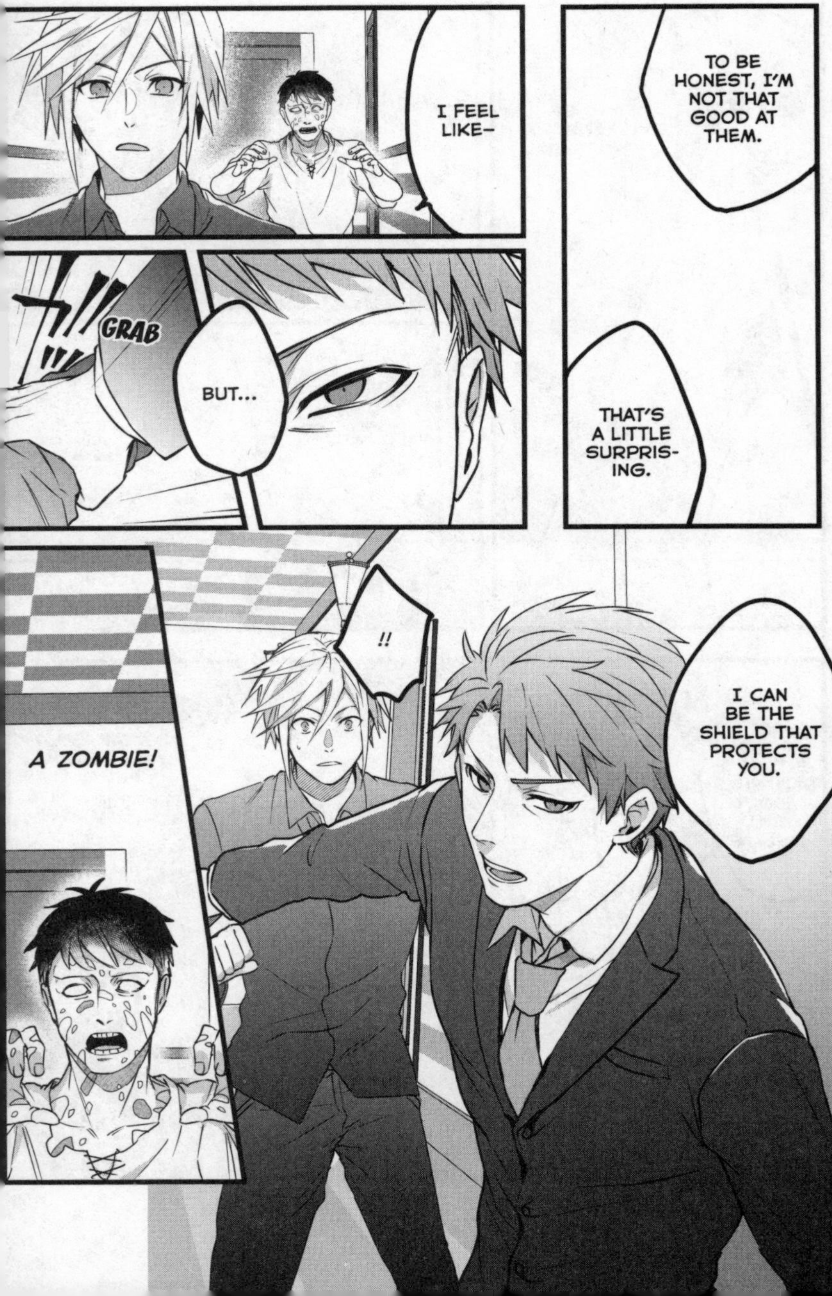
TO BE HONEST, I'M NOT THAT GOOD AT THEM.
THAT'S A LITTLE SURPRIS-ING.
I FEEL LIKE–
BUT...
GRAB
I CAN BE THE SHIELD THAT PROTECTS YOU.
!!
A ZOMBIE!

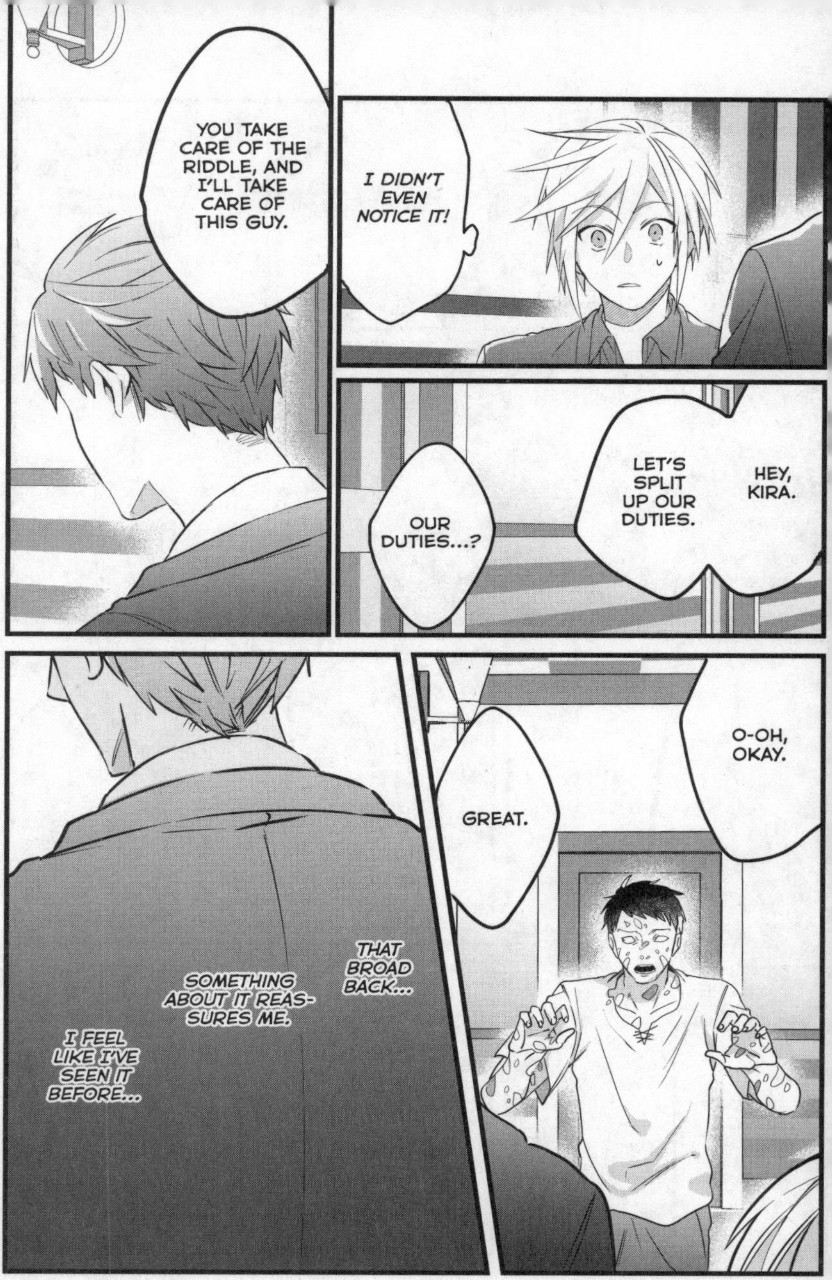
I DIDN'T EVEN NOTICE IT!
HEY, KIRA.
LET'S SPLIT UP OUR DUTIES.
OUR DUTIES...?
YOU TAKE CARE OF THE RIDDLE, AND I'LL TAKE CARE OF THIS GUY.
O-OH, OKAY.
GREAT.
THAT BROAD BACK...
SOMETHING ABOUT IT REAS-SURES ME.
I FEEL LIKE I'VE SEEN IT BEFORE...

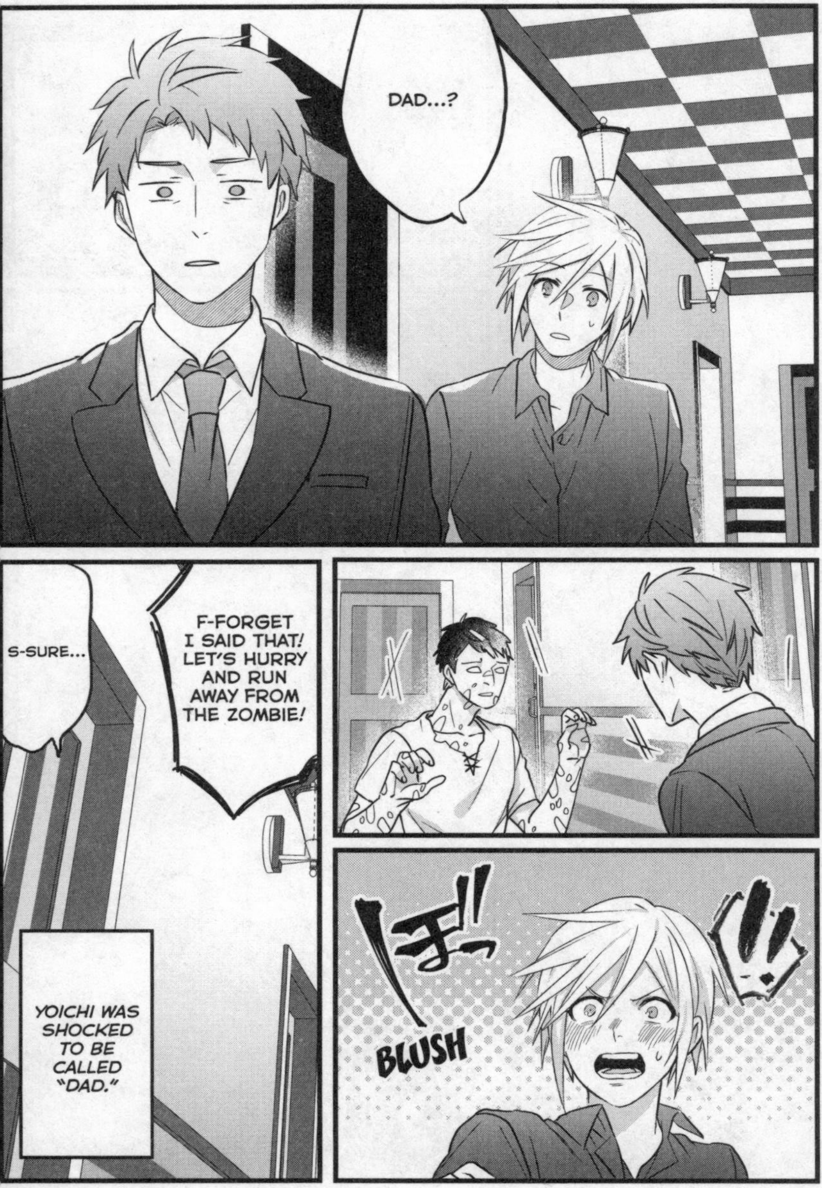
DAD...?
BLUSH
F-FORGET I SAID THAT! LET'S HURRY AND RUN AWAY FROM THE ZOMBIE!
S-SURE...
YOICHI WAS SHOCKED TO BE CALLED "DAD."

Chapter 35

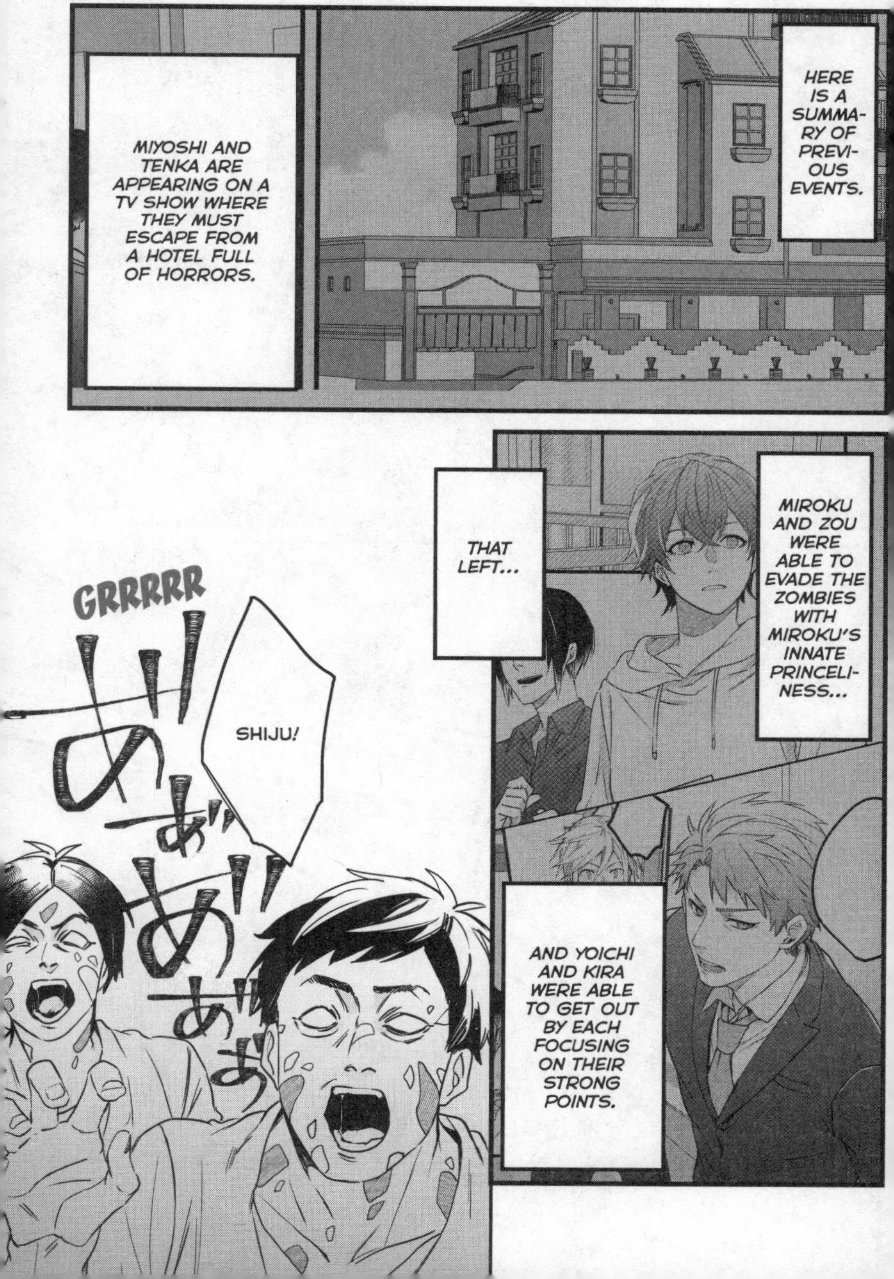
HERE IS A SUMMARY OF PREVIOUS EVENTS.
MIYOSHI AND TENKA ARE APPEARING ON A TV SHOW WHERE THEY MUST ESCAPE FROM A HOTEL FULL OF HORRORS.
MIROKU AND ZOU WERE ABLE TO EVADE THE ZOMBIES WITH MIROKU'S INNATE PRINCELINESS...
THAT LEFT...
AND YOICHI AND KIRA WERE ABLE TO GET OUT BY EACH FOCUSING ON THEIR STRONG POINTS.
SHIJU!
GRRRRR

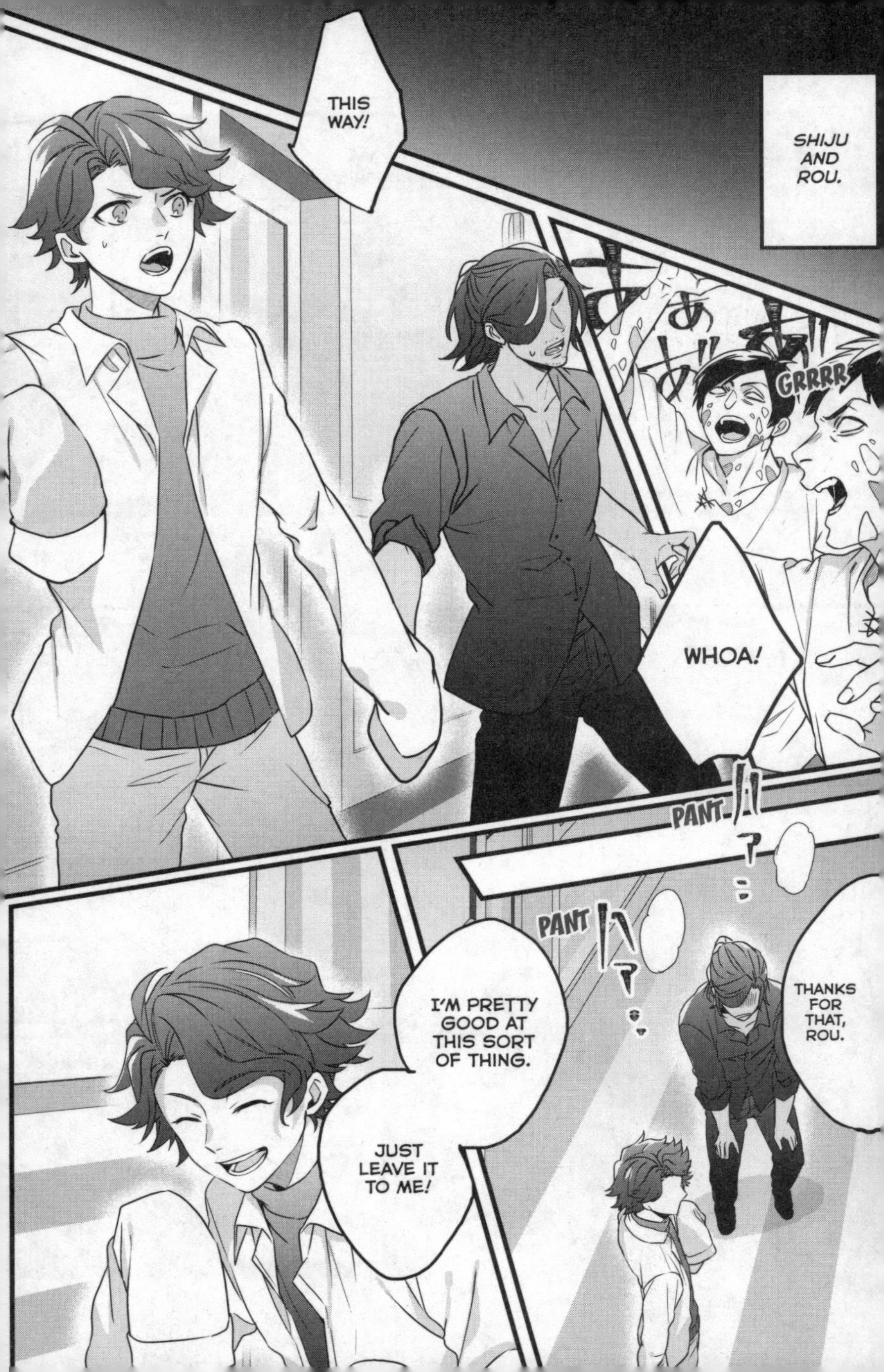
SHIJU AND ROU.
GRRRR
WHOA!
THIS WAY!
PANT
PANT
THANKS FOR THAT, ROU.
I'M PRETTY GOOD AT THIS SORT OF THING.
JUST LEAVE IT TO ME!

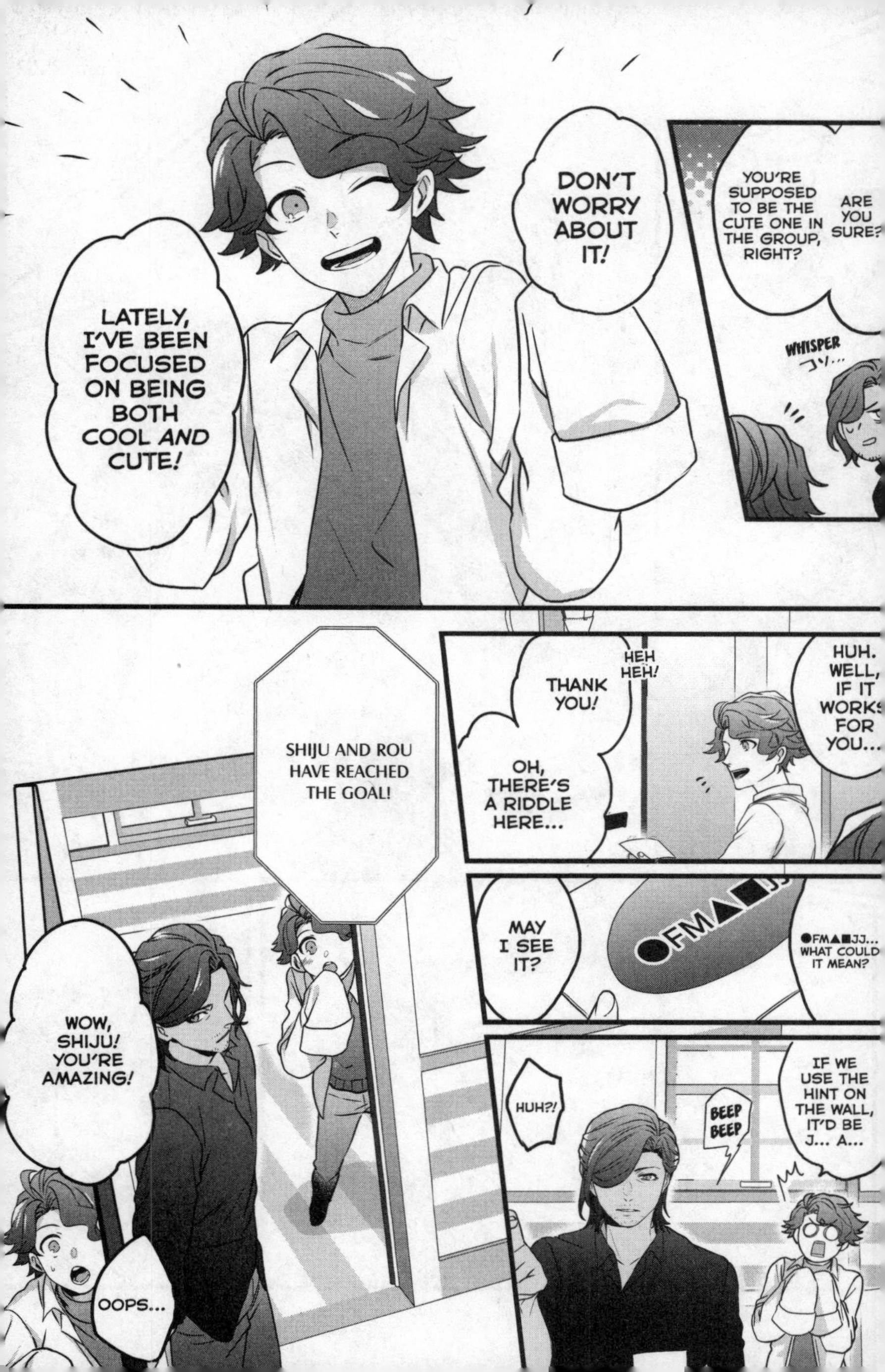

YOU'RE SUPPOSED TO BE THE CUTE ONE IN THE GROUP, RIGHT?
ARE YOU SURE?
WHISPER
コソ…
DON'T WORRY ABOUT IT!
LATELY, I'VE BEEN FOCUSED ON BEING BOTH COOL *AND* CUTE!
HUH. WELL, IF IT WORKS FOR YOU...
HEH HEH!
THANK YOU!
OH, THERE'S A RIDDLE HERE...
●FM▲■JJ... WHAT COULD IT MEAN?
MAY I SEE IT?
IF WE USE THE HINT ON THE WALL, IT'D BE J... A...
BEEP BEEP
HUH?!
SHIJU AND ROU HAVE REACHED THE GOAL!
WOW, SHIJU! YOU'RE AMAZING!
OOPS...

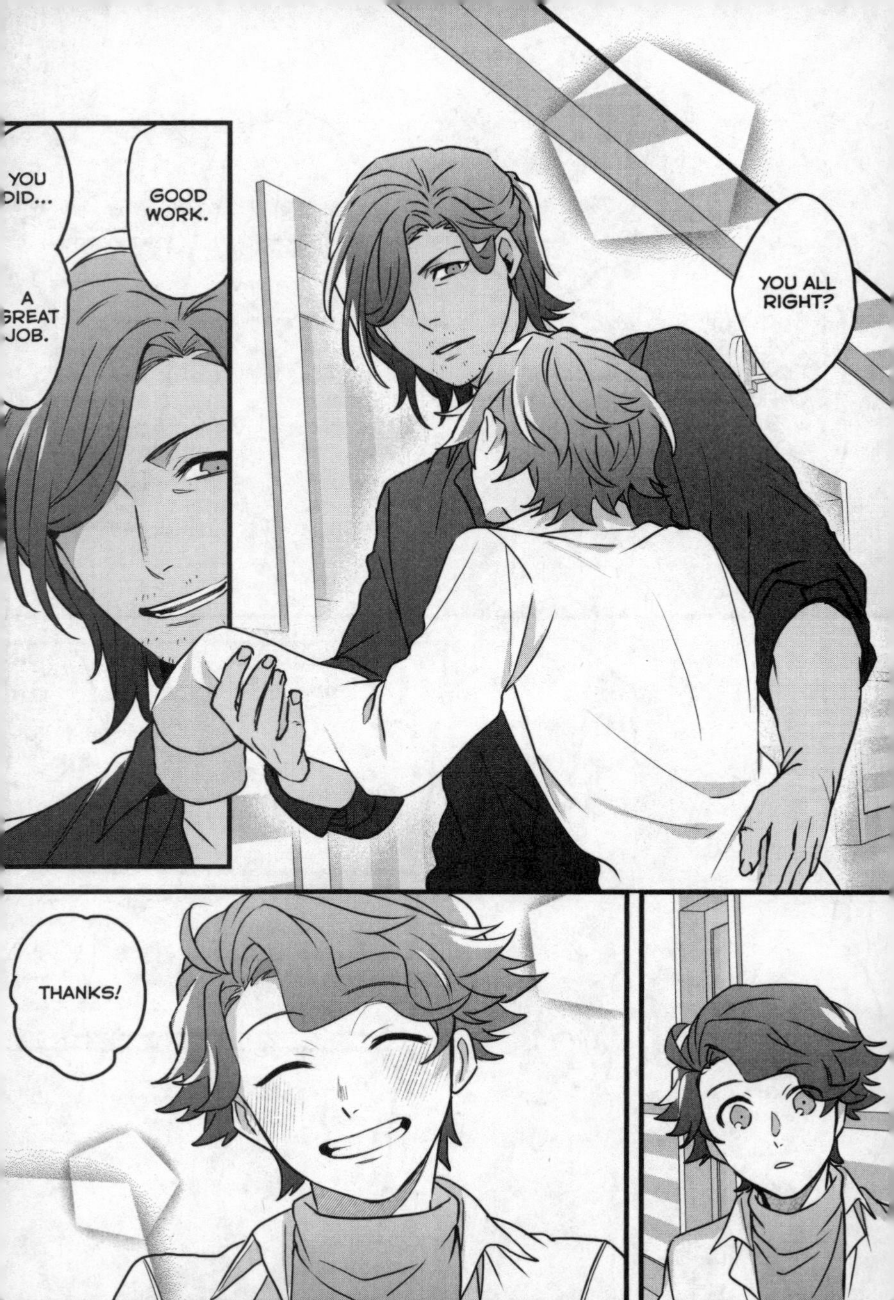
YOU ALL RIGHT?
GOOD WORK.
YOU DID... A GREAT JOB.
THANKS!

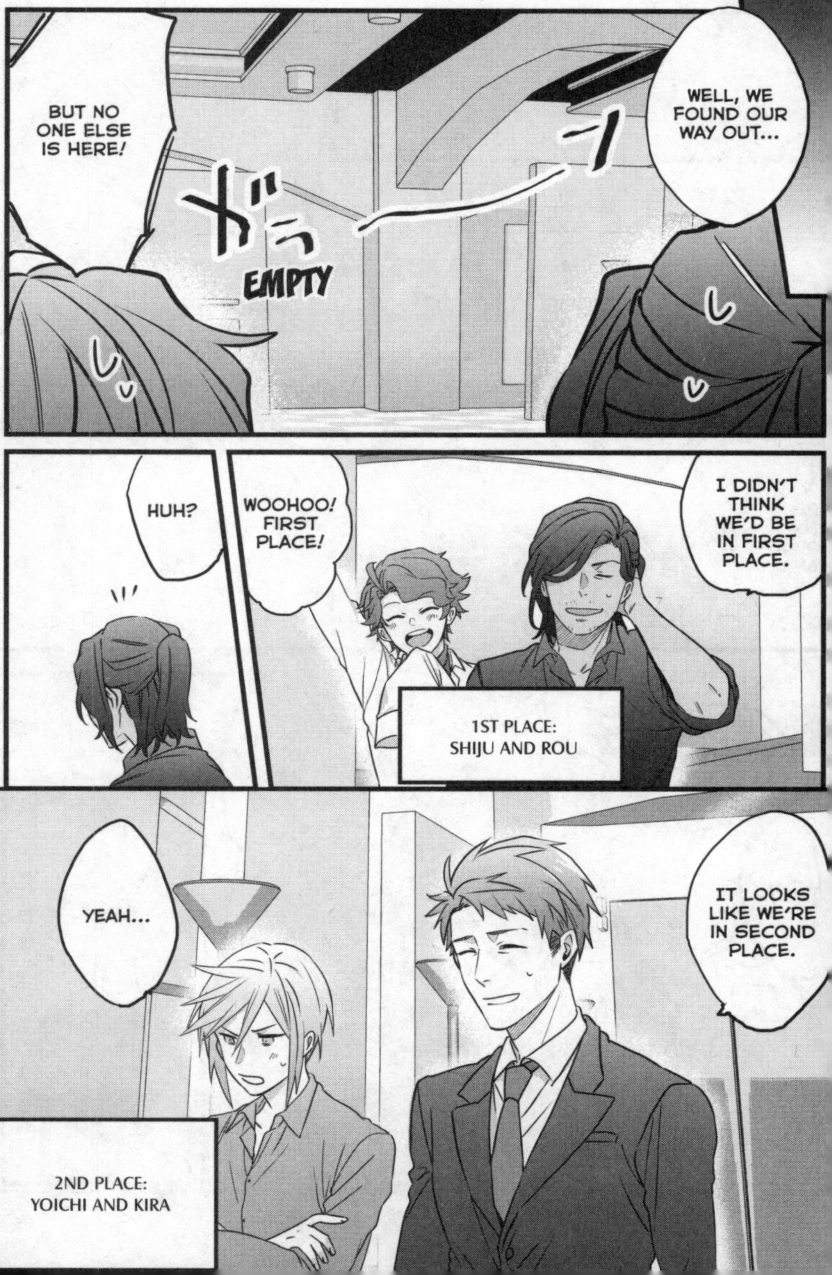
WELL, WE FOUND OUR WAY OUT...
EMPTY
BUT NO ONE ELSE IS HERE!
I DIDN'T THINK WE'D BE IN FIRST PLACE.
WOOHOO! FIRST PLACE!
1ST PLACE: SHIJU AND ROU
HUH?
IT LOOKS LIKE WE'RE IN SECOND PLACE.
YEAH...
2ND PLACE: YOICHI AND KIRA

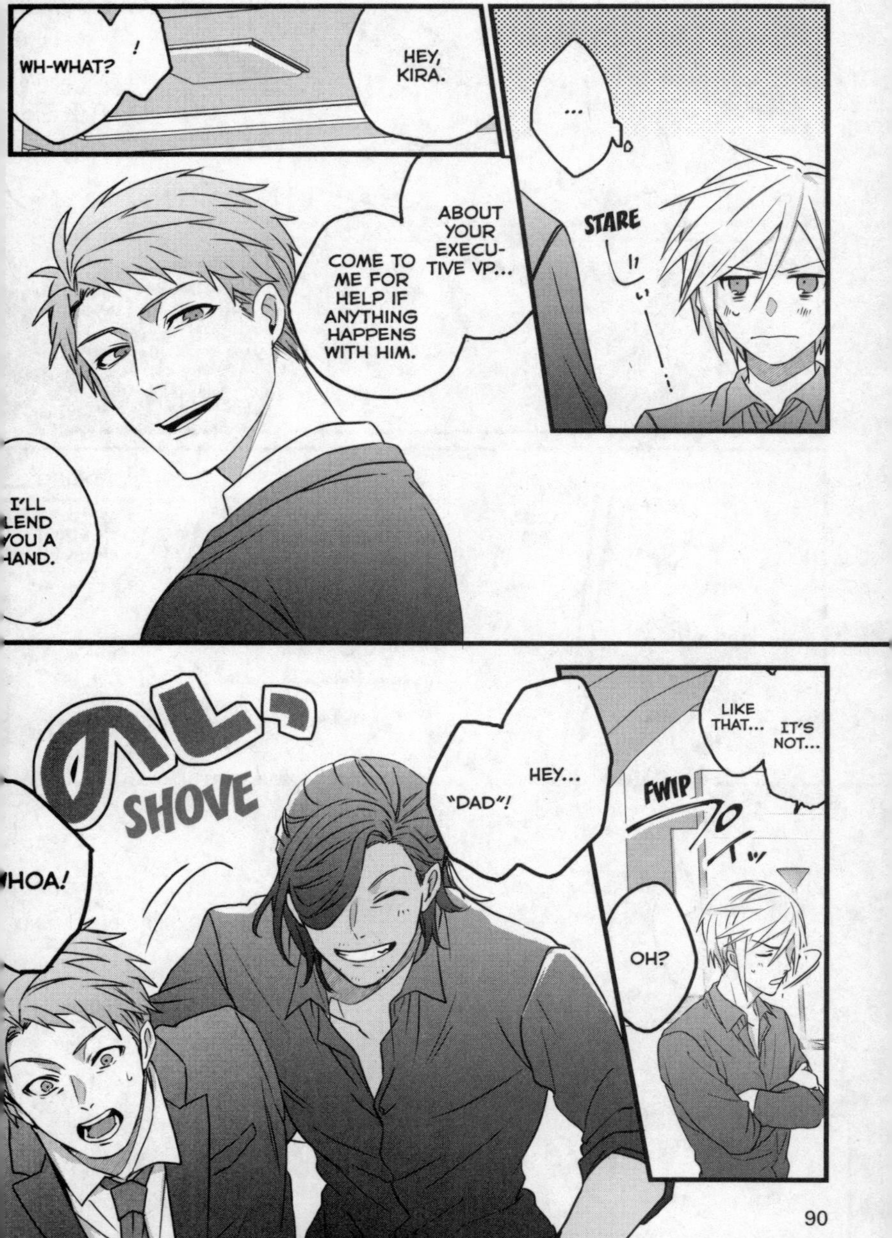
...
STARE
HEY, KIRA.
WH-WHAT?
!
ABOUT YOUR EXECUTIVE VP...
COME TO ME FOR HELP IF ANYTHING HAPPENS WITH HIM.
I'LL LEND YOU A HAND.
LIKE THAT... IT'S NOT...
FWIP
OH?
HEY... "DAD"!
SHOVE
WHOA!

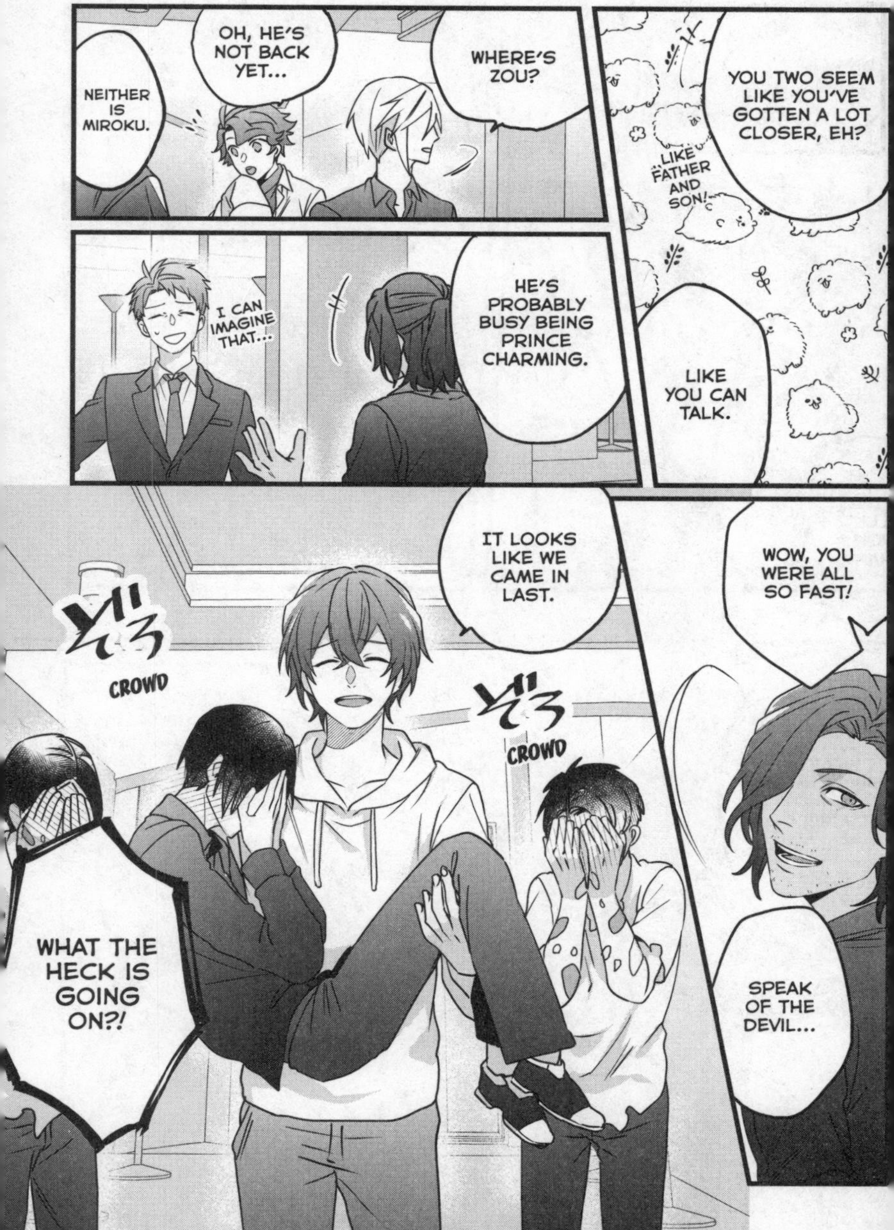

YOU TWO SEEM LIKE YOU'VE GOTTEN A LOT CLOSER, EH?
...LIKE FATHER AND SON!
LIKE YOU CAN TALK.
WHERE'S ZOU?
OH, HE'S NOT BACK YET...
NEITHER IS MIROKU.
HE'S PROBABLY BUSY BEING PRINCE CHARMING.
I CAN IMAGINE THAT...
WOW, YOU WERE ALL SO FAST!
SPEAK OF THE DEVIL...
IT LOOKS LIKE WE CAME IN LAST.
ぞろ
CROWD
ぞろ
CROWD
WHAT THE HECK IS GOING ON?!

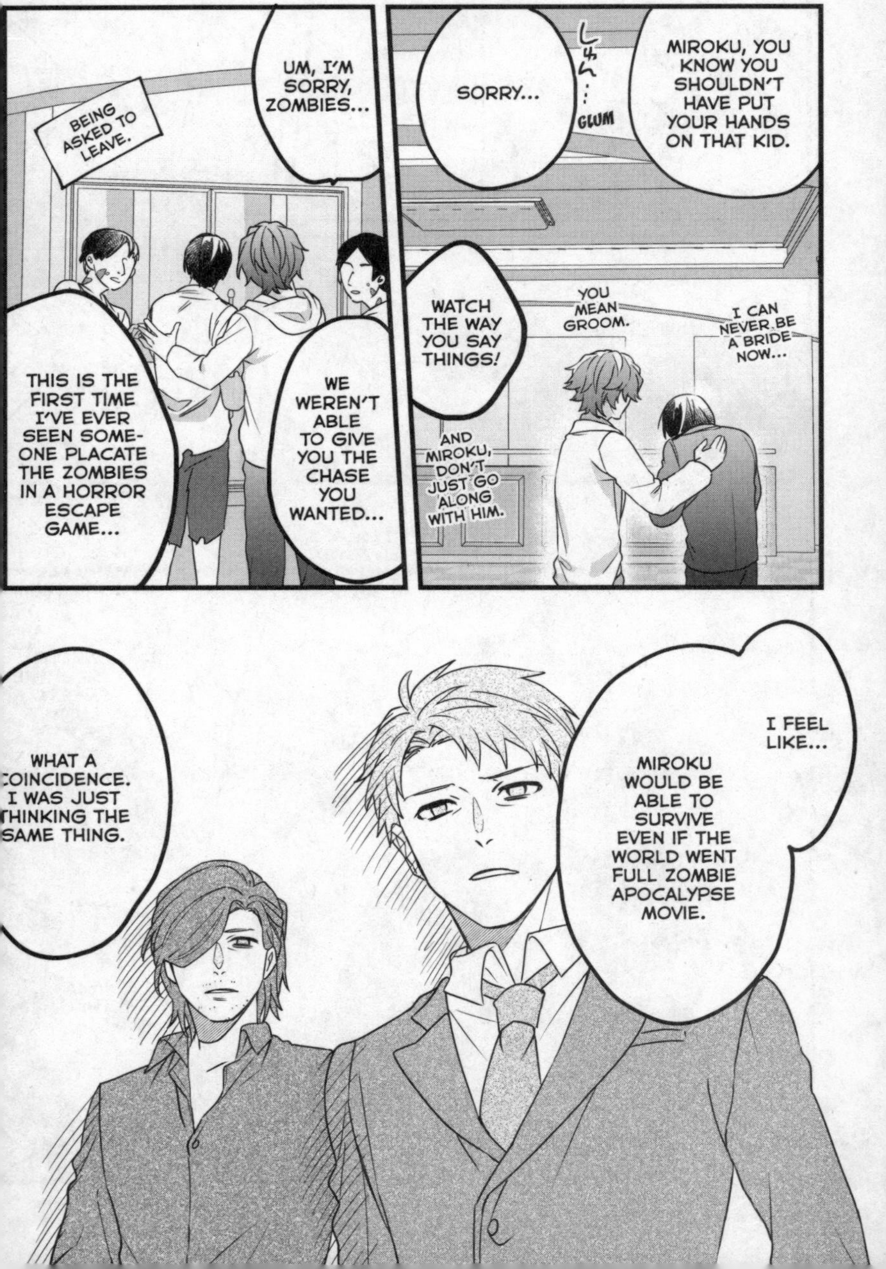
MIROKU, YOU KNOW YOU SHOULDN'T HAVE PUT YOUR HANDS ON THAT KID.
しゅん…
GLUM
SORRY...
I CAN NEVER BE A BRIDE NOW...
YOU MEAN GROOM.
WATCH THE WAY YOU SAY THINGS!
AND MIROKU, DON'T JUST GO ALONG WITH HIM.
UM, I'M SORRY, ZOMBIES...
BEING ASKED TO LEAVE.
WE WEREN'T ABLE TO GIVE YOU THE CHASE YOU WANTED...
THIS IS THE FIRST TIME I'VE EVER SEEN SOME-ONE PLACATE THE ZOMBIES IN A HORROR ESCAPE GAME...
I FEEL LIKE...
MIROKU WOULD BE ABLE TO SURVIVE EVEN IF THE WORLD WENT FULL ZOMBIE APOCALYPSE MOVIE.
WHAT A COINCIDENCE. I WAS JUST THINKING THE SAME THING.

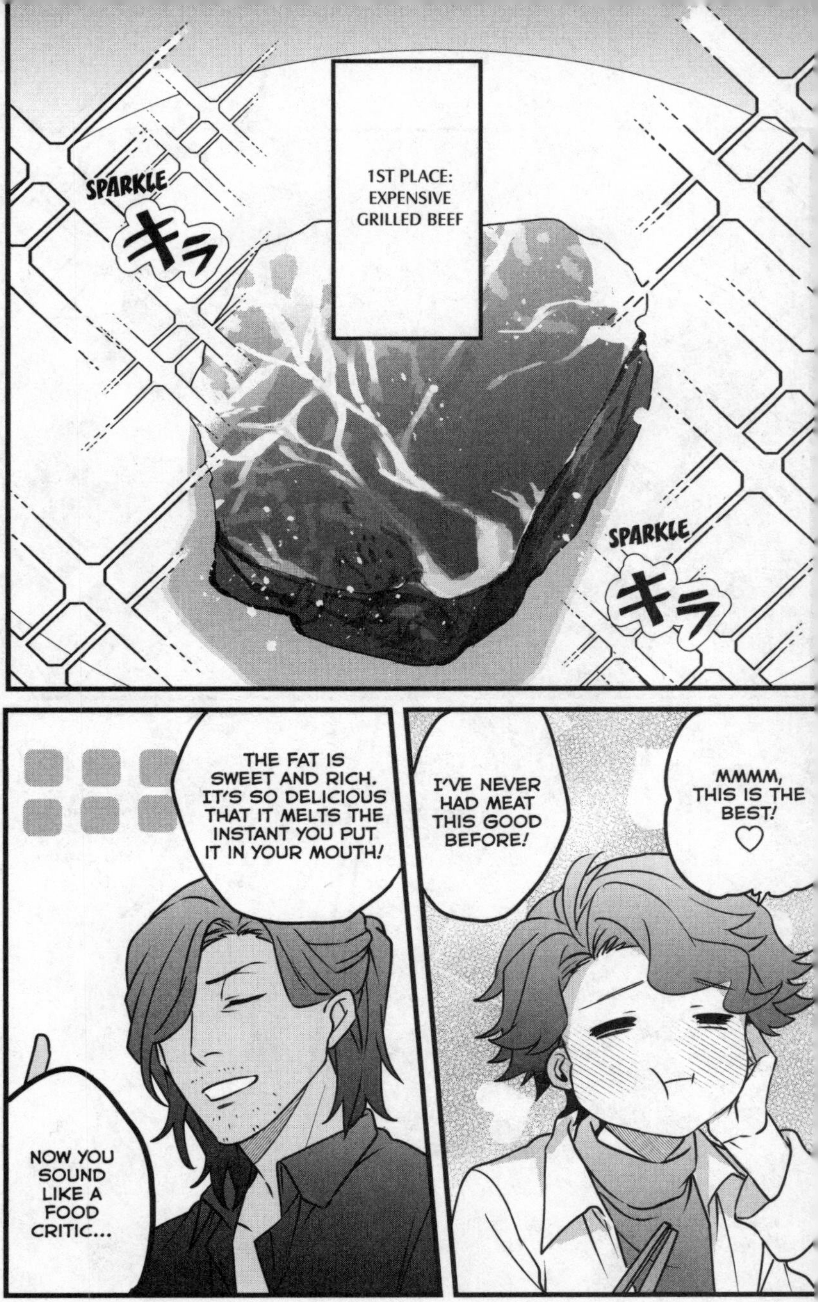
1ST PLACE: EXPENSIVE GRILLED BEEF
SPARKLE
キラ
SPARKLE
キラ
MMMM, THIS IS THE BEST! ♡
I'VE NEVER HAD MEAT THIS GOOD BEFORE!
THE FAT IS SWEET AND RICH. IT'S SO DELICIOUS THAT IT MELTS THE INSTANT YOU PUT IT IN YOUR MOUTH!
NOW YOU SOUND LIKE A FOOD CRITIC...

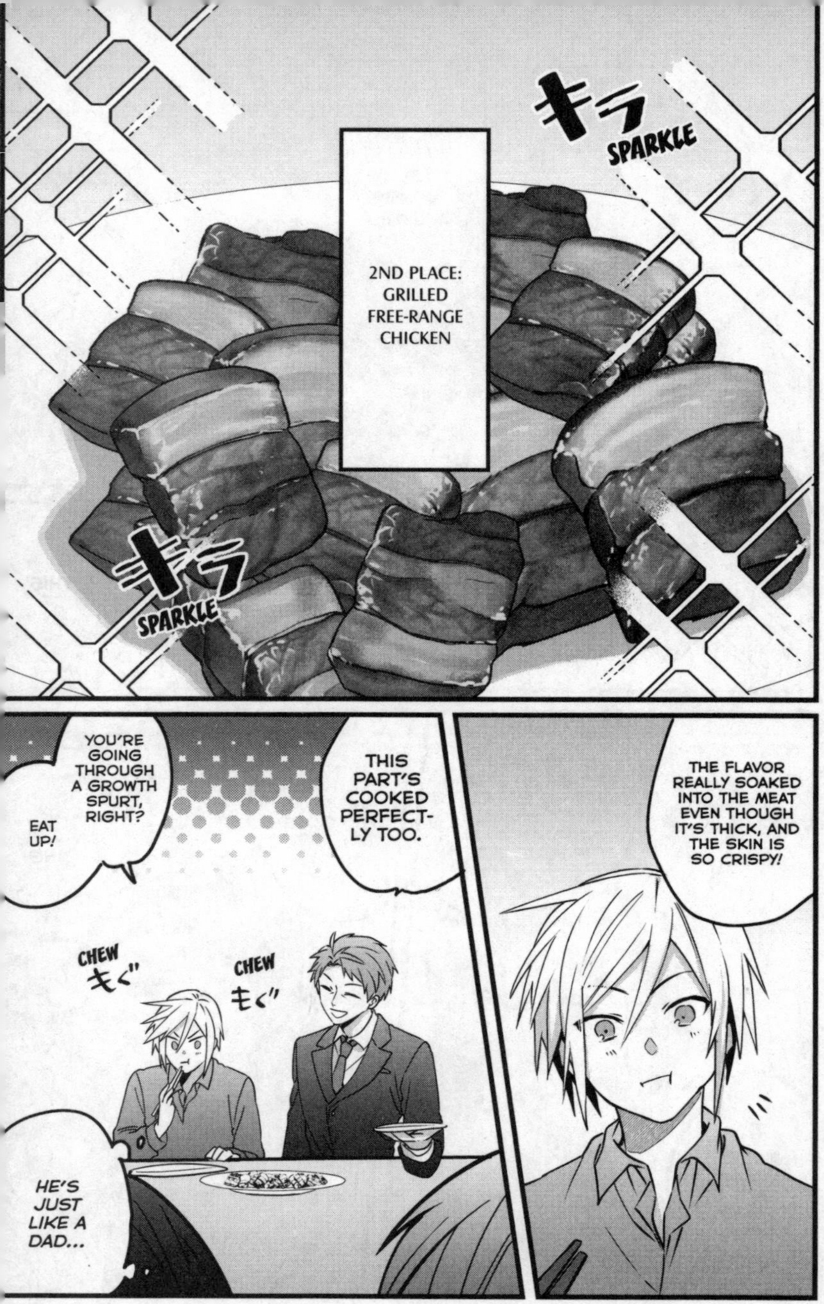
キラ
SPARKLE
2ND PLACE: GRILLED FREE-RANGE CHICKEN
キラ
SPARKLE
THE FLAVOR REALLY SOAKED INTO THE MEAT EVEN THOUGH IT'S THICK, AND THE SKIN IS SO CRISPY!
THIS PART'S COOKED PERFECT-LY TOO.
YOU'RE GOING THROUGH A GROWTH SPURT, RIGHT?
EAT UP!
CHEW
もぐ
CHEW
もぐ
HE'S JUST LIKE A DAD...

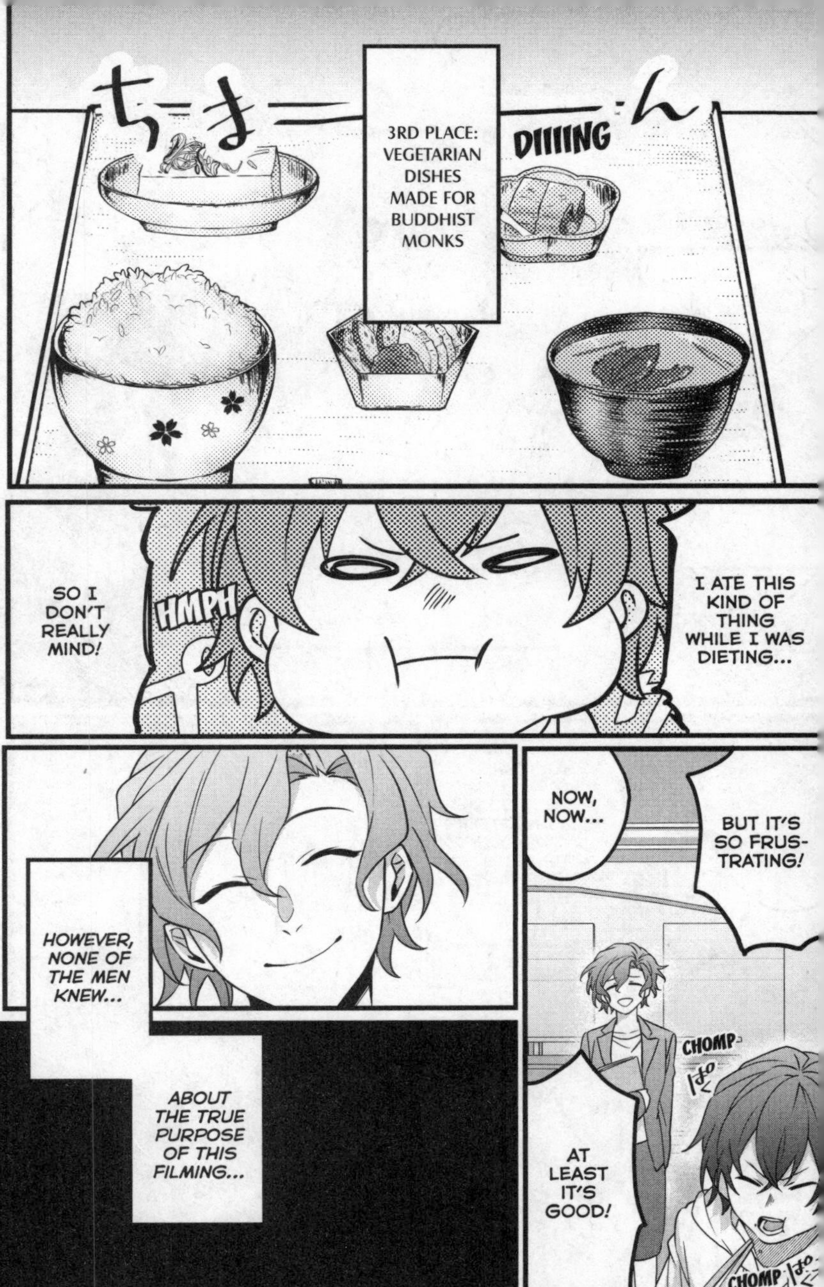
ちまーーーん
DIIIING
3RD PLACE: VEGETARIAN DISHES MADE FOR BUDDHIST MONKS
I ATE THIS KIND OF THING WHILE I WAS DIETING...
HMPH
SO I DON'T REALLY MIND!
BUT IT'S SO FRUS-TRATING!
NOW, NOW...
CHOMP
ぱく
AT LEAST IT'S GOOD!
CHOMP
ぱく
HOWEVER, NONE OF THE MEN KNEW...
ABOUT THE TRUE PURPOSE OF THIS FILMING...

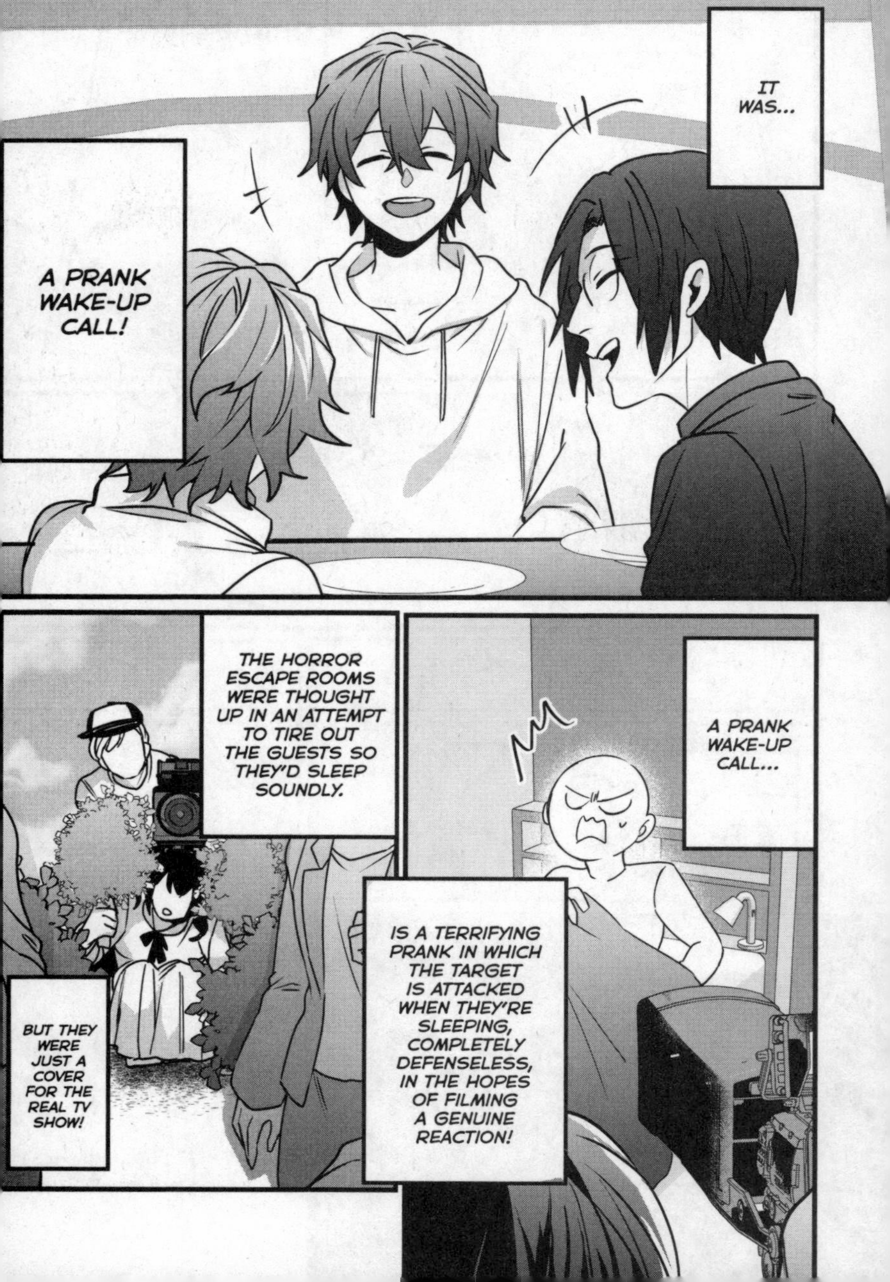
IT WAS...
A PRANK WAKE-UP CALL!
A PRANK WAKE-UP CALL...
IS A TERRIFYING PRANK IN WHICH THE TARGET IS ATTACKED WHEN THEY'RE SLEEPING, COMPLETELY DEFENSELESS, IN THE HOPES OF FILMING A GENUINE REACTION!
THE HORROR ESCAPE ROOMS WERE THOUGHT UP IN AN ATTEMPT TO TIRE OUT THE GUESTS SO THEY'D SLEEP SOUNDLY.
BUT THEY WERE JUST A COVER FOR THE REAL TV SHOW!

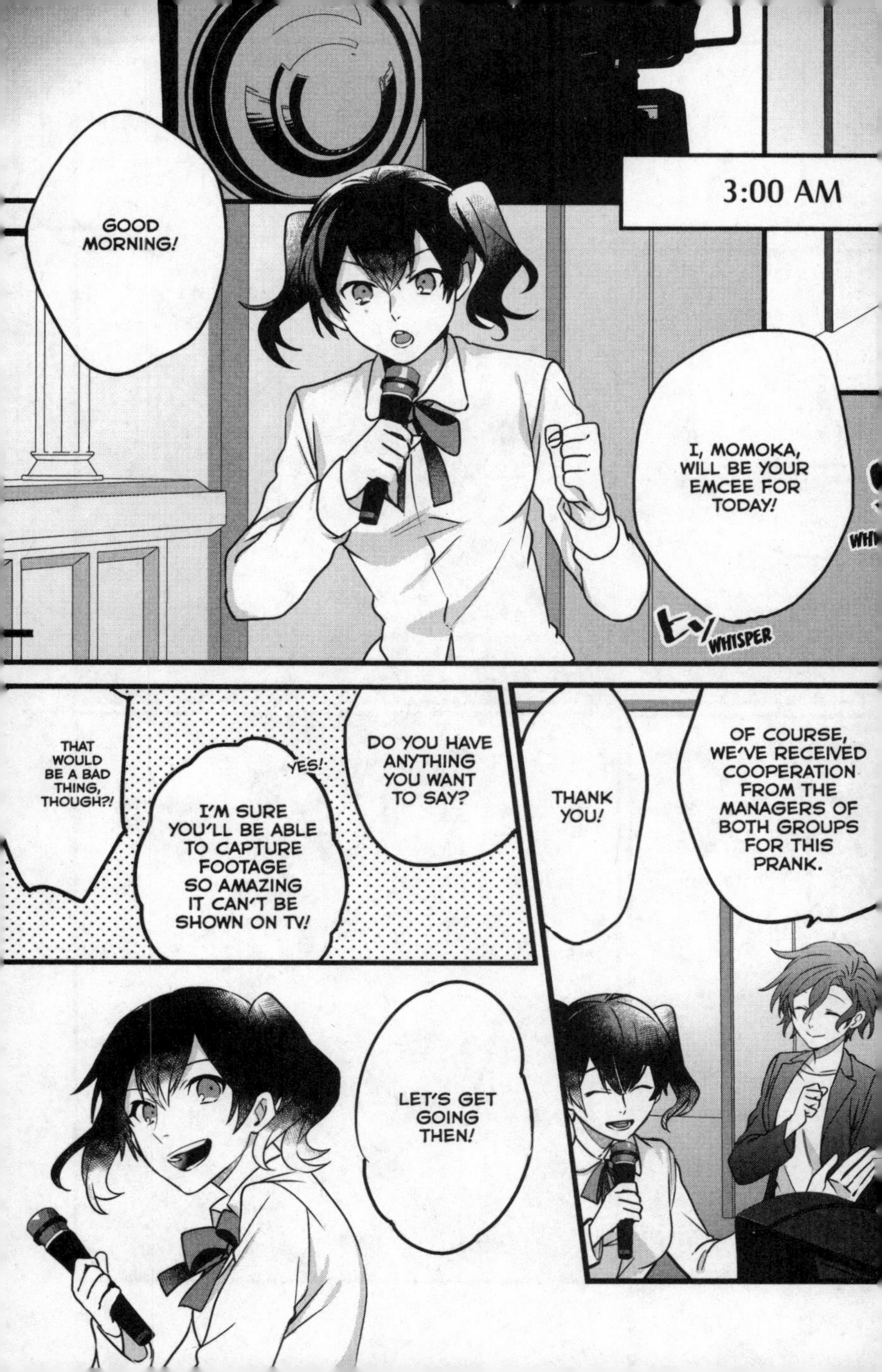
3:00 AM
GOOD MORNING!
I, MOMOKA, WILL BE YOUR EMCEE FOR TODAY!
WHISPER
OF COURSE, WE'VE RECEIVED COOPERATION FROM THE MANAGERS OF BOTH GROUPS FOR THIS PRANK.
THANK YOU!
DO YOU HAVE ANYTHING YOU WANT TO SAY?
YES!
I'M SURE YOU'LL BE ABLE TO CAPTURE FOOTAGE SO AMAZING IT CAN'T BE SHOWN ON TV!
THAT WOULD BE A BAD THING, THOUGH?!
LET'S GET GOING THEN!

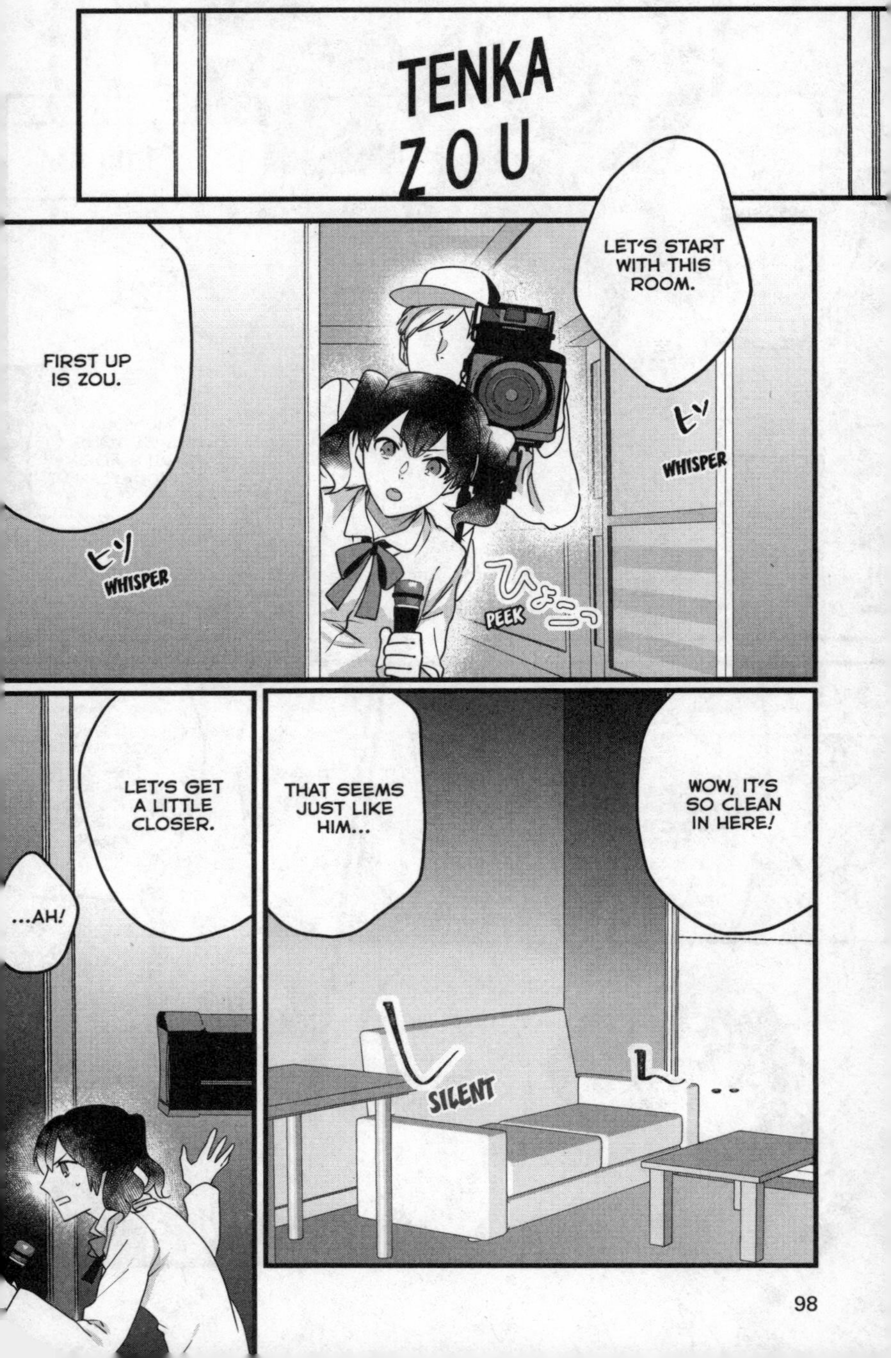
TENKA
ZOU
LET'S START WITH THIS ROOM.
ヒソ
WHISPER
FIRST UP IS ZOU.
ヒソ
WHISPER
ひょこっ
PEEK
WOW, IT'S SO CLEAN IN HERE!
THAT SEEMS JUST LIKE HIM...
シ〜ん...
SILENT
LET'S GET A LITTLE CLOSER.
...AH!

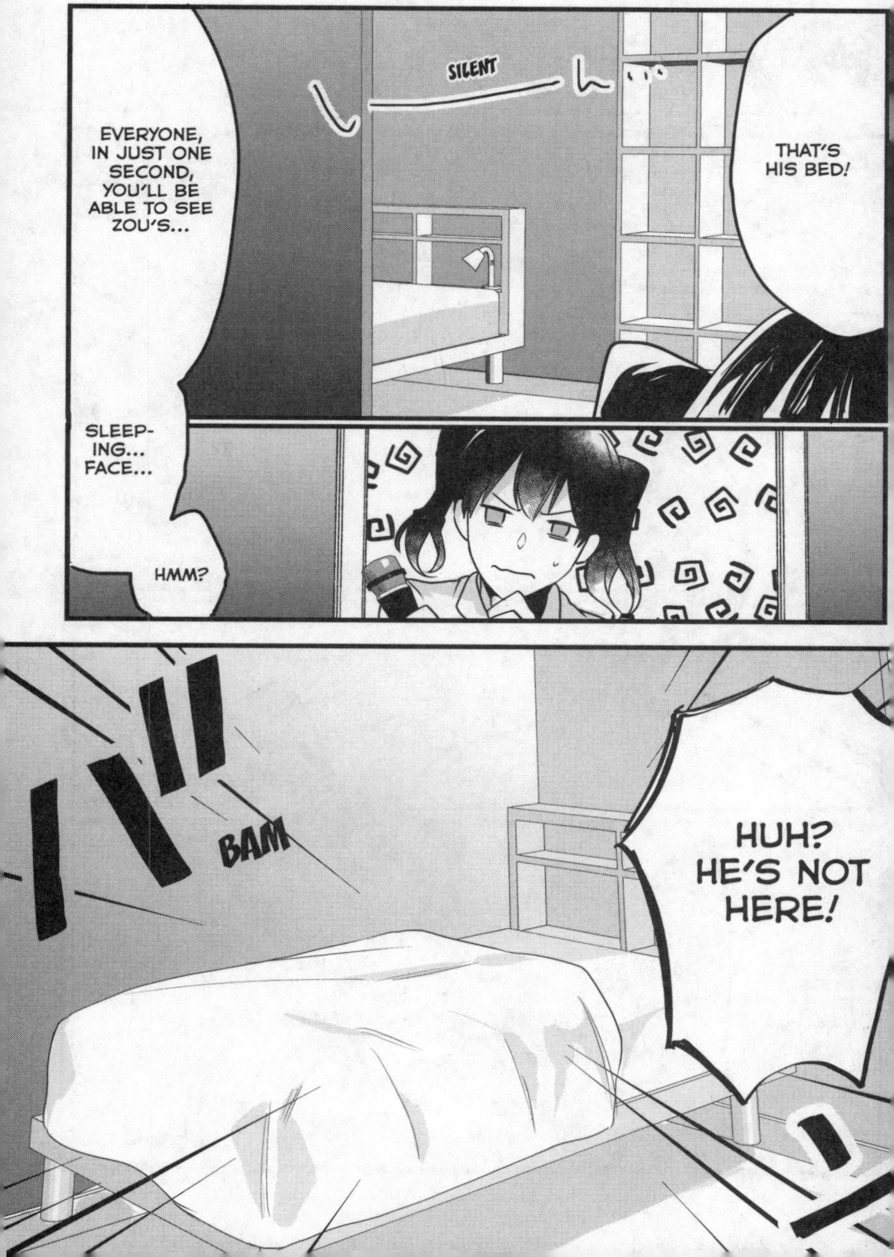
THAT'S HIS BED!
SILENT
EVERYONE, IN JUST ONE SECOND, YOU'LL BE ABLE TO SEE ZOU'S...
SLEEPING... FACE...
HMM?
HUH? HE'S NOT HERE!
BAM

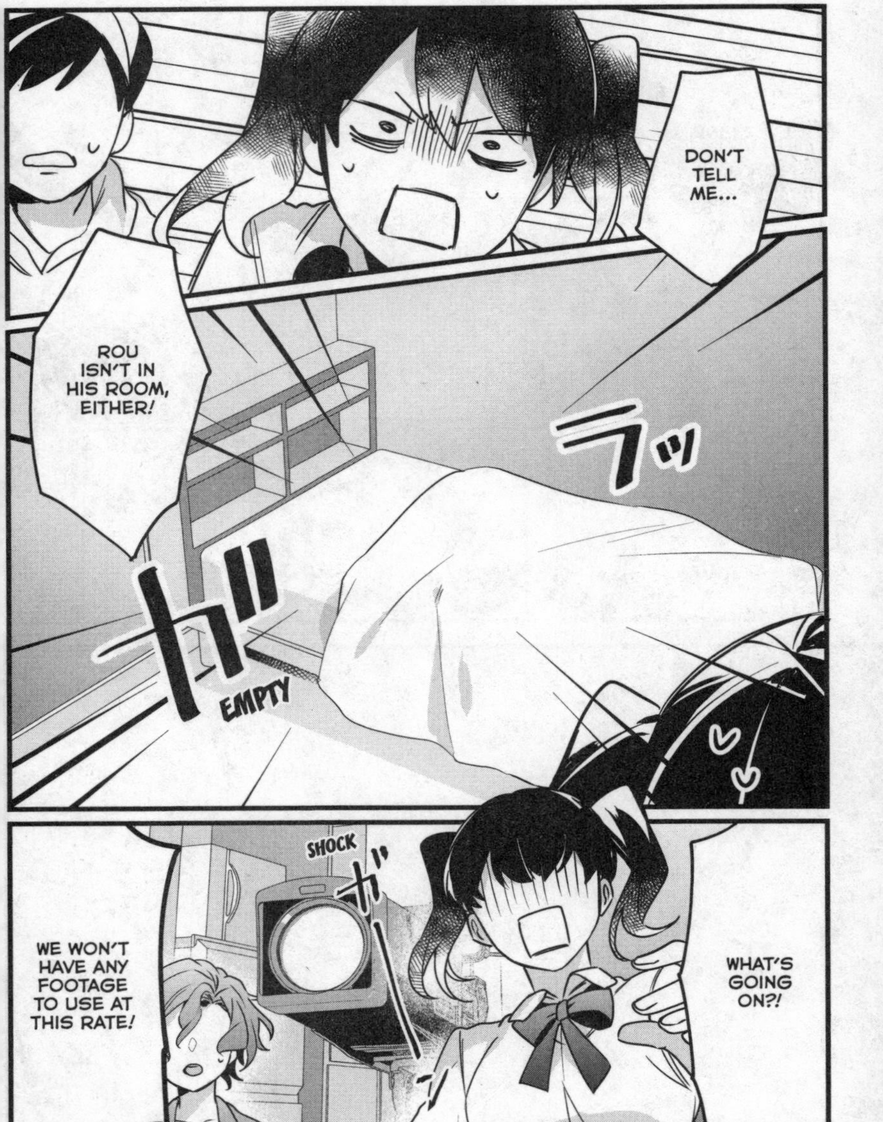
DON'T TELL ME...
ROU ISN'T IN HIS ROOM, EITHER!
ラッ
EMPTY
WHAT'S GOING ON?!
SHOCK
WE WON'T HAVE ANY FOOTAGE TO USE AT THIS RATE!

Chapter 36

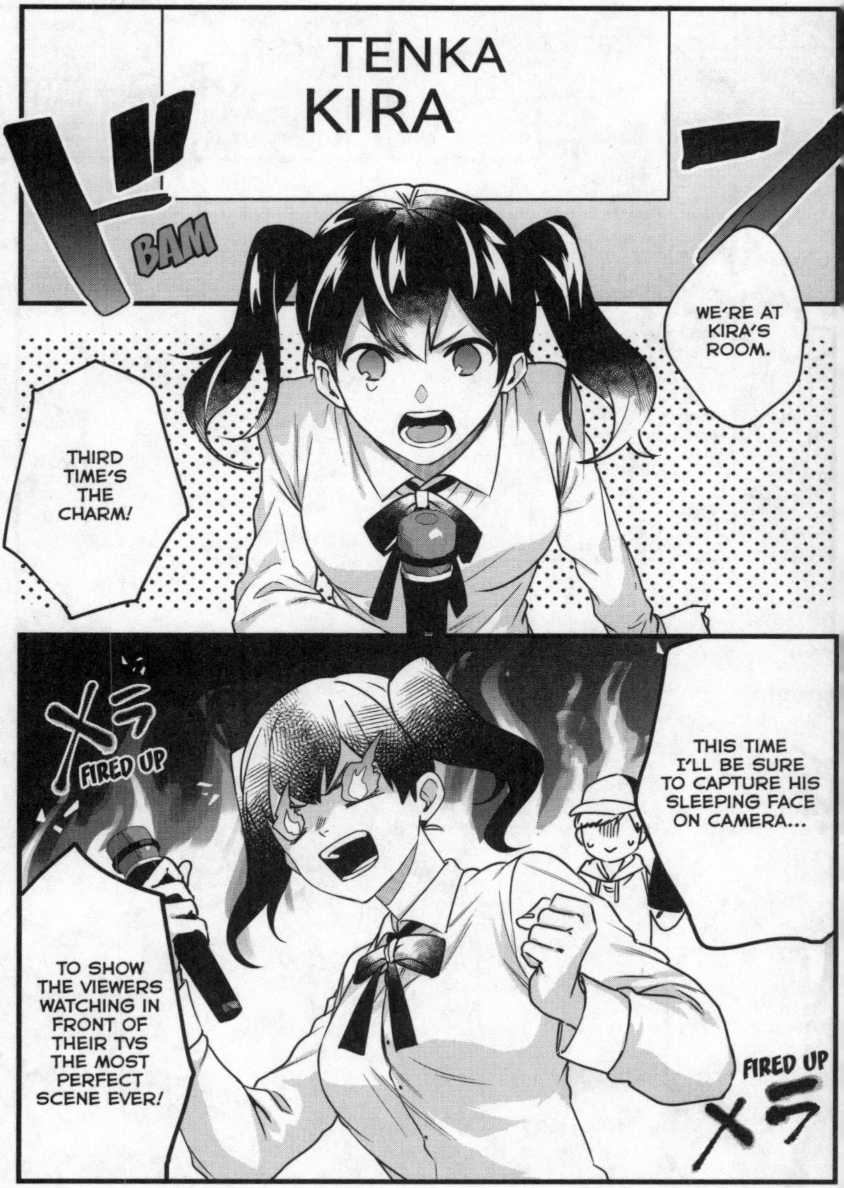
TENKA
KIRA
BAM
WE'RE AT KIRA'S ROOM.
THIRD TIME'S THE CHARM!
THIS TIME I'LL BE SURE TO CAPTURE HIS SLEEPING FACE ON CAMERA...
メラ
FIRED UP
TO SHOW THE VIEWERS WATCHING IN FRONT OF THEIR TVS THE MOST PERFECT SCENE EVER!
FIRED UP
メラ

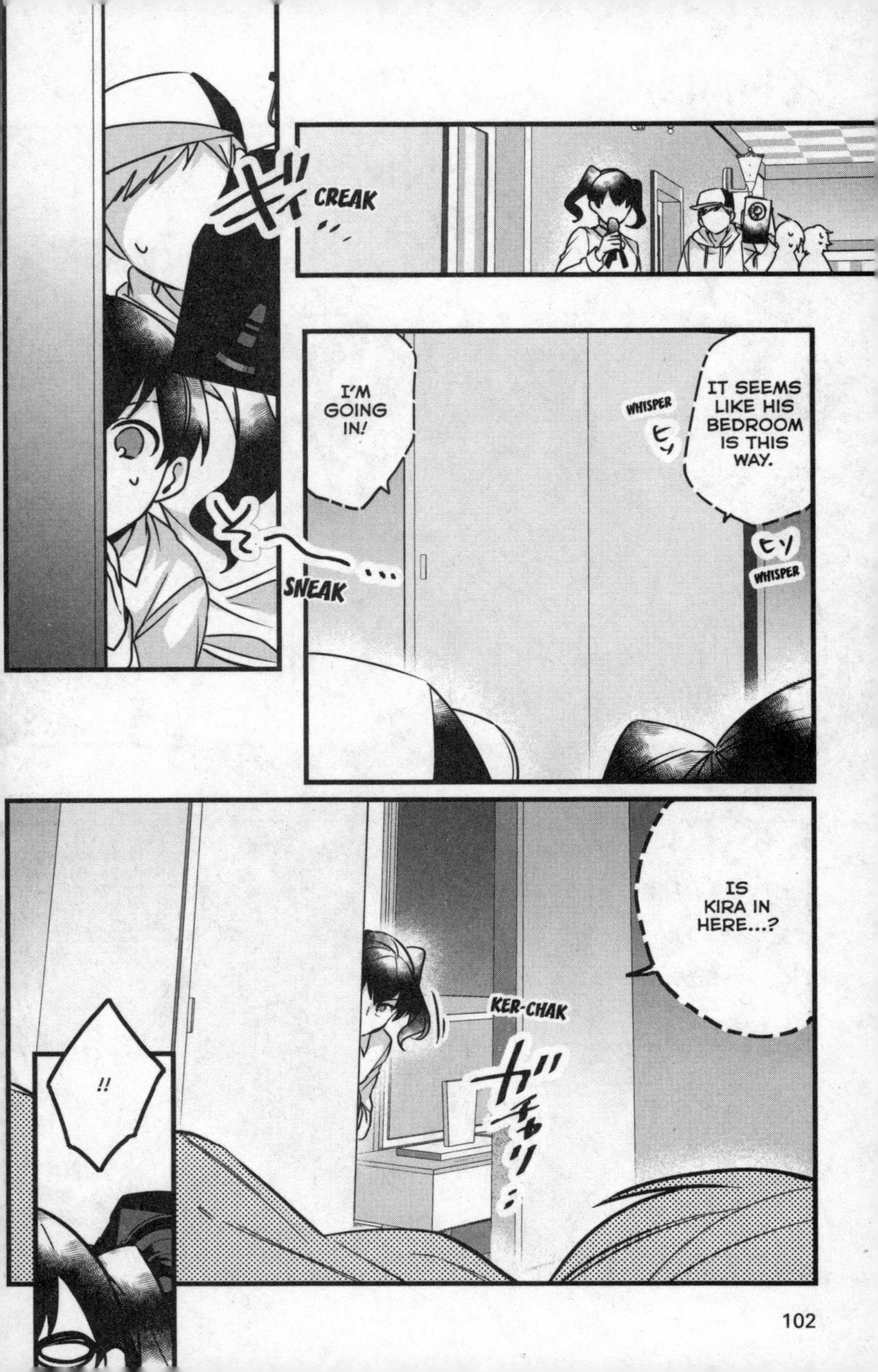
WHISPER
IT SEEMS LIKE HIS BEDROOM IS THIS WAY.
WHISPER
I'M GOING IN!
CREAK
SNEAK
...
IS KIRA IN HERE...?
KER-CHAK
!!

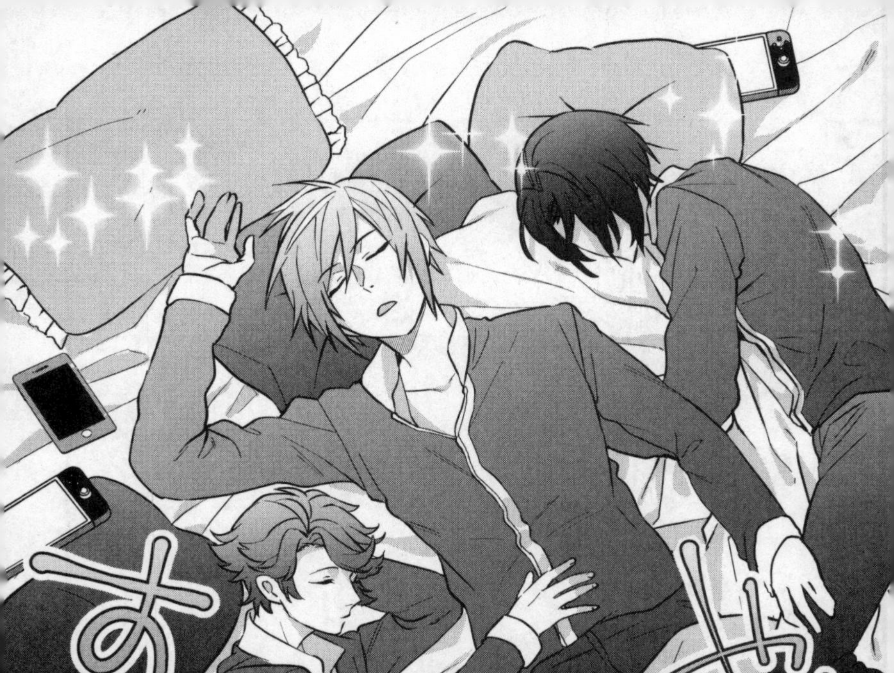

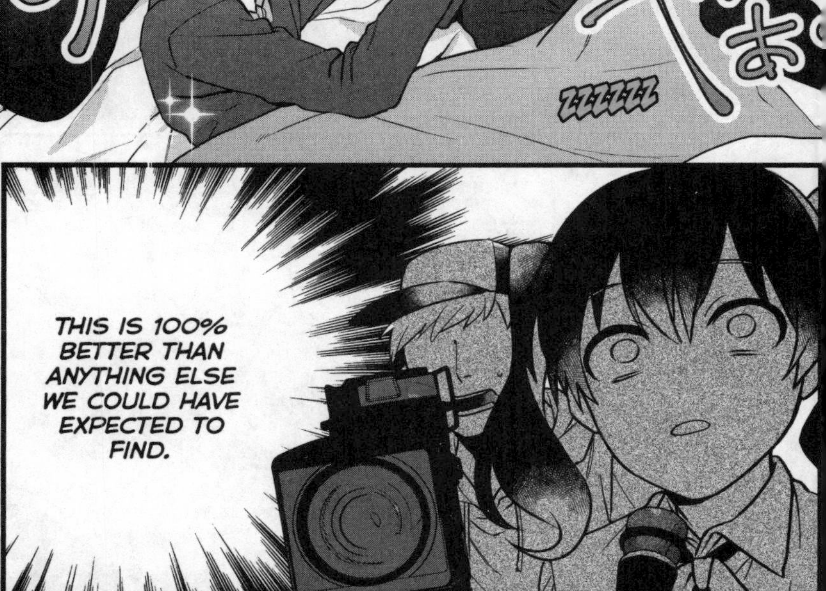
THIS IS 100% BETTER THAN ANYTHING ELSE WE COULD HAVE EXPECTED TO FIND.

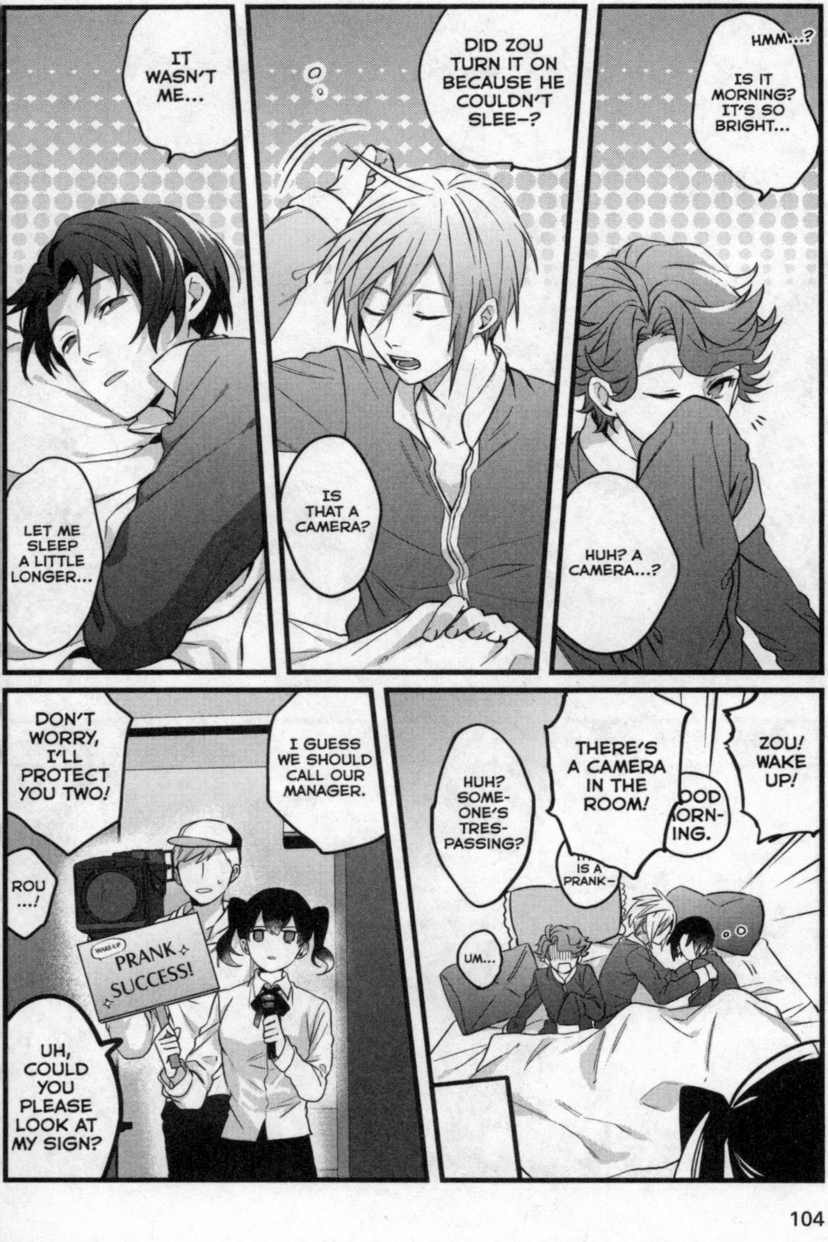
HMM...?
IS IT MORNING? IT'S SO BRIGHT...
HUH? A CAMERA...?
DID ZOU TURN IT ON BECAUSE HE COULDN'T SLEE–?
IS THAT A CAMERA?
IT WASN'T ME...
LET ME SLEEP A LITTLE LONGER...
ZOU! WAKE UP!
OOD ORN-ING.
THERE'S A CAMERA IN THE ROOM!
HUH? SOME-ONE'S TRES-PASSING?
IS A PRANK–
UM...
I GUESS WE SHOULD CALL OUR MANAGER.
DON'T WORRY, I'LL PROTECT YOU TWO!
ROU ...!
WAKE-UP PRANK SUCCESS!
UH, COULD YOU PLEASE LOOK AT MY SIGN?

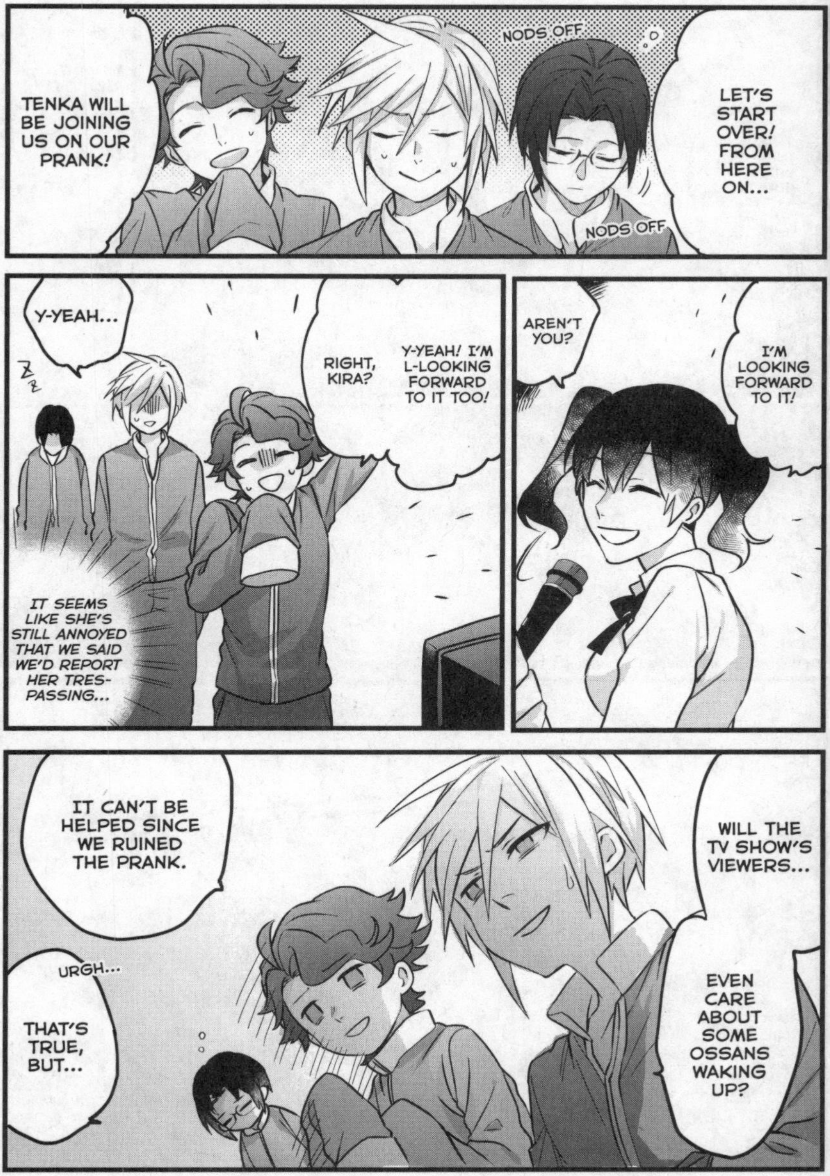
NODS OFF
LET'S START OVER! FROM HERE ON...
TENKA WILL BE JOINING US ON OUR PRANK!
NODS OFF
I'M LOOKING FORWARD TO IT!
AREN'T YOU?
RIGHT, KIRA?
Y-YEAH! I'M L-LOOKING FORWARD TO IT TOO!
Y-YEAH...
IT SEEMS LIKE SHE'S STILL ANNOYED THAT WE SAID WE'D REPORT HER TRES-PASSING...
WILL THE TV SHOW'S VIEWERS...
EVEN CARE ABOUT SOME OSSANS WAKING UP?
IT CAN'T BE HELPED SINCE WE RUINED THE PRANK.
URGH...
THAT'S TRUE, BUT...

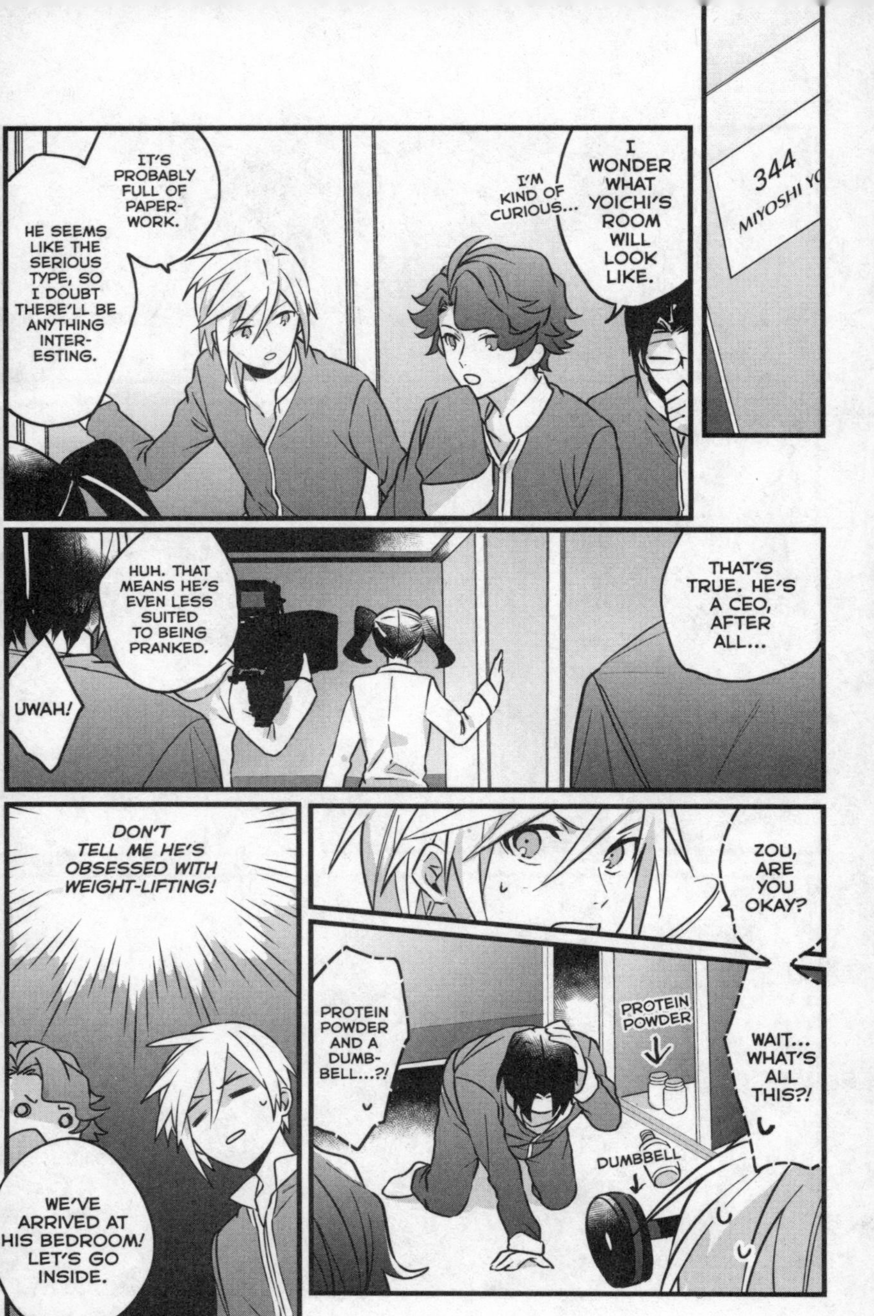
344
MIYOSHI YO
I WONDER WHAT YOICHI'S ROOM WILL LOOK LIKE.
I'M KIND OF CURIOUS...
IT'S PROBABLY FULL OF PAPER-WORK.
HE SEEMS LIKE THE SERIOUS TYPE, SO I DOUBT THERE'LL BE ANYTHING INTER-ESTING.
THAT'S TRUE. HE'S A CEO, AFTER ALL...
HUH. THAT MEANS HE'S EVEN LESS SUITED TO BEING PRANKED.
UWAH!
ZOU, ARE YOU OKAY?
WAIT... WHAT'S ALL THIS?!
PROTEIN POWDER
PROTEIN POWDER AND A DUMB-BELL...?!
DUMBBELL
DON'T TELL ME HE'S OBSESSED WITH WEIGHT-LIFTING!
WE'VE ARRIVED AT HIS BEDROOM! LET'S GO INSIDE.

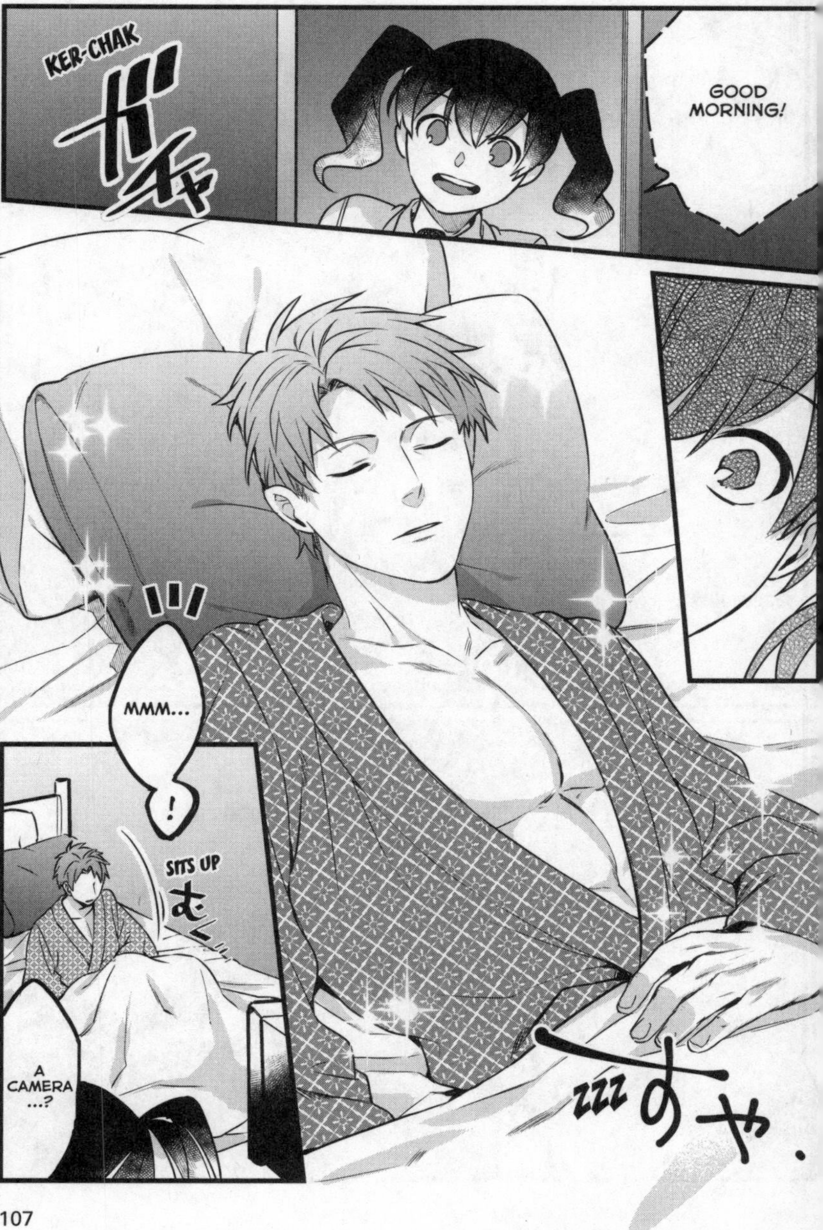
GOOD MORNING!
KER-CHAK
ZZZ
MMM...
!
SITS UP
A CAMERA ...?

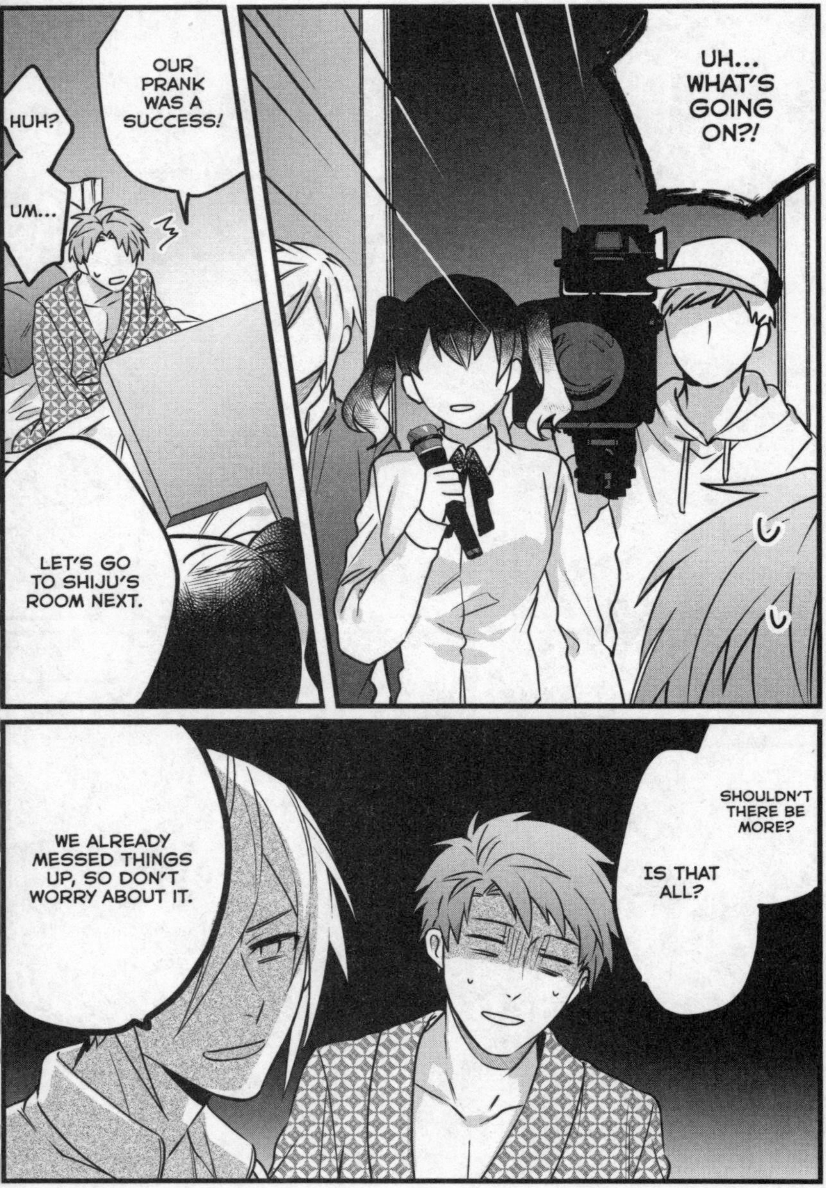
UH... WHAT'S GOING ON?!
OUR PRANK WAS A SUCCESS!
HUH?
UM...
LET'S GO TO SHIJU'S ROOM NEXT.
SHOULDN'T THERE BE MORE?
IS THAT ALL?
WE ALREADY MESSED THINGS UP, SO DON'T WORRY ABOUT IT.

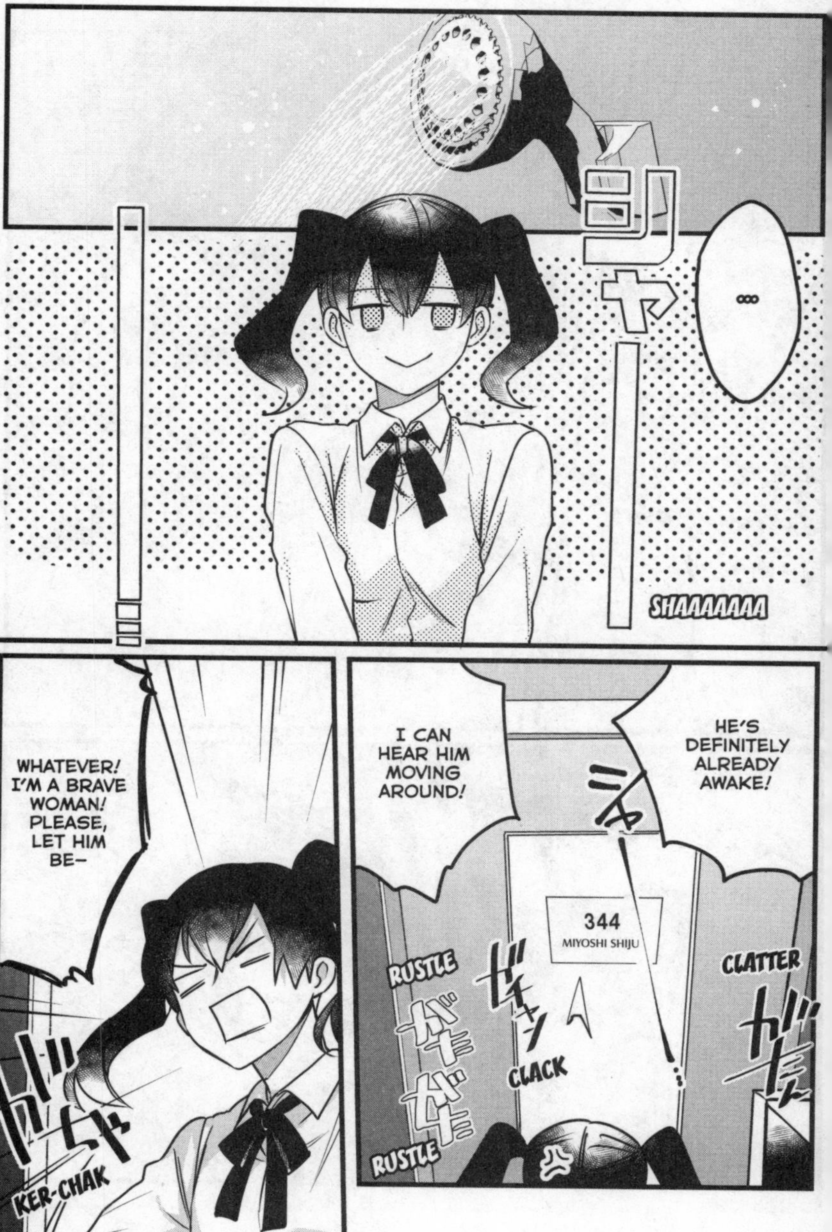
...
SHAAAAAAA
HE'S DEFINITELY ALREADY AWAKE!
I CAN HEAR HIM MOVING AROUND!
344
MIYOSHI SHIJU
CLATTER
RUSTLE
CLACK
RUSTLE
WHATEVER! I'M A BRAVE WOMAN! PLEASE, LET HIM BE–
KER-CHAK

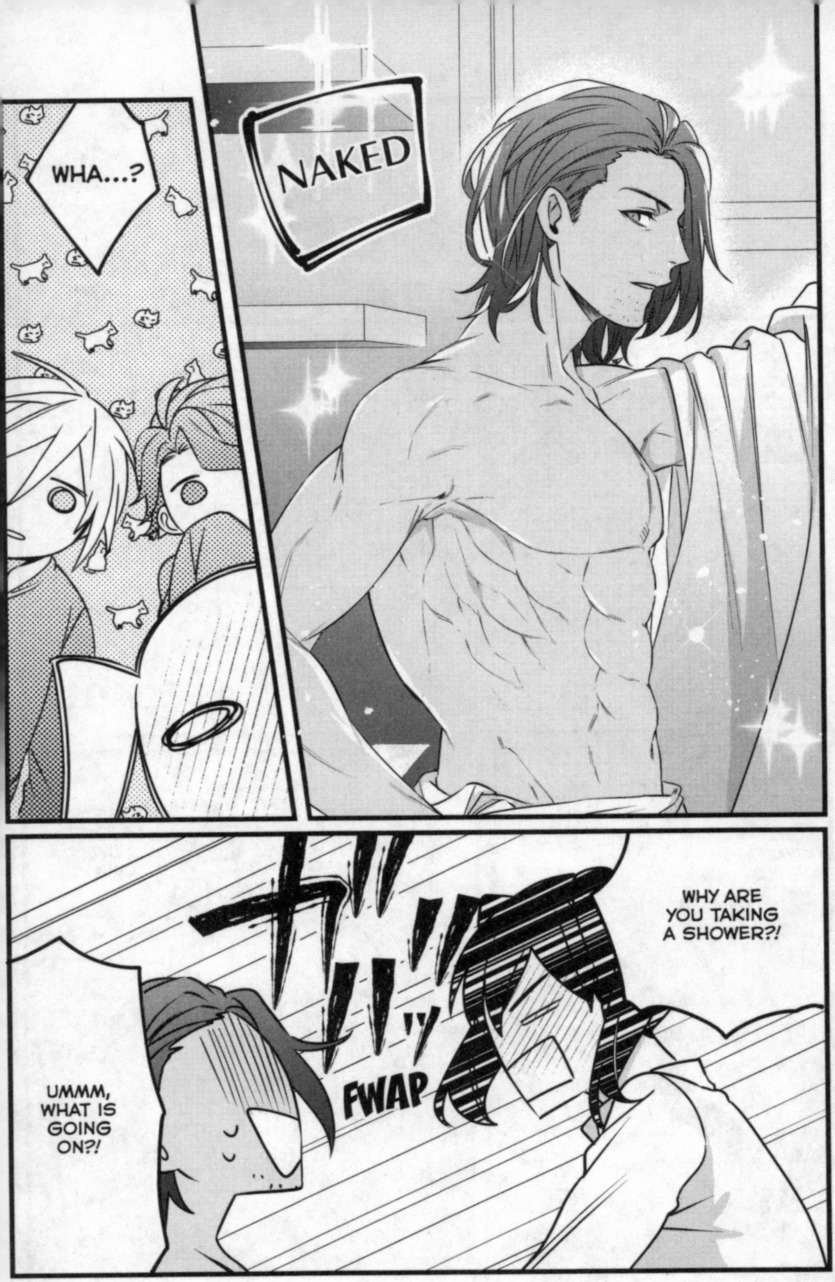
NAKED
WHA...?
WHY ARE YOU TAKING A SHOWER?!
FWAP
UMMM, WHAT IS GOING ON?!

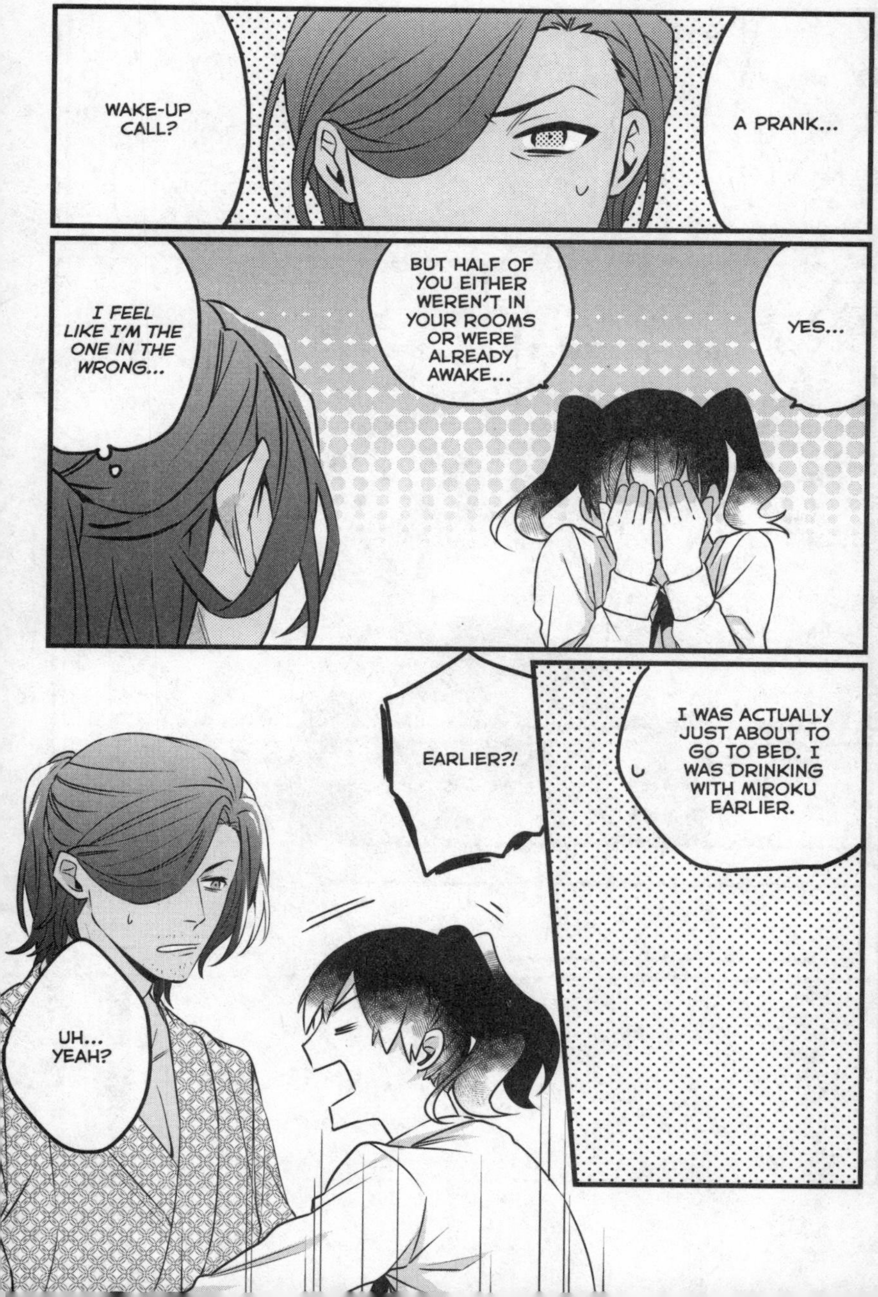
A PRANK...
WAKE-UP CALL?
YES...
BUT HALF OF YOU EITHER WEREN'T IN YOUR ROOMS OR WERE ALREADY AWAKE...
I FEEL LIKE I'M THE ONE IN THE WRONG...
I WAS ACTUALLY JUST ABOUT TO GO TO BED. I WAS DRINKING WITH MIROKU EARLIER.
EARLIER?!
UH... YEAH?

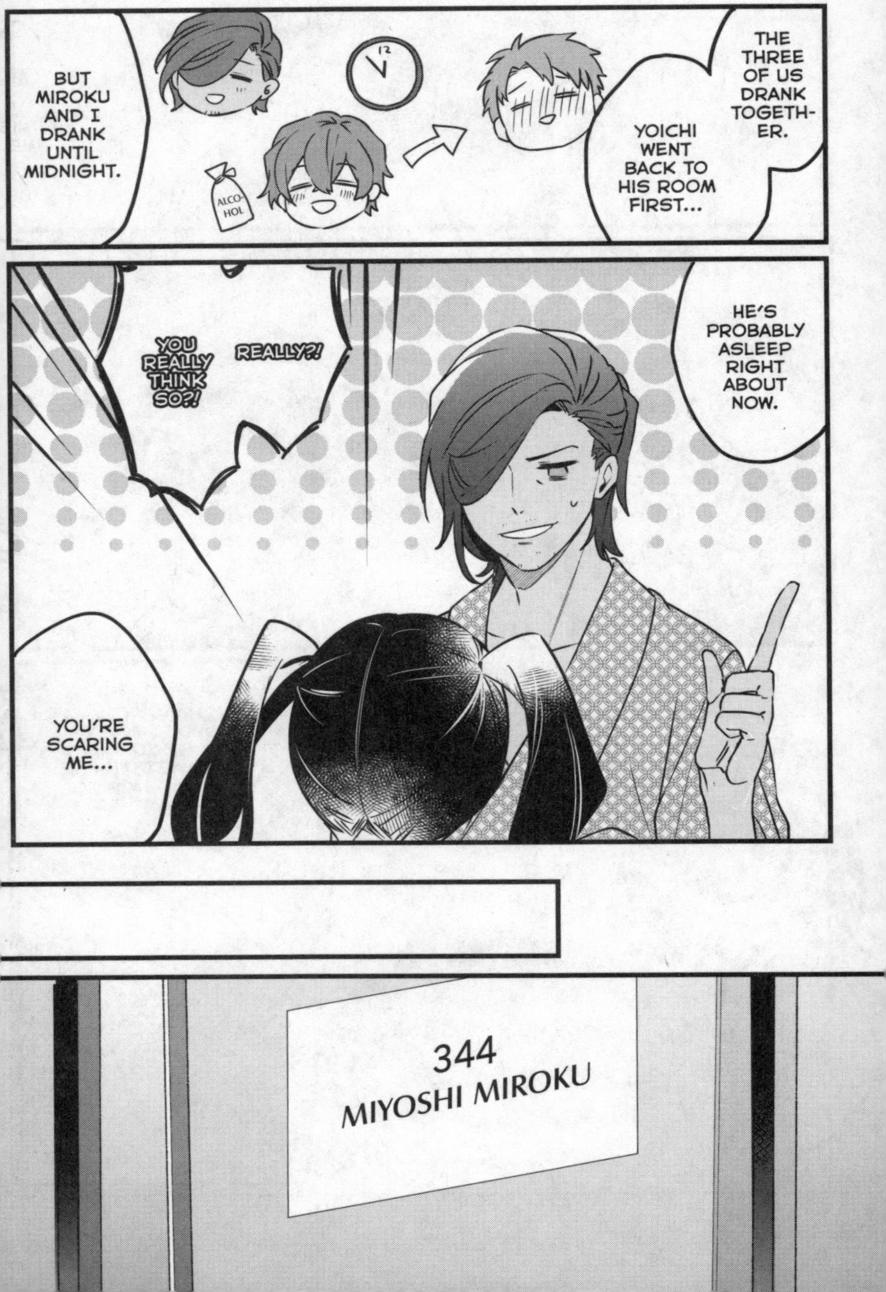
THE THREE OF US DRANK TOGETHER.
YOICHI WENT BACK TO HIS ROOM FIRST...
BUT MIROKU AND I DRANK UNTIL MIDNIGHT.
ALCOHOL
HE'S PROBABLY ASLEEP RIGHT ABOUT NOW.
REALLY?!
YOU REALLY THINK SO?!
YOU'RE SCARING ME...
344
MIYOSHI MIROKU

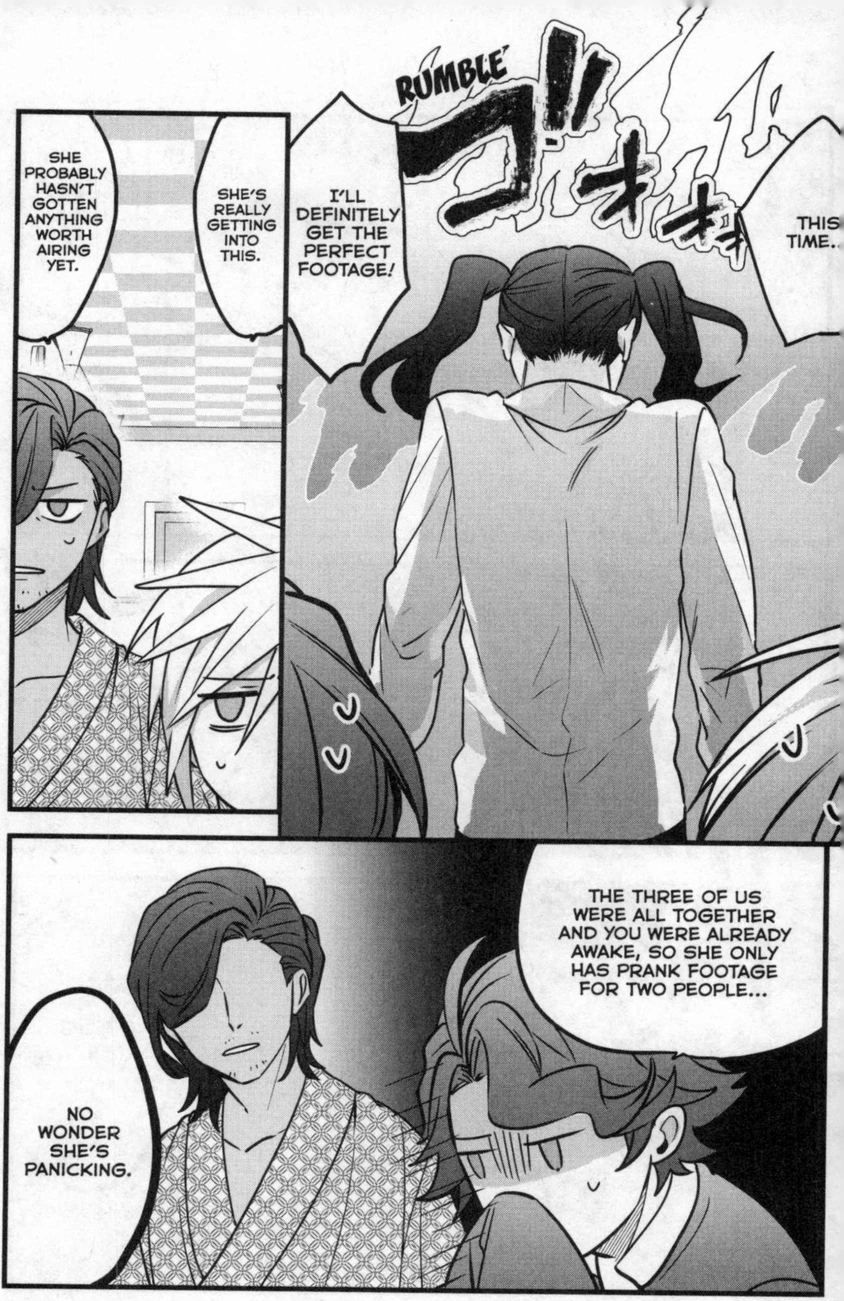

THIS TIME...
RUMBLE
I'LL DEFINITELY GET THE PERFECT FOOTAGE!
SHE'S REALLY GETTING INTO THIS.
SHE PROBABLY HASN'T GOTTEN ANYTHING WORTH AIRING YET.
THE THREE OF US WERE ALL TOGETHER AND YOU WERE ALREADY AWAKE, SO SHE ONLY HAS PRANK FOOTAGE FOR TWO PEOPLE...
NO WONDER SHE'S PANICKING.

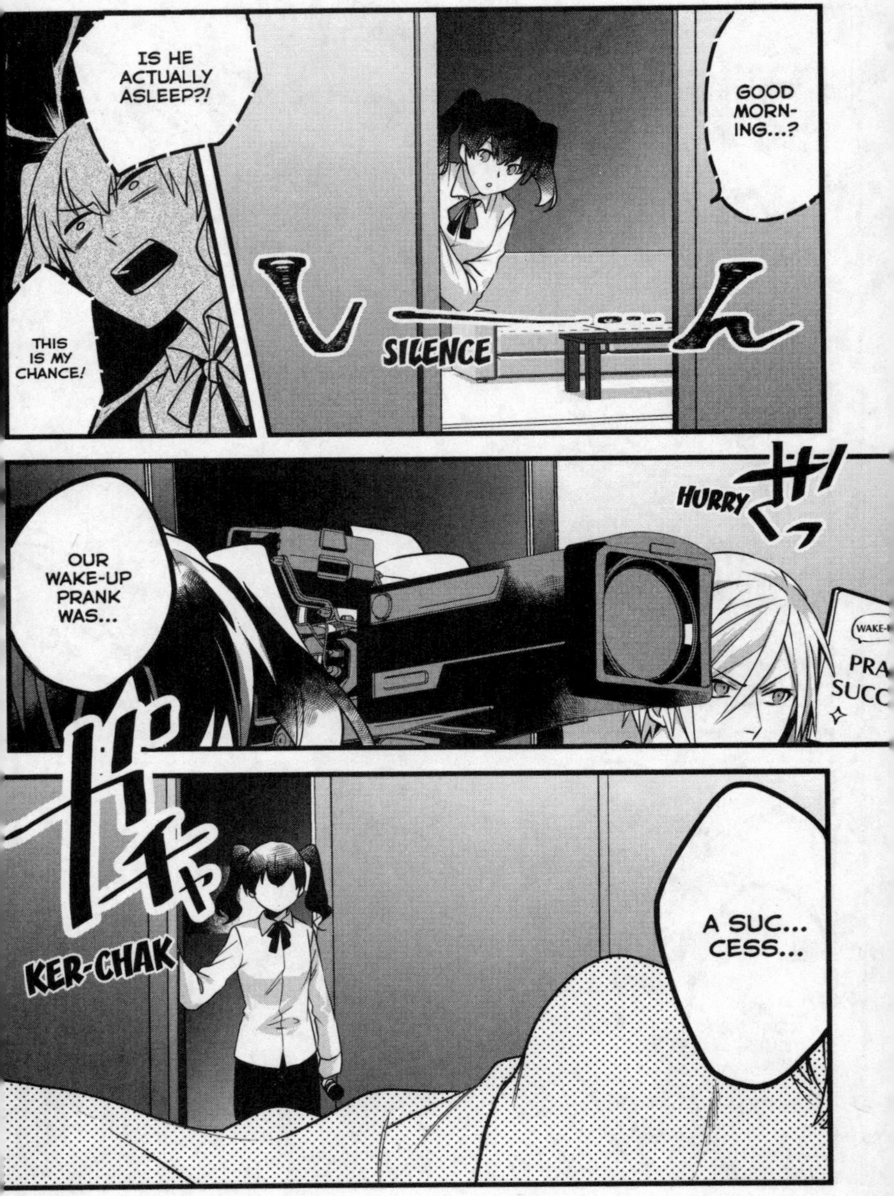
GOOD MORN-ING...?
SILENCE
IS HE ACTUALLY ASLEEP?!
THIS IS MY CHANCE!
HURRY
OUR WAKE-UP PRANK WAS...
A SUC... CESS...
KER-CHAK

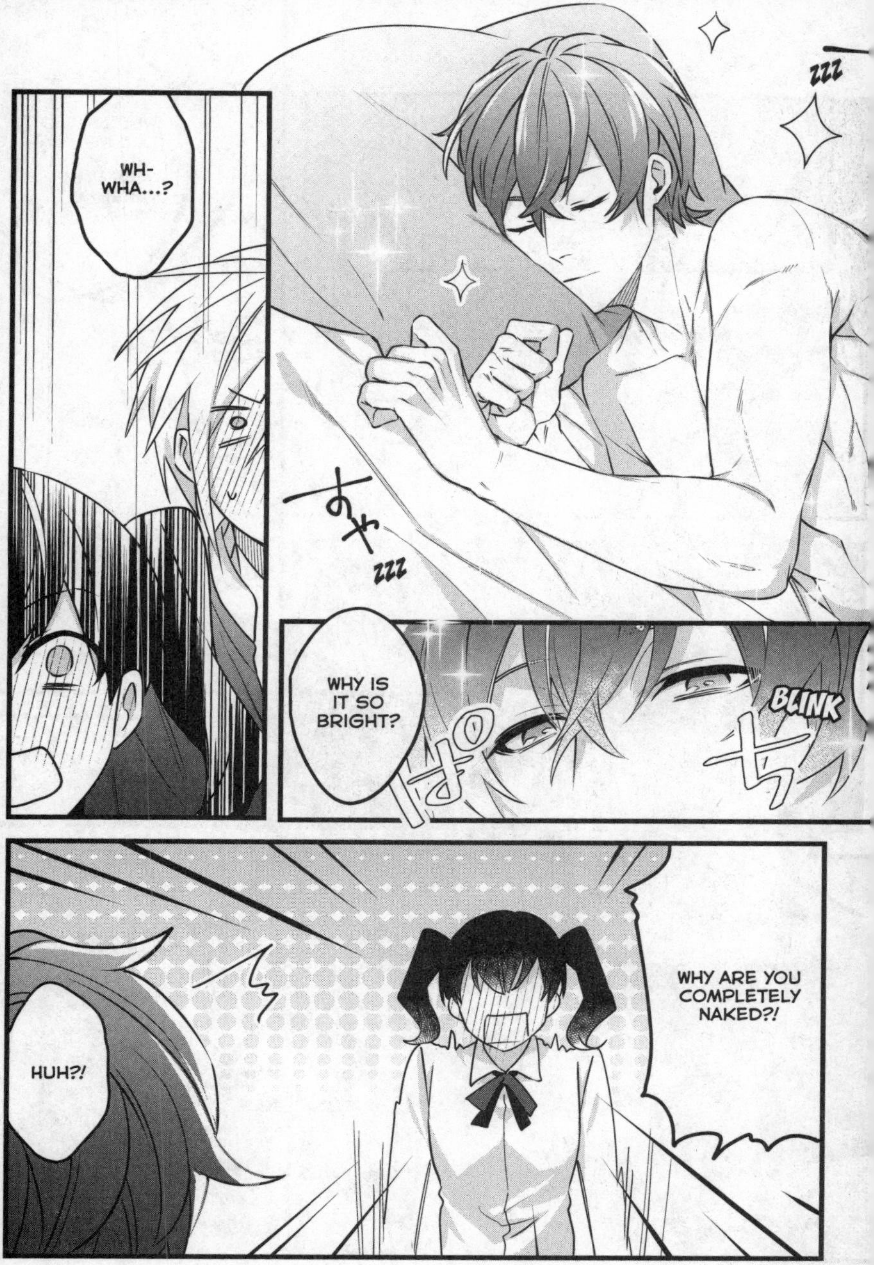
ZZZ
ZZZ
WHY IS IT SO BRIGHT?
BLINK
ぱち
WH-WHA...?
WHY ARE YOU COMPLETELY NAKED?!
HUH?!

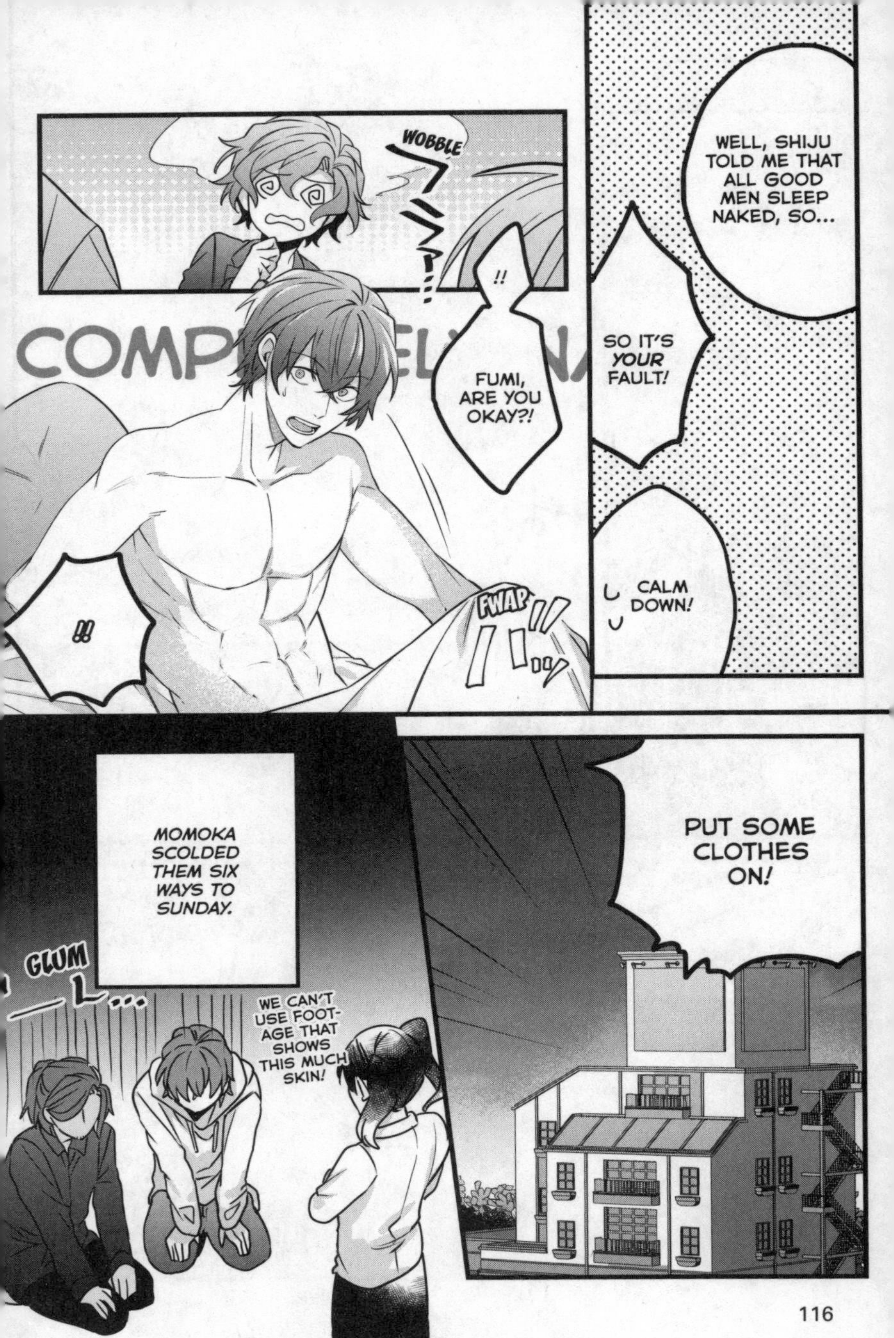
WELL, SHIJU TOLD ME THAT ALL GOOD MEN SLEEP NAKED, SO...
SO IT'S *YOUR* FAULT!
CALM DOWN!
WOBBLE
!!
FUMI, ARE YOU OKAY?!
FWAP
!!
PUT SOME CLOTHES ON!
MOMOKA SCOLDED THEM SIX WAYS TO SUNDAY.
WE CAN'T USE FOOT-AGE THAT SHOWS THIS MUCH SKIN!
GLUM

Chapter 37

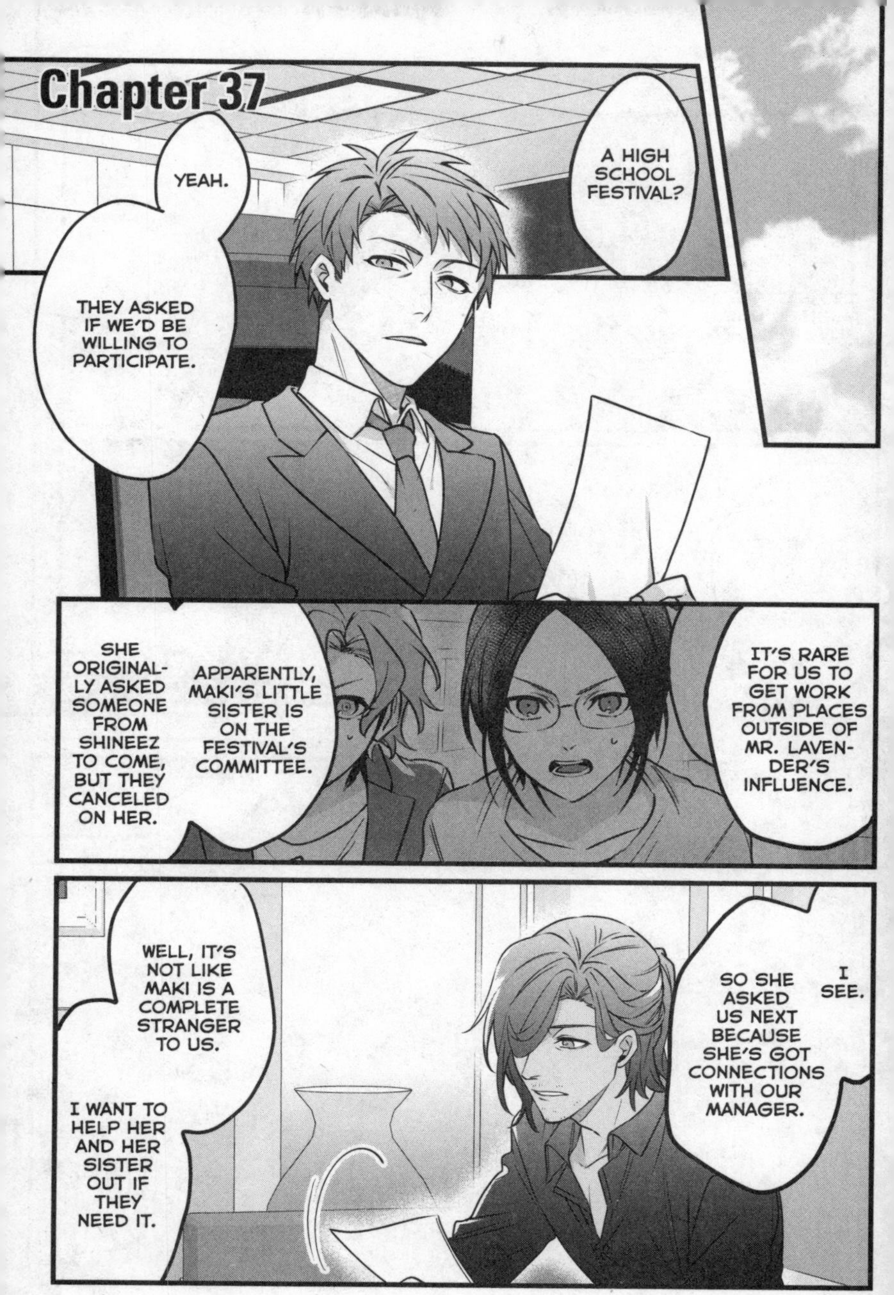
A HIGH SCHOOL FESTIVAL?
YEAH.
THEY ASKED IF WE'D BE WILLING TO PARTICIPATE.
IT'S RARE FOR US TO GET WORK FROM PLACES OUTSIDE OF MR. LAVENDER'S INFLUENCE.
APPARENTLY, MAKI'S LITTLE SISTER IS ON THE FESTIVAL'S COMMITTEE.
SHE ORIGINALLY ASKED SOMEONE FROM SHINEEZ TO COME, BUT THEY CANCELED ON HER.
I SEE.
SO SHE ASKED US NEXT BECAUSE SHE'S GOT CONNECTIONS WITH OUR MANAGER.
WELL, IT'S NOT LIKE MAKI IS A COMPLETE STRANGER TO US.
I WANT TO HELP HER AND HER SISTER OUT IF THEY NEED IT.

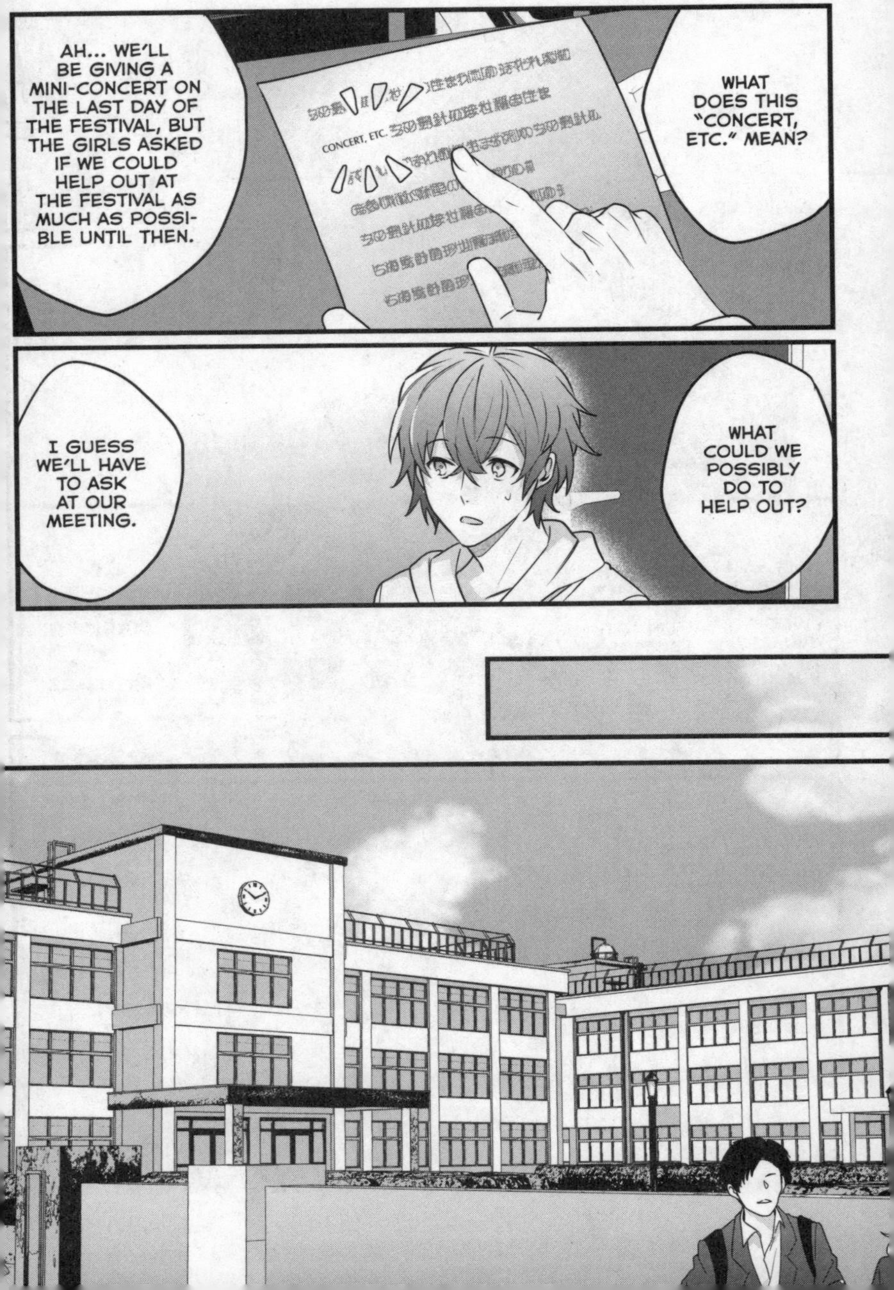
WHAT DOES THIS "CONCERT, ETC." MEAN?
CONCERT, ETC.
AH... WE'LL BE GIVING A MINI-CONCERT ON THE LAST DAY OF THE FESTIVAL, BUT THE GIRLS ASKED IF WE COULD HELP OUT AT THE FESTIVAL AS MUCH AS POSSI-BLE UNTIL THEN.
WHAT COULD WE POSSIBLY DO TO HELP OUT?
I GUESS WE'LL HAVE TO ASK AT OUR MEETING.

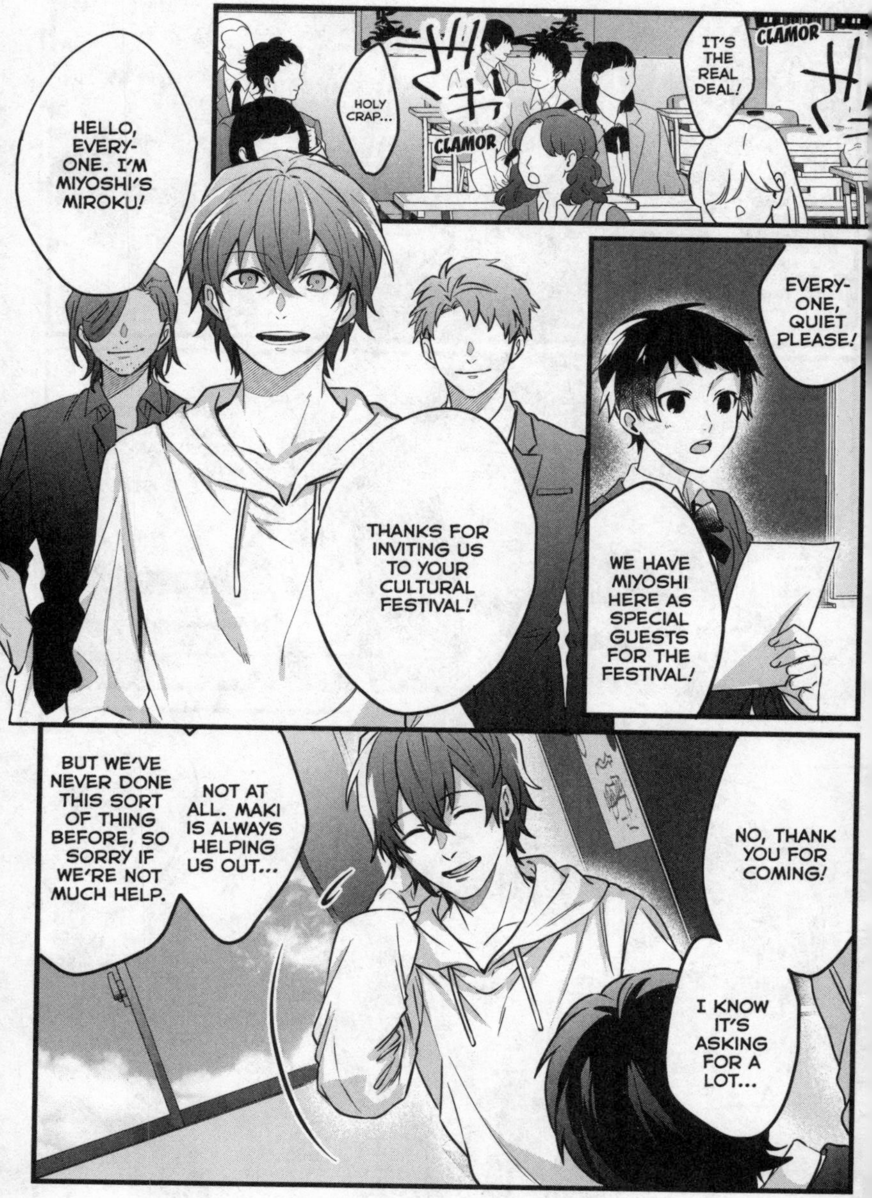
CLAMOR
IT'S THE REAL DEAL!
HOLY CRAP...
CLAMOR
EVERY-ONE, QUIET PLEASE!
WE HAVE MIYOSHI HERE AS SPECIAL GUESTS FOR THE FESTIVAL!
HELLO, EVERY-ONE. I'M MIYOSHI'S MIROKU!
THANKS FOR INVITING US TO YOUR CULTURAL FESTIVAL!
NO, THANK YOU FOR COMING!
I KNOW IT'S ASKING FOR A LOT...
NOT AT ALL. MAKI IS ALWAYS HELPING US OUT...
BUT WE'VE NEVER DONE THIS SORT OF THING BEFORE, SO SORRY IF WE'RE NOT MUCH HELP.

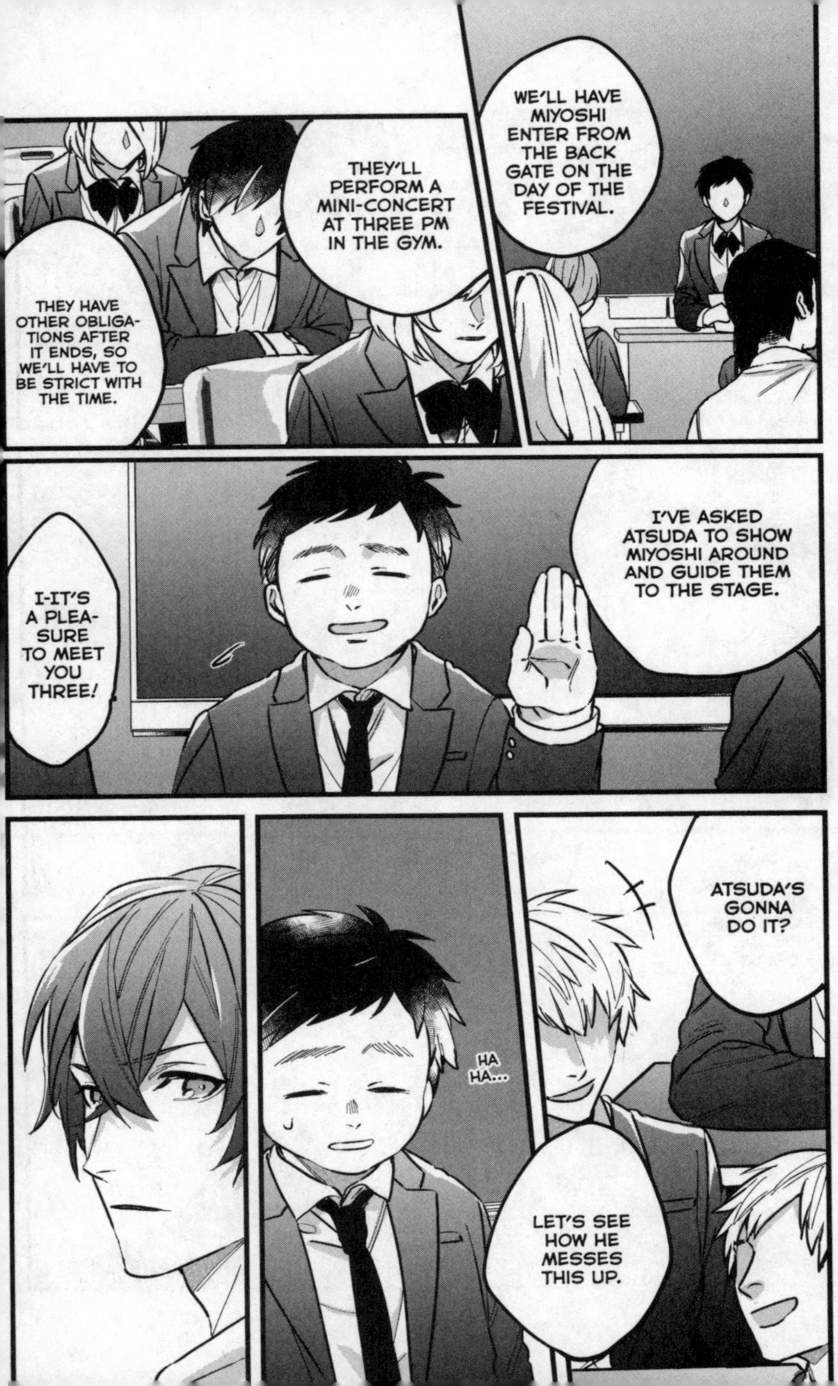
WE'LL HAVE MIYOSHI ENTER FROM THE BACK GATE ON THE DAY OF THE FESTIVAL.
THEY'LL PERFORM A MINI-CONCERT AT THREE PM IN THE GYM.
THEY HAVE OTHER OBLIGATIONS AFTER IT ENDS, SO WE'LL HAVE TO BE STRICT WITH THE TIME.
I'VE ASKED ATSUDA TO SHOW MIYOSHI AROUND AND GUIDE THEM TO THE STAGE.
I-IT'S A PLEASURE TO MEET YOU THREE!
ATSUDA'S GONNA DO IT?
LET'S SEE HOW HE MESSES THIS UP.
HA HA...

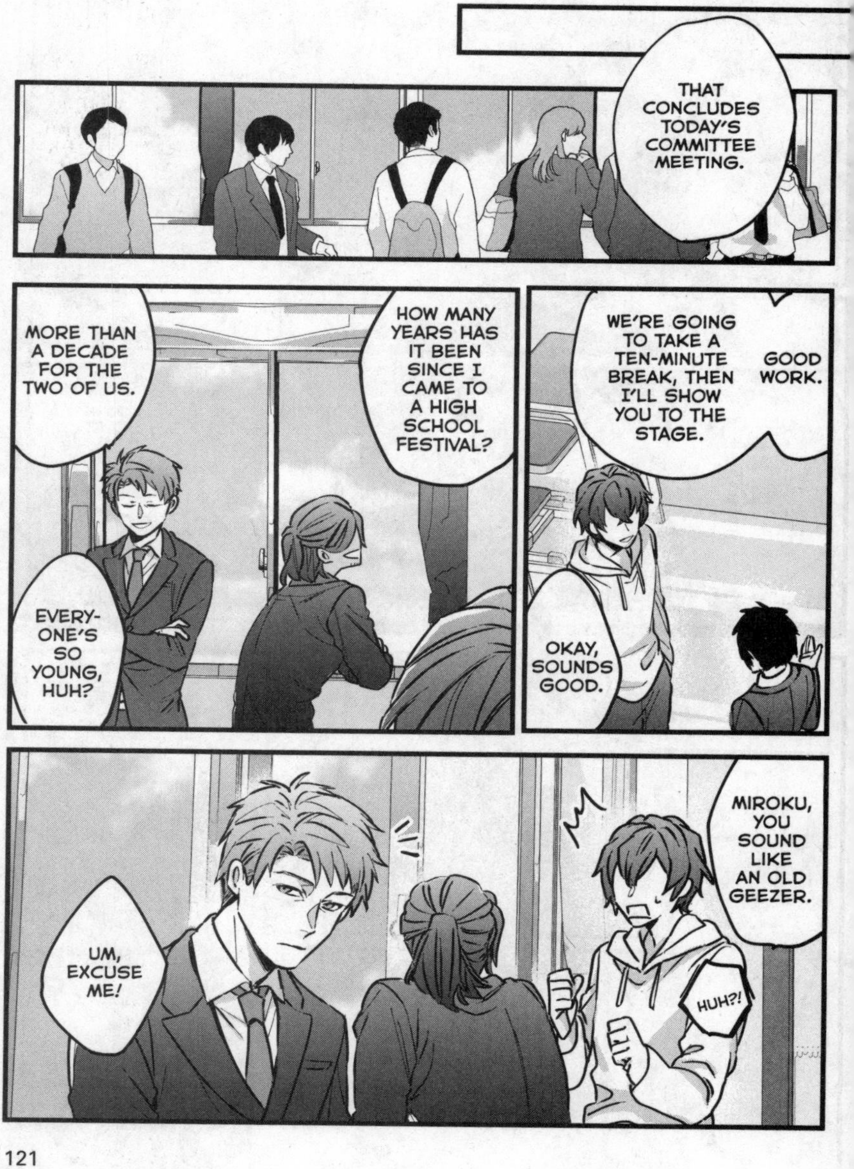
THAT CONCLUDES TODAY'S COMMITTEE MEETING.
GOOD WORK.
WE'RE GOING TO TAKE A TEN-MINUTE BREAK, THEN I'LL SHOW YOU TO THE STAGE.
OKAY, SOUNDS GOOD.
HOW MANY YEARS HAS IT BEEN SINCE I CAME TO A HIGH SCHOOL FESTIVAL?
MORE THAN A DECADE FOR THE TWO OF US.
EVERY-ONE'S SO YOUNG, HUH?
MIROKU, YOU SOUND LIKE AN OLD GEEZER.
HUH?!
UM, EXCUSE ME!

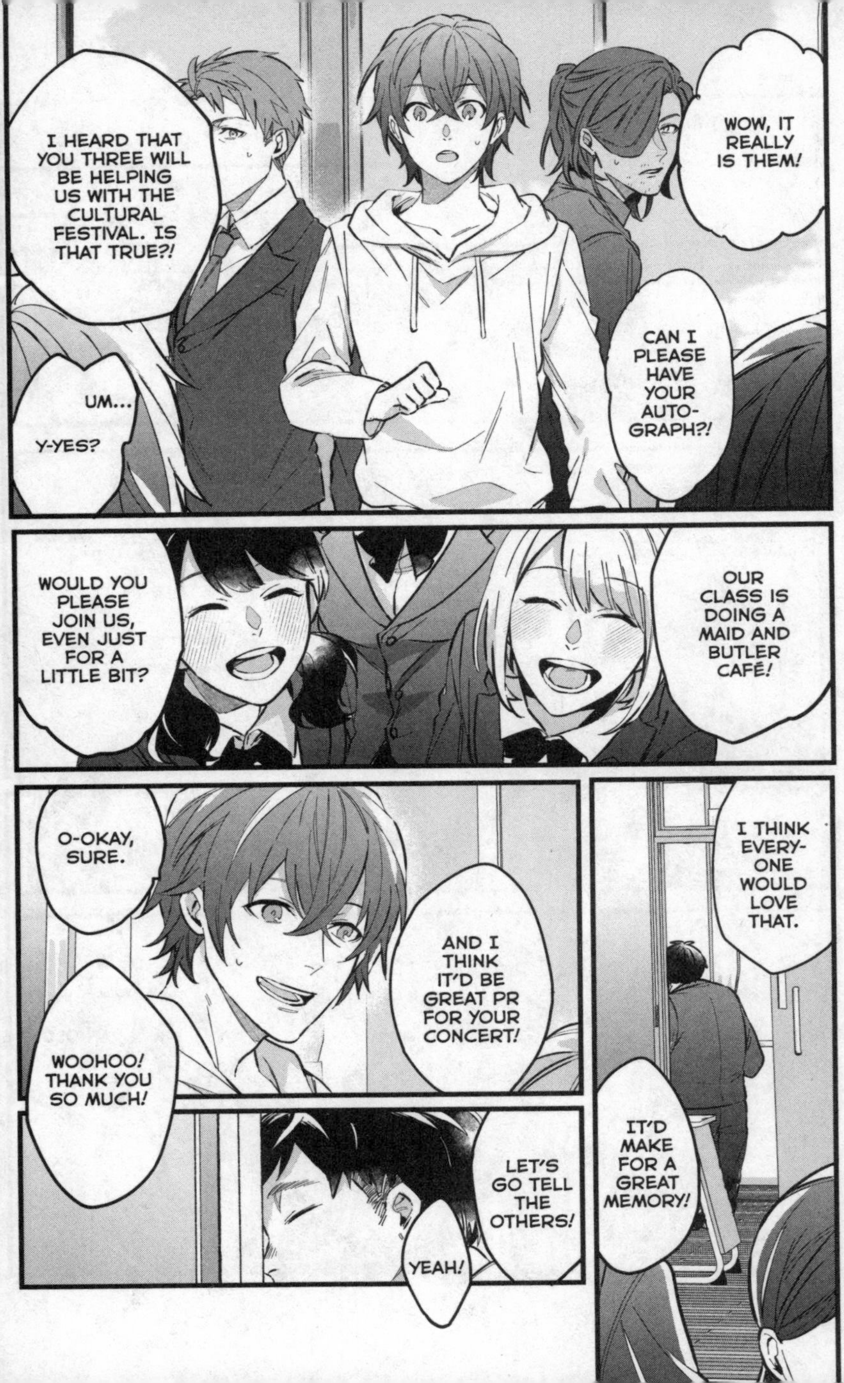
WOW, IT REALLY IS THEM!
I HEARD THAT YOU THREE WILL BE HELPING US WITH THE CULTURAL FESTIVAL. IS THAT TRUE?!
CAN I PLEASE HAVE YOUR AUTO-GRAPH?!
UM...
Y-YES?
OUR CLASS IS DOING A MAID AND BUTLER CAFÉ!
WOULD YOU PLEASE JOIN US, EVEN JUST FOR A LITTLE BIT?
I THINK EVERY-ONE WOULD LOVE THAT.
IT'D MAKE FOR A GREAT MEMORY!
O-OKAY, SURE.
AND I THINK IT'D BE GREAT PR FOR YOUR CONCERT!
WOOHOO! THANK YOU SO MUCH!
LET'S GO TELL THE OTHERS!
YEAH!

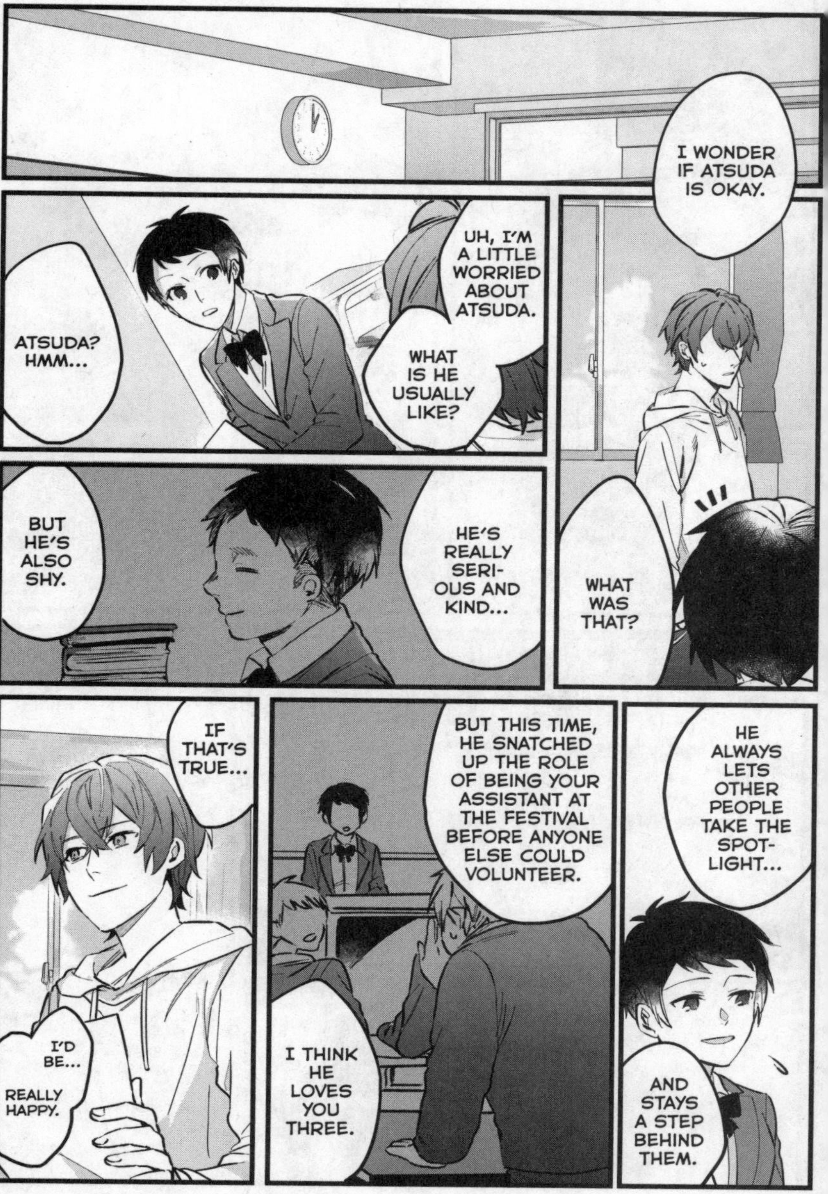
I WONDER IF ATSUDA IS OKAY.
WHAT WAS THAT?
UH, I'M A LITTLE WORRIED ABOUT ATSUDA.
WHAT IS HE USUALLY LIKE?
ATSUDA? HMM...
HE'S REALLY SERI- OUS AND KIND...
BUT HE'S ALSO SHY.
HE ALWAYS LETS OTHER PEOPLE TAKE THE SPOT- LIGHT...
AND STAYS A STEP BEHIND THEM.
BUT THIS TIME, HE SNATCHED UP THE ROLE OF BEING YOUR ASSISTANT AT THE FESTIVAL BEFORE ANYONE ELSE COULD VOLUNTEER.
I THINK HE LOVES YOU THREE.
IF THAT'S TRUE...
I'D BE...
REALLY HAPPY.

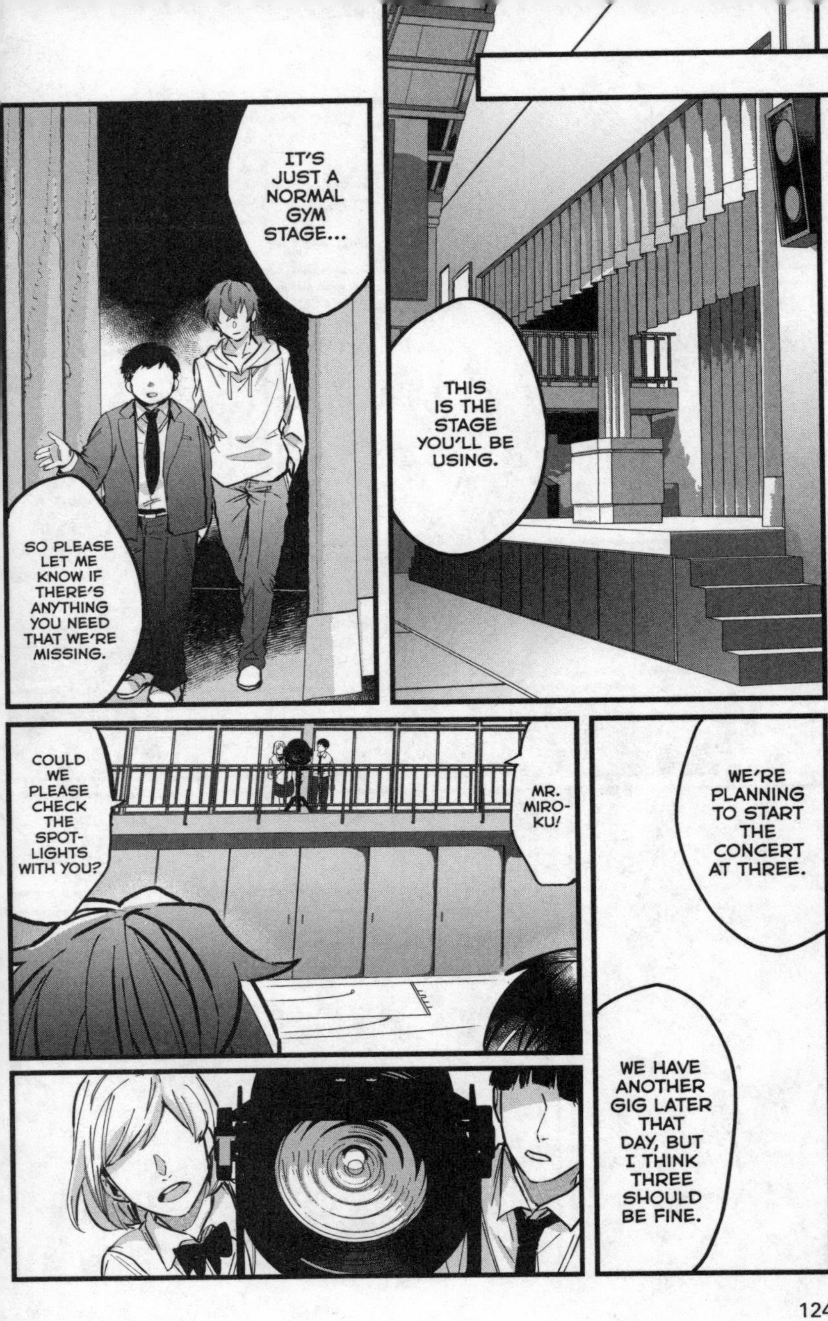
THIS IS THE STAGE YOU'LL BE USING.
IT'S JUST A NORMAL GYM STAGE...
SO PLEASE LET ME KNOW IF THERE'S ANYTHING YOU NEED THAT WE'RE MISSING.
WE'RE PLANNING TO START THE CONCERT AT THREE.
WE HAVE ANOTHER GIG LATER THAT DAY, BUT I THINK THREE SHOULD BE FINE.
MR. MIRO-KU!
COULD WE PLEASE CHECK THE SPOT-LIGHTS WITH YOU?

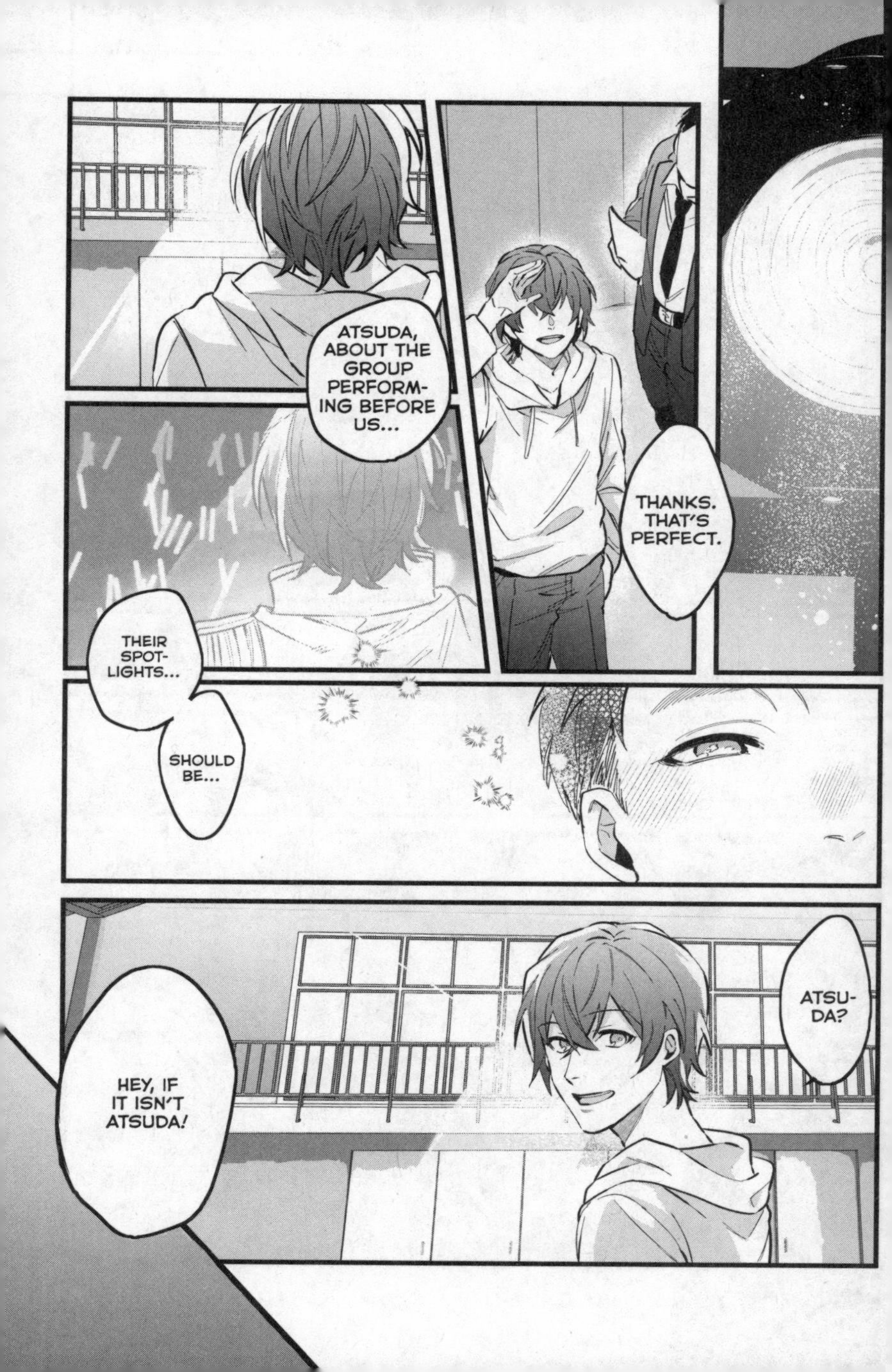
THANKS. THAT'S PERFECT.
ATSUDA, ABOUT THE GROUP PERFORMING BEFORE US...
THEIR SPOT-LIGHTS...
SHOULD BE...
ATSU-DA?
HEY, IF IT ISN'T ATSUDA!

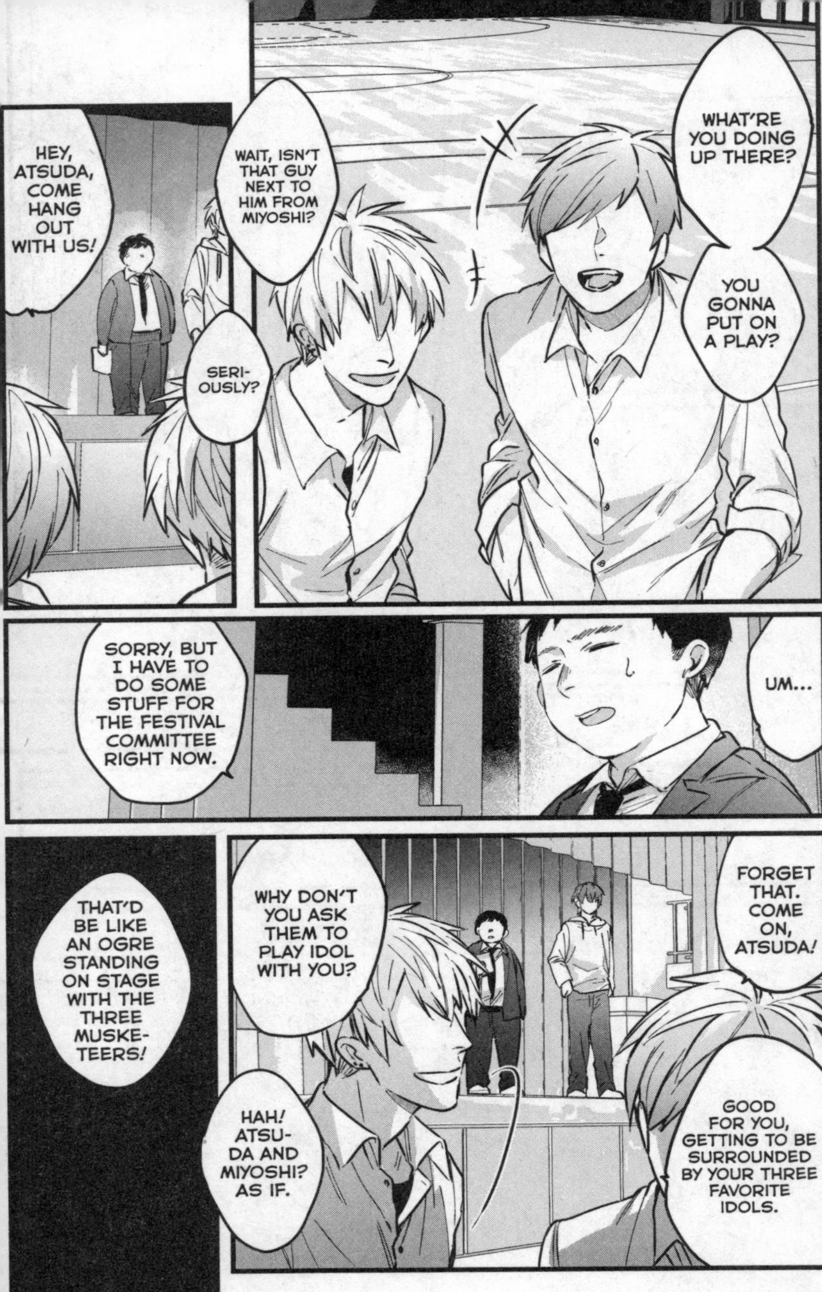
WHAT'RE YOU DOING UP THERE?
YOU GONNA PUT ON A PLAY?
WAIT, ISN'T THAT GUY NEXT TO HIM FROM MIYOSHI?
SERIOUSLY?
HEY, ATSUDA, COME HANG OUT WITH US!
UM...
SORRY, BUT I HAVE TO DO SOME STUFF FOR THE FESTIVAL COMMITTEE RIGHT NOW.
FORGET THAT. COME ON, ATSUDA!
WHY DON'T YOU ASK THEM TO PLAY IDOL WITH YOU?
GOOD FOR YOU, GETTING TO BE SURROUNDED BY YOUR THREE FAVORITE IDOLS.
HAH! ATSUDA AND MIYOSHI? AS IF.
THAT'D BE LIKE AN OGRE STANDING ON STAGE WITH THE THREE MUSKETEERS!

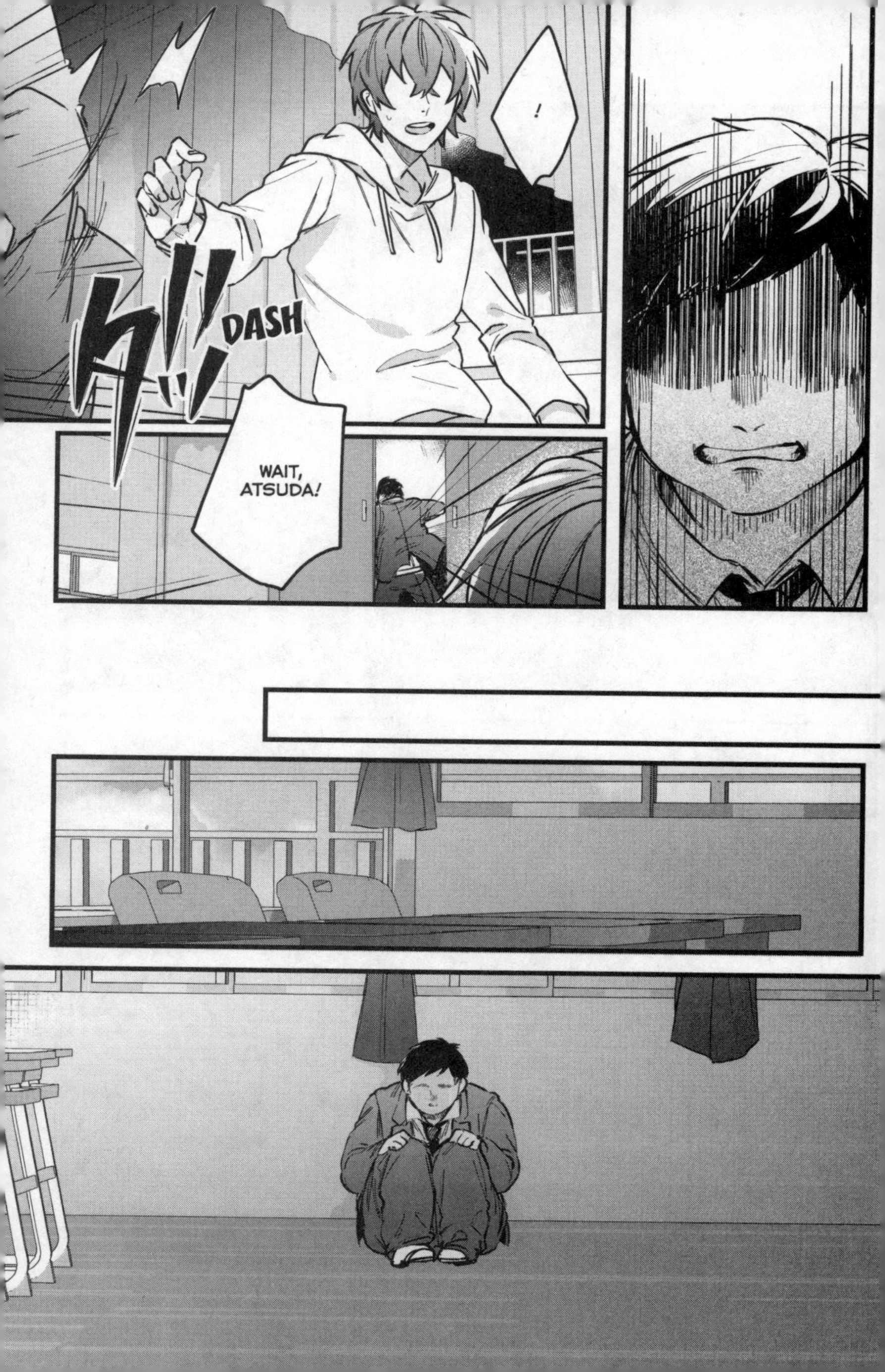
!
DASH
WAIT, ATSUDA!

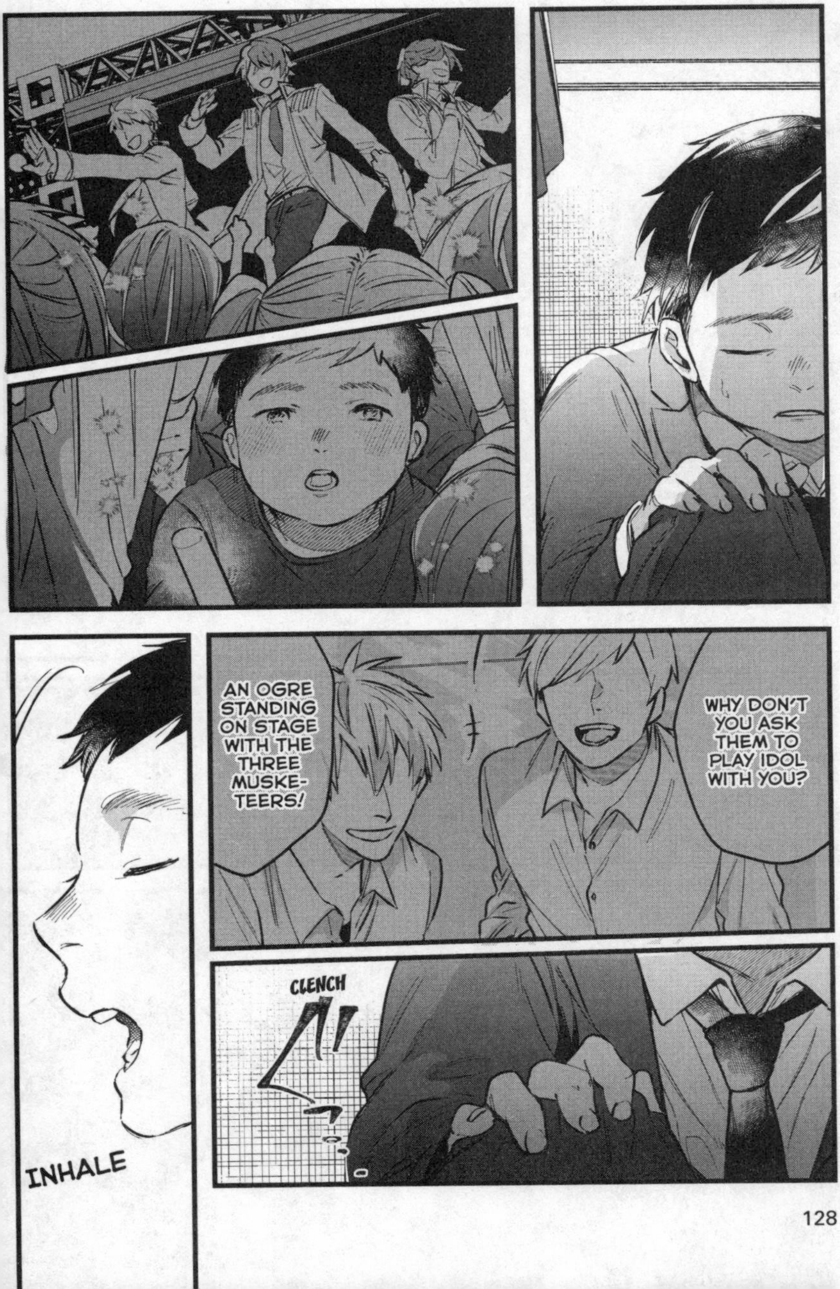
WHY DON'T YOU ASK THEM TO PLAY IDOL WITH YOU?
AN OGRE STANDING ON STAGE WITH THE THREE MUSKE-TEERS!
CLENCH
INHALE

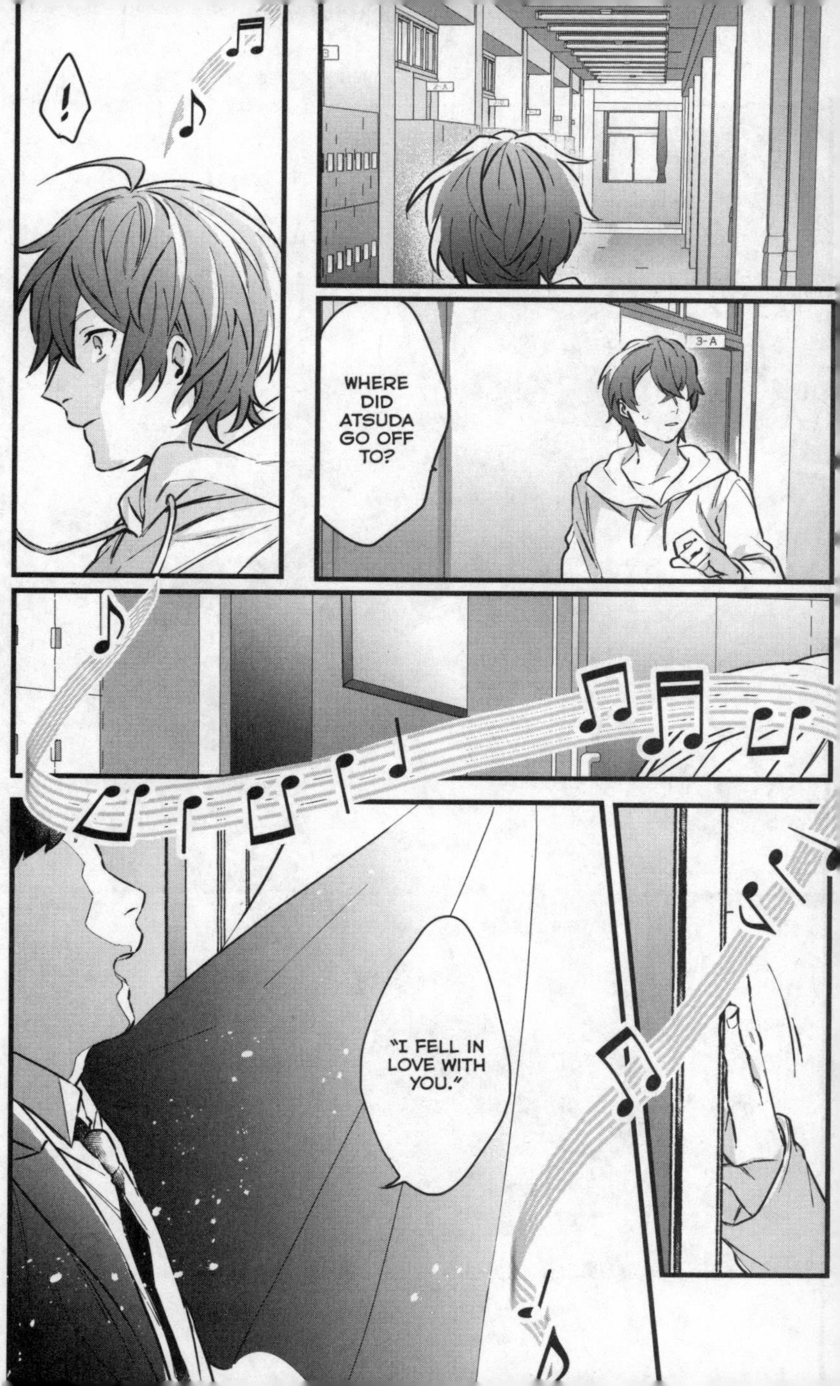
3-A
WHERE DID ATSUDA GO OFF TO?
!
"I FELL IN LOVE WITH YOU."

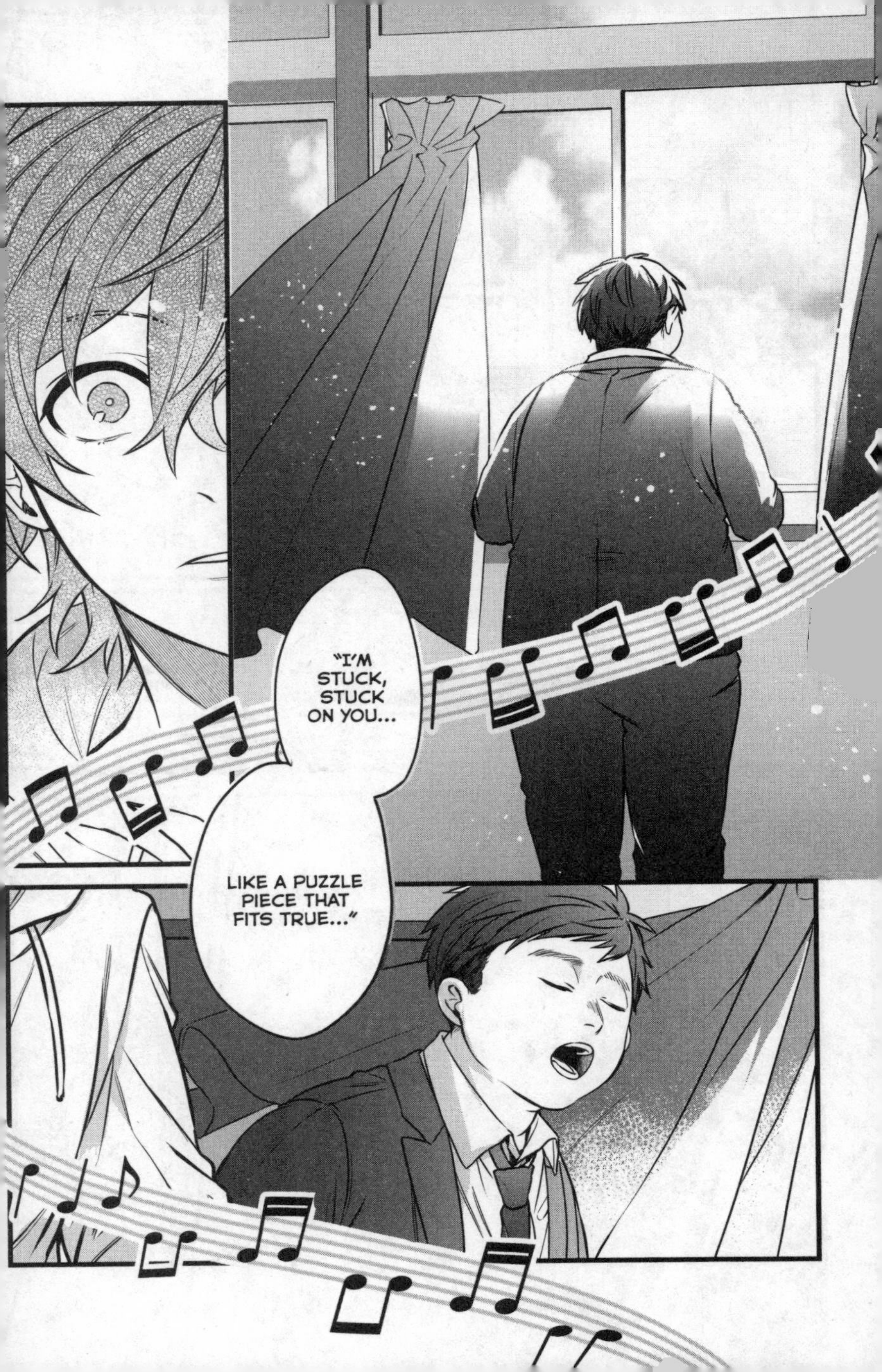
"I'M STUCK, STUCK ON YOU...
LIKE A PUZZLE PIECE THAT FITS TRUE..."

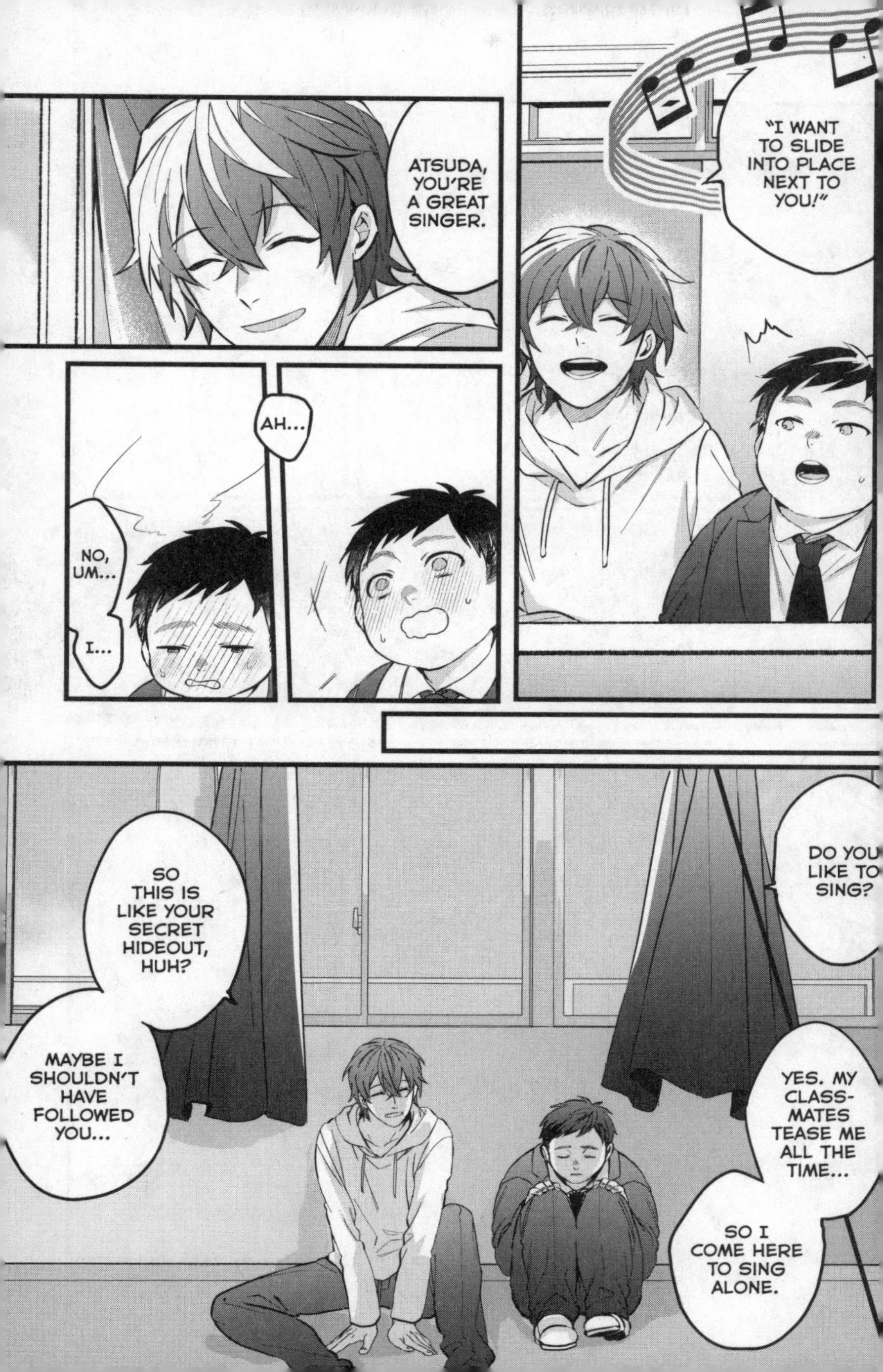
"I WANT TO SLIDE INTO PLACE NEXT TO YOU!"
ATSUDA, YOU'RE A GREAT SINGER.
AH...
NO, UM...
I...
DO YOU LIKE TO SING?
YES. MY CLASSMATES TEASE ME ALL THE TIME...
SO I COME HERE TO SING ALONE.
SO THIS IS LIKE YOUR SECRET HIDEOUT, HUH?
MAYBE I SHOULDN'T HAVE FOLLOWED YOU...

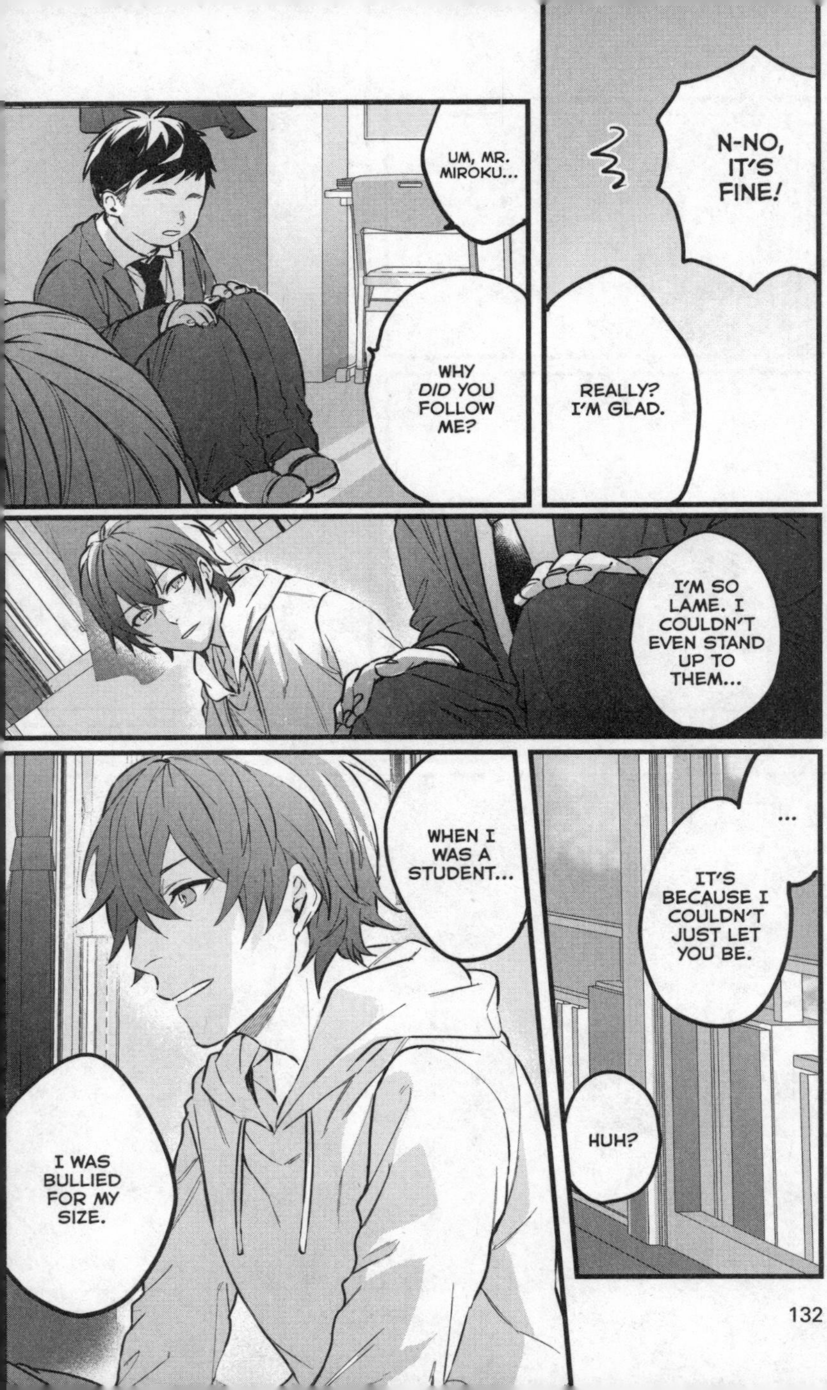
N-NO, IT'S FINE!
REALLY? I'M GLAD.
UM, MR. MIROKU...
WHY *DID* YOU FOLLOW ME?
I'M SO LAME. I COULDN'T EVEN STAND UP TO THEM...
...
IT'S BECAUSE I COULDN'T JUST LET YOU BE.
HUH?
WHEN I WAS A STUDENT...
I WAS BULLIED FOR MY SIZE.

Chapter 38

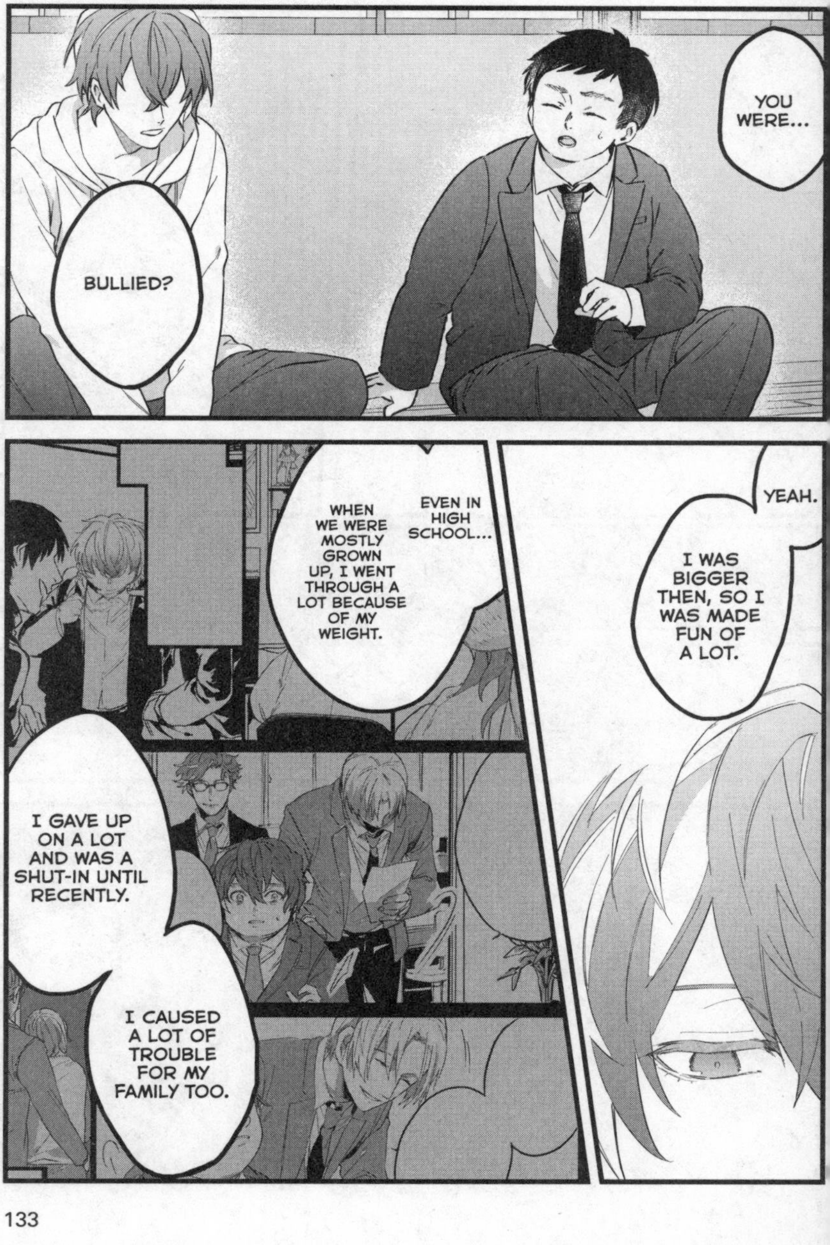
YOU WERE...
BULLIED?
YEAH.
I WAS BIGGER THEN, SO I WAS MADE FUN OF A LOT.
EVEN IN HIGH SCHOOL...
WHEN WE WERE MOSTLY GROWN UP, I WENT THROUGH A LOT BECAUSE OF MY WEIGHT.
I GAVE UP ON A LOT AND WAS A SHUT-IN UNTIL RECENTLY.
I CAUSED A LOT OF TROUBLE FOR MY FAMILY TOO.

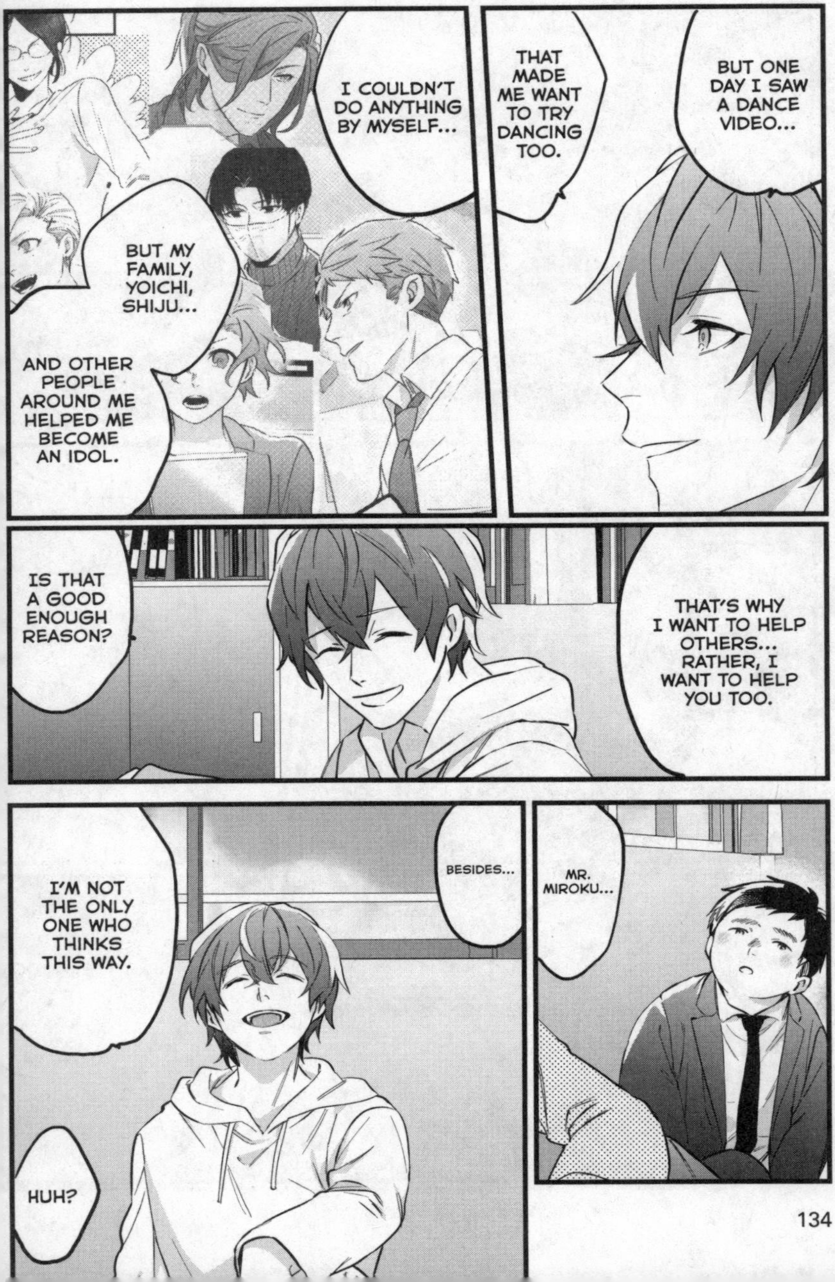
BUT ONE DAY I SAW A DANCE VIDEO...
THAT MADE ME WANT TO TRY DANCING TOO.
I COULDN'T DO ANYTHING BY MYSELF...
BUT MY FAMILY, YOICHI, SHIJU...
AND OTHER PEOPLE AROUND ME HELPED ME BECOME AN IDOL.
THAT'S WHY I WANT TO HELP OTHERS... RATHER, I WANT TO HELP YOU TOO.
IS THAT A GOOD ENOUGH REASON?
MR. MIROKU...
BESIDES...
I'M NOT THE ONLY ONE WHO THINKS THIS WAY.
HUH?

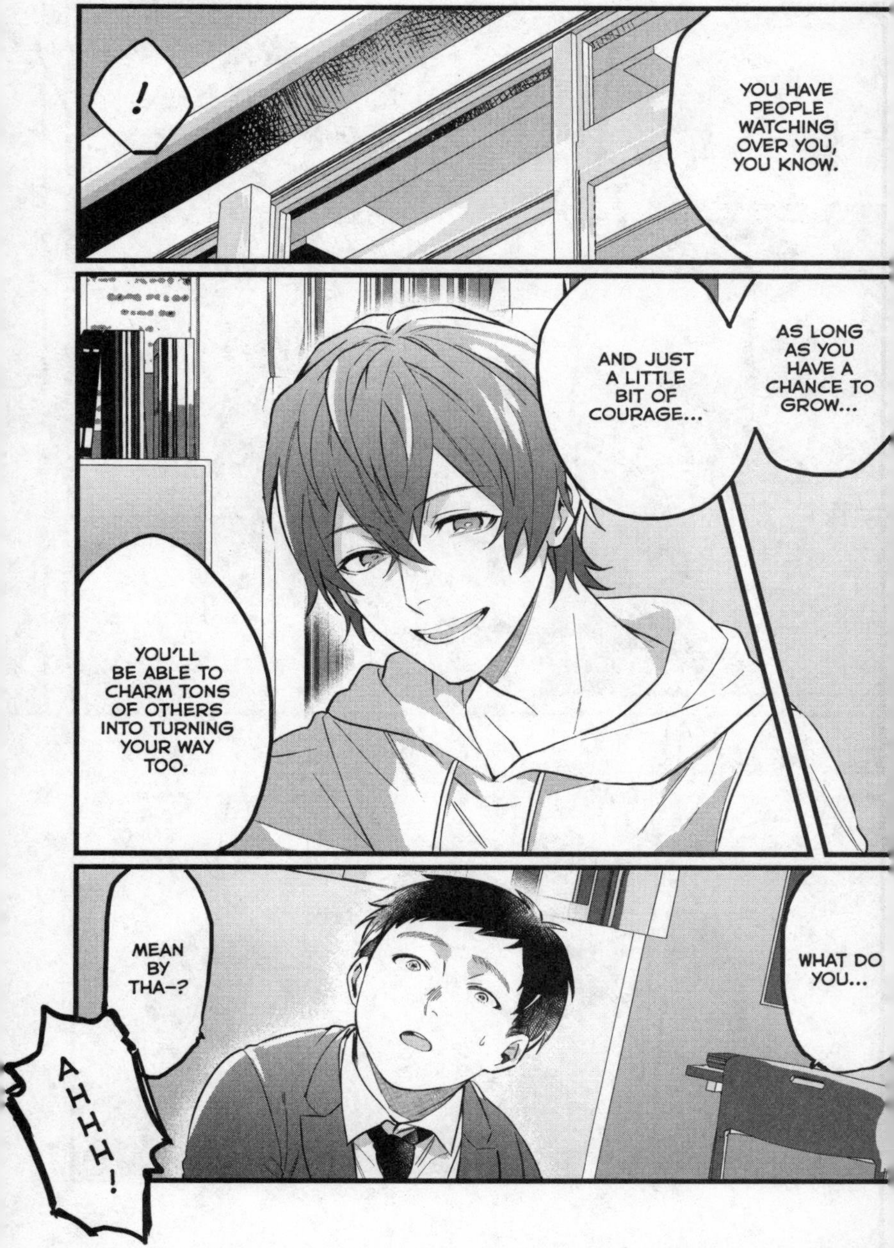
YOU HAVE PEOPLE WATCHING OVER YOU, YOU KNOW.
!
AS LONG AS YOU HAVE A CHANCE TO GROW...
AND JUST A LITTLE BIT OF COURAGE...
YOU'LL BE ABLE TO CHARM TONS OF OTHERS INTO TURNING YOUR WAY TOO.
WHAT DO YOU...
MEAN BY THA-?
AHHH!

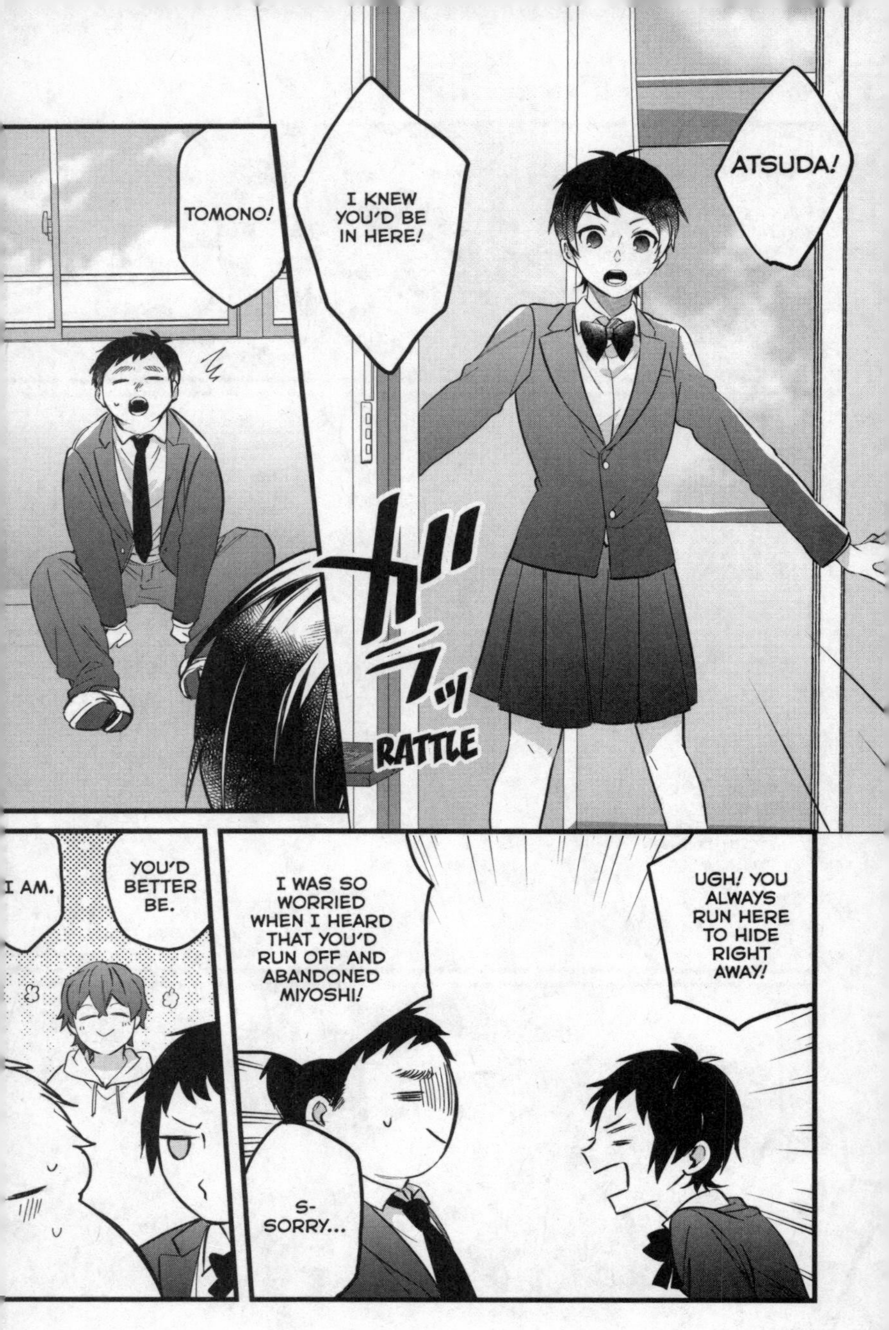

ATSUDA!
I KNEW YOU'D BE IN HERE!
RATTLE
TOMONO!
UGH! YOU ALWAYS RUN HERE TO HIDE RIGHT AWAY!
I WAS SO WORRIED WHEN I HEARD THAT YOU'D RUN OFF AND ABANDONED MIYOSHI!
S- SORRY...
YOU'D BETTER BE.
I AM.

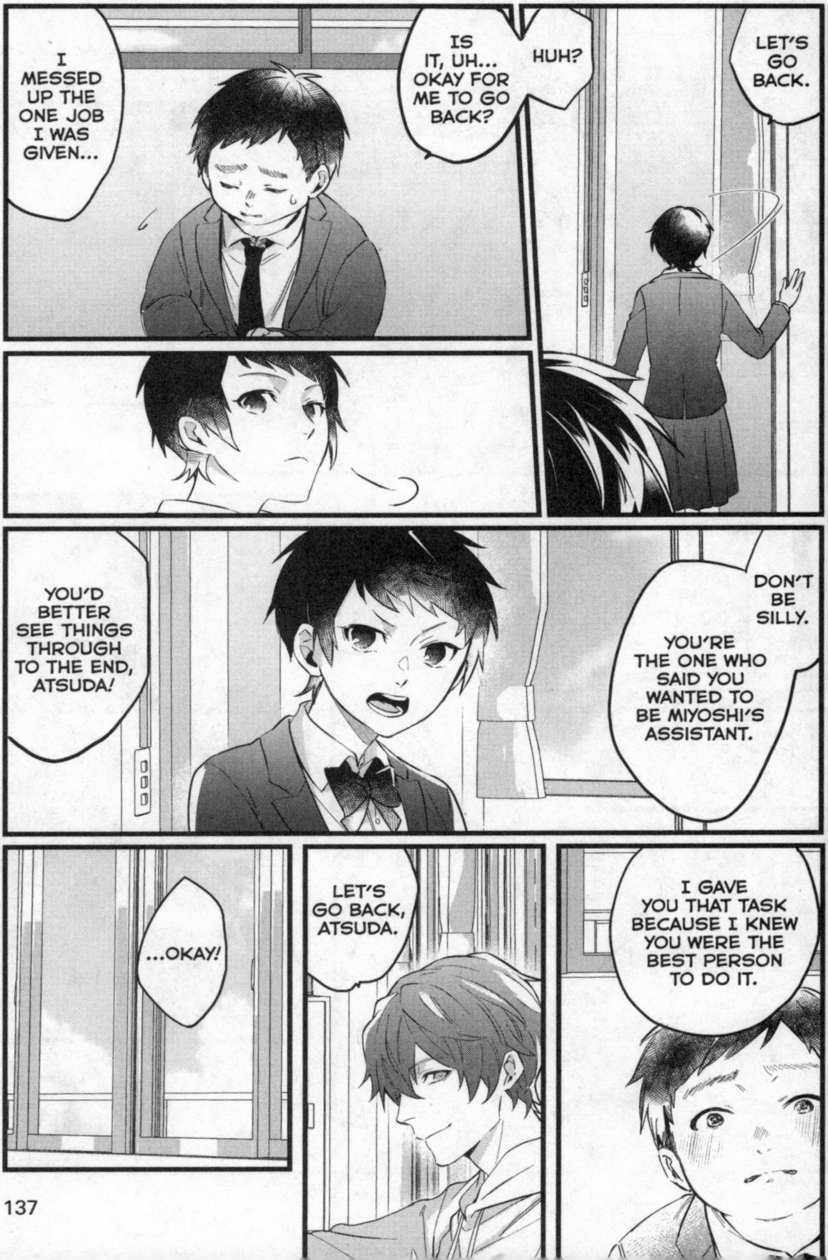
LET'S GO BACK.
HUH?
IS IT, UH... OKAY FOR ME TO GO BACK?
I MESSED UP THE ONE JOB I WAS GIVEN...
DON'T BE SILLY.
YOU'RE THE ONE WHO SAID YOU WANTED TO BE MIYOSHI'S ASSISTANT.
YOU'D BETTER SEE THINGS THROUGH TO THE END, ATSUDA!
I GAVE YOU THAT TASK BECAUSE I KNEW YOU WERE THE BEST PERSON TO DO IT.
LET'S GO BACK, ATSUDA.
...OKAY!

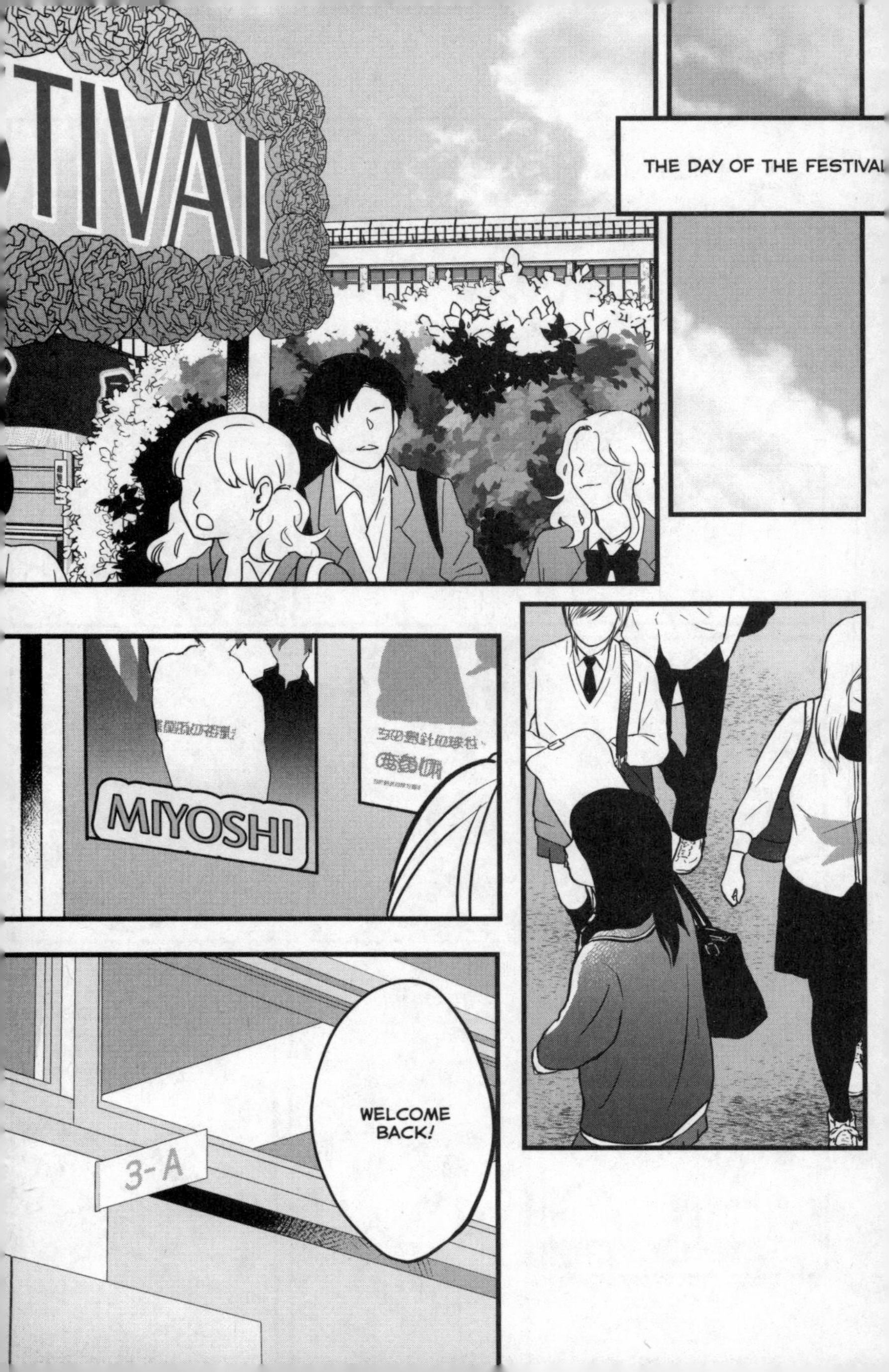
THE DAY OF THE FESTIVAL
TIVAL
MIYOSHI
3-A
WELCOME BACK!

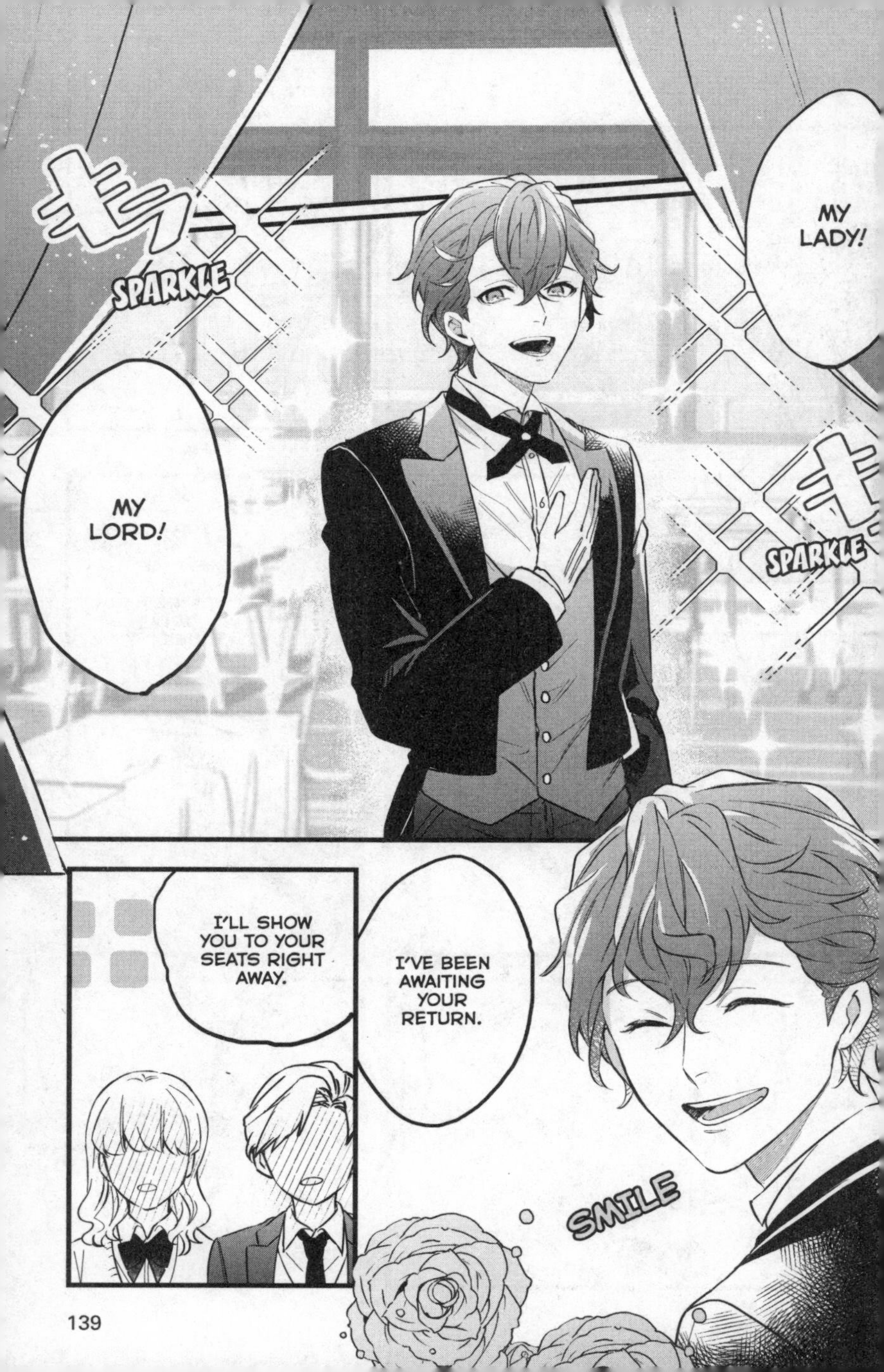
MY LADY!
キラ
SPARKLE
MY LORD!
SPARKLE
I'VE BEEN AWAITING YOUR RETURN.
SMILE
I'LL SHOW YOU TO YOUR SEATS RIGHT AWAY.

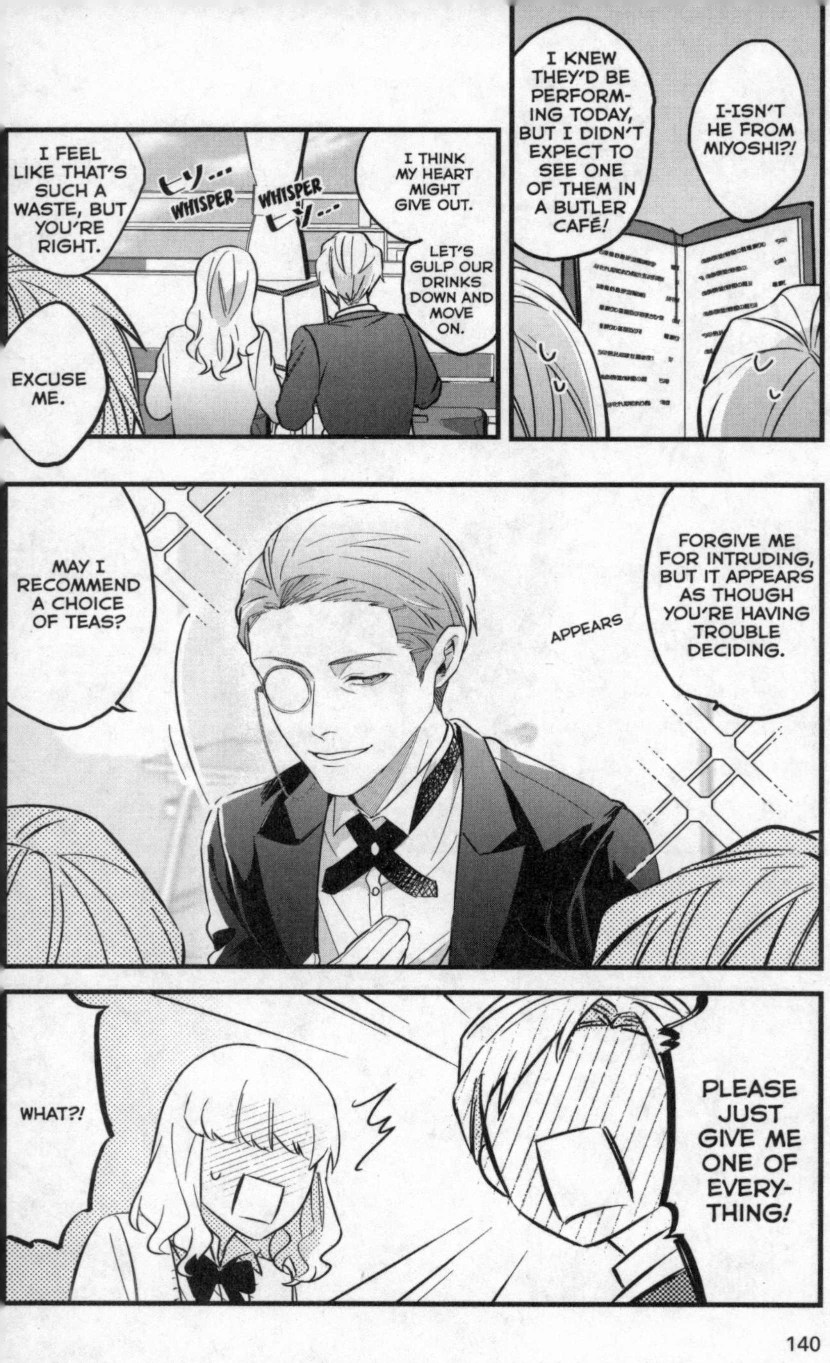
I-ISN'T HE FROM MIYOSHI?!
I KNEW THEY'D BE PERFORM-ING TODAY, BUT I DIDN'T EXPECT TO SEE ONE OF THEM IN A BUTLER CAFÉ!
I THINK MY HEART MIGHT GIVE OUT.
LET'S GULP OUR DRINKS DOWN AND MOVE ON.
ヒソ... WHISPER
WHISPER ヒソ...
I FEEL LIKE THAT'S SUCH A WASTE, BUT YOU'RE RIGHT.
EXCUSE ME.
FORGIVE ME FOR INTRUDING, BUT IT APPEARS AS THOUGH YOU'RE HAVING TROUBLE DECIDING.
APPEARS
MAY I RECOMMEND A CHOICE OF TEAS?
PLEASE JUST GIVE ME ONE OF EVERY-THING!
WHAT?!

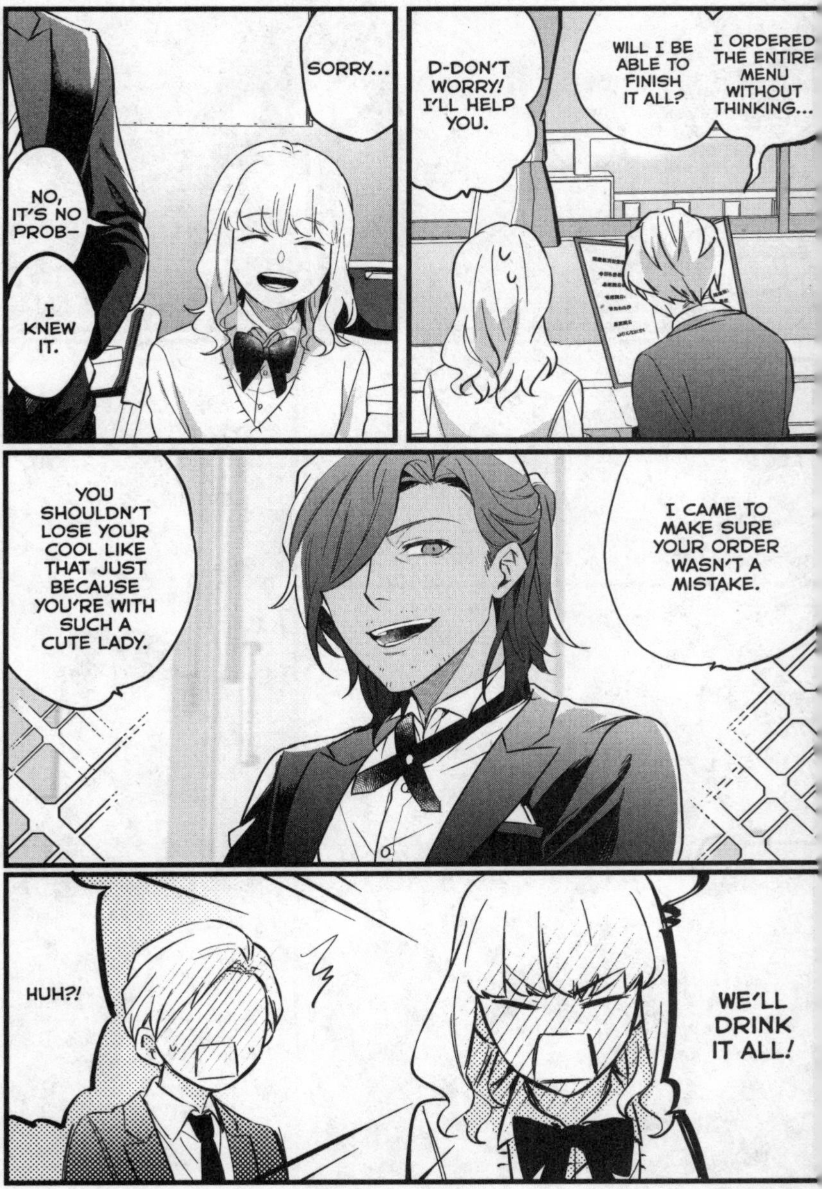
I ORDERED THE ENTIRE MENU WITHOUT THINKING...
WILL I BE ABLE TO FINISH IT ALL?
D-DON'T WORRY! I'LL HELP YOU.
SORRY...
NO, IT'S NO PROB–
I KNEW IT.
I CAME TO MAKE SURE YOUR ORDER WASN'T A MISTAKE.
YOU SHOULDN'T LOSE YOUR COOL LIKE THAT JUST BECAUSE YOU'RE WITH SUCH A CUTE LADY.
WE'LL DRINK IT ALL!
HUH?!

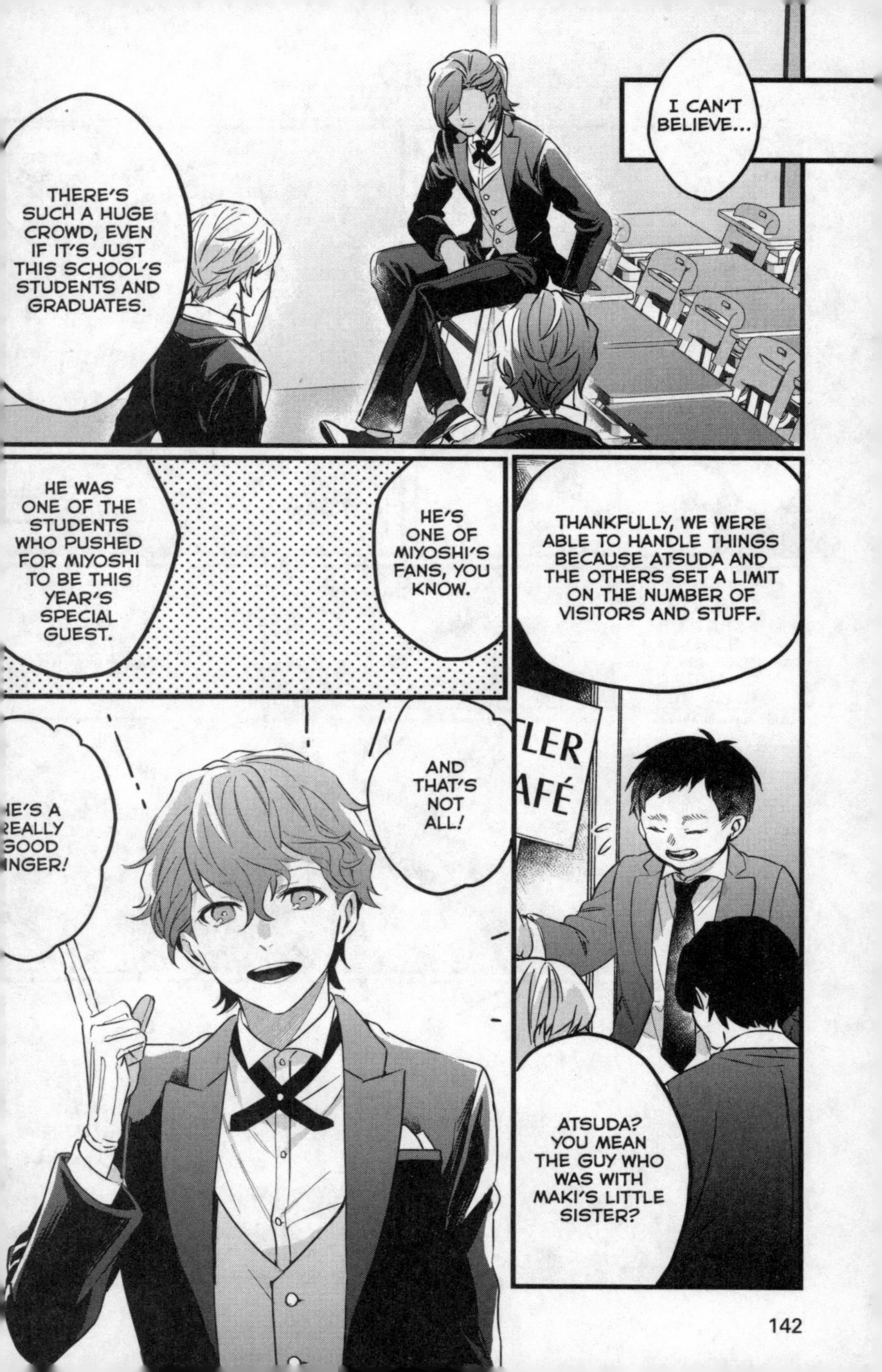
I CAN'T BELIEVE...
THERE'S SUCH A HUGE CROWD, EVEN IF IT'S JUST THIS SCHOOL'S STUDENTS AND GRADUATES.
THANKFULLY, WE WERE ABLE TO HANDLE THINGS BECAUSE ATSUDA AND THE OTHERS SET A LIMIT ON THE NUMBER OF VISITORS AND STUFF.
TLER
AFÉ
ATSUDA? YOU MEAN THE GUY WHO WAS WITH MAKI'S LITTLE SISTER?
HE'S ONE OF MIYOSHI'S FANS, YOU KNOW.
HE WAS ONE OF THE STUDENTS WHO PUSHED FOR MIYOSHI TO BE THIS YEAR'S SPECIAL GUEST.
AND THAT'S NOT ALL!
E'S A REALLY GOOD INGER!

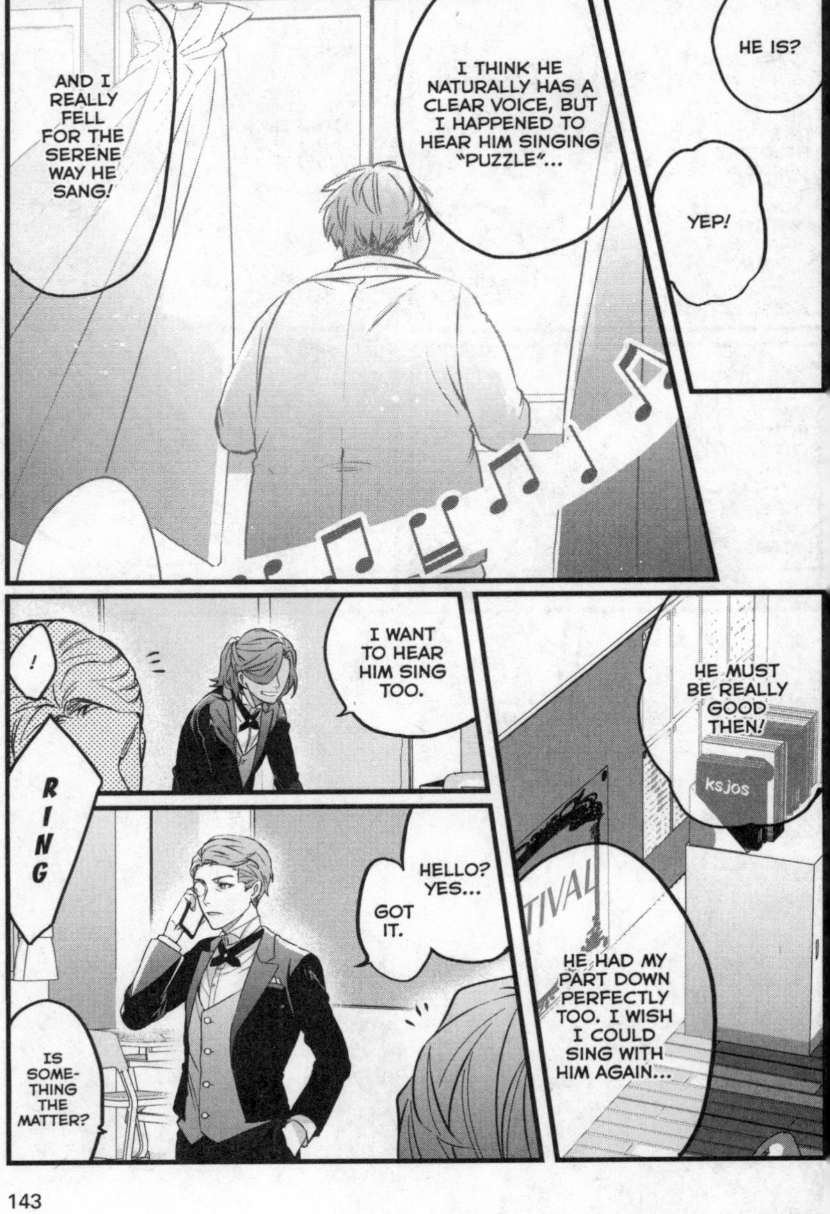
HE IS?
YEP!
I THINK HE NATURALLY HAS A CLEAR VOICE, BUT I HAPPENED TO HEAR HIM SINGING "PUZZLE"...
AND I REALLY FELL FOR THE SERENE WAY HE SANG!
HE MUST BE REALLY GOOD THEN!
ksjos
HE HAD MY PART DOWN PERFECTLY TOO. I WISH I COULD SING WITH HIM AGAIN...
I WANT TO HEAR HIM SING TOO.
!
RING
HELLO? YES...
GOT IT.
IS SOME-THING THE MATTER?

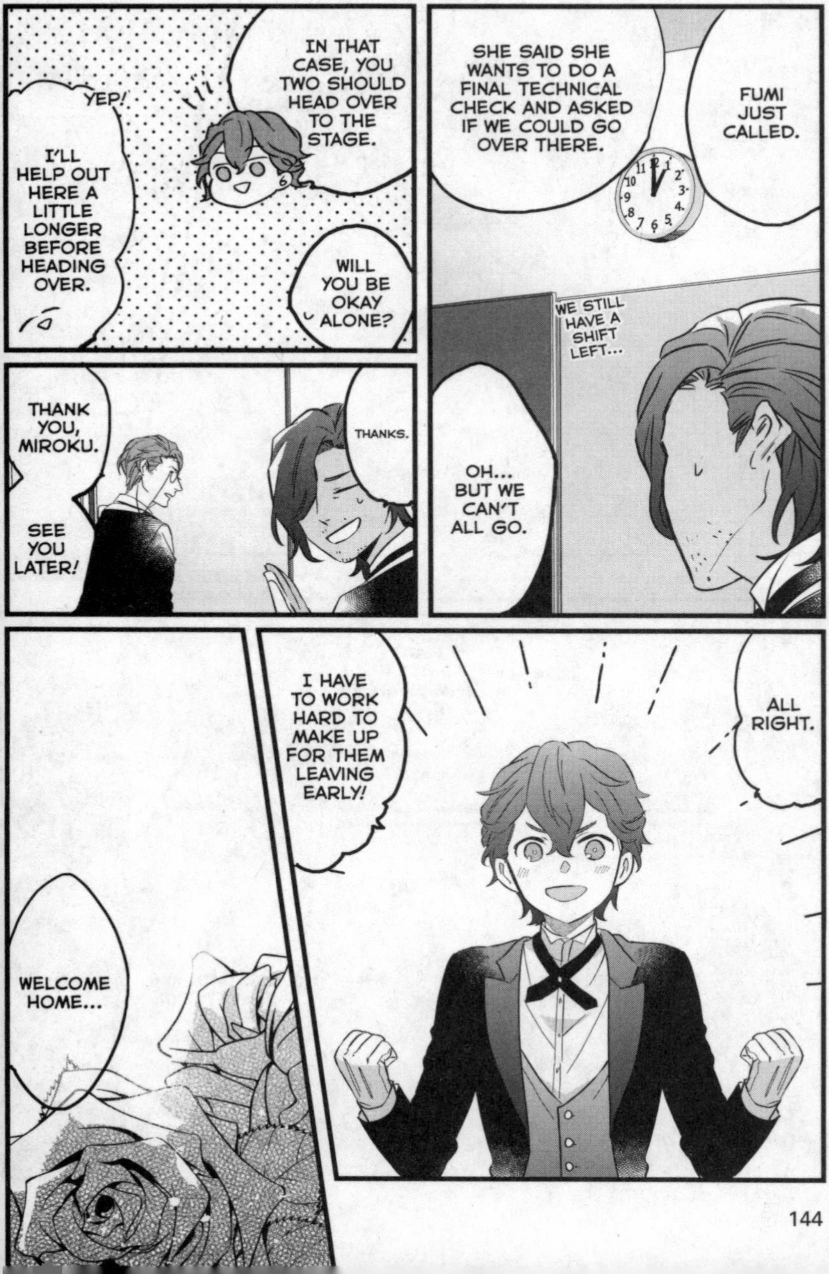
FUMI JUST CALLED.
SHE SAID SHE WANTS TO DO A FINAL TECHNICAL CHECK AND ASKED IF WE COULD GO OVER THERE.
WE STILL HAVE A SHIFT LEFT...
OH... BUT WE CAN'T ALL GO.
IN THAT CASE, YOU TWO SHOULD HEAD OVER TO THE STAGE.
WILL YOU BE OKAY ALONE?
YEP!
I'LL HELP OUT HERE A LITTLE LONGER BEFORE HEADING OVER.
THANKS.
THANK YOU, MIROKU.
SEE YOU LATER!
ALL RIGHT.
I HAVE TO WORK HARD TO MAKE UP FOR THEM LEAVING EARLY!
WELCOME HOME...

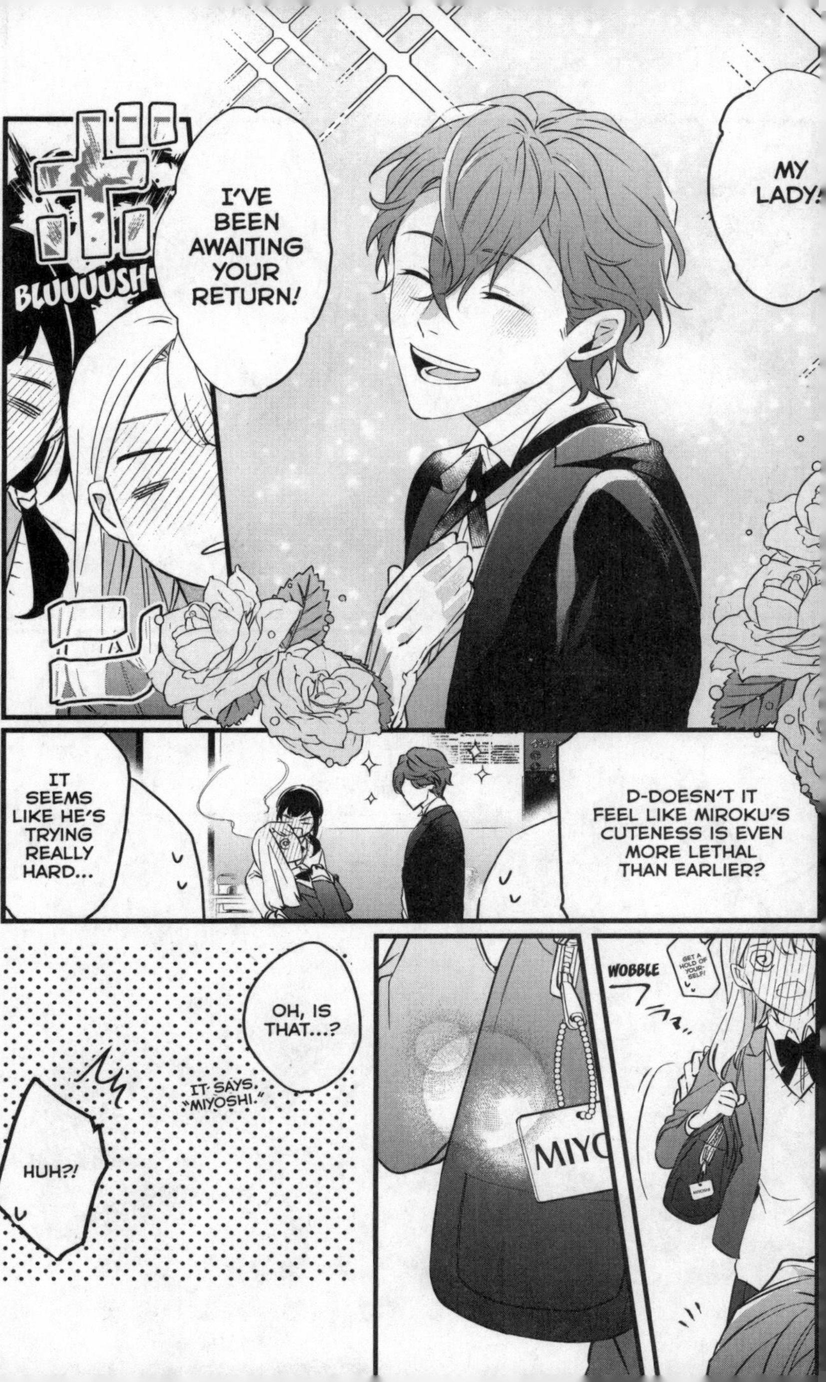
MY LADY!
I'VE BEEN AWAITING YOUR RETURN!
BLUUUUSH
D-DOESN'T IT FEEL LIKE MIROKU'S CUTENESS IS EVEN MORE LETHAL THAN EARLIER?
IT SEEMS LIKE HE'S TRYING REALLY HARD...
GET A HOLD OF YOURSELF!
WOBBLE
MIYO
OH, IS THAT...?
IT SAYS, "MIYOSHI."
HUH?!

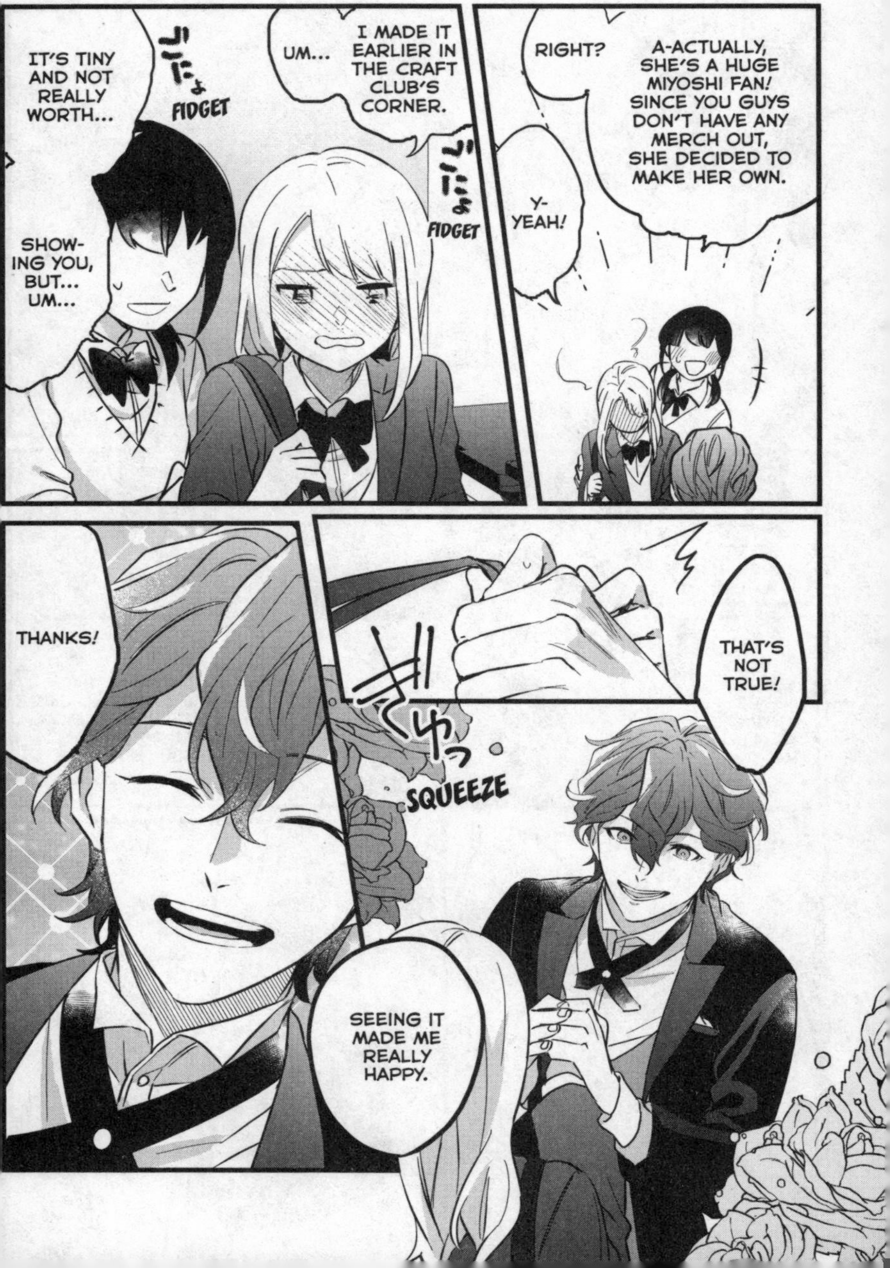
A-ACTUALLY, SHE'S A HUGE MIYOSHI FAN! SINCE YOU GUYS DON'T HAVE ANY MERCH OUT, SHE DECIDED TO MAKE HER OWN.
RIGHT?
Y-YEAH!
I MADE IT EARLIER IN THE CRAFT CLUB'S CORNER.
UM...
ごにょ FIDGET
ごにょ FIDGET
IT'S TINY AND NOT REALLY WORTH...
SHOWING YOU, BUT... UM...
THAT'S NOT TRUE!
ぎゅっ SQUEEZE
THANKS!
SEEING IT MADE ME REALLY HAPPY.

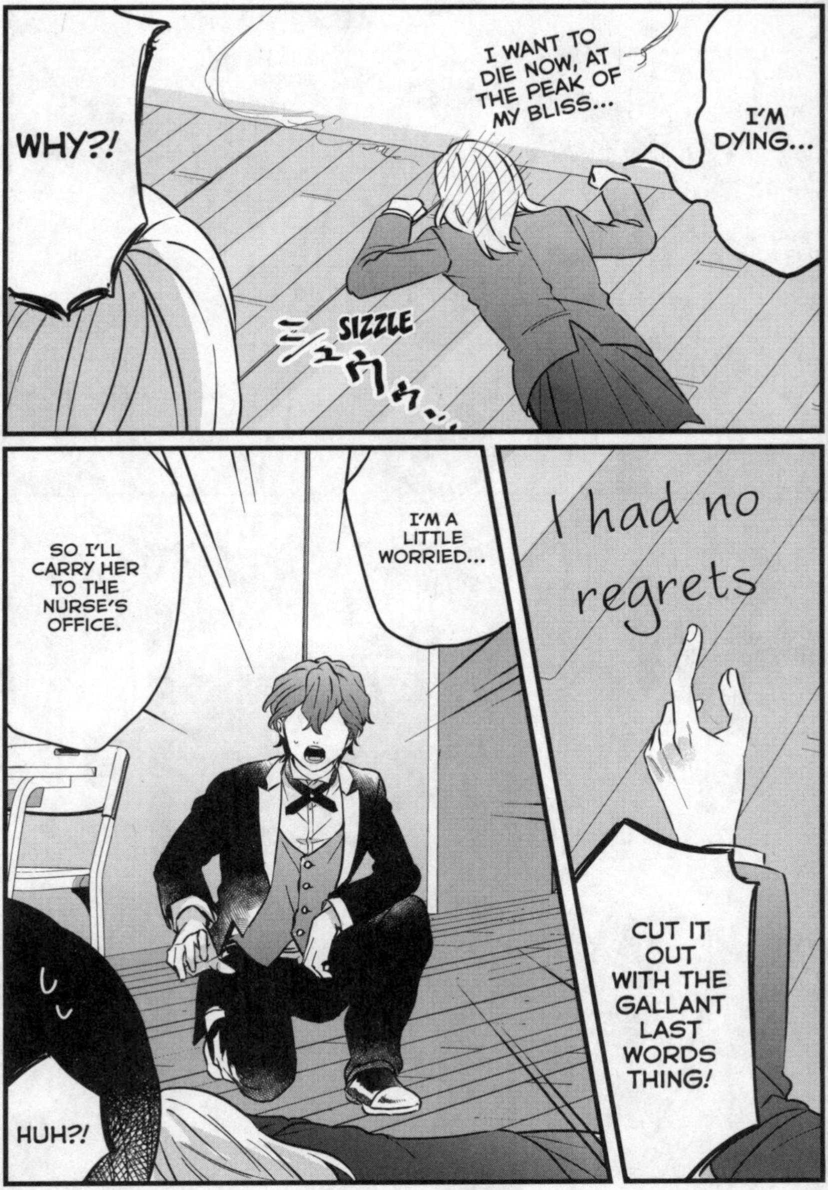
I'M DYING...
I WANT TO DIE NOW, AT THE PEAK OF MY BLISS...
SIZZLE
WHY?!
I had no regrets
CUT IT OUT WITH THE GALLANT LAST WORDS THING!
I'M A LITTLE WORRIED...
SO I'LL CARRY HER TO THE NURSE'S OFFICE.
HUH?!

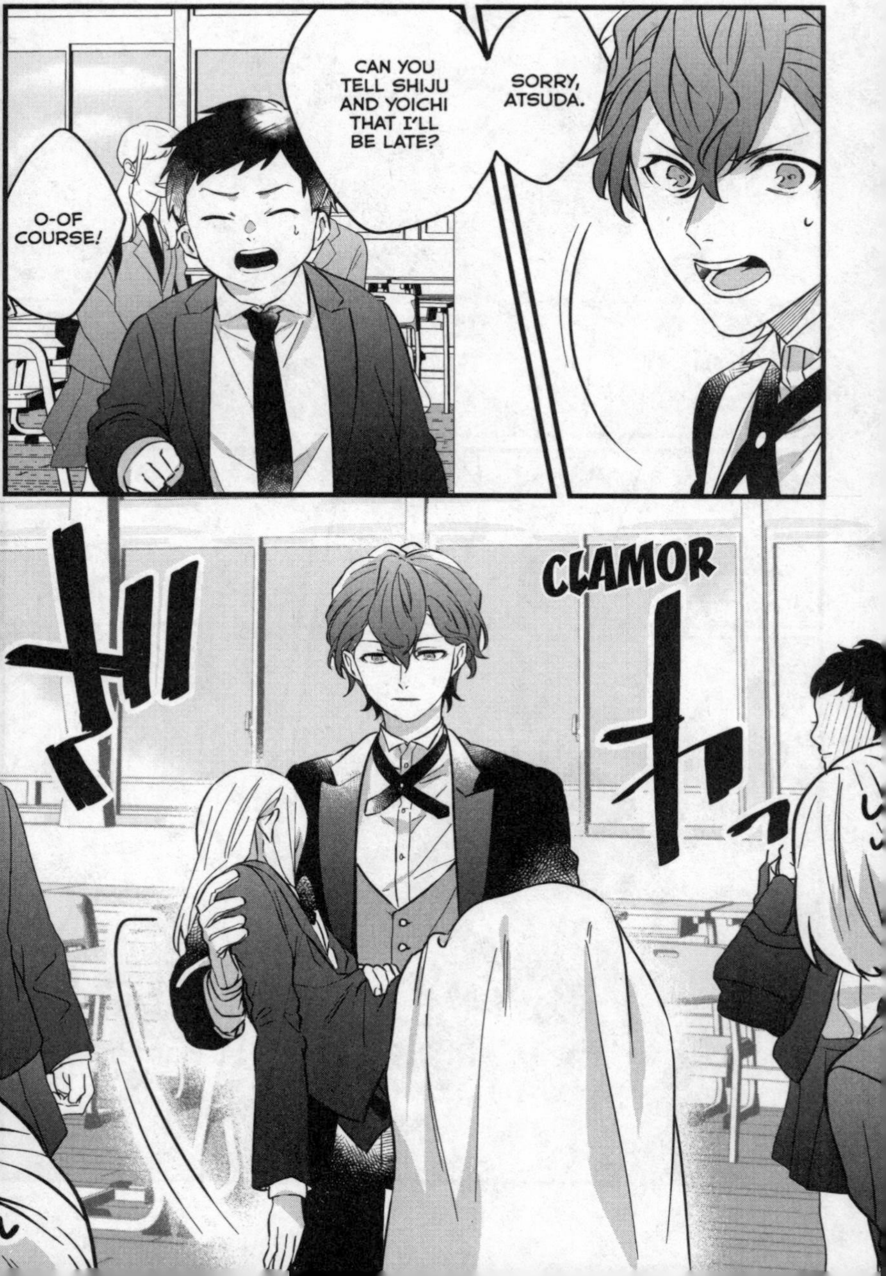
SORRY, ATSUDA.
CAN YOU TELL SHIJU AND YOICHI THAT I'LL BE LATE?
O-OF COURSE!
CLAMOR

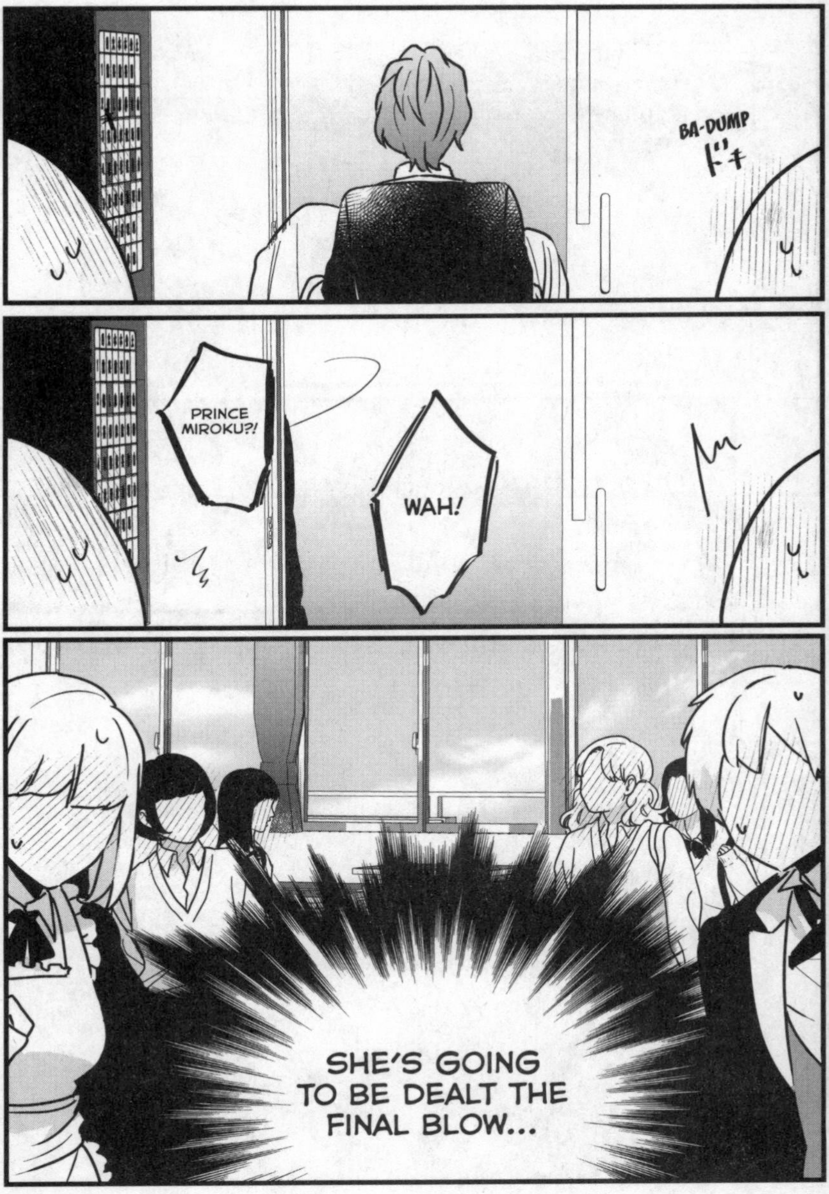
BA-DUMP
ドキ
WAH!
PRINCE MIROKU?!
SHE'S GOING TO BE DEALT THE FINAL BLOW...

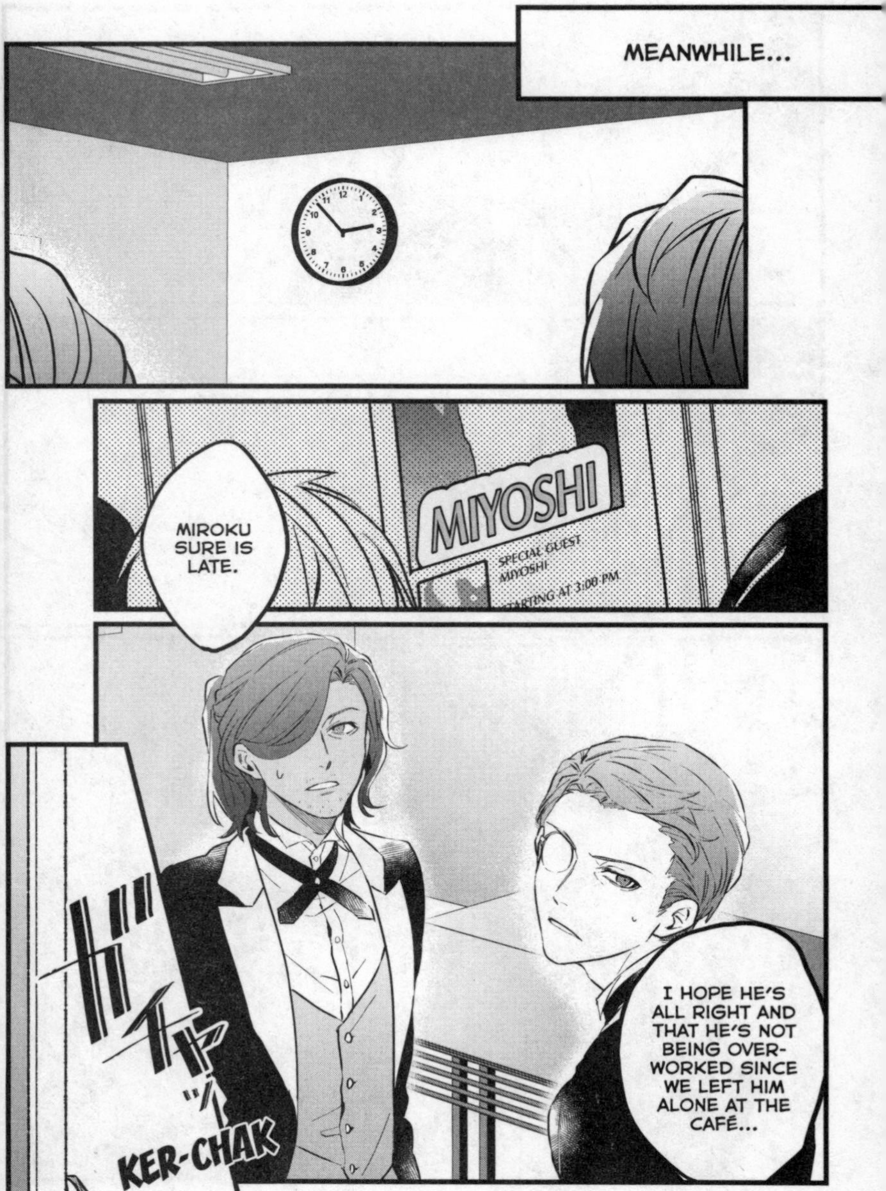
MEANWHILE...
MIYOSHI
SPECIAL GUEST
MIYOSHI
MIROKU SURE IS LATE.
I HOPE HE'S ALL RIGHT AND THAT HE'S NOT BEING OVER-WORKED SINCE WE LEFT HIM ALONE AT THE CAFÉ...
KER-CHAK

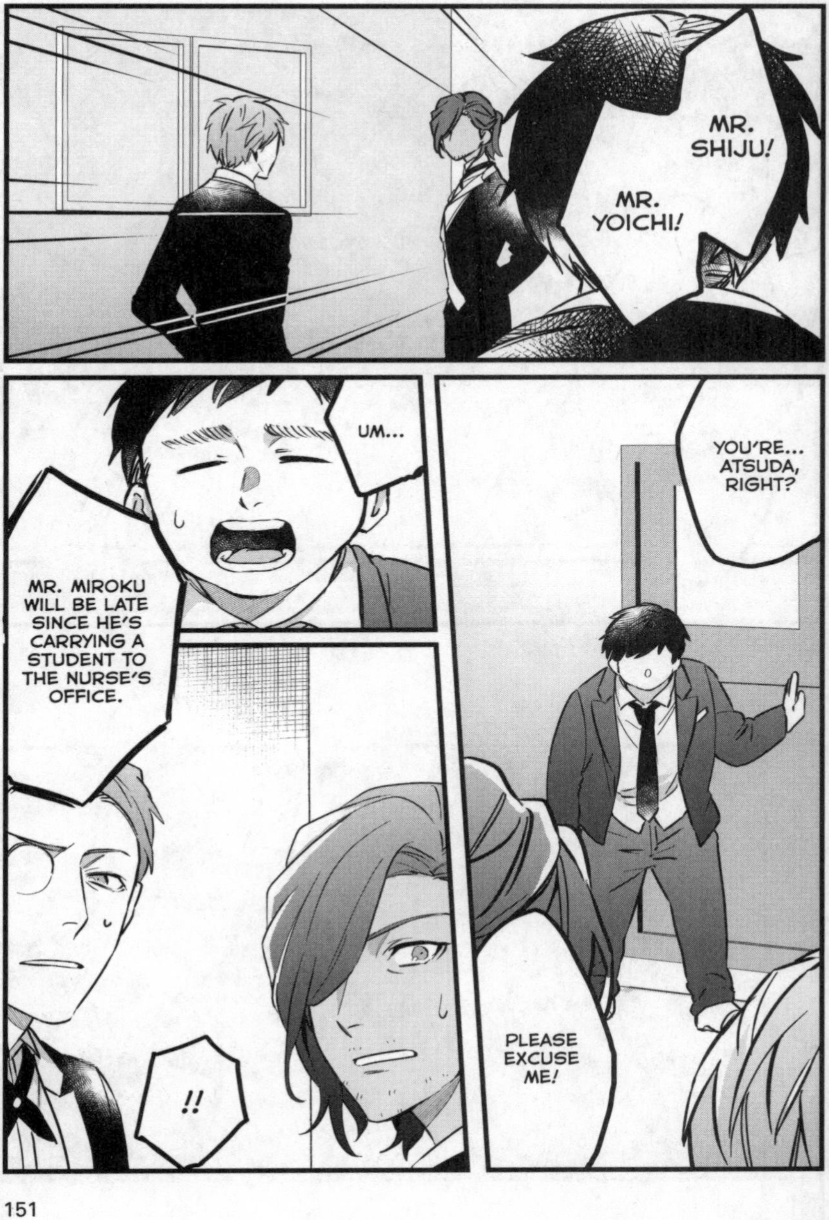
MR. SHIJU!
MR. YOICHI!
YOU'RE... ATSUDA, RIGHT?
PLEASE EXCUSE ME!
UM...
MR. MIROKU WILL BE LATE SINCE HE'S CARRYING A STUDENT TO THE NURSE'S OFFICE.
!!

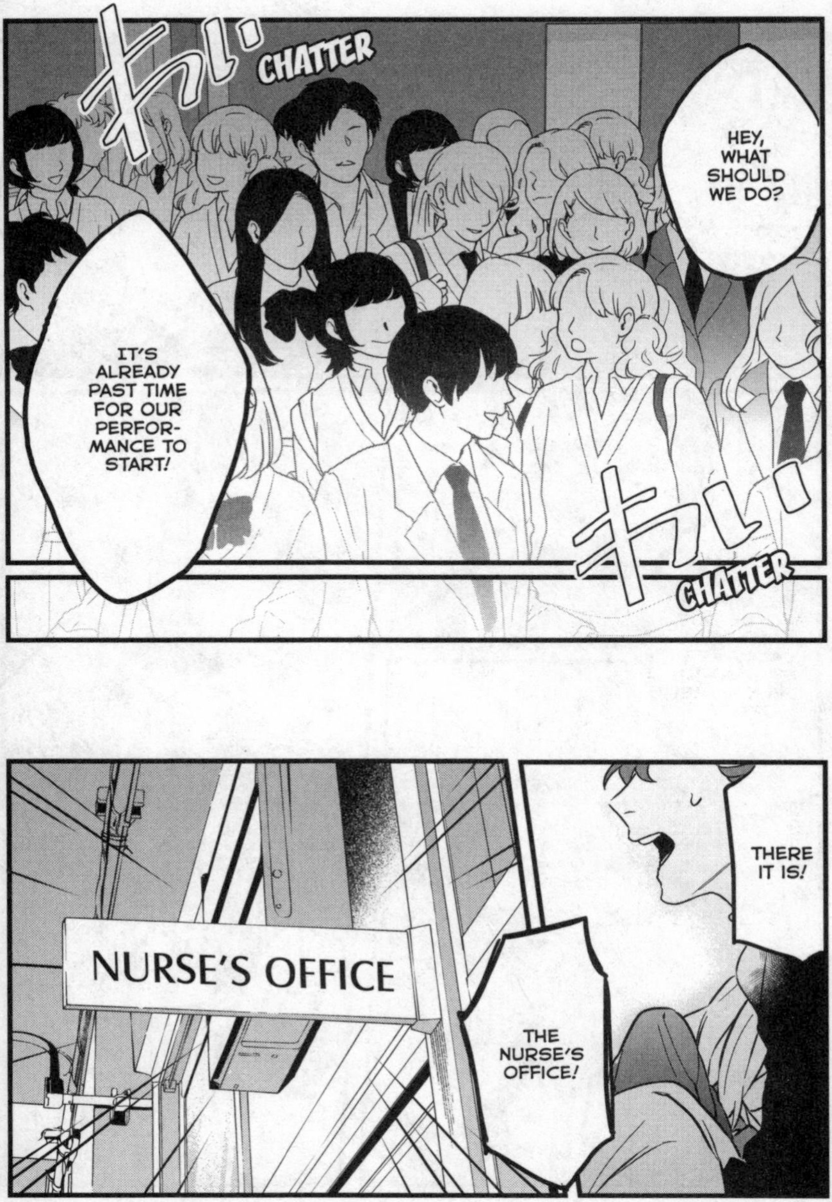
HEY, WHAT SHOULD WE DO?
わい
CHATTER
IT'S ALREADY PAST TIME FOR OUR PERFORMANCE TO START!
わい
CHATTER
THERE IT IS!
THE NURSE'S OFFICE!
NURSE'S OFFICE

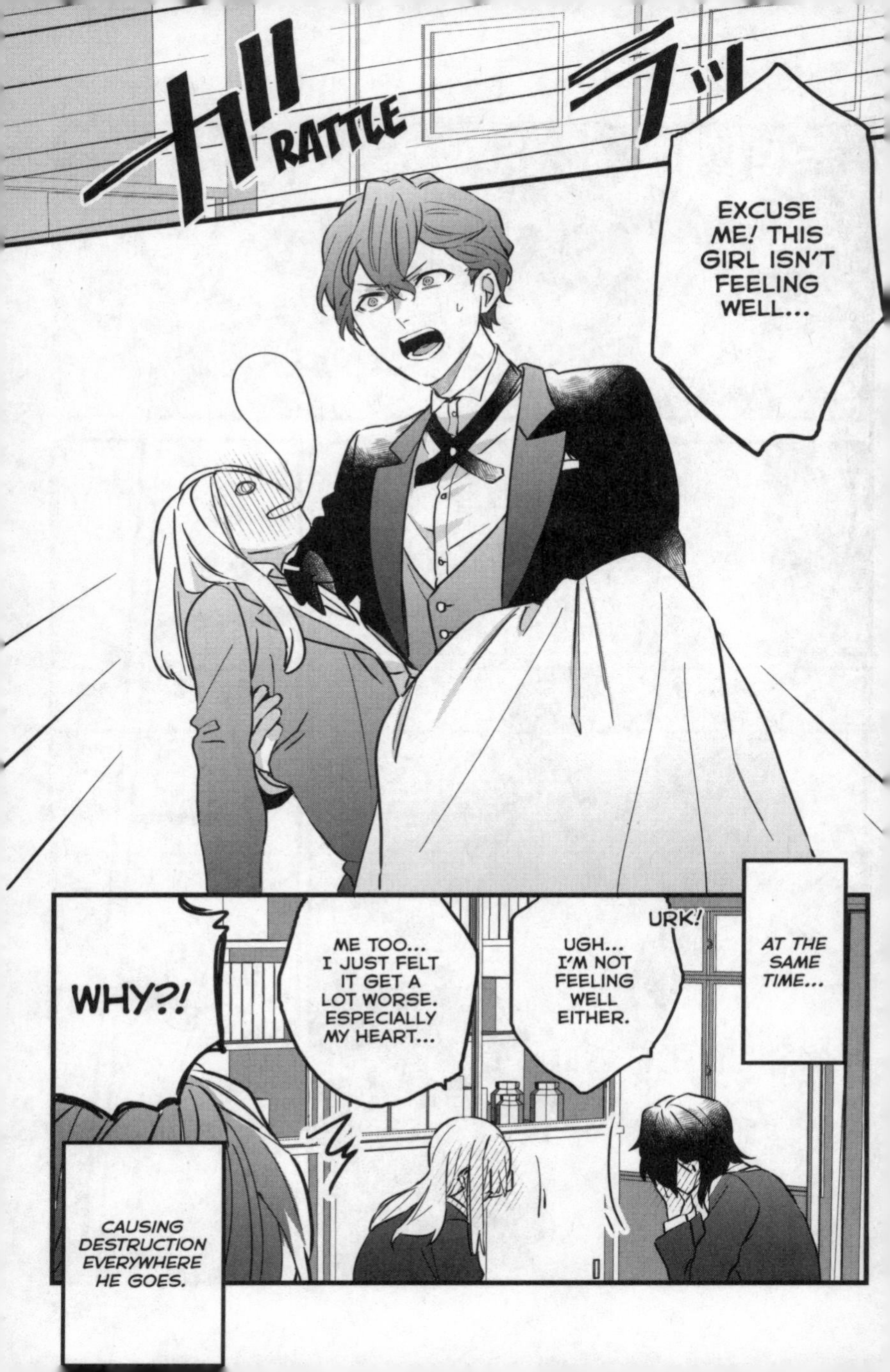
ガラッ
RATTLE
EXCUSE ME! THIS GIRL ISN'T FEELING WELL...
AT THE SAME TIME...
URK!
UGH... I'M NOT FEELING WELL EITHER.
ME TOO... I JUST FELT IT GET A LOT WORSE. ESPECIALLY MY HEART...
WHY?!
CAUSING DESTRUCTION EVERYWHERE HE GOES.

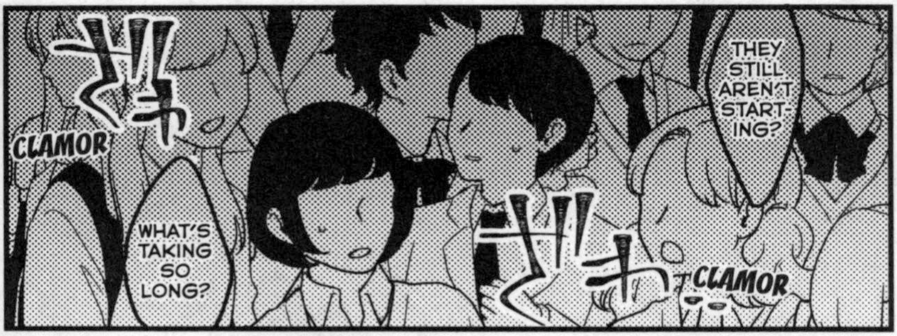
THEY STILL AREN'T STARTING?
CLAMOR
WHAT'S TAKING SO LONG?
CLAMOR

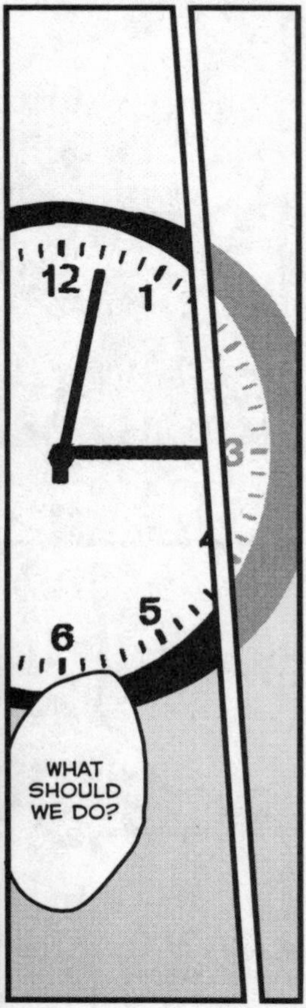
WHAT SHOULD WE DO?

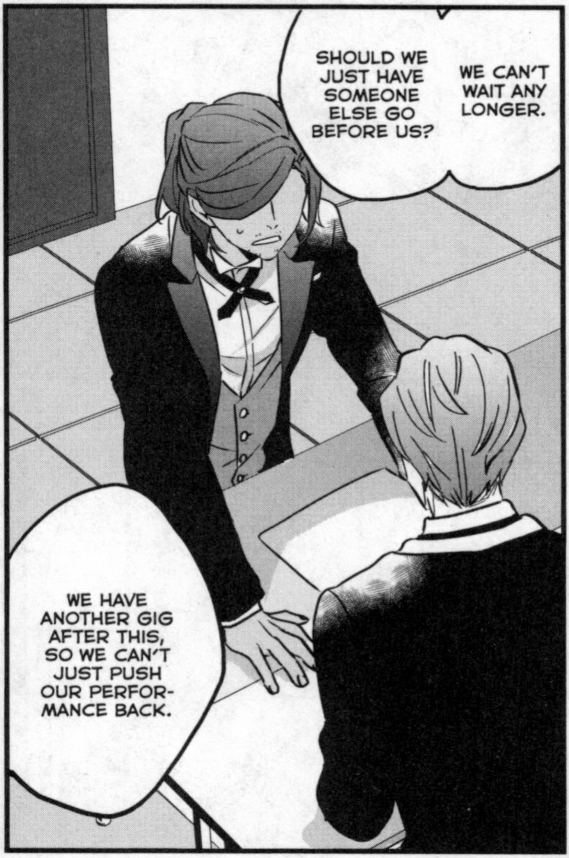
WE CAN'T WAIT ANY LONGER.
SHOULD WE JUST HAVE SOMEONE ELSE GO BEFORE US?
WE HAVE ANOTHER GIG AFTER THIS, SO WE CAN'T JUST PUSH OUR PERFORMANCE BACK.

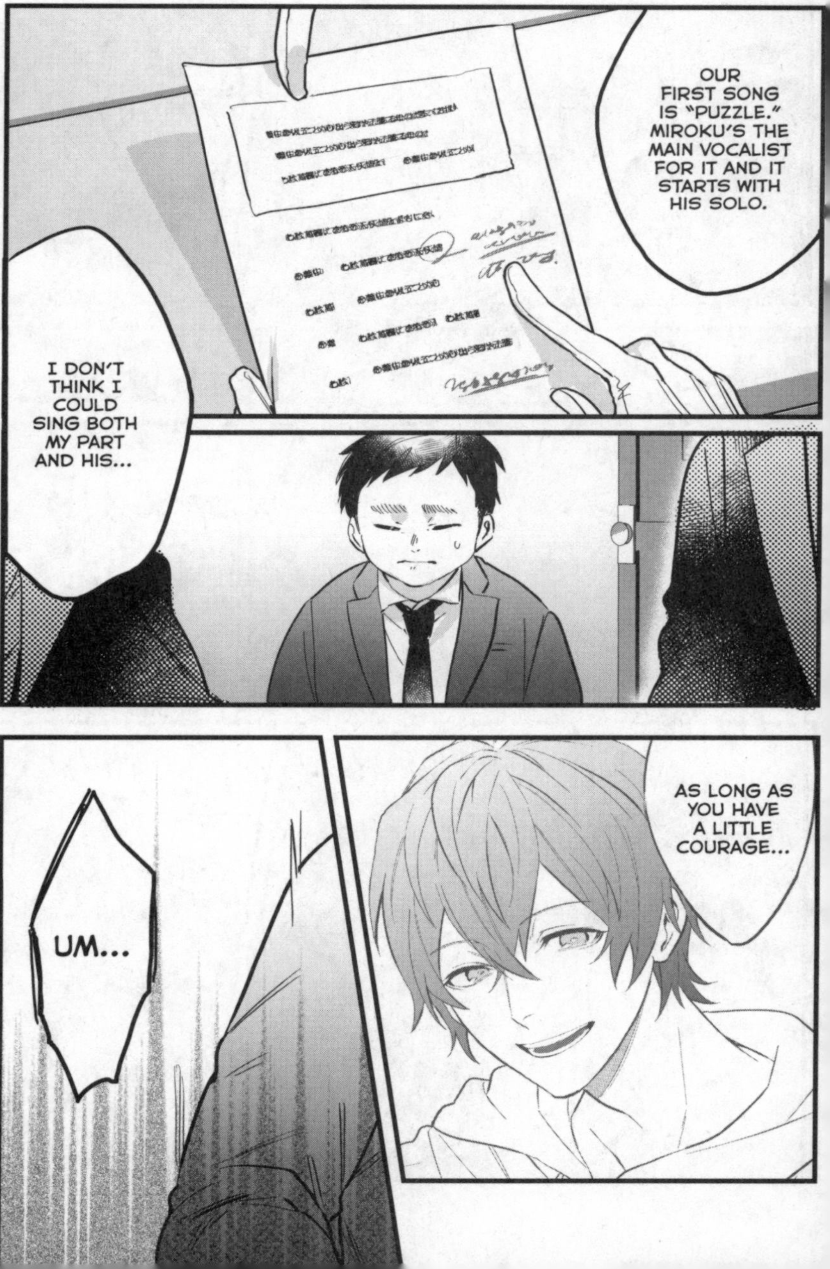
OUR FIRST SONG IS "PUZZLE." MIROKU'S THE MAIN VOCALIST FOR IT AND IT STARTS WITH HIS SOLO.
I DON'T THINK I COULD SING BOTH MY PART AND HIS...
AS LONG AS YOU HAVE A LITTLE COURAGE...
UM...

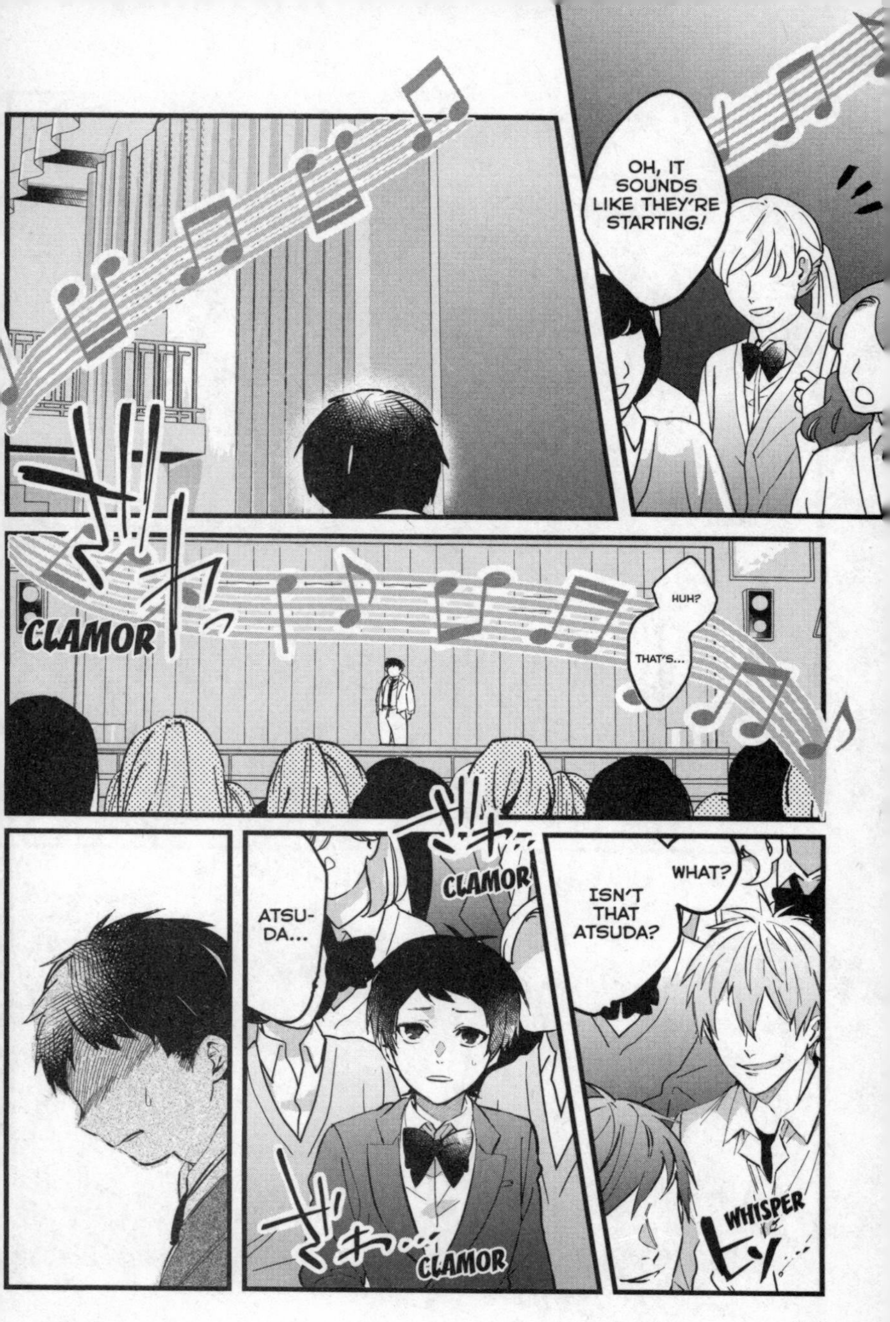
OH, IT SOUNDS LIKE THEY'RE STARTING!
CLAMOR
HUH?
THAT'S...
CLAMOR
WHAT?
ISN'T THAT ATSUDA?
WHISPER
ATSU-DA...
CLAMOR

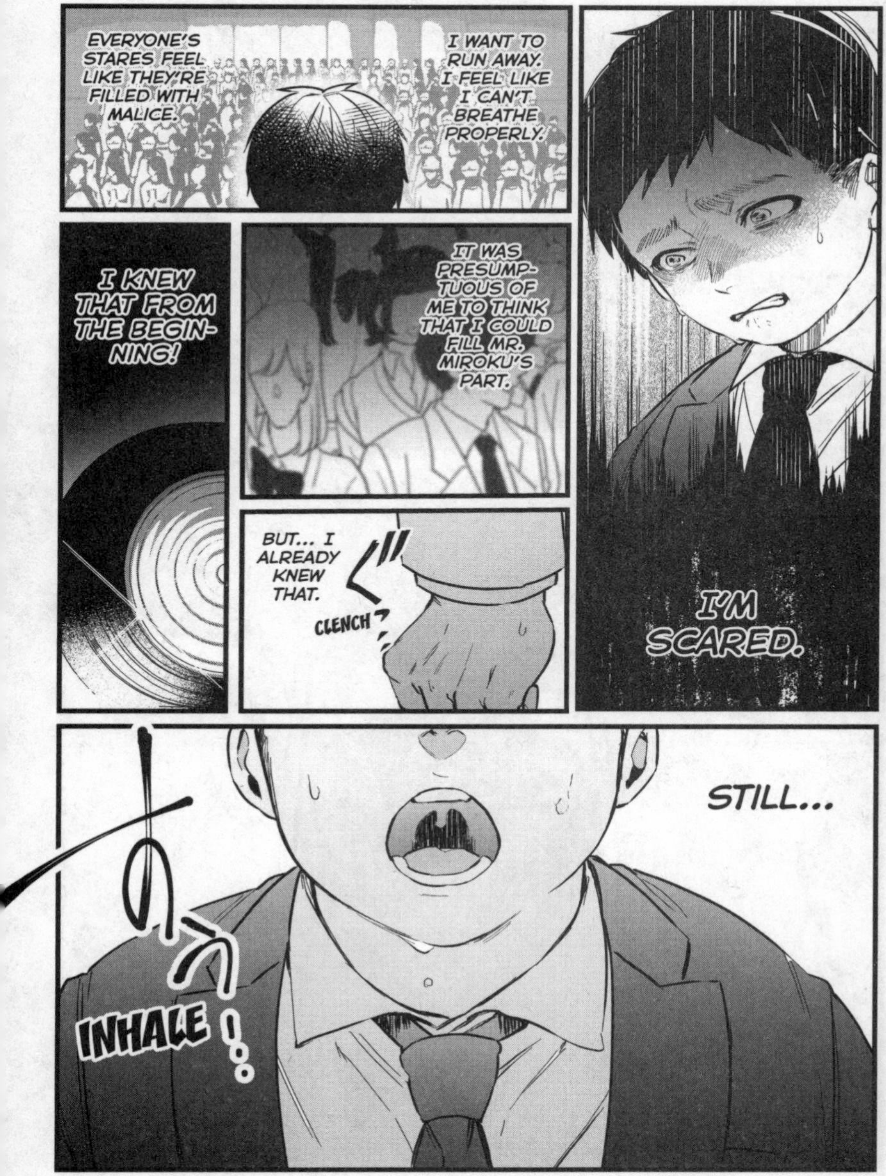
I'M SCARED.
I WANT TO RUN AWAY. I FEEL LIKE I CAN'T BREATHE PROPERLY.
EVERYONE'S STARES FEEL LIKE THEY'RE FILLED WITH MALICE.
IT WAS PRESUMPTUOUS OF ME TO THINK THAT I COULD FILL MR. MIROKU'S PART.
BUT... I ALREADY KNEW THAT.
CLENCH
I KNEW THAT FROM THE BEGINNING!
STILL...
INHALE

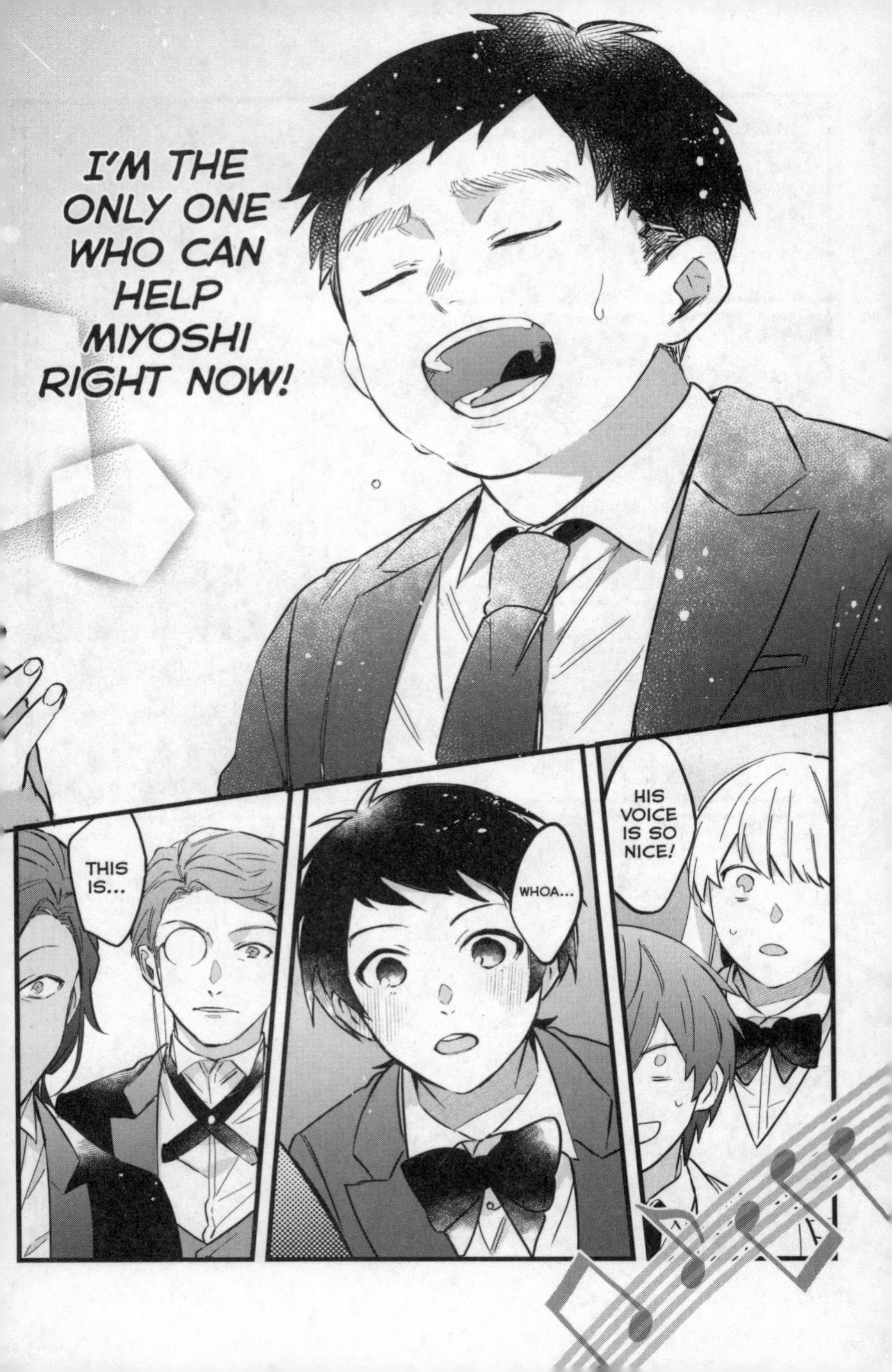
I'M THE ONLY ONE WHO CAN HELP MIYOSHI RIGHT NOW!
HIS VOICE IS SO NICE!
WHOA...
THIS IS...

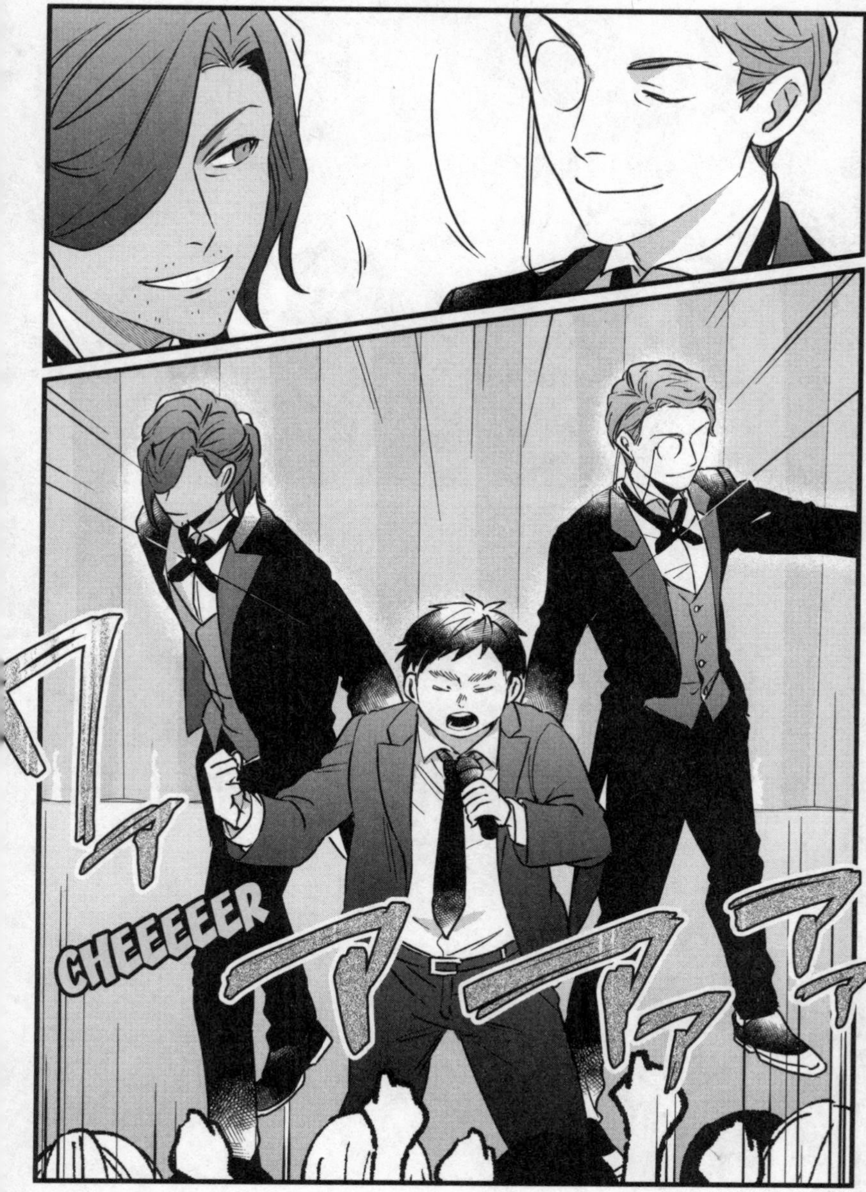
CHEEEEER

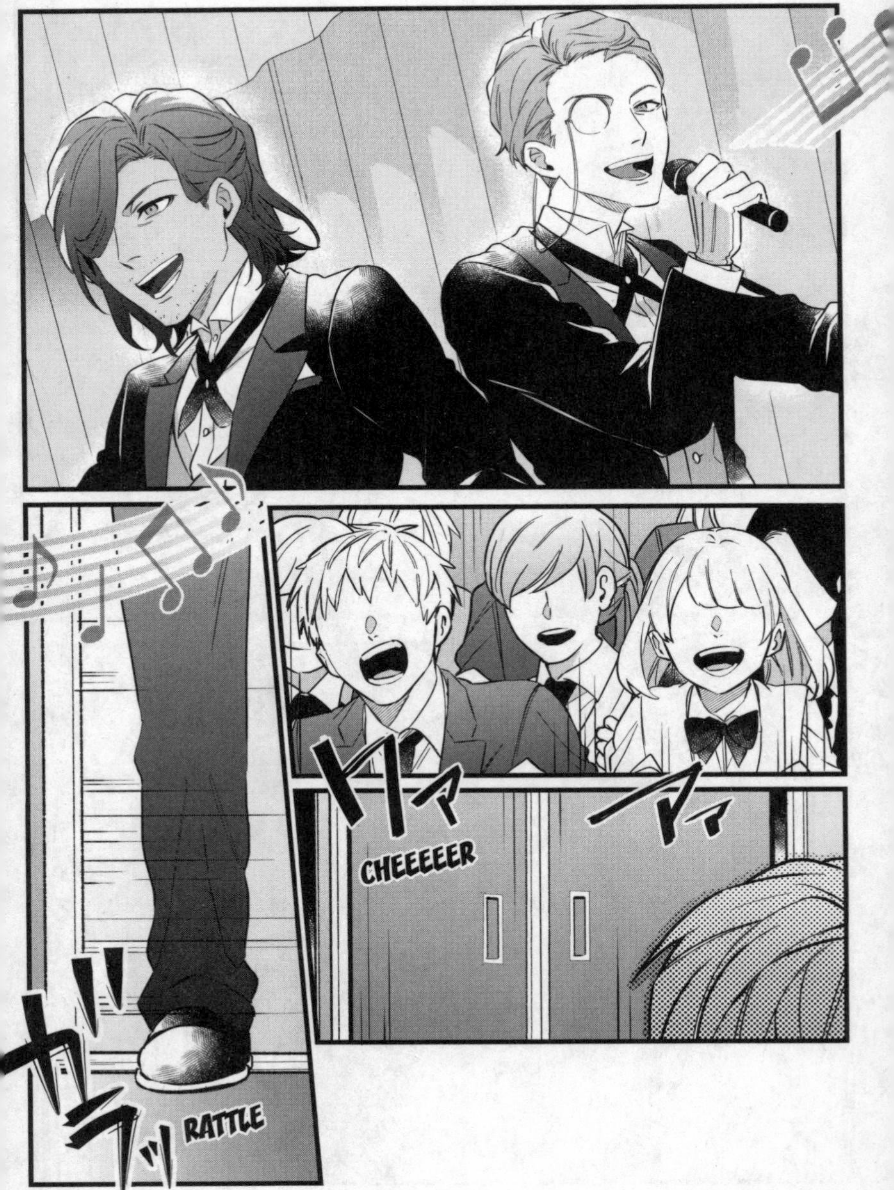
CHEEEEER
RATTLE

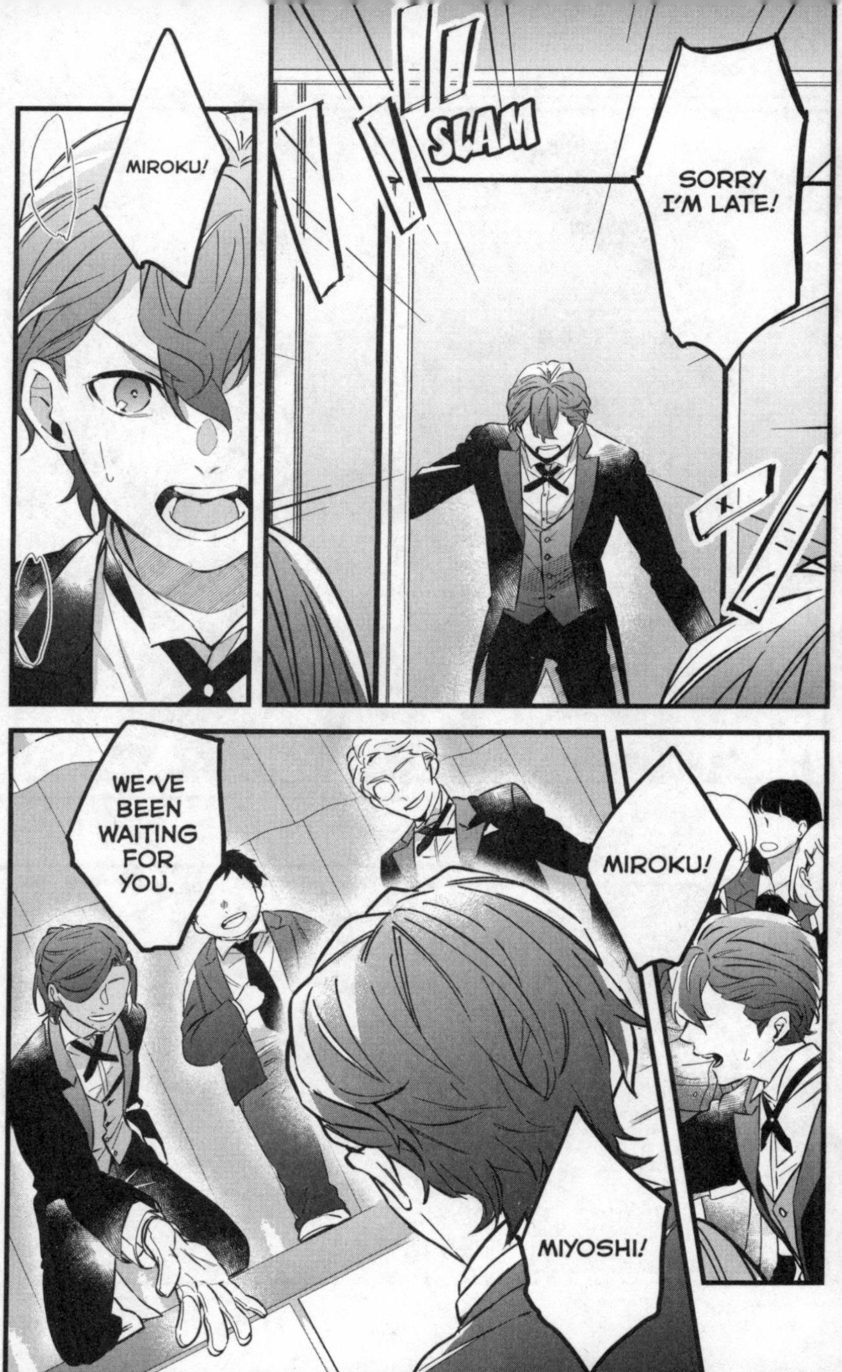
SLAM
SORRY I'M LATE!
MIROKU!
MIROKU!
WE'VE BEEN WAITING FOR YOU.
MIYOSHI!

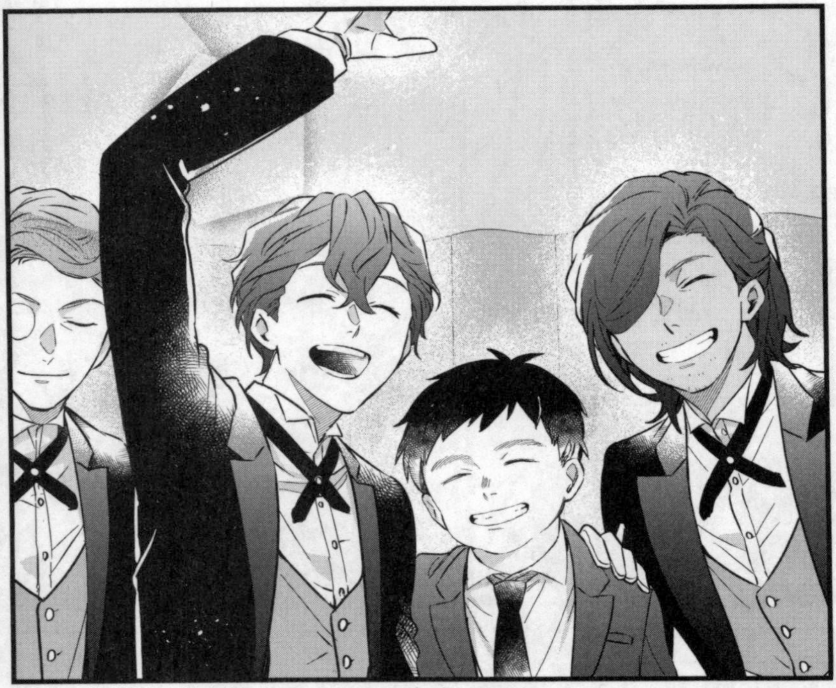
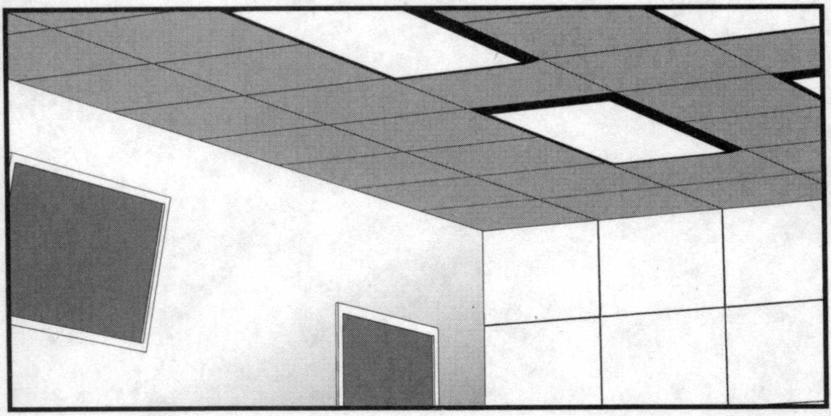

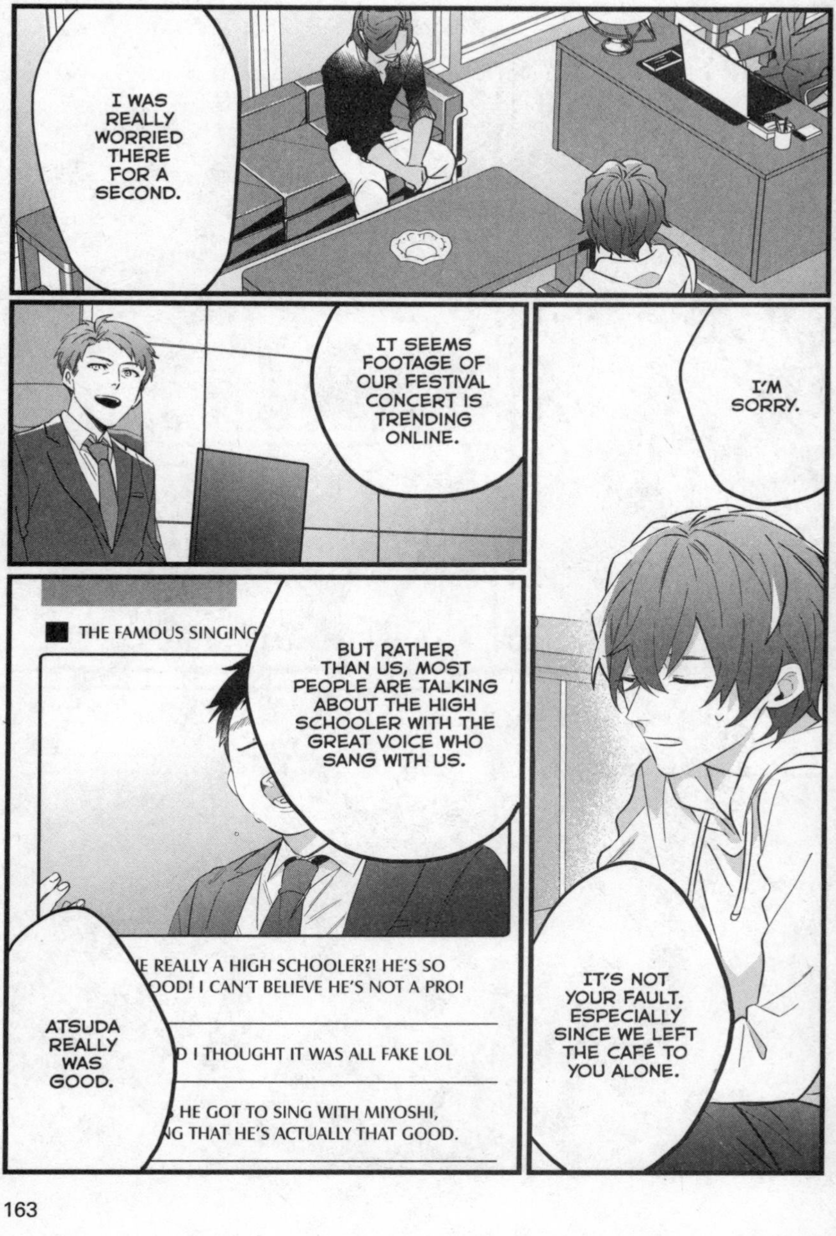
I WAS REALLY WORRIED THERE FOR A SECOND.
I'M SORRY.
IT'S NOT YOUR FAULT. ESPECIALLY SINCE WE LEFT THE CAFÉ TO YOU ALONE.
IT SEEMS FOOTAGE OF OUR FESTIVAL CONCERT IS TRENDING ONLINE.
BUT RATHER THAN US, MOST PEOPLE ARE TALKING ABOUT THE HIGH SCHOOLER WITH THE GREAT VOICE WHO SANG WITH US.
THE FAMOUS SINGING
E REALLY A HIGH SCHOOLER?! HE'S SO
OOD! I CAN'T BELIEVE HE'S NOT A PRO!
D I THOUGHT IT WAS ALL FAKE LOL
HE GOT TO SING WITH MIYOSHI,
NG THAT HE'S ACTUALLY THAT GOOD.
ATSUDA REALLY WAS GOOD.

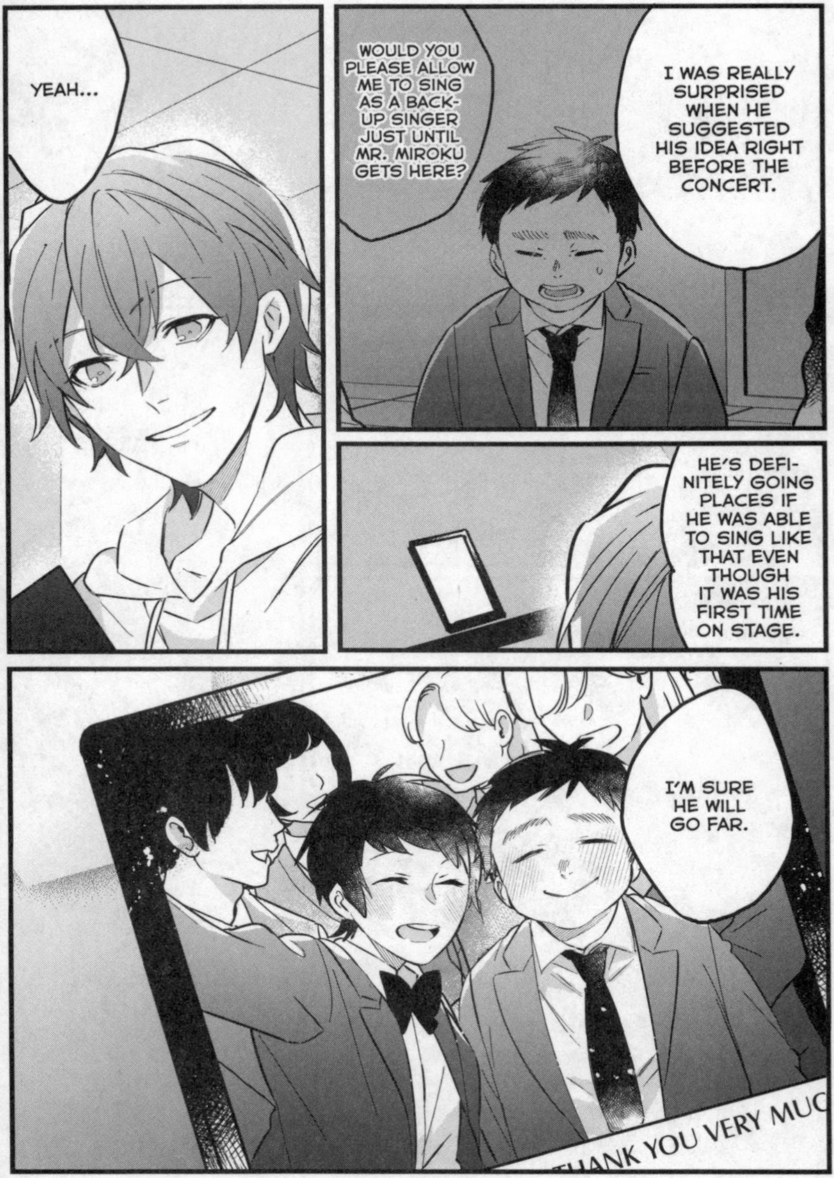
I WAS REALLY SURPRISED WHEN HE SUGGESTED HIS IDEA RIGHT BEFORE THE CONCERT.
WOULD YOU PLEASE ALLOW ME TO SING AS A BACK-UP SINGER JUST UNTIL MR. MIROKU GETS HERE?
HE'S DEFINITELY GOING PLACES IF HE WAS ABLE TO SING LIKE THAT EVEN THOUGH IT WAS HIS FIRST TIME ON STAGE.
YEAH...
I'M SURE HE WILL GO FAR.
THANK YOU VERY MUC

OSSAN IDOL!

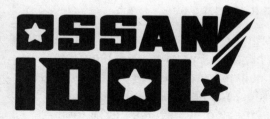

Original Short Story
"The Events of That Day"
by Mochiko Mochida

I guess I can sing. It's not like I hate it.

Dancing is hard, but I kind of enjoy it.

I love putting smiles on other people's faces.

Being surrounded by girls that fawn over me… To be honest, I'm still not sure how to feel about that.

I hate working out in the summer. Moving continuously in the heat makes my energy just seep out of me, even when we practice indoors with the A/C on full blast.

"Ugh, this sucks…"

"Just a little more, Yoichi. Keep at it."

"Bro, how do you have this much energy?"

"Since I don't have to focus on smiling while I practice, I'm able to direct all my attention to working out."

Apparently, my older brother requires a lot of energy to plaster an idol-worthy smile on his face. But what's the logic in not putting effort into one small thing so you can put more effort into something even harder? My head is filled with biting remarks, but I don't have the energy to voice any of them.

"Excuse me! Your backup dancers are here." At our manager's words, I remember that today we have a meeting with our backup dancers in order to get ready for the concerts we'll be putting on this autumn. We don't usually practice with them.

We quickly greet them before getting right into our lessons.

Since we're idols that belong to the major talent agency Shineez, most people are really courteous around us. I feel like we're barely famous, but the CEO of our agency has told me we're a lot more popular than we think.

"You okay?"

"Yeah. I just can't handle this heat." My brother must have been worried seeing me deep in thought, so I flash him a smile.

We are idols.

We are Alpha, the greatest idols of all time.

We have to become stars that others can only dream about.

"Hey, do you like to dance?"

"Huh?" I'm surprised by a question from one of our backup dancers during a short break.

That dancer really stood out. I didn't start learning how to dance until I became an idol with my brother, but even to my untrained eye, this guy's talent made him shine brighter than the others. He had sunkissed skin and wavy black hair and stared at me with gleaming eyes.

"I asked if you like it. You look like you're suffering."

"Uh… because it's… hot?" I tilt my head, and the guy in front of me bursts out laughing.

"Why did you say that like it's a question? You're so weird."

Immediately, the backup dancer's friends grab at his clothes, looking flustered.

"H-Hey!"

"What?"

"Don't you remember that we were told not to talk to Alpha before we came here?!"

"Oh, were we?" The other dancers start to drag the man away, but before they can, I call out to him.

"Hey, my name's Yoichi."

"Pfft! I know. You're part of Alpha, after all."

"Oh, right."

I forgot.

I'm a famous idol.

"I'm Shiju. It's nice to meet ya." His gleaming eyes sparkle with a grin that takes over his entire face.

Thinking back, that meeting might have been the start of everything.

Our concerts were all successes, and my brother and I started to plan a nationwide tour despite being the first ever idol group to have one decided so quickly after debuting. Everything was going well, but I felt panicked.

I hadn't been able to get Shiju's concerned words out of my head since that summer.

"Hey, do you like to dance?"

I always aimed for perfection. As an idol, as a person, as the sibling who supported his older brother… but in doing so, I could feel my sense of enjoyment leave everything I did. Before, I had pushed myself to go faster to make up for my youth and inexperience, but those words had me slowing my steps.

"What're you doing, Yoichi?"

"…Shiju?"

"Hey. Long time no see."

After my older brother collapsed and was hospitalized for fatigue, no one had been brave enough to talk to me, leaving me to attend a recording for a TV show by myself. Shiju didn't seem to notice how the others were tiptoeing around me— or rather, he didn't seem to care— and that was perhaps what made him so special.

"Is your brother okay?"

"Yeah. Thanks for asking."

Actually, my brother had a girlfriend. They were eager to finally have time together and were flirting in my brother's hospital room, but I couldn't exactly say that, so I answered curtly and asked why Shiju was here.

"I'm about to perform in the final round for a national dance battle."

"Huh? Should you really be talking with me then?"

"I have three hours until I'm on, and it's not like I can prepare any more than I already have."

"You're not going to practice up until the last minute? If it were me, I'd want to perfect things so I didn't make a single mistake…"

"Dummy, it'd be boring to have to think about stuff like that while dancing."

"Boring?"

"I'm not saying it's wrong to want to be perfect. But I'm worried about you. That's all I have to say, but I'm pretty sure your fans would agree with me."

I felt like I finally understood the thing that had been buzzing around at the back of my mind.

Oh, I get it.

"…I've always wanted to hurry up and become a perfect adult."

"What? There's no such thing."

"Heh, that's true."

Yeah. We can shine even if we're incomplete. I think I want to start enjoying myself more.

"You okay?"

"Yeah, thanks. I feel like that really helped. If you ever need a hand in the future, it'll be my turn to help you, Shiju."

"Pfft, like that would ever happen."

I didn't think I'd mind helping, being helped, or turning into an imperfect adult if I were with Shiju. I was willing to bet we would shine bright together, forever.

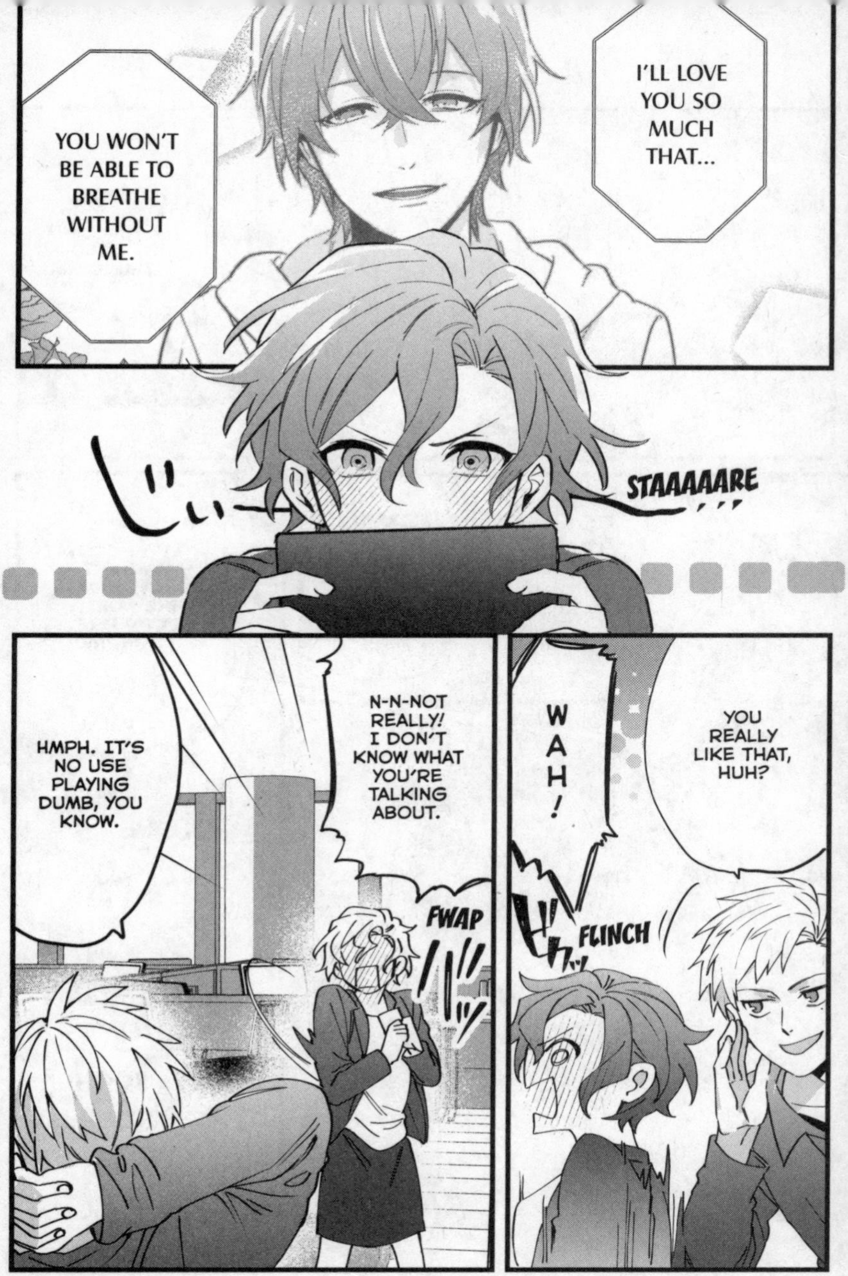
I'LL LOVE YOU SO MUCH THAT...
YOU WON'T BE ABLE TO BREATHE WITHOUT ME.
じぃ
STAAAAARE...
YOU REALLY LIKE THAT, HUH?
WAH!
FLINCH
N-N-NOT REALLY! I DON'T KNOW WHAT YOU'RE TALKING ABOUT.
FWAP
HMPH. IT'S NO USE PLAYING DUMB, YOU KNOW.

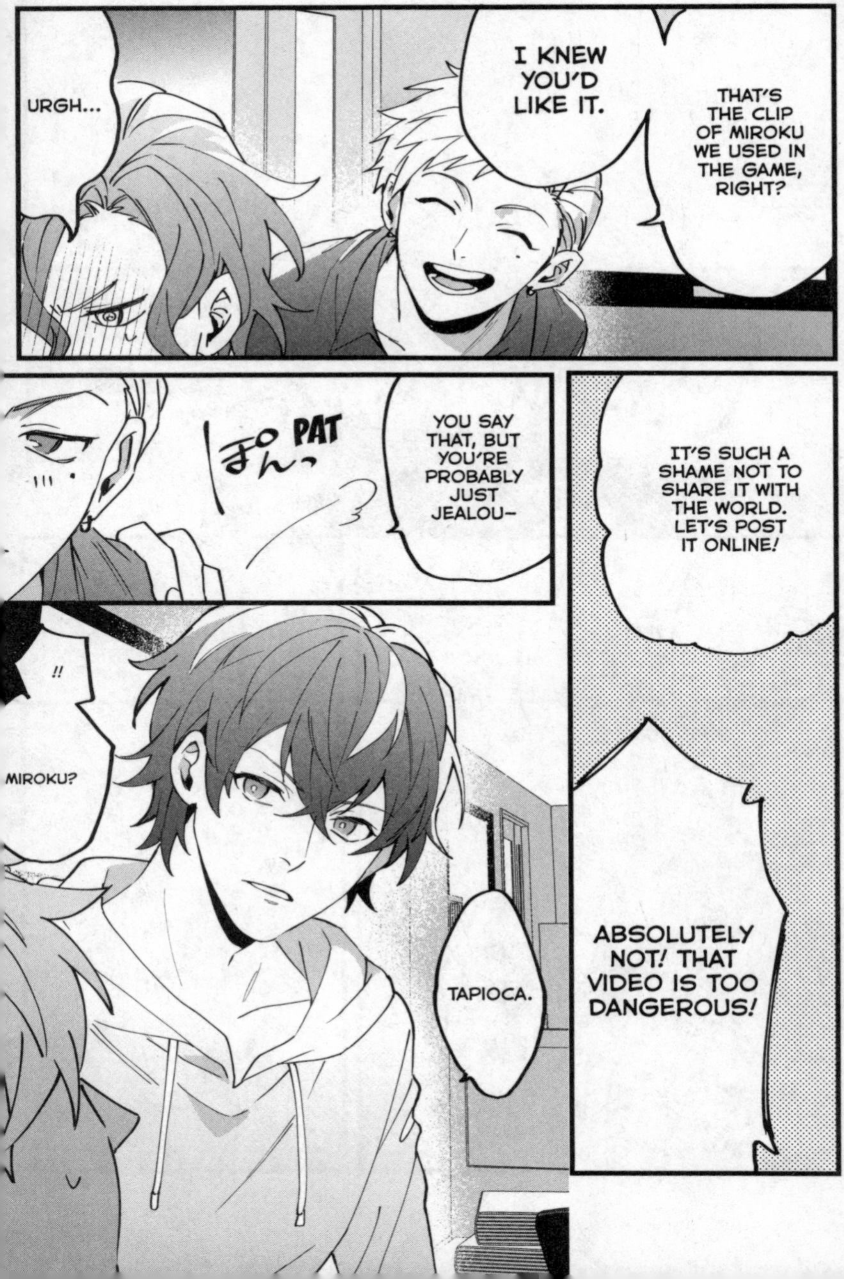
THAT'S THE CLIP OF MIROKU WE USED IN THE GAME, RIGHT?
I KNEW YOU'D LIKE IT.
URGH...
IT'S SUCH A SHAME NOT TO SHARE IT WITH THE WORLD. LET'S POST IT ONLINE!
ABSOLUTELY NOT! THAT VIDEO IS TOO DANGEROUS!
YOU SAY THAT, BUT YOU'RE PROBABLY JUST JEALOU-
PAT
ぽんっ
!!
MIROKU?
TAPIOCA.

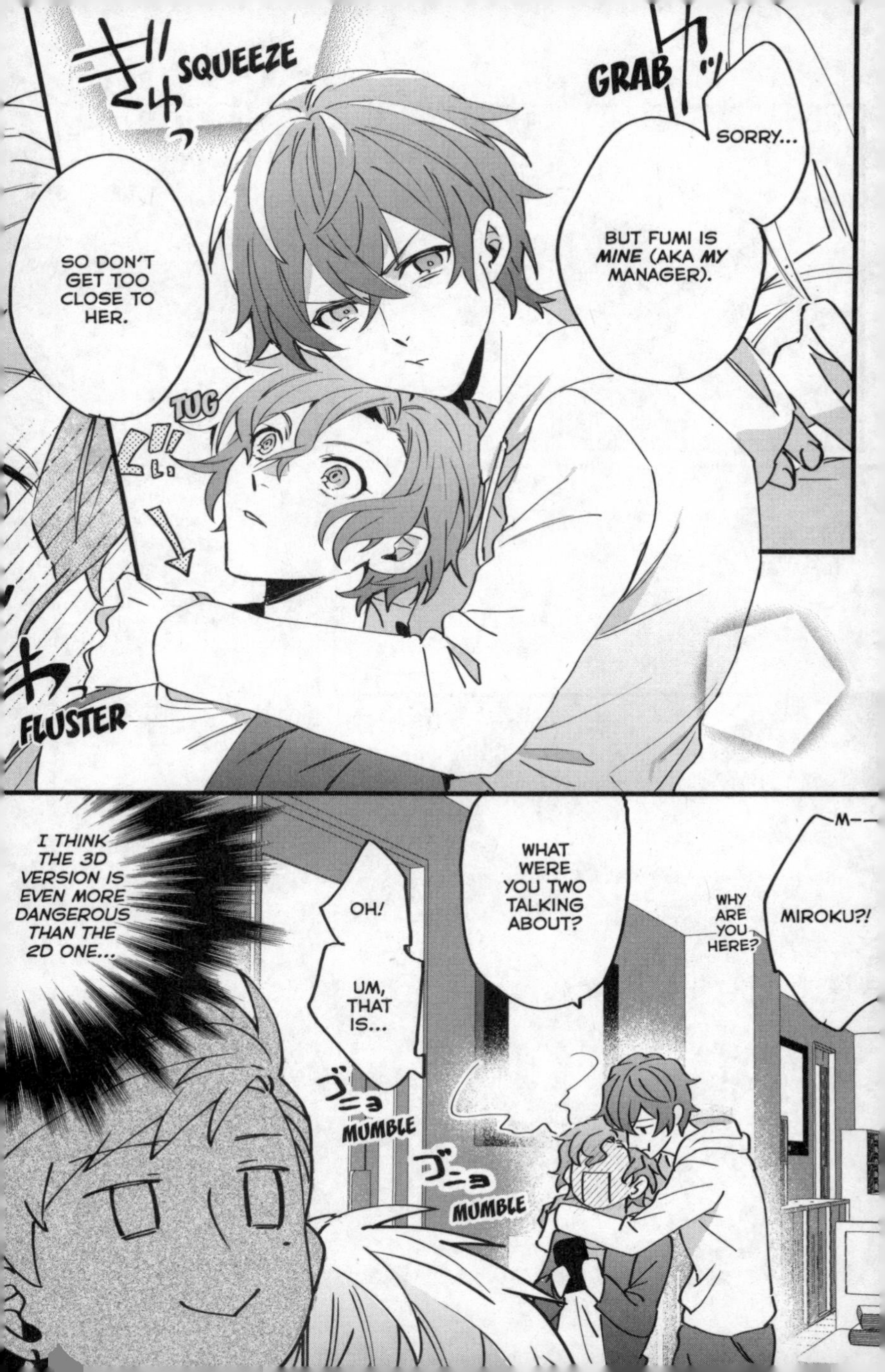
GRAB
SORRY...
BUT FUMI IS *MINE* (AKA *MY* MANAGER).
SQUEEZE
SO DON'T GET TOO CLOSE TO HER.
TUG
FLUSTER
M--
MIROKU?!
WHY ARE YOU HERE?
WHAT WERE YOU TWO TALKING ABOUT?
OH!
UM, THAT IS...
MUMBLE
MUMBLE
I THINK THE 3D VERSION IS EVEN MORE DANGEROUS THAN THE 2D ONE...

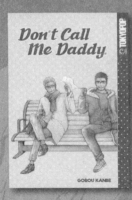

LOVE x LOVE

TOKYOPOP believes all types of romances deserve to be celebrated. *LOVE x LOVE* was born from that idea and our commitment to representing a variety of stories and voices as diverse as our fans.

MAME COORDINATE, VOLUME 1

Sachi Miyabe

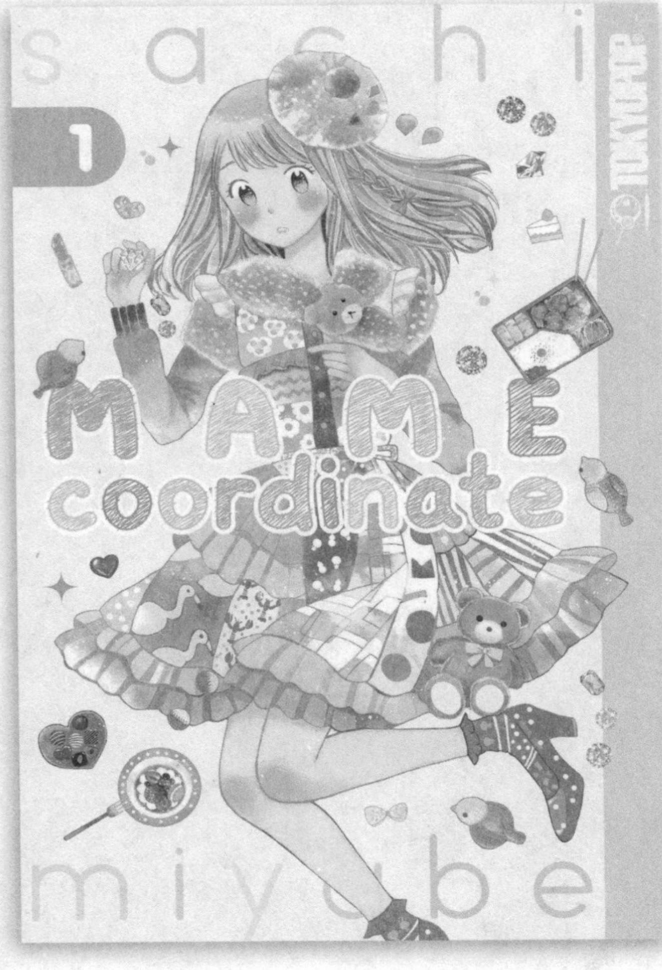
sachi
1
MAME
coordinate
miyabe
TOKYOPOP

SLICE OF LIFE

She loves meat and fried foods, and eats only karaage bento. Wearing exclusively clothes with weird characters printed on them, her fashion sense is practically non-existent. No confidence in her own looks. Extreme social anxiety. She speaks with a country drawl, and even her name is unusual. But then Mame (born in Tottori prefecture) was discovered by an intimidating, bespectacled rookie manager, and now begins the arduous task of getting her ready for auditions! The road to Top Model looks awfully steep from here.

TOKYOPOP

ALICE IN KYOTO FOREST, VOLUME 1

Mai Mochizuki, Haruki Niwa

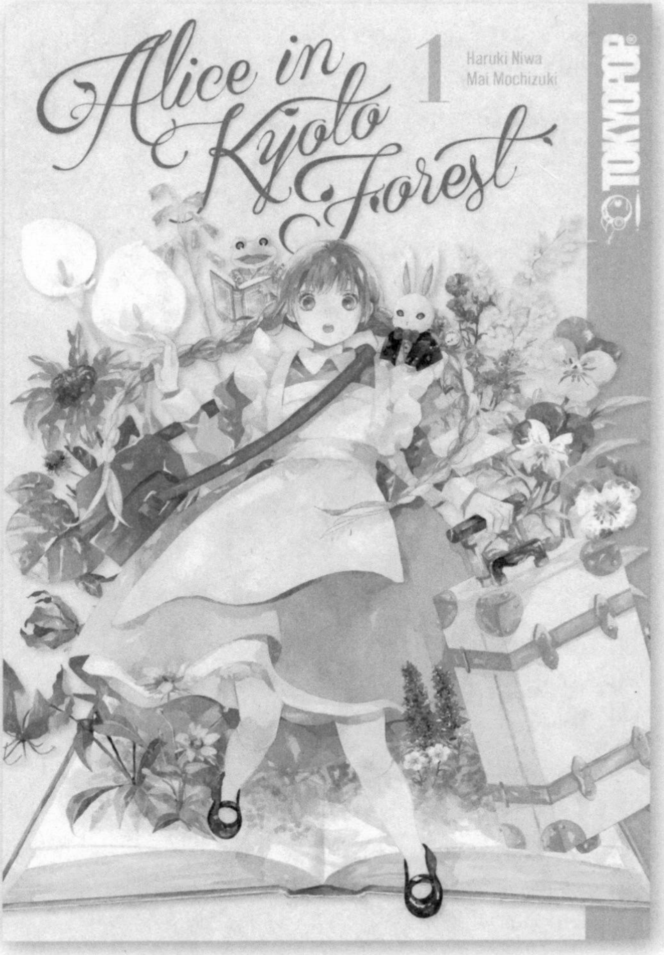
Alice in Kyoto Forest
1
Haruki Niwa
Mai Mochizuki
TOKYOPOP

TOKYOPOP

SLICE OF LIFE FANTASY

Orphaned at a young age, Alice has lived with her aunt for most of her childhood. But her uncle is abusive and resentful, and at fifteen years old, Alice decides to return home to Kyoto and train as a maiko, eventually hoping to become a geisha. But when she arrives back to the city where she was born, she finds that Kyoto has changed quite a bit in the eight years since she left it. Almost as if it's a completely different world...

LAUGHING UNDER THE CLOUDS, VOLUME 3

KarakaraKemuri

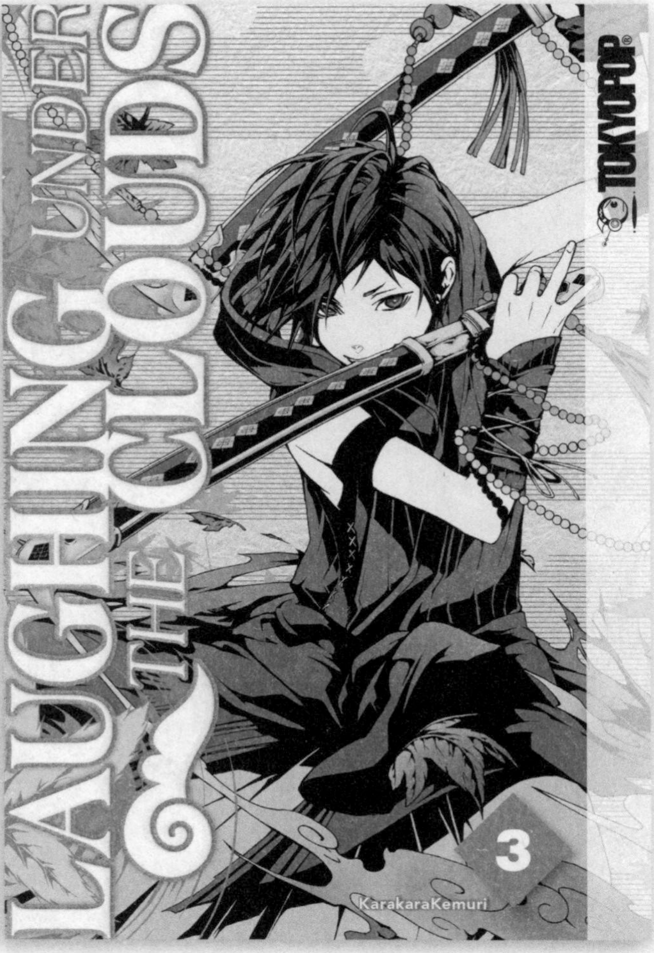
TOKYOPOP
LAUGHING UNDER THE CLOUDS
3
KarakaraKemuri

ACTION FANTASY

Soramaru's quest to grow stronger brings him to the leader of the Yamainu, Abe no Sousei. Sousei proposes a trade: training in exchange for information. In search of the information required, Soramaru disguises himself and — with the help of youngest brother Chutaro — infiltrates the very prison he's taken so many criminals to: Gokumonjo. But nothing is ever as easy as it seems, and although Soramaru finds the information he needs to make a deal, the eldest Kumo brother Tenka suddenly finds himself under arrest and in dire straits...

TOKYOPOP

DOUBLE, VOLUME 1

Ayako Noda

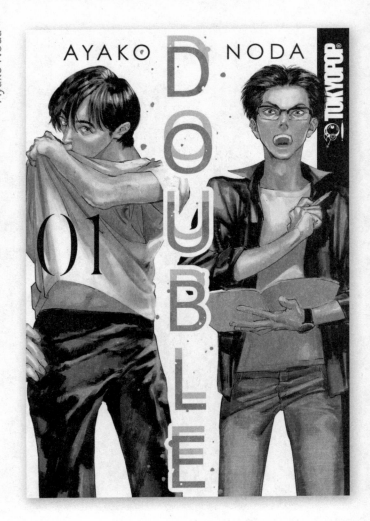

AYAKO NODA

DOUBLE

01

TOKYOPOP®

DRAMA

Scatterbrained Takara Takarada is an undiscovered genius actor who fully embodies every character he's cast as, delivering unforgettable performance after performance onstage. But this genius can only be brought forth by his best friend and fellow actor, Yuujin Kamoshima, who cares for Takara even as he envies him for his innate talent. When it takes the two of them together to bring a character to life, what will happen when Takara is scouted away from their small-time theater troupe and thrust into the new world of television instead?

TOKYOPOP®

ISEKAI FANTASY

Lizel and Gil finally flush out their mysterious attacker and settle the score with him... but it seems the assailant isn't quite the threat they initially believed him to be. Is it possible this former foe could actually be a new ally? Maybe so... but first he'll have to convince them to give him the chance he knows he deserves!

A GENTLE NOBLE'S VACATION RECOMMENDATION, VOLUME 5

Misaki, Momochi & Sando

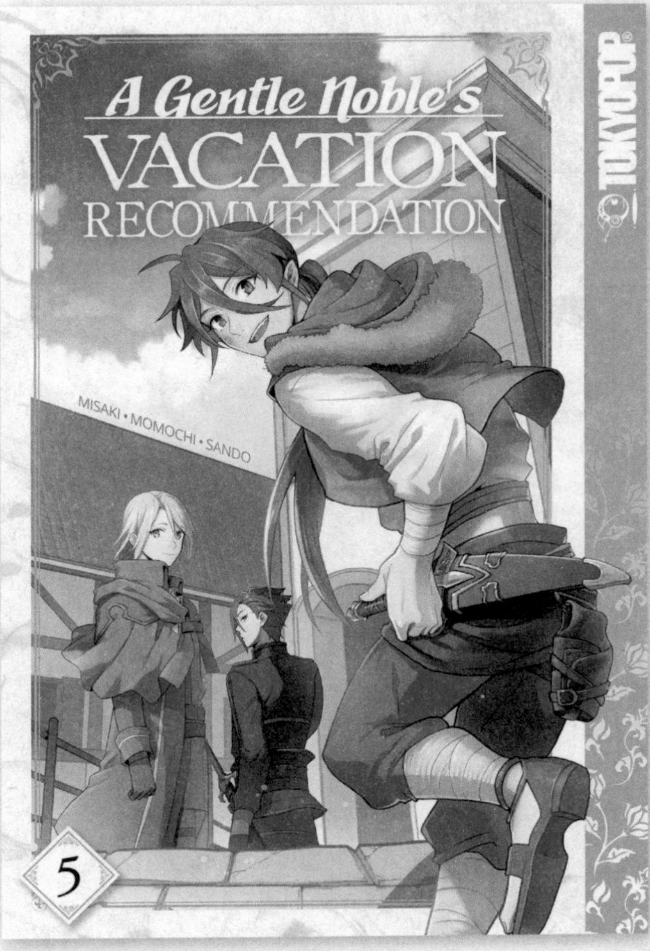

A Gentle Noble's
VACATION
RECOMMENDATION
MISAKI • MOMOCHI • SANDO
5
TOKYOPOP

ISEKAI FANTASY

Lizel's adventuring party grows by one! With thieves on the prowl and questionable characters skulking about in the night, Lizel and Gil finally come to an agreement with Eleven. Little by little, they begin to accept him as he is... and although there are some who might disagree, can anyone ever say no to Lizel when he sets his mind to something?

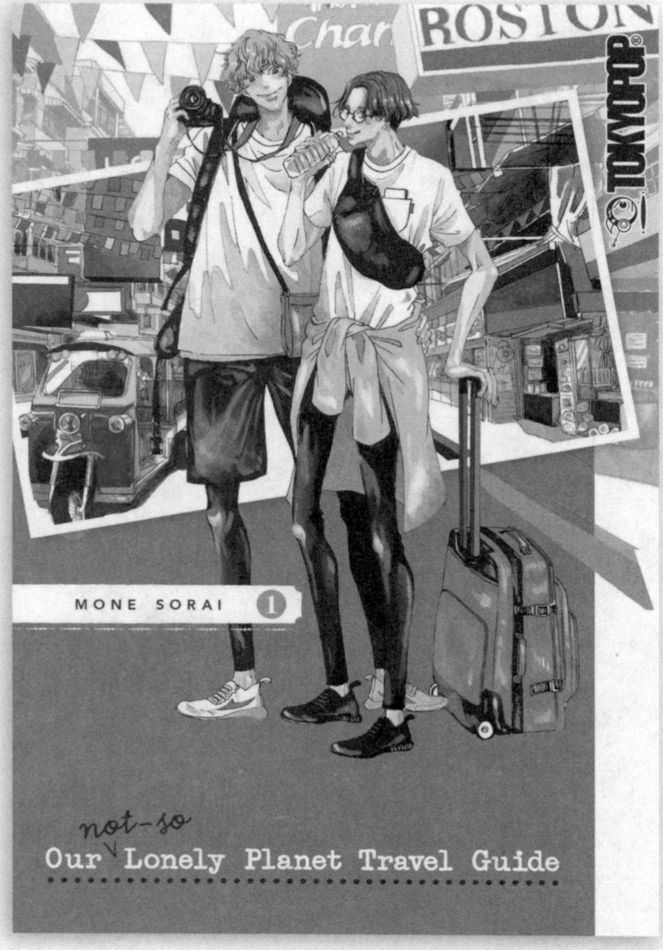
TOKYOPOP
MONE SORAI 1
Our not-so Lonely Planet Travel Guide

OUR NOT-SO-LONELY PLANET TRAVEL GUIDE, VOLUME 1

Mone Sorai

LOVE x LOVE

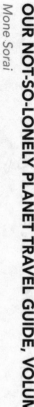

After quitting his job, Asahi tells his boyfriend Mitsuki that he'll marry him if they go on a trip around the world together first. Though Asahi's cautious nature often clashes with Mitsuki's carefree ways, the two grow steadily closer as they sightsee and eat their way through the first three countries on their world tour: Thailand, India, and Georgia. The people they meet and places they see will forever change their lives.

TOKYOPOP

OUR NOT-SO-LONELY PLANET TRAVEL GUIDE, VOLUME 2

Mone Sorai

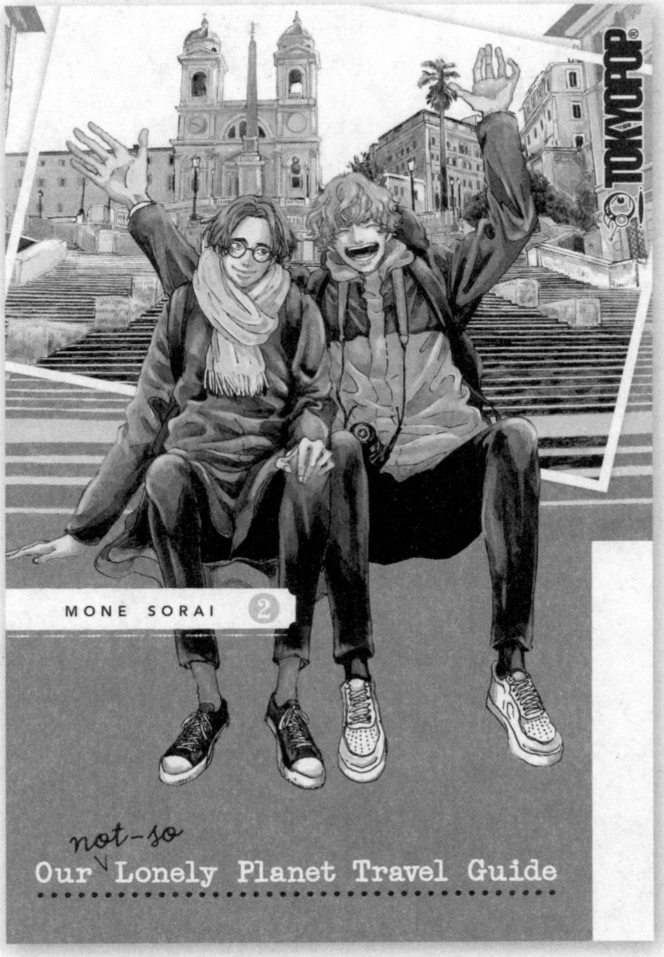
TOKYOPOP
MONE SORAI 2
Our not-so Lonely Planet Travel Guide

LOVE x LOVE

Super-serious Asahi Suzumura and easygoing Mitsuki Sayama may seem like an odd couple, but they made a deal — they'll vacation together around the world, and when they return to Japan, they'll get married. Even though they're far from home, each new destination is an opportunity to become closer to each other.

ALICE IN BISHOUNEN-LAND, VOLUME 1

Yushi Kawata, Yukito

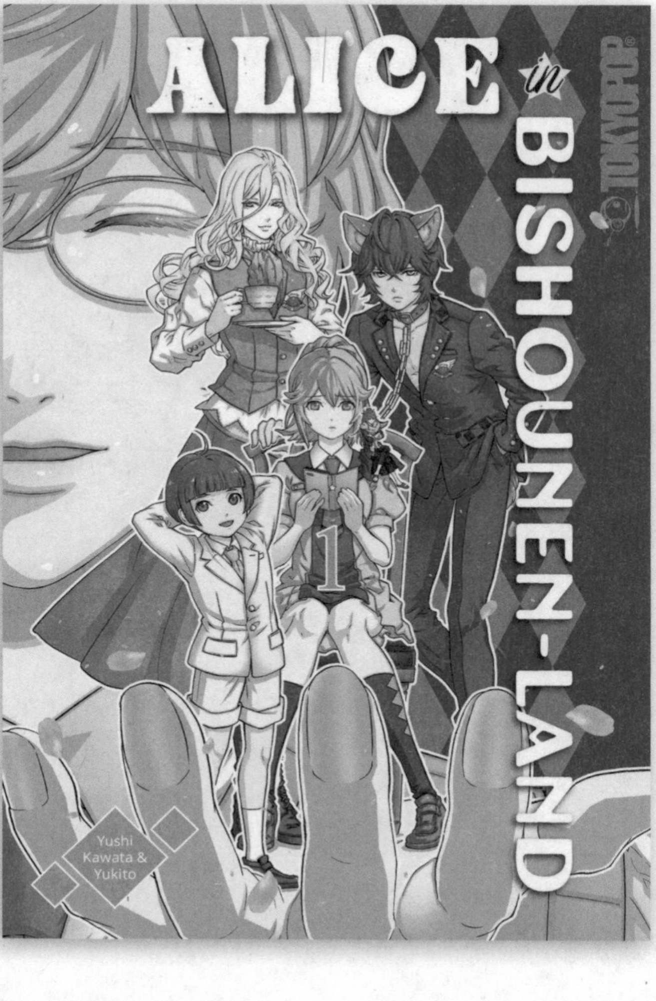
ALICE in BISHOUNEN-LAND
TOKYOPOP
1
Yushi Kawata & Yukito

COMEDY

Alice Kagami is an ordinary high school girl who doesn't really get her friend Tamami's obsession with idol games. There's more to life than handsome digital boys, dating sims, and mini-games, right? But then, Tamami is "chosen" as one of the top idol fangirls in the country and gets drawn into the game — and hapless Alice gets pulled in too! Between dealing with the mismatched members of her idol group to intense pressure to spend real money on gachas, how is a total idol game newbie supposed to take them to the top?

TOKYOPOP

ALICE IN BISHOUNEN-LAND, VOLUME 2

Yushi Kawata, Yukito

COMEDY

After getting unexpectedly drawn into an idol dating sim, total newbie Alice Kagami doesn't have a clue how she's supposed to act like a proper producer, let alone save herself and her idol-obsessed friend Tamami. Together with her mismatched group of handsome boys, Alice learns to brave the gacha, level up her idols, and join in summer festival fun. But will their group's newfound success transform digital dreams into reality? Includes excerpts from artist Yukito on the design and production process of the elegant FIORE Rose plastic model by popular kit-and-doll-making company VOLKS!

STILL SICK, VOLUME 1

Akashi

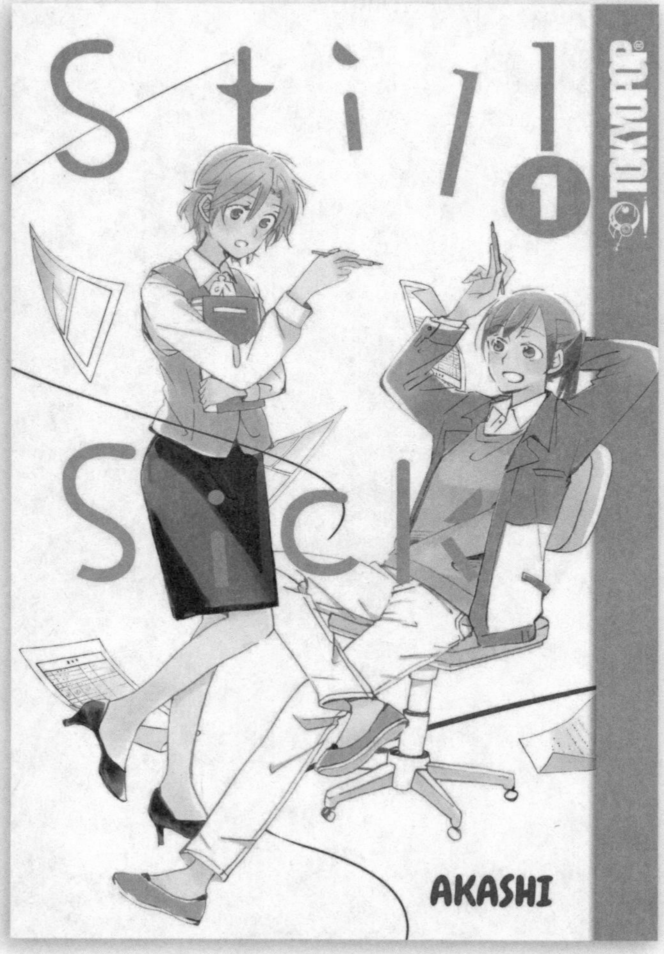

Still Sick
1
TOKYOPOP
AKASHI

LOVE x LOVE

Makoto Shimizu is just an ordinary office worker, blending in seamlessly with her colleagues on the job... That is, until her coworker Akane Maekawa discovers her well-hidden secret: in her spare time, she draws and sells girls' love comics! Akane is the last person Makoto would think of as a nerd, but as the two grow closer, it starts to seem like Akane may have a secret of her own...

TOKYOPOP

STILL SICK, VOLUME 2

Akashi

After finding out that her coworker Akane used to be a manga creator, Makoto encourages her new friend to recapture that dream. As an amateur comic artist herself, Makoto looks up to Akane and tries to help her overcome the difficulties that made her give up that profession in the past. Although Akane is often her own worst critic, Makoto inspires her to try reshaping her attitude toward her art. But matters become more complicated when Makoto realizes that, somewhere along the way, what started out as a professional friendship over a common interest has developed into... a serious crush!

Ossan Idol, Volume 6

Manga by Ichika Kino
Original story by Mochiko Mochida

Editor - Lena Atanassova
Translator - Katie Kimura
Quality Check - Shingo Nemoto
Proofreader - Caroline Wong
Copyeditor - M. Cara Carper
Editorial Associate - Janae Young
Marketing Associate - Kae Winters
Cover Design - Sol DeLeo
Retouching and Lettering - Vibrraant Publishing Studio
Licensing Specialist - Arika Yanaka
Editor-in-Chief & Publisher - Stu Levy

A **TOKYOPOP** Manga

TOKYOPOP and 🐸 are trademarks or registered trademarks of TOKYOPOP Inc.

TOKYOPOP Inc.
4136 Del Rey Ave., Suite 502
Marina del Rey, CA 90292-5604

E-mail: info@TOKYOPOP.com
Come visit us online at www.TOKYOPOP.com

f www.facebook.com/TOKYOPOP
🐦 www.twitter.com/TOKYOPOP
📷 www.instagram.com/TOKYOPOP

OSSAN 36 GA IDOL NI NARUHANASHI 6
©2021 Kino Ichika ©2021 Mochico Mochida

First published in Japan in 2021 by Shufu To Seikatsu Sha Co., Ltd.
English translation rights reserved by TOKYOPOP. under the license from Shufu To Seikatsu Sha Co., Ltd.

ISBN: 978-1-4278-6925-8
First TOKYOPOP Printing: May 2022
Printed in CANADA

STOP

THIS IS THE BACK OF THE BOOK!

How do you read manga-style? It's simple! Let's practice -- just start in the top right panel and follow the numbers below!

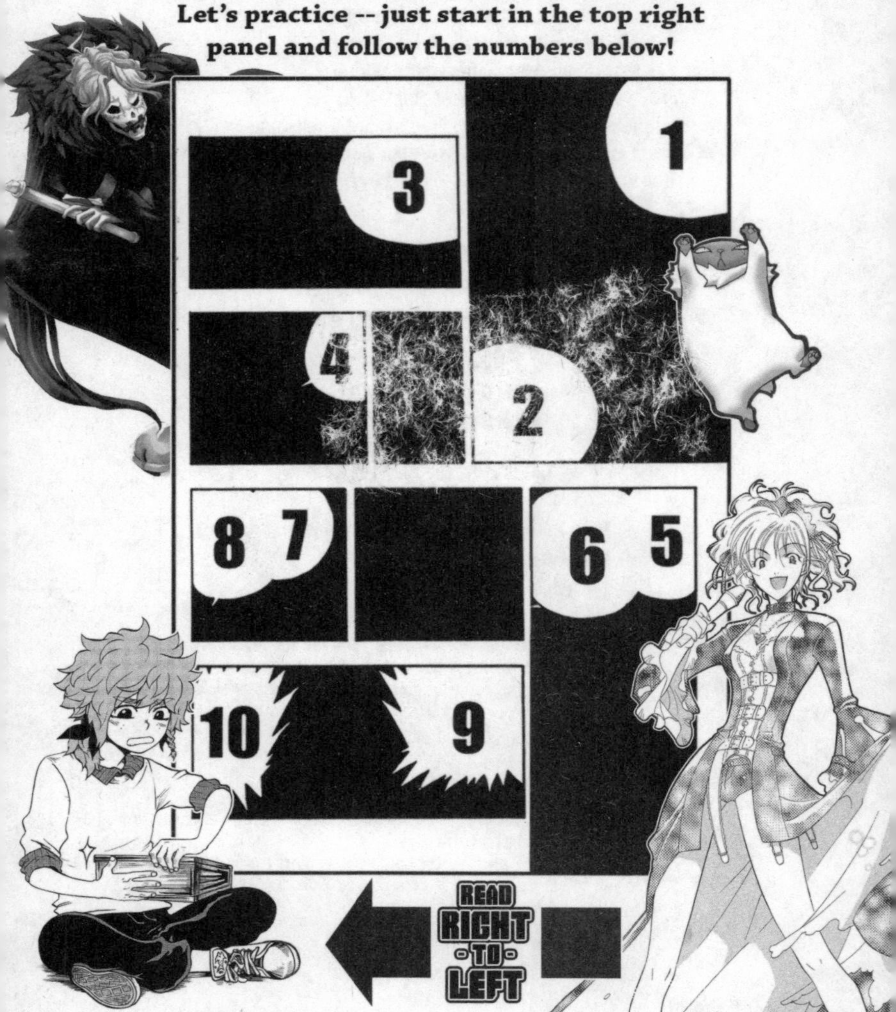

1
2
3
4
5
6
7
8
9
10
READ
RIGHT
-TO-
LEFT

Crimson from ***Kamo*** / Fairy Cat from ***Grimms Manga Tales***
Morrey from ***Goldfisch*** / Princess Ai from ***Princess Ai***